HISTORY OF THE NEW ZEALAND ENGINEERS

OFFICIAL HISTORY

OF THE

NEW ZEALAND ENGINEERS

DURING THE GREAT WAR
1914-1919.

A RECORD OF THE WORK CARRIED OUT BY THE FEILD COMPANIES, FIELD TROOPS, SIGNAL TROOP, AND WIRELESS TROOP, DURING THE OPERATIONS IN SAMOA (1914-15); EGYPT, GALLIPOLI, SINAI, AND PALESTINE (1914-1918); FRANCE, BELGIUM AND GERMANY (1916-1919); AND MESOPOTAMIA (1916-1918).

MCMXXVII
EVANS, COBB & SHARPE, LTD.
Wanganui, N.Z.

Foreword

At a New Zealand Expeditionary Force Senior Officers' conference, held in Wellington some time ago, it was decided to have Regimental Histories prepared.

Unfortunately a large number of war diaries, the notes prepared for the Field Troops' history, and various other records never reached New Zealand. Many of the maps and plans sent back from the field were also missing, and even the records of men decorated or commended for gallant action were incomplete.

To such an extent is this true that the Committee in charge of publication, greatly averse to running any risk of drawing invidious distinction, almost decided to make no reference by name to any member of the Regiment save a bare list of honours and awards gained.

However, it was realised that this would greatly lessen the general interest in the book, and it was finally decided to set forth appropriate details of gallant actions and faithful service where such particulars were known. This decision of the Committee was further strengthened by their conviction that the men most worthy of special mention would be the last to complain of its absence, and the first to realise that many another just as deserving as themselves had missed recognition through unavoidable force of circumstances or had received but an obscure wooden cross as his share of the material gains of the mighty conflict.

The bare material available from existing diaries and records was not sufficient to produce a history which would appeal to and retain the interest of ex-members and others concerned in the work of the Engineers. It was therefore decided that a personal note should be introduced.

With a view to obtaining all the necessary information a circular was prepared and addressed to Officers, Warrant Officers and Senior N.C.O.'s who had served with this branch of the Force asking for information which was not likely to have been included in the war diaries. The following were particularly asked for.—

(a) Any noteworthy exploits in the field carried out by any individual member of the party.

(b) Any incidents of a sensational, amusing, or humorous nature.

(c) Any facts concerning the N.Z.E. which it was considered should be chronicled.

(d) Any suggestions which would tend towards the general improvement of the Regimental History.

Foreword

The loan was also solicited of photographs, postcards, and sketches of places, works, etc., associated with the Engineers, from which to make a selection.

The assistance given by certain officers, N.C.O.'s and others in response to this appeal is gratefully acknowledged, but whether owing to short memories or as a result of war weariness the great majority failed even to reply to the circular which was addressed to them. This is to be regretted, as it is felt that, had all the information which was in the possession of those to whom the communication was addressed, been placed at the disposal of the compiler, the book could have been made much more interesting.

Considerable help, notes and photos relating to the Field Companies were received from Lt.-Col. G. Barclay, Lt.-Col. L. M. Shera, Lt. A. H. Bogle, Sergt. A. Goss and Corpl. A. Williams. In fact the Field Companies' history has, to a large extent, been compiled from contributions by these officers and N.C.O.'s.

Lt. R. T. G. Patrick undertook the task of writing the History of the Signal Troop.

Writers for the Histories of the Field Troop in Palestine and the Wireless Troop in Mesopotamia could not be found amongst the ex-members of these units and, owing to the loss of most of the diaries and records, this was regrettable. Many notes and photos were received from Lieuts. H. G. Alexander and H. A. Lockington and assistance was given by Colonel Commandant C. G. Powles. Short Histories of the Troops' work, based on the information available, were finally written.

Major L. C. Forgie and Capt. Jervis were found to be untiring in their efforts to help with official records.

The assistance received from all the above-mentioned Officers and N.C.O.'s, also Lieut. I. Davey, is gratefully acknowledged. Although the compiling and writing was difficult, it would have been considerably harder without their help.

The delay in the issue of the History has been attributable to various causes. Many of the records required did not reach New Zealand until some time after the demobilization of the Forces, and the daily avocation of those associated in the work necessarily curtailed the time which they could devote to the completion of the History. It is trusted that the reader will make due allowance for any shortcomings which may be observed, and credit the writers and others responsible with doing their best under somewhat difficult circumstances.

N. ANNABELL,
Major N.Z.E.

Introductory

FIELD COMPANIES

Though the complete establishment of New Zealand Divisional troops included several units quite entitled to come under the heading "New Zealand Engineers," and some of which wore both the N.Z.E. badge and the distinctive blue and Khaki puggaree, yet the use of the term "Engineers" at the front generally referred to the personnel of the New Zealand Field Companies or Field Troop, and it is with the fortunes of these Units that the word is used throughout this story.

According to R.E. regulations a Field Company consists of five sections: Nos. 1, 2, 3 and 4, actually engaged in field work, and a headquarters' section concerned with the duties of organisation and supply. The whole company of 210 men is commanded by a Major, with a Captain as second in command, whose especial duty is the control of headquarters. A subaltern is in charge of each of the four field sections. In practice, the drivers from each section are almost invariably combined into one transport section, commanded by the Captain or by an officer supernumerary to the given establishment.

The number of Field Companies normally attached to a Division is three, all under the control of an Engineer Colonel or Lt.-Colonel, whose official designation is C.R.E. (Officer Commanding Royal Engineers) to the Division, and who is assisted by an Adjutant and a small Headquarters' staff. In addition to supervision of all Divisional Engineers, the C.R.E. acts as the technical adviser of the G.O.C. Division and his Staff in all matters concerned with engineering activities, and is therefore in such constant touch with Divisional Headquarters that he is practically acting as a member of the Staff. In warfare such as has recently been experienced, where the armies were almost stationary for years, there was ample scope for the constant employment of every resource known to engineering skill, and though many of the highly scientific branches of modern military engineering were conducted by specialised Units created for the purpose, the post of a Divisional C.R.E. remained an extremely onerous and exacting charge.

In a defensive sector he had to decide upon the best and quickest means of translating the Divisional policy into terms of trenches, posts and entanglements and so on, with all the minor modifications entailed by questions of time, material and labour available; when an attack was pending, he was called

Introductory

upon to exercise the same judgment in the numberless problems of preparation; while the attack was going on and after its completion, the questions of consolidation, new communication tracks and trenches, roads, bridges and tramways, water supply, dugout accommodation, aid posts and dressing stations, organisation of main sources of supply and establishment of forward dumps of material, reconnaissance of captured areas, utilisation of local resources and a dozen other contingencies impossible to foresee, had all to be dealt with in the office of the C.R.E.

Throughout the story continual references are made to works as undertaken or performed by the Field Companies which it is quite obvious could not actually have been handled unaided by the limited number of sappers in the field on any occasion. It has generally been expressed, and always understood, that the Engineers had the assistance of working parties drawn from the Infantry battalions; in any case it may be gladly emphasised here that the Engineers were indebted to the willing labour of the Infantry for a great part of any success which attended their efforts, and fully recognised that the fighting men of the Division were as handy with a shovel as they were irresistible with a bayonet.

It became more and more apparent as the war dragged on, that the establishment of three Field Companies allowed to a C.R.E. as outlined above, was quite inadequate for the efficient handling of the work entailed by his position. Divisional Pioneers, though often placed under the control of the C.R.E., were liable to be called away at any moment, with the result that for works of any extensive nature calls had to be made upon the Infantry battalions for working parties. This invariably led to delays and to a certain amount of misunderstanding. The average soldier who had just been through severe fighting, or was expecting to be called on in a few hours to take his place in the firing line, showed a pardonable lack of interest in many of the tasks he was called upon to perform.

Some recognition of this state of affairs was allowed in France by the general plan of making brigades in lines responsible for a definite programme of work laid down by the Division in their own advanced areas, with skilled labour available from the Field Companies only in such amount as the nature of the work demanded. But the approximate conclusion reached by most of the Divisional C.R.E.'s long before the end of hostilities was that the three Field Companies allowed should be expanded to include 350 men each, making a Battalion of Engineers, and that a Divisional Pioneer Battalion consisting of three Companies of 300 men each should come

Introductory

under the definite command of the C.R.E. With a Pioneer Company attached, the officers and N.C.O.'s of which would be trained as Engineers, and whose channel of promotion would be through the Field Companies, each Field Company would have sufficient labour to handle most of its jobs with speed and certainty, with a fair reserve of men available for supervision and control of work undertaken by infantry working parties under their own officers.

This arrangement, had it been carried out in the late war, would possibly not have appealed to the New Zealand Divisional Pioneers, whose ranks included many officers and men of a high standard of engineering skill and training, and who, from the nature of their case, were the happy possessors of a keen spirit of esprit-de-corps, but as an indication of the general conclusions reached after much experience, it may hope to receive further consideration in the future. As a matter of fact several Engineer N.C.O.s had already been appointed to commissions in the Pioneer Battalion before the end of hostilities, and had the war continued longer, no doubt the practice would have become general.

Contents

Chapter	Page
I.—Formation and Training	1
II.—Gallipoli	15
III.—Summer at Anzac	32
IV.—The Attack on Sari Bair and the Evacuation	42
V.—Reorganisation in Egypt	55
VI.—Summer at Armentieres	61
VII.—The Battle of the Somme, 1916	85
VIII.—Winter on the Lys	99
IX.—The Battle of Messines	115
X.—Passchendaele	146
XI.—Winter in Ypres	160
XII.—German Offensive, 1918	178
XIII.—The Final Advance	195
XIV.—The Reserve Depot in England	227
XV.—Signal Troop N.Z.E.	237
XVI.—N.Z. Field Troop Engineers in Palestine	273
XVII.—Personnel of Field Troop Engineers	294
XVIII.—N.Z. Wireless Troop in Mesopotamia and Persia	299

Appendix	Page
"A"—Roll of Honour	305
"B"—Honours and Rewards	309
"C"—Officers Who Served With The N.Z. Engineers	313

List of Maps

Anzac Sector, Gallipoli	17
Apex Defences, Gallipoli	47
Portions of France, Belgium and Germany Traversed by N.Z. Engineers	62
Armentieres, Bois Grenier and Sailly Sectors	68
Flers and Longueval Sector	88
Main Towns Between Estaires and Ypres	103
Messines Sector	120
Zonnebeke Sector	162
Area Captured by N.Z. Division Between August 5th and November 4th, 1918	200
North-West Europe	(Under Separate Cover)

List of Illustrations

	Page
Lieut.-Colonel G. R. Pridham, D.S.O.	1
Anzac Cove	16
North Beach	16
The Sphinx	16
Lieut.-Colonel G. Barclay, O.B.E.	17
The Second Field Company in Trentham	32
Horse Lines at Moascar	48
A Pontoon and Trestle Bridge at Moascar	48
Engineers on Camels	48
Major D. J. Gibbs, D.S.O.	96
A Shrine and Ruined Church at Nouville Houplines	112
Forming a Plank Road near Ypres	112
Lieut.-Colonel H. L. Bingay, D.S.O.	128
Ypres Cloth Hall before the Great War	144
Ypres Cloth Hall after Bombardment	145
Sergt. Samuel Forsyth, V.C.	160
Lieut.-Colonel L. M. Shera, O.B.E., M.C.	176
Major N. Annabell, M.C.	192
Lieut.-Col. E. J. Hulbert, D.S.O.	240
Despatch Riders of A.N.Z.A.C. Mounted Division	248
Signal Officers and N.C.O.'s at Serapium	248
A Signal Station	248
The Signal Troop at Jaffa	248
Nos. I. and II. Well-clearing Parties, Khalassa	249
Canvas Reservoirs and Horse Trough at Khalassa	249
Bridges Erected over the River Rubin	256
The Party which Demolished the Asluj Bridge	273
Demolishing the Railway South-East of Beersheba	273
Asluj Railway Station	273
Demolition of the Asluj Bridge	288

Lieut. Colonel G. R. Pridham, D.S.O.

CHAPTER I.

FORMATION AND TRAINING.

On August 6th, 1914, two days after the outbreak of the Great War, the following message from the Secretary of State for War in London was received by His Excellency the Governor-General of New Zealand:—"If your Ministers desire and feel themselves able to seize the German wireless station at Samoa, we should feel that this was a great and urgent Imperial service. . ." By August 15th, a force of some 1400 men, volunteers from territorial units in Auckland and Wellington, was already on its way to strike an early blow for the cause of the Homeland. With this force there sailed from Wellington two sections of an Engineer Field Company under Captain D. J. Gibbs, and, with the entry of those few sappers into the crowded lists, commences the story of the Field Companies of the New Zealand Engineers as set out in these pages.

Convoyed by three aged cruisers, strengthened later by warships of the Australian Squadron, the transports sailed by way of New Caledonia and Fiji, and on August 29th took possession of German Samoa without firing a shot.

From the moment of landing the sappers were actively employed on the many and varied jobs that fall to the lot of a Field Company. Defensive lines were put in hand about the town of Apia, while the wireless station was organised as a defensive post, and adequately protected by the erection of stone sangars and wire entanglements. On the score of organisation and supply, numerous works required attention. Adequate water supplies for the various units were arranged by pumping from springs and wells into water carts, a bridge was built across the Vaisingano River, and a road was cut through the forest to provide an alternative line of communication with the defences. The lighthouse and beacon destroyed by the enemy were rebuilt and maintained; a signal station was erected; barracks to accommodate 250 men each were built with stores and bakehouses in close proximity; and the wireless station, which the enemy had attempted to put out of action, was again placed in commission after much difficulty in the improvisation of missing parts. Sapper Maynard, who took a prominent part in this latter enterprise, was mentioned in orders, and received monetary recognition later from the Government. Other especially valuable men in the sappers' ranks were four trained ship's officers, who took charge of four

Field Companies and Field Troop.

motor patrol launches, and were particularly useful in landing stores and so on through the surf. On one occasion a mounted patrol of Engineers was sent inland to quell a disturbance, but on arrival the expected trouble faded away.

Seven months after the landing, all New Zealand Engineers were relieved, and returned home preparatory to enlisting for further service on more distant fields.

On August 7th, the services of a New Zealand Expeditionary Force were offered to the Imperial Government, and immediately accepted. Men poured into the district concentration camps from all parts of the country and from every walk of life. The much debated territorial system of compulsory training at once showed its value, in that it supplied a basis of organisation and equipment for this emergency, and the majority of the men chosen for the Main Body were from the Territorial ranks, with at least some degree of military knowledge and training. No Field Companies were sent with this first Force, but the men required for a Field Troop to complete the establishment of a full mounted brigade were chosen from volunteers from the Territorial Field Companies, which also supplied the engineering equipment required by the Troop.

Mobilised at Awapuni Racecourse near Palmerston North, under command of Captain L. M. Shera, of No. 3 Field Company (Territorial) Auckland, the Field Troop had little time for training. In any case the men all had knowledge of field works, and the period immediately preceding embarkation was generally utilised in acquiring knowledge of horse management, and in enduring the good humoured though sadly time-worn jokes and jibes of the Sergeant Instructors. A large number of these Instructors, both now and later on, were old Imperial soldiers, and a chance of having a share in the real thing once more was the wine of life to them. New Zealand owes a great deal to the Sergeant Instructors of the training camps, and no victim of their heavy shafts of wit really grudged them their brief strut in the centre of the stage.

Apart from the small trials of training and military discipline, the troops thoroughly enjoyed the camp life. To be in khaki in those early days ensured recognition as the hero of the hour and the centre of all attraction. The general public could not do enough to show its appreciation of its citizen soldiers, and gifts of every description immediately inundated the camps in a continual stream. Originally it had been intended that the Force should embark at the end of August, but the presence of German raiders in the Pacific delayed matters, and it was not till September 24th that the

Formation and Training.

Field Troop, along with other Wellington detachments, was finally inspected on Newtown Park, Wellington, and marched through the cheering crowds to the waiting transports, which immediately pulled out into the stream.

But next morning, acting on further information as to the German raiders, they all came quietly back to the wharves once more, there to await the arrival of a more powerful naval escort. It was the troops' first experience of the delays and disappointments inseparable from the complicated arrangements of a nation at war. In later years, on sandy deserts and in Continental troop trains, they were to become painfully familiar with the process of possessing their souls in patience, but on this first occasion they found it very hard. However, all things come to an end at last, even in the Army, and on the afternoon of Thursday, October 15th, all hands were again aboard, and at 6 a.m. next morning, with the "Minotaur" and "Ibuki" leading, the ten transports weighed anchor and passed out into the Straits. 9,000 chosen men sailed away from New Zealand that day, the first fruits of a young country laid willingly on the altar of duty and Empire, but long ere the grey line of ships had risen to the first swell of the open sea, they were but a confused blur to many a silent watcher on the crowded heights about the harbour. The troops themselves, most of whom knew no other land than their own, now watched her shores recede with mingled feelings. But youth and the spirit of adventure never marched long with sadness or repining, and the cares and details of immediate duties soon banished melancholy reflections.

The Field Troop, comprising 3 officers and 80 other ranks, were on the "Maunganui" along with their horses and transport and equipment. After six days at sea the coast of Tasmania loomed up ahead, and within a few hours the fleet was anchored at Hobart, where every possible kindness was received from the enthusiastic residents. Thence across the Great Australian Bight to Albany, with men and horses daily becoming more at home in their strange quarters, despite the long rolling swell peculiar to those distressing waters. At Albany the New Zealanders fell in with the troopships of the First Australian Division; an occasion memorable as the first meeting of the young untried forces so soon to be known by an imperishable name born of association in a desperate and glorious enterprise as yet hidden in the lap of the gods. As the united convoy put to sea again, some 40 ships in all, it presented a spectacle never before seen in southern seas, and probably never to be seen again, if only from the stand-

Field Companies and Field Troop.

point of the submarine menace existing in these later degenerate days. The German Pacific Fleet was still employed on its nefarious expeditions, and every care was taken to avoid accident. At Albany the fleet of protecting warships had been joined by the "Sydney" and "Melbourne." On the morning of Sunday, November 8th, the "Minotaur" signalled to the "Maunganui" :—" I am ordered on another service; wish you the very best of success when you land in France. Give the Germans a good shake up. It has been a great pleasure to escort such a well disciplined force and convoy.—Good-bye."

The Cocos Islands were to be passed that night, and special precautions were taken. Early next morning the "Sydney" was ordered away on unknown service, though sufficient had been picked up from the welter of wireless messages in the air to know that mischief was afoot not far away. Later in the day came the welcome news that the "Sydney" had engaged the "Emden" off Keeling Island in the Cocos Group, and had forced her ashore in a sinking condition. As evidence that the precautions against raiders had not been arbitrarily imposed, the news required no enlargement, and this early success of the Australian Navy was taken as a happy augury for the future achievements of the Colonial Forces.

Colombo was the next break in the monotony of the long voyage, which had already been somewhat relieved by the visit of Neptune, and by sports and concerts on board each ship. Ceylon was, to the great majority, their first experience of a tropical island, the calm blue coastal waters and graceful palm-clad hill slopes proving especially attractive after the long spell of unrelieved ocean. A brief spell of shore leave did nothing to dispel the favourable impressions of this beautiful land, and if the thousands of diseased beggars all over Colombo were a shock to the unsophisticated New Zealanders, that introduction to the seamy side of Eastern life was some preparation for the experiences awaiting them in Egypt. On November 17th, the New Zealand transports continued their journey, heading for Aden and the Red Sea.

By this time the delights of existence on a crowded troopship had completely palled on the travellers, and the warm weather and slow rate of steam made all hands extremely impatient. At Aden, rumours of Turkish hostilities against the Suez Canal prepared the way for the announcement, which was made in the Red Sea, that the troops would disembark in Egypt, though all ranks were disappointed at not being allowed to go straight on to service in France.

Formation and Training.

On November 30th, at 5 o'clock in the evening, the "Maunganui" entered the Suez Canal, and every eye on board was immediately trained eastward in vain expectation of seeing Turks, but no life was visible save the stately Indian sentries pacing their beats along the shore. On the African side the gorgeous tints of an Egyptian sunset, far more varied and beautiful than anything seen at sea during the long voyage, passed almost unnoticed. Nothing would have satisfied the eager fire-eaters that evening but the sight of an enemy; though as far as Turks were concerned, they were to see enough and to spare before many more months had passed. As the transports steamed slowly up the Canal, the troops were greatly interested in the various Indian units all along the banks, and in the numerous fortified posts they were to know so well for themselves later on. Anchor was dropped off Port Said. No shore leave was allowed, but crowds of Gyppos—as the natives were universally known then and for ever after, no matter what their particular gradations of breed—came down upon the ships like a flock of vultures, their lateen-sailed craft laden with atrocious cigarettes, fairly good fruit and a sticky conglomeration bearing a faint resemblance to turkish delight. Some of the bolder pirates managed to board the "Maunganui," and eventually penetrated to the deck where the Field Troop men were cleaning their harness. Here the leader of the band was invited to try some of the dubbin. He required some coaxing, though the dubbin certainly looked quite as attractive as did his turkish delight, but finally he ventured on a mouthful, and in a trice the whole gang were jabbering and falling over one another in their efforts to secure a share of the new delicacy.

No long stay was made at Port Said, and early on the 3rd of December the minarets of Alexandria were clearly discernible through the cold mists of the dawn. By breakfast time several transports were alongside the crowded wharves, and shortly afterwards advanced guards were on their way to the railway station, en route for Zeitoun, where camp was to be established on the desert outside Heliopolis, a wealthy suburb of Cairo. Despite the excellence of the Egyptian railways, some days elapsed before all the Colonial Forces were finally transported to Zeitoun. Those men who remained longest on the transports fared the best, since the camp, when first occupied, consisted of a bare desert unadorned by tent or blanket, and the winter nights proved bitterly cold to troops who had just come through the tropics. Before long, however, the newcomers were all comfortably settled, and training began in earnest. Morning after morning the bat-

Field Companies and Field Troop.

talions paraded in full marching order, and trudged for hours across the hot and weary sands, till every man was either fit and hard enough to go for his life, or else had been weeded out as unable to stand the strain.

The horses of the Field Troop, as of all other mounted units, required special attention for some time after landing, though on the whole they had stood their trials very well. Careful exercise and plenty of green food were the specifics employed to bring them up to normal form again, fit to take their share of the general training. A type of lucerne known as berseem was to be had in unlimited quantities from that most fertile of all agricultural regions—the Nile Delta, where three crops are gathered in a year—and long lines of camels or small donkeys wended their way daily to the stores, piled so high with enormous loads of the succulent feed, that, in the case of the donkeys at least, nothing could be seen but a pair of long ears and a pair of shining black eyes. The bandits in charge of these pack animals lost no chance of increasing the weight of their loads by a judicious use of stones or sticks, but even under the Southern Cross such little pleasantries are not unknown, and no one bore them any ill-will for their up-to-date trading methods.

For training in Engineering work, no ground could have been more suitable than the desert, which stretched away for illimitable miles, a waste of yellow sand. Circumstances were almost too ideal, since nowhere again were bridges erected with the ease and speed possible on the regular waterways of the Nile irrigation canals, nor were trenches dug under conditions comparable with the easy handling of this loose, convenient sand. Desert trenches we were certainly to know later, but the sand-storms which then filled them in and caused great labour and inconvenience, were matters of small moment during these early weeks, when demonstration of principles of construction was more important than the use of the finished article.

Some slight diversion from the attractions of the desert was furnished when a demonstration of armed force was made by the British military authorities to impress the native mind with the futility of any attempt at serious disturbances. This took place on December 23rd, three days after the coronation of His Highness Prince Hussein Kamel Pasha, who was proclaimed Sultan of Egypt under the protection of His Majesty the King, owing to the ill-advised action of the former Khedive in casting in his lot with Turkey and the Central Powers. Leaving camp in the early morning, the New Zea-

Formation and Training.

landers marched into the centre of Cairo, to the Opera Square, and out again through wide avenues and crowded bazaars, where the populace gave no sign of any ill-feeling, and appeared entirely unconcerned. The parade furnished some opportunity of gauging the appearance and organisation of the New Zealand troops, who unquestionably made a fine show. Horse, foot, and artillery, everything was there down to the collapsible boats of the Field Troop, and every man enjoyed the day's outing, whatever the effect on the poor Egyptians.

Meanwhile, in England, a small force was being organised and trained whose ultimate destinies were to be so closely connected with the New Zealand Engineers that its origin and composition must be investigated. On the outbreak of war, many New Zealanders either residing or visiting at Home, were in the first rush to join the forces. In spite of many enlistments in British regiments, there was a natural preference shown for such units as King Edward's Horse, and a Colonial battalion of the Royal Fusiliers, which already had definite colonial associations to commend them to the outlanders.

To Captain Lampen of the New Zealand Staff, who happened to be in London on furlough, fell the distinction of originating a scheme to raise a British Section of the New Zealand Expeditionary Force, an idea which at once received the approval of the New Zealand Government, and was supported in London by the authority and influence of its High Commissioner, the Hon. Sir Thomas Mackenzie. Men who responded to the advertisements placed in the London papers were sworn in at the High Commissioner's Office on September 28th, and went into training on the following day on Wandsworth Common, London, S.W. Captain Lampen was assisted in his task of breaking in the raw material by Captains Simpson, May and Wright, and by Messrs. Lucina, Skelsey, and Stocker, acting officers. Many New Zealanders who had already enlisted in other regiments now obtained transfers to this British Section, which ere long numbered 150 rank and file, all as good as the best so far as physical fitness and a keen desire to have a crack at the enemy might avail them.

Early in October, the Section moved into camp at Bulford on Salisbury Plain, which had been the original destination of the New Zealand Main Body, and was yet to become familiar with them or their successors as time rolled on. A week later a further move was made into huts at Sling. Many ex-New Zealanders were still arriving in England from

Field Companies and Field Troop.

various parts of the world, all anxious to bear their share of the national burden, and on hearing of the Section, these men were naturally drawn to their own people, with the result that by mid-November more than 200 names appeared upon the roll. Vigorous training went on daily with a view to joining up with the Main Body known to be then on the water. In further anticipation of its arrival, stores and gear were prepared ready for use, and if the force had reached England at that time, it would have entered a well-equipped camp.

The usual concerts and entertainments broke the monotony of drill and long winter evenings. On two occasions the members of the New Zealand War Contingent Association, formed under the Presidency of Lord Plunket, a former Governor of the Dominion, visited Sling and did much to increase the comfort of the men in camp. Platoon competitions with members of Canadian battalions now camped alongside the New Zealanders also added interest and zest to the day's proceedings.

Within a few days of the landing of the Main Body in Egypt, the British Section had received its marching orders, enjoyed a short period of final leave, and re-assembled for embarkation, 240 men of all ranks. On December 12th they marched out of camp to Bulford Station, escorted by a band and two battalions of Canadians, who did their best to make up for the absence of friends and relatives at the farewell ceremonies. At Southampton the men embarked on the transport "Dunera" along with Hants Territorials and a battalion of Wilts Artillery. In company with four other transports, escorted by H.M.S. "Talbot," the "Dunera" reached Alexandria without incident, and on Christmas Eve the members of the British Section found themselves in Zeitoun Camp, among the slouched hats, with the different coloured puggarees and well-known Territorial badges, of their fellow countrymen.

But not for long was the British Section to be known as such, or even to remain as an undivided unit. On parade next morning the men were informed by General Godley, commanding the New Zealand forces, that they would be disbanded forthwith, and used as the nucleus of an Engineer Field Company and for the Army Service Corps. Two days later the Section fell in for the last time, but already in two groups, one consisting of volunteers for the Engineers, the other for the Army Service Corps. Thus was the 1st Field Company launched on its honourable career. Full establishment was brought up by volunteer artisans and tradesmen from the

Formation and Training.

ranks of the 2nd Reinforcements, who reached Egypt about the end of January. Command of the new Company was given to Captain S. A. Ferguson, R.E., of the Army of Occupation in Egypt.

In the intervals of military fatigues and duties, there was no lack of opportunity to visit the cities of Cairo or Heliopolis, or to make closer acquaintance with the historic monuments and agricultural curiosities of the surrounding country. The whole atmosphere of Egypt, from the ultra-modern life of the gayer quarters of Cairo to the ancient records of bygone kings and dynasties, and the realisation that the countryside and the great River and even the peasantry themselves were much as they had been thousands of years ago, were peculiarly romantic to these sons of a country not yet passed its centenary; and exercised a charm whose memories can never wholly fade, despite the less favourable associations soon to make their appearance. Heliopolis was but a short walk from the camp and was a pleasure ground in itself, peaceful and restrained by day, but bursting into vivid life as soon as darkness settled down. Dozens of cafes were flung open, pictures were screened in the open air to attract the crowds, acrobats and conjurors aired their accomplishments on the street corners, and representatives of a hundred nationalities thronged the brilliantly lighted sidewalks. In Cairo, which could be reached by electric trams and trains leaving every few minutes, the same scenes were enacted on a more expansive scale. On Saturdays and Sundays more extended expeditions were undertaken—to the Zoo, to the ancient mosques, to the Egyptian Museum(where the captains and the kings of battles long ago were sleeping in their polished cases), or to the Pyramids of Ghizeh, there to marvel afresh at the achievements of an engineering knowledge long since lost in the mists of antiquity. A recreational institute was opened by the Y.M.C.A. in the Esbekieh Gardens in the heart of Cairo, where all kinds of concerts and other amusements were available daily. But most of the men's spare time was naturally spent in the streets watching the extraordinarily variegated life of the great Eastern city, or in the places of amusement which combined refreshment and entertainment under one roof. The desire to see life in as many new forms as possible, and a certain lack of restraint due to the restrictions and uncertainties of a soldier's existence, combined to tempt some men into undue familiarity with dancing halls and saloons not all above suspicion, but the keener wish to keep fit for the stern work ahead was a sufficient deterrent in the case of the great majority.

Field Companies and Field Troop.

It had already been decided to use the New Zealand Expeditionary Force as the basis of a Division, the additional units of which would be the 1st Australian Light Horse Brigade and the 4th Australian Infantry Brigade, now on the water en route to Egypt. Of the Divisional troops required (under direct control of Divisional Headquarters, as distinct from those under Brigade or other control), one Field Company was already in existence. A cable was now sent to New Zealand asking for another, and Lieutenant-Colonel G. R. Pridham, R.E., of the Army of Occupation, was appointed to the position of C.R.E. to the new composite New Zealand and Australian Division. In the meantime, the 1st Field Company was expected to function in whatever areas might be allotted to the New Zealand Infantry Brigade, while the Field Troop filled the same position with the New Zealand Mounted Rifles Brigade.

The matter of extra Engineer equipment for the 1st Field Company immediately became one of pressing moment. Ultimately waggons, tool carts, and pontoons were built at the Egyptian State Railway Workshops, while the harness was made at the Model Workshops in Cairo—tools, bicycles, and other gear had to be purchased in the local shops, since the Ordnance Stores at that stage contained nothing but the most ordinary articles of usual military equipment.

In the midst of training and preparation, Headquarters were hurriedly notified on January 25th, 1915, that the Infantry Brigade was urgently required on the Canal to assist in repelling a Turkish attack believed to be imminent. Amidst great excitement, next day was given up to entrainment, and the last of the infantrymen cleared Helmieh Siding before night. The 1st Field Company, owing to the incomplete state of its equipment and organisation, was not allowed to accompany the infantry battalions, and as the mounted men, to whom the Field Troop was attached, were not included in the New Zealand troops engaged either, the New Zealand Engineers were not represented in this first clash of arms. The Turks finally made a very half-hearted attempt to cross the Canal on the night of 2nd-3rd February, being easily repulsed and suffering some 3000 casualties. Among our trophies of war were several pontoons made in Germany.

Following this little skirmish with the enemy the New Zealanders resumed their training, which now began to take the form of Divisional manoeuvres. The desert was a wonderful stamping ground for the young battalions; hundreds of square miles were available without interference with valuable land or crops of any description, and the numerous deep hol-

Formation and Training.

lows and steep little sandhills, varied by rough precipitous wadis, and dotted here and there with palms and mud huts, made up an unexpected diversity of landscape which afforded ample scope for variety of scheme. One "attack" in particular is still held in affectionate remembrance by the gallant sappers engaged. Of this battle, the share allotted to the Engineers was to prepare a defensive position through which the attacking infantry had to break before they could engage the mass of the defending enemy behind. Nothing loath, the 1st Field Company and Field Troop loaded their pontoon waggons with wire and stakes, and sundry other weapons of their gruesome calling, and repaired to the scene of the projected operations. Here they erected a really fine entanglement. Plain wire only was the instruction, but a few strands of the barbed article were weaved in with loving care, for the sake of the more complete education of their infantry comrades. A complex system of trip wires, attached to old tins, and so arranged as to light flares and fire a few small and harmless mines on removal, were further expedients suggested by military science, and a desire to make a success of their minor part in the grand enterprise. With rifles loaded with blank ammunition, the sappers then took shelter behind their barrier, and awaited the onslaught with philosophic calm. Soon after dark a rattle among the tins proclaimed the usefulness of those munitions of war. Then a flare went up, and rapid fire opened all along the line. The oncoming patrols retired for private consultation, and apparently reached the decision to carry the position by frontal attack, for the whole force came on in serried ranks full of valour and determination. Up went the flares, bang went the mines, to the temporary discomfiture of the attackers, who had not anticipated those unfamiliar "extras."

However, by this time the attack was being unduly held up, and peremptory orders from the rear forced another onslaught. On came the faithful warriors again, and tried to haul away the entanglement by main force. In vain the Engineers shot them dead and told them so to avoid any misapprehension; the dead men still hauled on the wire, the flares and mines and rifle shots still filled the air, and the leaders of the thwarted assailants grew more and more annoyed. Eventually force of numbers prevailed, and the position fell. The sappers had thoroughly enjoyed their evening's work, and their opponents no less in reality, though the unexpected opposition met with was reputed to have lost them the honours of the sham fight.

As March drew on, the weather became so warm that

Field Companies and Field Troop.

parades were held only in the early mornings and evenings, and the Division, now thoroughly on its feet, began to pine for some chance of active service. There still seemed a prospect of going on to France, and all news from that quarter was eagerly sought for and discussed unceasingly. Then came rumours of a Mediterranean Expeditionary Force, and though no definite information was available to the troops now straining at the leash in Zeitoun, it soon became apparent that the two Colonial Divisions—the 1st Australian, and the New Zealand and Australian Divisions would soon be called upon to engage in whatever enterprise was afoot.

Towards the end of the month, the Division was inspected by the High Commissioner for Egypt, Sir H. McMahon, and a week later a final review was held in the desert before Sir Ian Hamilton. There was a general feeling in the air that this was in the nature of a final test as to the fitness of the troops to be sent on service, and every man did his utmost to prove that he had attained the requisite high standard. Sir Ian Hamilton was fully satisfied with his inspection, and has many times recorded in generous terms how little he ever had cause to regret his decision.

The training of the Engineers had necessarily been somewhat scanty, though considerable experience had been gained in the more general branches of field work, and all ranks had spared neither time nor effort to acquire knowledge of the main outlines of the full training laid down for sappers of the Royal Engineers. The rest was left perforce to luck, and to reliance on the essential grit and intelligence of the rank and file, who justified that faith full many a time in the days to come.

The closing days of our occupation of Egyptian camps were marked by a certain absence of that order and decorum for which all Colonial troops are justly celebrated. General physical fitness and suppressed excitement were the causes of any harmless fallings from grace; in the case of the more serious outburst resulting in the burning of one or two of the less desirable residences in a disreputable quarter, the troops concerned were under the impression that some of their fellows had been robbed or worse, and were in no mood for cold enquiry. In any case, had the whole street been destroyed, it would have been no miscarriage of justice. The authorities never wearied of impressing upon the men the evil results of undue freedom with the cosmopolitan crowd of harpies who thronged the city, but no serious effort was ever made to regulate or abate the nuisance. Everyone knew that in many parts

Formation and Training.

of Cairo there was nothing to be expected save dishonest dealing, bad liquor and disease, and as a simple matter of military expediency and conservation of man-power, those areas should have been controlled or abolished.

On 10th April, Headquarters of the Divisional Engineers, and the 1st Field Company entrained at Cairo for Alexandria, where the transports were already waiting in the harbour. The Field Troop, to its intense disgust, was left in the desert along with the mounted men. On arrival at Alexandria, the Engineers detrained at the coal wharf, where the transport "Goslar" immediately came alongside. This vessel was a German prize, and had never been much more than a dirty ocean tramp; now after some eight months in Alexandria Harbour she was even less than that. However, the journey was only to occupy three or four days, and a certain lack of cleanliness and comfort was not considered of great account. Eventually a short experience on board proved that alterations to the hull of the vessel were essential to the health of the troops, and three days were spent on arranging that matter. On the first day at Alexandria, the Engineers' stores and waggons were got aboard, but the men bivouacked in the coal yard for the night. Next day horses and men were embarked, and the night was spent out in the stream, close enough to the United States cruiser "Tennessee" for the "Goslar's" troops to enjoy the cinema show with which Yankee sailors afloat are instructed and amused. Finally at sunset on the 17th the old tub moved out of Alexandria Harbour, and followed in the wake of the numerous vessels that had already cleared the ancient port during the previous fortnight. Fire and boat drill, practice parades by echelons—each echelon representing a group of units which were all to land at the same time—and the rapid slinging of horses and waggons, were carried on assiduously; sufficient in themselves to show that the contemplated operations involved disembarkation in the face of the enemy. No perfection of boat drill could have greatly availed in the case of any disaster, since there were only sufficient boats to carry about 30 per cent. of the men afloat; similarly there was some scarcity of life-belts. However, the beautiful islands of the Aegean Sea were left one by one astern, and no Turkish torpedo disturbed the argonauts. The ancient monastery, clearly seen on the heights of Patmos, was an item of special interest to those conversant with Biblical history.

As regards personal comfort, the appointments of the "Goslar" were somewhat scanty. Every movement of the

Field Companies and Field Troop.

transport animals resounded through her iron decks, which in themselves furnished a poor bed after the sands of Egypt; the food was mostly bully beef and biscuit; while countless swarms of little brown insects, fortunately of vegetarian persuasion, explored the forms of the crowded sleepers.

On the morning of 20th April the "Goslar" steamed through the narrow entrance to Mudros Bay, Lemnos Island, and dropped anchor among the great fleet of vessels already assembled in that safe shelter, ranging from the "Queen Elizabeth" down to humble trawlers from the North Sea. Here for three days echelon parades and disembarkation in full marching order were practised until the troops would almost have preferred a real landing to any more of the climbing with heavy packs, clinging to slender ropes, and hopping on to the deck of a small tumbling boat at the psychological moment to avoid a watery grave, which made up the daily round. However, the proficiency acquired made for safety and despatch in the very near future.

Sir Ian Hamilton's famous Order, beginning :—

"Soldiers of France and the King—Before us lies an adventure unprecedented in modern war. Together with our comrades of the Fleet we are about to force a landing upon an open beach in face of positions vaunted by our enemy as impregnable. . . ."

was still the only official intimation to the troops of the nature of their coming trial, but it was now well understood by all that a landing was to be effected on Gallipoli Peninsula.

CHAPTER II.

GALLIPOLI.

On arrival at Mudros, the general plan of attack had been made known to the Divisional Staff. All hope of surprising the Turk had long since been dissipated by the previous naval efforts; some attempt to assist the actual landing was now to be made by a series of feints on other positions, calculated to confuse the enemy as to our final intentions and to pin down his local garrisons. The three outstanding features of the country about to be attacked were Achi Baba, a great hill on the southern end of the Peninsula overlooking Cape Helles; the lofty plateau of Kilid Bahr, guarding the approaches to the great fortresses of Kilid Bahr and Chanak, whose capture would largely have fulfilled the objects of the expedition; and further north, inland from Suvla Bay, the tangled knot of cliffs and ravines leading up to the heights of Sari Bair, 1000 feet above the sea. Both Achi Baba and Sari Bair commanded the central plateau, and had to fall before the control of the latter could be hoped for.

Two feint attacks were organised, one by portion of the Royal Naval Division up at Bulair, near the head of the Gulf of Saros, the other by the French Division, on Kum Kale and surrounding forts on the Asiatic shore at the entrance to the Straits. The main attack was entrusted to the only seasoned Division present, the immortal 29th, assisted by units of the Royal Naval Division. Their orders were to land at the extreme south-eastern tip of the Peninsula near Cape Helles, and to push on against Achi Baba and Krithia, a small village lying in the shadow of the great hill. Just south of Suvla Bay, between Gaba Tepe and Fisherman's Hut, the Australian and New Zealand Army Corps (to be known hereafter as Anzacs) were to tackle the cliffs, and if all went well would push on past the southern flank of Sari Bair to capture the roadlines running down the full length of the Peninsula from Gallipoli to Cape Helles, thus materially assisting the southern attack by threatening, if not cutting, the only line of retreat of the forces opposed to it, and also of the garrisons of the Kilid Bahr forts.

The Australian Division was to land before the New Zealand and Australian Division, and by afternoon of the 24th April, with the band on the "Queen Elizabeth" playing "Fall

Field Companies and Field Troop.

in and Follow Me," its transports had slipped their anchors, and were standing out of Mudros Bay for the rendezvous off the coast of the Peninsula. Here the troops were transferred to boats and destroyers and moved on quietly towards the beach. Sir Ian Hamilton's Despatch of 20th May, 1915, gives a vivid picture of the scene:—

"All these arrangements worked without a hitch, and were carried out in complete orderliness and silence. No breath of wind ruffled the surface of the sea, and every condition was favourable save for the moon, which, sinking behind the ships, may have silhouetted them against its orb, betraying them thus to the watchers on the shore.

"A rugged and difficult part of the coast had been selected for the landing, so difficult and rugged that I considered the Turks were not at all likely to anticipate such a descent. Indeed, owing to the tows having failed to maintain their exact direction, the actual point of disembarkation was more than a mile north of that which I had selected, and was more closely overhung by steeper cliffs. Although this accident increased the initial difficulty of driving the enemy off the heights inland, it has since proved itself to have been a blessing in disguise, inasmuch as the actual base of the force of occupation has been much better defiladed from shell-fire.

"The beach on which the landing was actually effected is a very narrow strip of sand, about 1000 yards in length, bounded on the north and south by two small promontories. At its southern extremity a deep ravine, with exceedingly steep scrub-clad sides, runs inland in a north-easterly direction. Near the northern end of the beach a small but steep gully runs up into the hills at right angles to the shore. Between the ravine and the gully the whole of the beach is backed by the seaward face of the spur which forms the north-western side of the ravine. From the top of the spur the ground falls almost sheer, except near the southern limit of the beach, where gentler slopes give access to the mouth of the ravine behind. Further inland lie in a tangled knot the under-features of Sari Bair, separated by deep ravines, which make a most confusing diversity of direction. Sharp spurs, covered with dense scrub, and falling away in many places in precipitous sandy cliffs, radiate from the principal mass of the mountain, from which they run north-west, west, south-west, and south to the coast.

"The boats approached the land in the silence and the darkness, and they were close to the shore before the enemy stirred. Then about one battalion of the Turks was seen run-

ANZAC COVE

NORTH BEACH

DUGOUTS NEAR THE SPHINX

Lieut. Colonel G. Barclay, O.B.E.

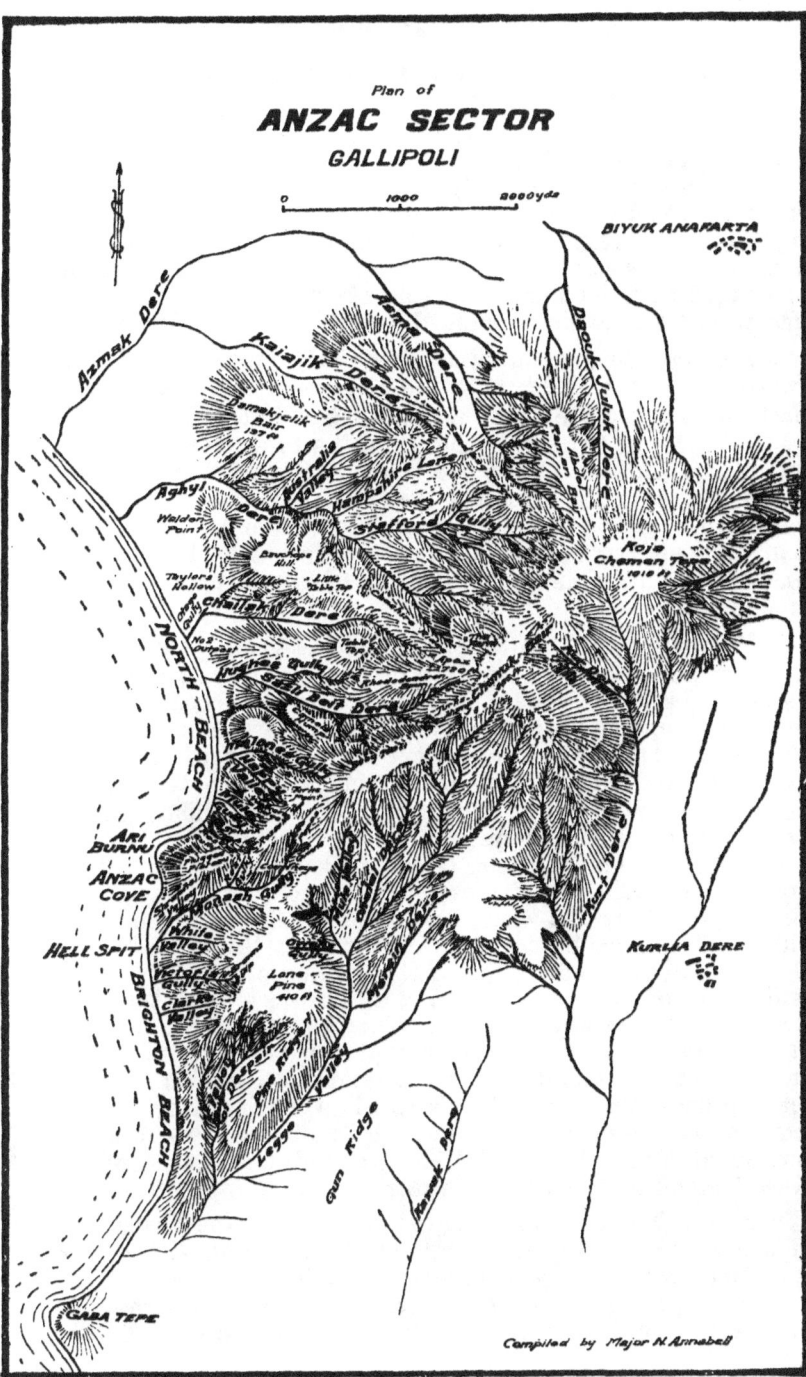

Field Companies and Field Troop.

ning along the beach to intercept the lines of the boats. At this so critical a moment, the conduct of all ranks was most praiseworthy. Not a word was spoken—everyone remained perfectly orderly and quiet awaiting the enemy's fire, which sure enough opened, causing many casualties. The moment the boats touched land, the Australians' turn had come. Like lightning they leapt ashore, and each man as he did so went straight as his bayonet to the enemy. So vigorous was the onslaught that the Turks made no effort to withstand it, and fled from ridge to ridge pursued by the Australian Infantry.''

All night long at Mudros the orderly procession of ships passed out of the harbour for the performance of their several parts in the great drama; a mighty and impressive pageant of the power of Britain. When morning broke they were still moving out, all too slowly for some of the eager spirits who could now hear the faint rumble of the guns 50 miles to the eastward. At 9 a.m. the "Goslar," with the 1st Field Company among the occupants of her crowded decks, weighed anchor, and took her appointed place in the departing line of ships.

Meanwhile the Australians had made good their glorious landing, and were now fighting desperately among the rocky ridges and scrubby valleys of the hills behind the beach. Their leading troops had struck east and south-east from the landing place—Anzac Cove hereafter—and had forced their way over the first ridge (Maclagan's Ridge) and to the further side of the next gully, which from the early hours of the assault was known as Shrapnel Valley. By evening they had established a line of posts, Quinn's, Courtney's, and others, from Pope's Hill, the farthest point reached up Maclagan's Ridge, stretching fan-wise in a southerly direction round the ridge line on the farther side of Shrapnel Valley and so to the beach about a mile south of the landing place. The centre and right of their newly-won position were thus tolerably defined, if by no means secure. The position on the left was far less satisfactory, with an actual gap between the troops and the sea. A well-defined ridge, known as Walker's Ridge, leading down from near Pope's Hill in a north-westerly direction to the beach some distance north of the Cove, was the obvious defensive line in this locality, and here several of the New Zealand battalions were sent on landing.

As the New Zealand transports neared Cape Helles, the men enjoyed a clear view of their distant goal, and of the operations immediately in progress. Under a blue and cloudless sky, apparently almost treeless, but swathed in the verdure of Spring, lay the gaunt ridges of the Peninsula. Tower-

Gallipoli.

ing above them the heights of Achi Baba and Sari Bair rose calm and serene, wearing even then an air of stern detachment unmoved by the advancing hosts. Farther off the snow-capped ranges on the Asiatic shore looked down upon the beginnings of this titanic struggle. To the north-west, like gems on the breast of the calm sea, lay the beautiful islands of Imbros and Samothrace, while in the blue haze of the dim distance the Turkish mainland was faintly discernible. The whole scene was strongly reminiscent of New Zealand on a calm day in early December. But close at hand the battleships, both French and British, were heavily bombarding the coastal forts and Turkish positions further inland, the whole air a-quiver with the recurring detonations, and filled with dust and smoke. On the beach in the immediate foreground, the famous "River Clyde," that modern Horse of Troy, was clearly seen aground, surrounded by smaller craft valiantly pushing troops ashore. Here, too, fountains of earth and water marked the crash of innumerable shells, grim testimony that the Turkish gunners were by no means disabled, and that many of the 29th Division would never see another landing.

But on went the "Goslar" and her sister transports, and within the hour the sight of a concentration of ships beyond Gaba Tepe headland was sufficient evidence of our own approaching trials to distract the mind from consideration of the landscape or the sufferings of others. Here also the guns boomed unceasingly, while a rattle of rifle fire from the nearer cliffs showed that the gallant Australians had gained at least a footing. A captive balloon swayed above one ship, while vigilant seaplanes were circling between the warships and Sari Bair, spotting for the Turkish guns. Destroyers steamed from ship to ship collecting men, and when fully loaded, dashed for the beach, then out again for another load. But the never-ceasing procession of boats to the hospital ships at the end of the line gave some indication of the price of progress.

The glory and sacrifice of that immortal day of landing have been told elsewhere on several occasions, and no attempt at elaboration will be made here. At 3.30 p.m. the destroyer "Foxhound" drew alongside the "Goslar," and an hour later, the 1st Field Company was on its way to the shore. Closer in it was transferred to large cutters which were run aground on the beach. Men leaped into the water and after landing picks, shovels and other gear, the Field Company was lined up in the

Field Companies and Field Troop.

shelter of a cliff while arrangements were made for their immediate employment.

Finally, all but two small detachments were sent to dig support trenches on Plugge's Plateau, a flat knoll on the seaward end of Maclagan's Ridge overlooking the mouth of Shrapnel Valley. Of those left behind, one part was set to prepare gun emplacements for two Australian howitzer batteries, while the other was detailed to construct machine gun posts covering either flank. On Plugge's Plateau, though by no means in the foremost line, the whistle of machine-gun bullets and the constant crash of shrapnel conspired to assist the untried sappers to put up a record first performance in the way of digging trenches under fire. As the trench sank into the kindly earth, and they found themselves with a little decent cover and not yet all dead men, they found time to draw breath and take stock of their surroundings. Out in the bay the battleships were still bombarding the Turkish positions, and the flashes of the guns showed redly through the gathering gloom. Pinnaces and lighters were running to and fro incessantly, with shrapnel lashing the water like hail around them. On the beach below stores and men were accumulating; troops were hurried off as soon as they landed to one or other of the critical points in the uncertain line, but their places were filled immediately by the constant stream of wounded. The ground from the beach came up steeply in sharp narrow ridges, composed of a gravelly soil and covered with short wiry scrub in which, a few hours earlier, the Turkish snipers and machine-gunners had screened themselves while they took toll of the first intrepid landing parties. Further inland the ground rose more gradually, still much cut up by spurs and gullies, to the dominating peak of Sari Bair, some two or three miles away. Everything was seen through a haze of smoke and dust, while the acrid fumes of various explosives polluted the whole atmosphere. Night was falling, and nothing could be seen of either friend or foe up towards the fighting line, but the rattle of rifle and machine-gun fire never ceased.

By midnight trench and emplacements were complete, but there was no sleep at Anzac that night. The sappers manned the trench they had just dug and stood by till dawn, in momentary expectation of being called upon to withstand the enemy, who had received reinforcements and kept up incessant activity along the whole line. The beach gradually became one long hospital ward, but without appliances and almost without attendants, though the weary doctors did all that men might do.

Gallipoli.

With daylight, road reconnaissance was immediately undertaken and later in the day the Field Company commenced to form a track out to the front line positions at Walker's Ridge on the left. That night parties were again employed on howitzer emplacements, but by the afternoon of Tuesday, the 27th, every available man was required for the front line. Half the Field Company was sent to Walker's Ridge and the remainder to Quinn's Post, where they alternately took spells of front line duty, and bent their energies to the provision of communication and firing trenches. At Walker's Ridge, in particular, the garrison had been too busy skirmishing and fighting ever since the landing to have spent any time on their trenches, which were practically non-existent in some places, and only a series of shallow disconnected pits in others. The sappers began at once to deepen and connect these early efforts, but were soon forced to drop their shovels and help to repel a determined attack. For his coolness and resource in this little brush, Corporal C. W. Saunders was awarded the first decoration won by a New Zealand Engineer—the D.C.M.

On the other side of the Divisional sector, at Quinn's Post, the sappers were immediately in the very forefront of the battle, in a spot notorious throughout the whole of the Gallipoli operations. This position had been taken on the day of the landing by Captain Quinn and his party of the 15th Australian Battalion, and had been held since despite all efforts by the Turks, entrenched not more than 20 yards away. Situated right on the rim of the ridge at the head of Monash Gully, as the top end of Shrapnel Valley was already named, this Post was the only point in our whole line where our position could be said to excel the Turks', and the fact appeared to annoy the sons of the Prophet beyond belief. As at Walker's, there were no trenches when the sappers arrived, and a very limited field of fire. The existing pits were soon deepened and connected up into a serviceable firing line. Saps were then pushed steadily forward to just over the crest of the ridge, when by joining up from saphead to saphead a new trench was formed, giving the superiority of fire and observation, which alone enabled us to hold Quinn's right through the campaign. These sapping operations were greatly assisted by the command given by a small observation post erected under fire by Corporal C. W. Salmon, which was afterwards extremely useful to both infantry and artillery observers. Salmon received the D.C.M. for his fine work. On completion of this front line trench, parties were set on to the problem

Field Companies and Field Troop.

of communications, and numerous tracks gradually made their appearance, breaking off up the spurs to the firing line from the convenient main track afforded by the line of Shrapnel Valley.

The Turk was fully alive to the possibilities of this deep, narrow valley running up into the heart of our position; in fact, it was due to his assiduous attentions that the place came by its expressive name. Though no amount of shelling could hinder us from using this natural access, the gully soon became a veritable Valley of Tribulation, strewn with every kind of equipment and flanked by stinking dead mules, with a never-ending stream of the pathetically cheerful walking wounded, or of more serious cases on stretchers, many of them doomed to die long ere the transports reached Alexandria from sheer lack of accommodation and necessary attendance.

With these improvements, the need for a comprehensive survey of the whole position became acute, and by the beginning of May, the C.R.E. was able to furnish G.H.Q. with a serviceable plan showing the whole of the Divisional position. Apart from the continual conflict against superior numbers, conditions of life were still pleasant enough. The great heat of summer had not yet come, and the invigorating breath of spring was still in the air, with birds singing in the bushes, and wild flowers growing on the open ridges.

Down on the beach some sort of order was gradually being evolved, with Headquarters, Field Ambulance Hospitals and Ordnance Stores nestling under the precarious shelter of the low cliffs. The Engineers' Stores of explosives, wire, sandbags, timber and so on, were not so fortunate, and were relegated to Hell Spit, a narrow point jutting out at the southern extremity of Anzac Cove, and receiving all attention going in the way of fire from both flanks. The position had its advantages in that stores were terribly scarce and the unhealthy locality of the depot may have deterred some importunate applicants for material. For a time the Turks enjoyed uninterrupted observation of all our movements at the Cove from positions they had established on two promontories—Nibrunesi Point, about four miles to the north, and Gaba Tepe, about two miles south. Expeditions were ultimately organised to deal with these offensive lookouts. The Adjutant and two N.C.O's of the 1st Field Company accompanied a New Zealand force to Nibrunesi Point, where everything was destroyed and the garrison captured. Australians attacking Gaba Tepe found the position heavily wired,

Gallipoli.

and were forced to withdraw, and the place remained in enemy hands till the evacuation.

The horses belonging to the 1st Field Company were left for some days on the "Goslar," and were then returned to Lemnos and Egypt. Many of the drivers, however, returned from Lemnos and served in the line as sappers. For some days after landing, officers and men of the Engineers, in common with all other troops on the Peninsula, had slept when and where they could, but with the first easing of the constant pressure of work some attempt was made to establish definite bivouacs—in Walker's Rest Gully and on Pope's Hill—for the respective parties of left and right sectors. These "bivvies" or "possies" were simply ledges and holes cut out in the rear slopes of the hills, but day after day in spare moments men worked away at their little shelters till some became quite pretentious residences fitted with many conveniences. Later on these mansions were quite commonly put up to auction; in fact, one enterprising sapper made a regular business of it, and spent all his spare time and energy in building up-to-date shelters to trade to the cash aristocrats of the moment. The flies were the most persistent enemy on Gallipoli; it was occasionally possible to avoid Turkish attentions, but even in the few hours allowed for sleep, generally in the day time, the fly was always on hand and always a source of irritation and discomfort. Food of course was never free from the plague, and the cumulative evil effects of a protracted diet of bully beef and biscuits were inevitably heightened in that sordid environment by the disease-carrying tendencies of the myriad flies.

At the beginning of May, the impression still remained general that we would commence a successful advance again before very long, if only because the positions won on the first day were now proving themselves so perilously insecure. A minor attack was in fact arranged for the evening of May 2nd, with the intention of improving our line between Walker's and Quinn's. The Turks still held the head of a small gully forking from Monash Gully and running up between Pope's Hill and Walker's Ridge, where, in addition to fine observation of all our movements in the vicinity, they prevented any direct communication between Pope's and Walker's. Again between Pope's Hill and Quinn's Post there ran out a sharp narrow ridge, so far unoccupied, but likely to prove very dangerous to us if the Turks should establish a hold upon it. A mixed force of Australians, New Zealanders, and men of the Royal Naval Division was detailed for the

Field Companies and Field Troop.

assault, which took place at 7 p.m., assisted by bombardment from the warships off-shore. Some delays undoubtedly occurred in assembly, so that the first attackers from Quinn's Post were advancing "on their own," but this could hardly have affected the ultimate result. From none of our positions was it possible for more than a handful of men to come into action at the same time; and as soon as they showed on the crest of the ridge they fell riddled with a stream of machine-gun bullets. All night vain efforts to advance were continued till morning showed the hopelessness of the attempt, and the precarious position of the gallant few who were now out in front in improvised pits or lying behind rocks. Two parties of Engineers were attached to the attacking forces. Of one party attempting to dig a forward line about midnight all were killed or wounded save two, and the other party was early requisitioned to carry the wounded back to the shelter of our side of the ridge, and later to cut a track to get them down to the beach. In this work they were assisted by the Royal Navals still waiting to support the already hopeless attack on the hills above. Soon the Navals were ordered to make a final effort up the ridge between Pope's and Quinn's, and up to the ridge they went, to die as soon as they came within view of the waiting Turks. At 8 a.m. orders came to withdraw. The attack had failed, and Dead Man's Ridge, as it was rightly known thereafter, became a Turkish post. Captain F. Waite, of the New Zealand Engineers, who had led forward a party at a critical period in the early morning, was awarded the D.S.O., while Sapper Scrimshaw received the D.C.M. for coolness and gallantry throughout the proceedings. Sergeant Wallace and Sapper A. S. Carlyon were recommended at the same time, but were unfortunately killed before any action could be taken in the way of awards. Both men had been prominent in all activities of the Company right from the day of the landing.

This reverse showed plainly that for the present at any rate our activities were to be confined to the ground already held, and detailed plans were laid for consolidation and improvement of each portion. In particular an inner line of defences were determined upon, and immediately put under construction in those areas where no trench already existed. Starting at Hell Spit this inner line ran up Maclagan's Ridge, over Plugge's Plateau, and then down the cliffs to Ari Burnu, as the small point at the northern extremity of Anzac Cove was known. No alteration was possible in the line of the outer defences; all that could be done there was to improve them—a task that would have taxed the energies of six times

Gallipoli.

the number of sappers available. The normal equipment of a Division on active service is three Field Companies—here on Anzac one only was available, and that one already sadly depleted by wounds and sickness.

The defences of the outer line were now divided into four distinct sectors, of which No. 3 comprised the cluster of Posts at Quinn's, Courtney's, and Pope's, while Walker's Ridge constituted No. 4. Nos. 1 and 2 were under control of the purely Australian Division further south, and do not enter into this account. On the three Posts mentioned, and at Walker's Ridge, great efforts were now made. All trenches were deepened and widened, some deviated, and other isolated portions joined up by judicious sapping, while communications were improved and shelters provided, and the whole front put into as permanent a form as possible under the circumstances. Quinn's Post, as ever, was the centre-piece of the daily harassing efforts of the enemy, and the occupants actually took their lives in their hands every time they entered the front line. However, some measure of relief was close at hand.

Back in Egypt the men of the Australian Light Horse and the New Zealand Mounted Rifles had been daily growing more and more impatient as time went on and no prospect appeared of joining in the struggle on the Peninsula. Finally they were all sent to serve as infantry, leaving a handful of men to care for the horses in Egypt. With them came the Field Troop as reinforcements to the Field Company; with them also came the horses of the Field Troop for reasons more difficult to explain, since no transport had ever been used at Anzac. These finally found themselves back in Egypt after some weeks cruising in the Mediterranean. The Field Troop on the 13th May took over all Engineering works on Walker's Ridge, where the Mounted men also relieved the Infantry garrisons. A considerable portion of their time at this stage was occupied in digging wells. Water could generally be had for a day or two, then slowly but surely the well dried up, and more digging had to be carried on. At the same time the track up to Russell's Top, on the summit of Walker's Ridge, was re-graded and widened, and in certain places the firing line was being improved by pushing out sap heads to be joined up later.

The Turks were not long in providing a full-dress performance for the benefit of the newcomers, who now held most of the line, the original garrison having been withdrawn to take part in the great attack at Helles on the 7th May. For a week our line had been perilously thinly held, but the enemy

Field Companies and Field Troop.

had been in ignorance of his opportunity. On the evening of the 18th a heavy bombardment appeared to presage another enemy attempt to drive the unbelievers into the sea, and with the dawn of the 19th it commenced. Covered by intense rifle and machine-gun fire and a cloud of snipers, the Turks came on along the whole line in droves, crying vigorously on Allah as they advanced. But the united efforts of Allah and his faithful followers were powerless against the machine-guns of the infidels. Well posted in hopeful anticipation of just such an opportunity, the Mounteds mowed them down in swathes. The advancing line would ebb and flow and finally break, but ere long a fresh line took its place, coming steadily down to meet the withering hail of lead. The Turk is a bonny fighter, but valour alone has little chance against machine-guns, and it is to be hoped that his belief in the special corner of Paradise reserved for those who die in battle has some foundation in fact. Only the merest trickle of men ever reached our trenches, and by 11 a.m. the attack had completely broken down. Soon after a white flag appeared, and appeals were made for an armistice to bury the dead. While negotiations were proceeding, opportunity was taken by the soldiers on both sides to have a good look at one another and at the ground so recently fought over. Very soon, however, the Turks were observed to be collecting rifles and bayonets outside their trenches, and when a fat German major, with the original notions of honour peculiar to his species, commenced solemnly to pace the distance between the opposing lines, proceedings were hurriedly broken off and firing went on as before.

The activities of ordinary trench warfare once more held the stage right along the front, marked by continual effort on our side to improve our inferior positions against the ceaseless firing and bomb-throwing of the better-posted enemy. Bombing, particularly at Quinn's, was practised by the Turks incessantly, their supply of the cricket ball variety being apparently unlimited. To meet this constant menace, the sappers erected the systems of overhead cover, which became such a feature of all front line work on Gallipoli where the trenches were close enough to enable hand-thrown bombs to be used.

Later on, as steel loopholed plates became available for letting into the parapet, the front trench was more like a long closed-in gallery than anything else. Such a system could only have been possible in a place like Quinn's, where hostile artillery was powerless to operate owing to the proximity of the opposing trenches.

Gallipoli.

The overhead cover and sandbag walls were carried down right into the small gullies behind, where there was almost as much need for them as in the front trench. The ridge was so narrow that any bomb thrown a little too far came bounding on down the steep hillside to explode among the garrison off duty in rear. Bombing operations of course were not entirely a prerogative of the Turk. We had used bombs from the start, but where the Turks seemed well supplied with the manufactured article, we were forced to make our own from jam tins and bulk explosive in the Engineer's Stores, a job which was always waiting down on the beach for any men of the Headquarters' section temporarily unemployed. One humourist up at Quinn's amused himself by throwing over lightly-loaded bombs supplied with a long slow-burning fuse. When a few of these had gone across the Turks hit on the bright idea of heaving them back again. After timing their efforts for a few minutes, the operator substituted a full-powered projectile armed with a short piece of slow fuse spliced to a length of "instantaneous." His vis-a-vis and his admiring friends enjoyed the joke exceedingly, if the squeals and jabbering that followed the burst were any criterion. But that little notion could only succeed once or twice, and generally speaking, the Turk had the best of the bombing exchanges.

On the 21st May, the enemy again renewed his requests for an armistice, and though reluctant on general grounds, our authorities decided to take the opportunity of burying and identifying the dead, arrangements being finally made for a truce all day on the 24th. Burial parties from either side were to meet in neutral territory, and to mark out the ground by a line of white flags midway between trenches. Each party would work on its own side, but would hand over strange dead to be buried by their own compatriots. In practice this was found impossible; in some places the dead lay so thickly and so intermingled, that there was no time to sort them out if they were to be buried at all. A certain number of Anzac dead were thus buried by the Turks, unidentified, and these were the men afterwards recorded "missing, believed killed," by the Court of Enquiry. Down on the beach the majority of their surviving brethren were celebrating their temporary freedom from care with a glorious wash!

After the armistice work went on as before, the only departure from routine lines being the commencement of mining operations on an extended scale. At Walker's, the improved firing line formed by the joining of the sap heads was now complete. In point of fact further saps were already being driven out, which within a few days provided this sub-

Field Companies and Field Troop.

sector with an additional trench line, which, added to internal improvements, left the position pretty secure. Support lines were also in progress at all other points along the front.

At Pope's Hill, New Zealand Engineers were working with a garrison composed of men of the 4th Australian Infantry Brigade, whose C.O., Colonel Monash, went to the trouble of forwarding special commendation of the good work done by Lieutenant Paine and the sappers working with him in that locality. The work consisted principally of sapping forward to improve the fire positions, and was carried on without cessation under constant shell fire, which caused many casualties, and ultimately resulted in the death of Lieutenant Paine before any official action could be taken to recognise his good work.

Several small mine tunnels had been pushed out by the sappers in front of Quinn's during May, with a view to protective rather than offensive action, since it was recognised that a Turkish mine of any magnitude would have practically had the effect of blowing the top clean off the small crest of the ridge held by our men. On the 25th sounds of enemy picks were heard at a distance estimated by several experienced miners to be only two feet. A charge of 32 lbs. of guncotton was therefore laid and fired, without much success, since the enemy was heard once more within a few hours. Next day he was again located, driving towards one of our loaded galleries, but apparently at the moment just above an empty chamber. A small charge was accordingly laid here and duly fired. Inspection revealed a hole in the roof leading into an enemy gallery, but the Turkish miners were on the alert and a shower of bombs precluded any attempts at closer investigation. To clear this unpleasant situation, a side drive was decided on from one of our existing galleries, from which, when sufficiently near, we might definitely destroy the Turks' gallery or at least close their entrance into our system. This was ultimately successful, but a small mine, fired at the same time in another gallery where suspicions had been aroused, again had the unlooked-for result of opening up a passage into another Turkish chamber. Two more small charges failed to close this, and ultimately we had to block the hole with packed sandbags and post a sentry, pending arrangements to drive under the chamber and wreck it from below.

Before this operation could be carried out, noises in another of our tunnels had become so loud that the miners became a trifle apprehensive, and one, on striking a soft patch with his pick, thought he had broken through into the Turks'

Gallipoli.

gallery. Being totally unarmed at the moment, he rushed hastily out of the tunnel, possibly to get a rifle, but his impetuous movements were not reassuring to other men nearer to the exit, who also made for the open air with stories of hostile invasion. On receipt of this news, 2nd Lieutenant the Hon. R. P. Butler, who was in charge of the general Engineering activities of the Post, led a small party bent on the eviction of the intruders, only to find that the only occupant of the still intact tunnel was a "listener" who had entered on the course of his usual rounds. He reported the enemy very close, however, so a charge of 100 lbs. of ammonal was laid and well tamped, an operation of some two anxious hours, but which, when fired, caused an excellent upheaval, which must have caught some Turks and shaken their fire trench considerably. Lieutenant Butler, accompanied by Captain McNeill and Sergeant A. W. Abbey, immediately entered our tunnel to investigate results, and, just as they reached the debris, were startled by a sudden burst of flame, which enveloped the whole area, but fortunately did not follow them in their retreat. While they were underground, a further explosion had been heard, which seemed to show that the Turks had been laying a charge when their efforts were frustrated by the explosion of ours. Nothing daunted, the enemy were heard again almost immediately on the other side of the Post, apparently determined to achieve results somewhere. Colonel Pridham took an early opportunity of visiting the Post and forming his own opinion of the situation on the spot. Next night we blew two more charges in selected localities, and thereafter, for a time at least, Turkish enthusiasm was considerably diminished.

The insignificant charges used by us naturally appear to invite comment, but the difficulty was that we dared not use large charges even had they been available, for fear of threatening the stability of the position. All we had in mind was to forestall the Turk by blowing in his galleries or exploding his charges while he was still as far as possible from our trenches. However he got in first in the early morning of the 29th May, when one of two mines fired wrecked a portion of the Post and broke a gap in the front line through which the Turks poured pell-mell. The crash of the explosion had been sufficient alarm to every man on Anzac, and while the machine-gunners on Pope's Hill and Russell's Top thrashed the ground in front of Quinn's, reinforcements hurried up from the reserve areas in rear. However, the surviving garrison was equal to the test, and very soon overpowered those

Field Companies and Field Troop.

of the enemy who had entered the Post, and by a sudden counter-attack dispersed the clamouring horde in front. To the sappers fell the ticklish task of clearing up and repairing the broken trench. As soon as darkness fell a party crept up to the job, but their disgruntled opponents in front kept up such a fusillade of bombs that no progress was possible and all hands save isolated sentries were forced to seek cover. Next morning work was again attempted. The only possible approach to the damaged trench in daylight was through a small tunnel, the end of which was almost completely blocked with debris of one sort and another. One man only could work at one time, and slowly and laboriously he cleared the exit, loading the spoil into bags which were dragged away by relays of men behind him. Once out in the trench, the dangerous position, and the unpleasant nature of the blood-soaked and fly-covered ruins, combined to effect a speedy clearance. Two sentries watched from adjacent stations, and on the warning cry of "Bomb!" the sapper engaged in the trench at the moment was forced to dive into his tunnel for cover. During that night the trench was practically reconstructed.

The Turk on his side had not been idle; in fact, for either gallantry or resource he was very hard to beat. During the same night he built a heavy blockhouse in the crater of the second mine fired on the 29th, about half-way between the opposing lines. From this he now began to make himself so extremely objectionable to the overwrought garrison that two men of the 1st Field Company—Lance-Corporal F. J. H. Fear, and Sapper E. A. Hodges—volunteered to attempt the demolition of his new stronghold. At 10 p.m. on the 1st June they crawled out over the parapet and wormed their way towards the blockhouse. Once on the spot the job was still one of extreme delicacy, since the Turks could be heard conversing below, and earth and sand had to be scraped away in order to lay their 12 lbs. of guncotton directly on the wooden roof. For 35 minutes they lay there quietly perfecting their arrangements, then after lighting the fuse under cover of a haversack they reached their own trench just as the blockhouse and garrison were destroyed with a loud bang. Both men received the D.C.M. for their courage and initiative.

Among men noted by Colonel Pridham, with special reference to gallantry and ability shown on these defences at Quinn's Post, was Sergeant H. A. Foote of the 1st Field Company, who ultimately received the Military Medal.

But critical as the situation at Quinn's undoubtedly always

Gallipoli.

was, the devoted occupants of that spear head of the defence had no monopoly of the dangers and excitements incidental to mining operations on the Peninsula. Thus the records note that on one occasion Sergeant H. W. Newman, of the 1st Field Company, while stationed at Courtney's Post worked for some hours with a bayonet enlarging a hole between one of our galleries and one of the enemy's. He later entered the Turkish tunnel and made a valuable reconnaissance, though enemy voices were plainly audible all the time, doubtless engaged in the philosophical discussions with which all soldiers while away the hours of trench duty. On Newman's return an attempt was made to lay a charge in the enemy's gallery, but the noise attracted their garrison, who immediately commenced investigations. Newman shot one of them and held up the others while the hole was blocked with sandbags, when the charge was laid behind the block and blown with disastrous results to the enemy's mine. Incidents of this description, while not frequent enough to become monotonous, were constantly occurring all through our period of occupation of the forward Posts, but very few have been actually recorded, and probably many others were never known save to the two or three principal actors in these underground dramas.

CHAPTER III.

SUMMER AT ANZAC.

At this point in the history of the Engineers, the 2nd Field Company joined forces with those on the Peninsula. A little break in the continuity of events is necessary to record the inauguration and earlier experiences of this Company—the first and only complete Field Company to leave the shores of New Zealand for a European battlefield.

About the end of January, 1915, announcements were made in the New Zealand papers that there were vacancies for suitable men in an Engineer Company about to be formed at Trentham, which by that time had become the established camp for the whole of New Zealand. By the middle of February sufficient men had been enlisted to commence the formation of the Company. Lieutenant-Colonel G. Barclay, V.D. Officer Commanding the North Island Railway Battalion, New Zealand Engineers, and formerly known in Southern military circles as Officer Commanding the Dunedin Engineers, took command of the Company with the rank of Major.

The trials of training and equipment followed, and the new Company rapidly improved. Model trenches, shelters and defence systems sprang into existence in the corner of Trentham reserved for these engineering feats, pontoon bridges were swung across the Hutt River on several occasions, and to crown their warlike preparations the Company took part in a fierce battle at Wallaceville on the 9th and 10th April. In the way of equipment—pontoons, toolcarts, waggons and limbers—they took away from New Zealand everything not already secured by the Field Troop. This was brought home vividly to later reinforcements, when, instead of pleasant bridging stunts on the cool waters of the Hutt, or learning the names and uses of the prehistoric weapons in the tool carts, they spent their days in sweat of brow and bitterness of soul digging trenches in the shingly soil of Trentham. Doubtless, the honest labour made them hard, one great consideration; but the time spent on those futile trenches, where every stone had to be dressed by the right, and the parapet was treated with a garden rake before the influx of Sunday visitors, became pathetic in later days. If the greater portion had been blown up once a week and then reconstructed, that

THE 2nd FIELD COMPANY IN TRENTHAM.

THIS WAS THE ONLY FULLY EQUIPPED FIELD COMPANY WHICH LEFT NEW ZEALAND.

Photo lent by Major N. Annabell.

Summer at Anzac.

approach to service conditions might have been of some advantage to the budding talent.

By the 17th April the 2nd Field Company was considered ready to face the final inspection, and received the already time-honoured compliment that it was "a fine body of men—probably the finest that had ever left New Zealand." On the same day the company embarked at Wellington with the 4th Reinforcements, 40 men on the transport "Knight Templar," and 200 more on the "Waitomo," the flagship "Willochra" completing the little squadron. The ships travelled without convoy straight to Albany, where they arrived at daybreak on the 29th.

Here the troops were disembarked for a three hours' route march and later for general leave in the town—a glorious day not soon forgotten. Albany will long have a place in the pleasant memories of thousands of New Zealanders, not only as being their last point of contact with Australasia before going on into the unknown, but also on account of the invariable hospitality received from the kindly townsfolk.

Next day the 4th Reinforcements continued their journey. The three weeks' run to Aden was uneventful, being occupied only by the ordinary easy routine of a troopship, which includes long hours of thoughtful study—with a pipe—of the foaming waters as they slip along the ship's sides. There were the usual deck games and concerts, and Neptune, as ever, cheerily paid his compliments.

At Aden, on the 20th May, some three weeks after the event, the flagship gave out the first hint of the Gallipoli landing in the terse statement, "There were 10,000 Colonial casualties at the Dardanelles." After a short and uninteresting halt of two hours, the troopships moved on again up the Red Sea to Port Tewfik, Suez, where the troops disembarked and entrained for Zeitoun.

The 4th Reinforcements wasted little time in Egypt. Within five days of landing, the 2nd Field Company, less 22 men detailed to look after the transport in Zeitoun, was aboard the "Minnetonka," which sailed from Alexandria on 30th May. At Lemnos it transhipped to the "Clacton" and pushed on for the Peninsula. By early morning of the 3rd June it was ashore at Anzac, and by night had taken up its quarters in Monash Gully.

The 1st Field Company had been relieved by Australian Engineers the previous day, and was down on the beach enjoying a brief period of such rest as could be obtained.

Field Companies and Field Troop.

Within three or four days, however, the Australians were recalled, and reorganisation of the New Zealand Engineers took place. The Field Troop was still left in charge of Walker's Ridge, Quinn's was undertaken by three sections from the 2nd Field Company and one from the 1st, while the further section from the 2nd Company gave its attention to wells and roads in Monash Gully. Pope's and Courtney's occupied a section each from the 1st Company, leaving their remaining section to build a pier and supervise various works going on along the waterfront.

The Engineers' Store down at Hell Spit was now in full blast, engaged on plumbing and carpentering operations, laying the foundation for a pumping plant, and making bombs, periscopes and movable wire entanglements under the direction of the Headquarters' staff. Grenade manufacturing had long since become a fine art, and the various types of tins originally tried had now given place to the green fuse tin from the 18-pounder guns. These tins were stout, and about the size of a condensed milk tin. Two holes punched in both top and bottom allowed passage of the wires, which were joined across the top after loading had taken place. A dry guncotton-primer or half a stick of gelignite was placed in the tin, surrounded by unexploded Turkish cartridges, and the whole equipped with a detonator and a five seconds' length of fuse. A heavier type of bomb was easily made by securing two or three pound slabs of guncotton to a piece of wood shaped like a hairbrush, the handle facilitating a longer throw. Where these could be got into the opposing trenches the results were highly satisfactory, and the destruction was not confined to personnel. As a general rule, however, the trenches were too far apart, and a demand sprang up for some kind of mechanical bomb-thrower. No springs were available on the Peninsula, and recourse was finally had to a trench mortar necessitating two fuses, one to detonate the bomb on arrival at its destination, and the other to ignite the propelling charge. After several favourable demonstrations the device was taken up to Quinn's, where the stout occupants of the opposing trenches had certainly earned some little extra attention. Unfortunately at one of the first attempts the bomb fuse lit but the propelling fuse failed to ignite. Sergeant R. R. Nairn of the 2nd Field Company saw the danger and immediately attempted to draw the detonator, but he was too late, and his unselfish effort to save his mates cost him his life.

As extra protection against enemy bombers in the more exposed Posts, where overhead cover was unobtainable or in-

Summer at Anzac.

advisable on account of the risk of the occupants being trapped, bomb screens were now introduced by the Sappers. Made of wire netting and erected on the parapet, these screens ensured that a bomb would either strike them and fall back into No Man's Land, or else would pass right over the trenches and burst harmlessly behind. The netting was constantly being cut by machine-gun fire and required endless repairing, but was a welcome advance on the old style of trying to dodge the missiles or of dropping an overcoat on them to attempt to blanket the explosion.

One portion of Quinn's Post known as the "Racecourse" had been so consistently harassed by the Turkish bombers, that on arrival of the 2nd Field Company, they found it temporarily abandoned—a fine opportunity to show the mettle of the new sappers, especially as the ground was well worth some risk in the reclaiming. Bomb screens minimised the risk of sudden dissolution, and little by little, with two or three men at a time working lying down, enough earth was scooped up to allow kneeling room. All dirt removed was filled into sandbags and dragged back for further use. From this slow laborious beginning the work progressed rapidly, gaining in speed as more room became available, until gradually the trench was sufficiently deepened and widened to enable work to be done in comparative comfort. Sandbags filled with gravel from the beach were built into a breastwork in which a steel loophole plate was fitted, with a crack shot posted to keep down the heads of too inquisitive Turks. Day and night the work went on till four loophole plates had been placed in position, and a section of the trench provided with overhead cover, when it again became part of the garrisoned defences of the Post. This particular corner of Quinn's was undoubtedly the most dangerous portion of the Anzac line at this time, and the constant casualties had been causing great concern. The improvements effected under the skilful supervision of the former Staff Sergeants-Major who had come with the new Field Company, earned the hearty commendation of the responsible authorities.

Apart from the particular enterprise just noted, one of many similar exploits on Anzac, the steady routine works of trench improvement and roading were going on all the time. In addition to the new bomb screens erected on the parapets, the system of overhead cover already in use in the front trenches was being extended to the support lines as labour and material became available. At Quinn's again, a new

Field Companies and Field Troop.

communication trench was required leading back over the crest of the ridge and down into the comparative safety of Monash Gully. From the Post up to the ridge any such work would lie in full view of the opposing Turks, who could be safely relied upon to improve their opportunity. The new C.T. was finally achieved by laboriously driving a small tunnel at the required depths of the trench, and later breaking in the top and removing the debris in a single night. ·At Pope's and Courteney's similar operations were in progress and similar methods were employed to overcome the numerous problems presented by the commanding positions of the energetic enemy, and by the tremendous natural difficulties of the country.

At Courtney's Post, the garrison hit upon a promising plan for returning some of the unwelcome attentions showered upon them. A Turkish battery, which shelled them with regularity and enthusiasm every morning and afternoon, was at length "spotted" in some tunnels facing them from a spur to the northward, and within easy range of our mountain guns. It was accordingly decided to introduce some light artillery into the front line to try the effect of close range shooting on the offending battery. The sappers forthwith prepared an underground chamber in the front line, with sacking across the opening in front, and there a 10-pounder gun from an Indian Mountain Battery was installed. The attendant "Janis" got off 20 rounds rapid, then hastily dismantled and removed their gun before reprisals commenced. The Turks were not noticeably cowed, but as a relief from the monotony of passive endurance of daily insults, these little enterprises had their merits.

Down at the Cove the new pier was already well out into deep water. Once there, the problem of pile driving added itself to the inexhaustible supply of unforeseen contingencies provided by Gallipoli. But not for nothing did the Field Companies include men who had served on many a far-off outpost of civilisation with little but a nimble brain and a ready hand to help them in their emergencies. A West African expert soon " came to light " with a monkey fashioned with the aid of the blacksmith from a dud Turkish 9.5 shell. This, despite the derisive comments of the onlookers and possibly to the secret relief of the inventor, failed to explode when used, and thereafter drove many piles most satisfactorily. The completion of the pier greatly facilitated the landing of all stores and troops.

At the Stores the making of chevaux-de-frise had been added to the list of local enterprises and was going on apace.

Summer at Anzac.

For some time efforts had been made to put out wire in front of all our positions, but in many places, for obvious reasons, it was quite impossible to send parties beyond the front trench, and chevaux-de-frise, or "knife-rests" in the vernacular, were the only alternative. Each section of this obstacle was composed of an iron or wooden framework very similar to the ordinary knife-rest of civilian life. Barbed wire was stretched across and tangled in between the end crosses of the frames, which were then ready for No Man's Land. They were carried up to the front line and carefully put out over the parapet at night, then anchored down as best they might be. To drive a stake or make any other sound was to invite interference of a sudden and intensely disagreeable nature, so the operation was a veritable deed of darkness. Such lightly-fastened obstructions were easily removed, and more than once the obstacles so carefully placed in the early hours of the night were adorning the enemy's parapet by daylight.

Mining, always a feature at Quinn's Post, had been carried on also at Pope's, Courtney's and Walker's Ridge since the beginning of June, and hardly a day passed without some small mine being blown either by the enemy or ourselves. Lieutenant R. Black of the Field Troop was the moving spirit of the Engineering operations on Walker's Ridge, where he was eventually "gassed" in one of the mine tunnels. As time wore on our galleries were extended and improved until it became apparent from the Turkish operations that they had abandoned the idea of blowing us up, and were now seeking to protect their own front line. This was the time when an adequate supply of explosives would have been welcome to the hard-working miners. As things were, we read in the official records such items as these: "A mine of 37 lbs. guncotton was fired at Quinn's—Result unknown." Or "A camouflet of 10 lbs. of guncotton was detonated. Result apparently satisfactory." Charges of this kind were often less than the amount of explosive contained in a 9-inch shell, and in their hopeless inadequacy merely afford one more instance to protect their own front line. This was the time when an by lack of proper material.

On the other hand, the great success often achieved with the insignificant resources at command throws into high relief the patient and heroic endeavours put forth by the indefatigable operators. In mining operations in particular success was ever to the brave. Judgment and skill and steady labour all played their part, but the hour had to come when everything depended on the final firing of the charge. A charge laid too soon would fail in its effect—if delayed too long

Field Companies and Field Troop.

there would be no chance to lay a charge at all. Very occasionally picks met in the middle, when the race was to the miner who got his rifle or bomb through the hole first.

The most ominous moment in the galleries was when enemy movement was noticed to have ceased—certain sign that the other man had decided to fire. Stripped to the waist, the miners would then work for their lives, laying and tamping the charge, confident of getting out before the enemy was ready. When all was in order the handle of the exploder was rammed home and a muffled report shook the air. A burst of flame or smoke rising from the Turkish trenches was sometimes the welcome intimation of a successful effort, showing that the charge had blown right through into their gallery. Craters were seldom blown since explosive was so scarce, and in any case a charge large enough to blow a crater was inadvisable near our own trenches; and in other parts of the line, the Turks who occupied the higher ground might have been able to use the crater as an advanced position. Many notable acts of courage and cool daring took place in these underground burrows. On one occasion when a corporal of the 2nd Field Company had broken a hole into a Turkish gallery and could see the inmates laying a charge, he took in a charge alone and succeeded in firing it first. At another time the same man was following two officers into a mine recently fired, when the leaders were overcome by noxious fumes, whereupon he got both of them out before succumbing himself.

An excellent piece of work was performed by the Field Troop during the night 22nd-23rd July in putting out wire entanglements on Russell's Top within 30 yards of the Turkish trenches. Corporal P. G. Pearce was mentioned in Army Corps Orders for gallantry on this occasion.

Down in Monash Gully the sappers hunting for water had all the excitement of gold mining. To strike water there was quite as thrilling as, and from some points of view much more valuable than, striking a reef in a gold area. Wells were sunk in every spot that showed any sign of proving favourable, but in general the experience here was the same as that of the seekers on the left flank—water could be found but seldom in any permanent form. Some wells did prove profitable, and yielded a fair flow all through the summer, but never enough for comfort. Water was also brought to Anzac in barges and pumped up into a storage reservoir on the hill 150 feet above the beach, whence it was led by a pipe-line into reserve tanks in Shrapnel Valley. Even then supplies were

Summer at Anzac.

scanty, and men even with a signed order often had to wait three or four hours before they could get their water-bottles filled.

Another illustration of the many-sided duties the sapper might be called upon to perform was afforded by the employment of one who happened to be an artist to draw and paint various aspects of the enemy position for the use of our artillery observers. In order to do this he was sent aloft in a captive balloon, where he made some splendid drawings, and fully availed himself of a unique opportunity to gather material for a further series of Anzac scenes, which were painted later, and many of which are now widely known and appreciated in New Zealand.

In June all drivers of the 1st Field Company were sent back to Alexandria, where the horses were reported to be losing condition owing to lack of attention. To make up this further defection from the available strength of the depleted Company, some 30 men of various trades were transferred from the Infantry battalions. Here at Anzac, as ever throughout the course of the war, the infantryman was the backbone of the whole structure, always in the thick of the trouble either working or fighting, and always bearing himself with a courage and cheerfulness beyond all praise.

As July wore on and the constant requests for reinforcements showed some likelihood of being in part fulfilled, preliminary preparations for a further great effort were put in hand. Engineering instructions bore special reference to the improvement of the communications leading out towards the left flank. The main existing communication trench, known as the Big Sap, was already cut right through to a suitable depth, but partly to save work and partly to avoid enfilade fire, had been left very narrow. This was now widened throughout to admit the passage of at least two men abreast, with recesses here and there to facilitate crossing. Portions of the trench especially liable to enfilade fire were deviated, and others were protected with overhead cover of timber and sandbags. Along the actual waterfront a new road was built northward, suitable for wheeled traffic. To avoid arousing enemy suspicions, with inevitable heavy casualties from the overlooking rifles and machine-guns, this road work had to be undertaken at night. The sandy beach alone gave an impossible surface. Stones had to be gathered along the shore and carried to form a foundation. Clay could be had in abundance on every hillside, and was carted down by the Indian mule-drivers. A certain amount of sand completed the list of available

Field Companies and Field Troop.

materials, and the "set" of the whole was imperfectly assisted by sea water carried up in petrol tins and poured over the surface. The difficulties of handling the men and materials in darkness and in silence were constantly increased by machine-gun fire, though there was no reason to believe that the Turks had any suspicion of what was going on.

The comparatively quiet conditions obtaining throughout July were reflected in the gradual accumulation of Engineering material at the Stores at Hell Spit, but with a view to future operations, everything was closely conserved. Timber, galvanised iron, loophole plates, tools, nails, sandbags and wire —no more than enough of each to support the contention that such things did exist—were brought across from a store-ship lying in Kephalos Bay, Imbros Island, two hours' steam from the Peninsula. Lighters 60 feet long, each in charge of a New Zealand sapper, were towed across to Imbros by pinnaces and trawlers, and loaded from the store-ship overnight. While so employed, the lucky captains of the lighters enjoyed a good feed and a bath, with perchance a sleep in a hammock—all luxuries unheard of on the mainland. At dawn every morning the loaded lighters were towed back by trawlers to within reasonable distance of the beach and then handed over to naval pinnaces which looked after the final dash for the shore. A certain amount of attention from the Turkish sharpshooters had generally to be endured, and occasionally "Beachy Bill" took a noticeable interest in the proceedings.

"Beachy" was a large gun, or battery of them, hidden in the Olive Groves behind Gaba Tepe Point, and notwithstanding constant shelling by the naval gunners, was never put out of action for more than two or three days at a time. Shells from "Beachy Bill" and from "Anafarta Annie," his active helpmate on the Suvla side, were particularly annoying to the bathers who crowded the beaches as the weather grew warmer. Midsummer found the inhabitants of Anzac generally reduced to hat, shorts, boots and socks. The exact extent of clothing favoured by each individual was at once shown by the amount of brown skin exhibited when he went into the water. Many men gave up shaving, and for general doubtful appearance there was soon little to choose on either side of the parapet. The heat and the flies made serious inroads on the general health of the garrison. Most men did their own cooking in their little bivvies, but there was so little to cook. Bully beef and biscuits were always available, but these dainties do not tempt any but the heartiest appetite. Prunes were dealt with singly, and rice by the spoonful, while the few stores of greater

Summer at Anzac.

variety which reached the Y.M.C.A. marquee on the beach were sold immediately to those lucky enough to be on hand at the moment. Very occasionally the gods distributed a few stray favours. Of this nature were the barrels once observed floating near Anzac Cove. The sappers, ever watchful for stores of military importance, secured four or more of them, all filled with good red wine, probably relict of some foundered ship; though no one allowed unhappy speculation to mar the simple pleasures of the ensuing hours.

CHAPTER IV.

THE ATTACK ON SARI BAIR AND THE EVACUATION.

Our last great throw for victory and the command of The Narrows was not undertaken without close investigation of all the possible avenues of attack. While none were particularly attractive, the plan finally adopted met most of the objections fatal to the others. Under this scheme a new landing was contemplated at Suvla Bay, where no special difficulties were anticipated by the naval authorities. Feint attacks, as usual, were to be delivered on the extreme flanks—on the Asiatic coastline, and away up at Bulair. On 6th August a more definite assault at Cape Helles, and by the Australian Division along the whole Anzac front from Russell's Top to the southern extremity at Chatham's Post, would engage the attention of the enemy sufficiently to hold fast any reserve troops he might have in those immediate vicinities, and would possibly attract others to the scenes of conflict. Meanwhile, early on the morning of the 7th, when these operations had committed the Turkish reserves, the New Zealand and Australian Division, reinforced by the newly-arrived 13th Division, and by an Indian Brigade, would advance up three deres or valleys leading to the summit of Sari Bair.

At the same time, the IX. Army Corps, comprising the bulk of the new troops now available, would land at Suvla Bay, smother any light opposition likely to be met on Suvla Flats, and linking up with the Anzacs' left flank, would converge on Sari Bair from the northward. Once we held possession of the main ridge, Maidos and the coast of the Straits should be within easy grasp. Shorn of elaboration, these were the main outlines of the coming attack. Numerically we were much inferior to the enemy, and inevitable difficulties would occur with water and supplies, but the scheme appeared, and probably was, within the range of possibility. Unfortunately it never had a fair chance of reaching fruition.

It must be understood that Sari Bair was not a hill but a great central ridge system, broken by numerous sharp rocky ridges, and a wilderness of precipitous water-courses. The three main spurs breaking out in the direction of Anzac from the nearer height of Chunuk Bair were the one running down

The Attack on Sari Bair and The Evacuation.

to Quinn's Post and Walker's Ridge; a second running due west called Rhododendron Spur and separated from Walker's by the Sazli Beit Dere; and a third called Cheshire Ridge, separated from Rhododendron by the Chailak Dere, and bounded again on the north by the Aghyl Dere. Rhododendron Spur and Cheshire Ridge met some 400 yards from Chunuk Bair at a point called the Apex, then ran as one steep ridge up to the heights.

The forces from Anzac were to attack in two columns, one up the Aghyl Dere, the other by way of Sazli Beit and Chailak Deres, each preceded by a covering force to remove obstacles, and generally to ensure as far as might be that the men detailed for the final assault should arrive near the summit as fresh as possible. The Field Troop was assigned to the Right Covering Force, while the 1st and 2nd Field Companies formed part of the Right and Left Assaulting Columns respectively. Their particular duties were to be the removal of mechanical obstacles, the consolidation of positions captured, and above all to find water. For several nights before the attack, fresh troops from the English New Army Divisions were landed at Anzac, and hidden away in positions already prepared among the numerous little gullies and fissures abutting on the coast. On the 5th August the bulk of the New Zealand Engineers moved out to Happy Valley, where they lay all next day in the scrub.

On the 6th our attacks broke out at Cape Helles and along the line of the Anzac Posts, where the Australians in particular suffered frightful losses, but all successfully fulfilled their share of the major operation. As darkness fell, the waiting troops on the left began to file off up the beach to the mouths of the deres. Heavy wire of great height and depth was found in several places up Chailak Dere, but gallant work by Lieutenant Oakey and a party from the Field Troop, assisted by some of the Maoris, resulted in a track being cleared for our advancing troops. This splendid work largely assisted the Right Assault Column in its attack on Rhododendron Spur, where their advanced troops finally reached the Apex. The 1st Field Company spent the night in Chailak Dere completing the clearance of obstacles and commencing a mule track up the valley. With the dawn they moved on towards the Apex. Wounded and prisoners began to pour down from both the Apex and Cheshire Ridge, and all tracks in the bottom of the valley were soon hopelessly blocked. The Indian Mountain Batteries were urgently needed in front, and to get

Field Companies and Field Troop.

them forward the sappers were set on the formation of a 10ft. track from the dere up the slopes of Cheshire Ridge and so to the Apex.

The Left Assaulting Column, composed of Australian and Indian Brigades, met with considerable opposition, but pushed on up the Aghyl Dere to where the valley forked about 2000 yards from the sea. The Australians here took the northern fork and by dawn had reached the ridge at the head of Asma Dere. The Indians went on up the southern fork towards the Farm, just under the crest of Chunuk Bair. As they went their flanks spread right and left, and succeeded in establishing touch with the New Zealanders and Australians on either side.

By this time it was full daylight, and the exhausted troops were everywhere held up by seemingly endless hordes of Turks. Still, a considerable advance had been made, and the tired men were given fresh heart by the sight of Suvla Bay full of ships, and apparently quite undisturbed by the Turks. Help must be near at hand. By the Australians on the far left in particular, with their flank entirely in the air, it was urgently required. All day the men lay out on the parched hillsides, where any attempt at movement was instantly shot down. The 2nd Field Company was employed digging wells in the Aghyl Dere, though no supplies of water could go forward till darkness fell. That night reorganisation was effected and a fresh attack planned for the morning. Only on the right did it succeed, where the New Zealanders took the crest of Chunuk Bair in the early dawn. All day again the fight went on with tremendous slaughter but little success. However, Chunuk Bair still lay in our hands at night. Still no sign of any troops from Suvla. Once more fresh arrangements were made to exploit our hold on Chunuk Bair, quite the most important gain of the whole campaign.

On Sunday, the 9th, fresh efforts were put forth all along the exhausted line, but far from advancing our gains, the only men still holding their own at nightfall were again on the grimly-contested Chunuk Bair. That night these worn-out troops were relieved by two battalions of English troops. With dawn on the 10th came a decisive counter-stroke by the Turks, who, pouring down the hill shoulder to shoulder in several lines, completely overran everything on Chunuk Bair, and were only held up at the Apex by the most strenuous efforts of the garrison.

Once their attack was broken, the enemy were forced to

The Attack on Sari Bair and The Evacuation.

retire up the steep slopes in full view of every man on our side able to fire a shot, and only a mere handful ever crossed over the ridge. But Chunuk Bair was lost to us and was never regained. During the three days' fighting the sappers were used as reinforcements in the firing line between spells of consolidation on Rhododendron Spur and of digging for water in the deres, and suffered very severe losses.

The failure at Suvla was complete. The only battalion which did make any material gain on the first day moved forward and occupied Scimitar Hill. During the night, owing to the general confusion reigning, it was recalled to attack somewhere else in the morning, and this valuable position was abandoned never to be again occupied by us.

With no early prospect of gaining Sari Bair in sight, nothing remained for the Anzacs but to establish connection with the troops round about Suvla Bay, to put such trenches as had been gained into a proper state of defence, and to make good their lines of communication. As many sappers as could be spared from the pressing needs of the water supply situation were at once put on to supervise these new works. The water question was soon greatly relieved by the finding of new wells on the beach and in Aghyl Dere, and by the installation of an oil engine and pumping plant.

The old Turkish well at No. 2 Post had always been a mainstay of the water supply system, but now it became one of the most important features of the whole local situation, since by pumping 20 hours a day enough water could be obtained to supply approximately two Divisions. On several occasions the overworked engines broke down. Fortunately the New Zealand sappers included men who could be relied on to make a job of any engine that could move at all, but their ingenuity was severely taxed. New bearings were filed up out of spare parts of abandoned service pumps, then the cylinder rings burnt on to the piston and had to be broken off. New rings were made by cutting up a Turkish 4.5 shell with a hacksaw. Luckily these were exactly the right size, and a supply was kept in stock thereafter. These are samples of the little problems confronting the sappers all through the occupation of the Peninsula, but few of which were long able to withstand the resource and skill brought to bear upon them.

Cables for reinforcements met with the reply that none were available. A further attempt to advance was accordingly made with troops on the spot, the long-suffering "regulars" of the faithful 29th Division being brought up from Cape

Field Companies and Field Troop.

Helles to stiffen the raw battalions at Suvla Bay. Scimitar Hill and Hill 60 were the objectives of this fresh assault, the first to be attacked by the troops at Suvla, the other by a force of Australian Infantry and New Zealand Mounted Rifles, with a sprinkling of other details. Scimitar Hill cost 5000 casualties and then was not occupied, an ironical contrast with the ease with which it was taken and abandoned some days earlier.

The attack from the Anzac side met with better fortune, but even then, after tremendous losses we only carried a portion of the crest of Hill 60. The 2nd Field Company was closely concerned digging consolidation trenches during the week occupied by these operations, while the Field Troop, despite heavy casualties, put out a large amount of barbed wire protection with their usual energy and skill. These struggles were the last pitched battles on the Peninsula. Simple honesty forces the admission that after four long months of ceaseless effort and continual bloodshed we were still nowhere past the outer fringe of the Turkish positions.

September found defensive works well in hand all along the front. Welcome assistance arriving on the 16th, nominally the 5th Reinforcements, but the first as far as the Engineers were concerned, put fresh heart into all activities. At the same time, the arrival of the 2nd Australian Division made it possible to relieve all Australian or New Zealand infantrymen of long standing for a spell of rest at Mudros.

The 1st Field Company had been employing half its forces widening the Big Sap running out from Anzac past No. 2 Post and so on towards Suvla, a track which ultimately became more like a sunken road than a communication trench. The remainder of the Company was improving trenches and erecting wire from Camel Hump to Destroyer Hill, two knolls commanding the mouth of the Sazli Beit Dere. These comparative veterans were now relieved by the greater portion of the fresh sappers, and sent to Mudros with the infantry. The following men of the 1st Company are noted in the records of the time as having been conspicuous for consistent good service:—Sergeants D. Ross, G. Masters, and A. K. Fyson; Corporal J. Caird, Second-Corporals W. J. McLaughlin, J. S. Cripps, and J. McKay; Lance-Corporals J. Woodhall and E. St. G. Gorton; Sappers F. Bridgewater and V. R. Maney.

The rest camp at Mudros was at Sarpi on the outskirts of the town, and despite some small inconveniences at the start, in

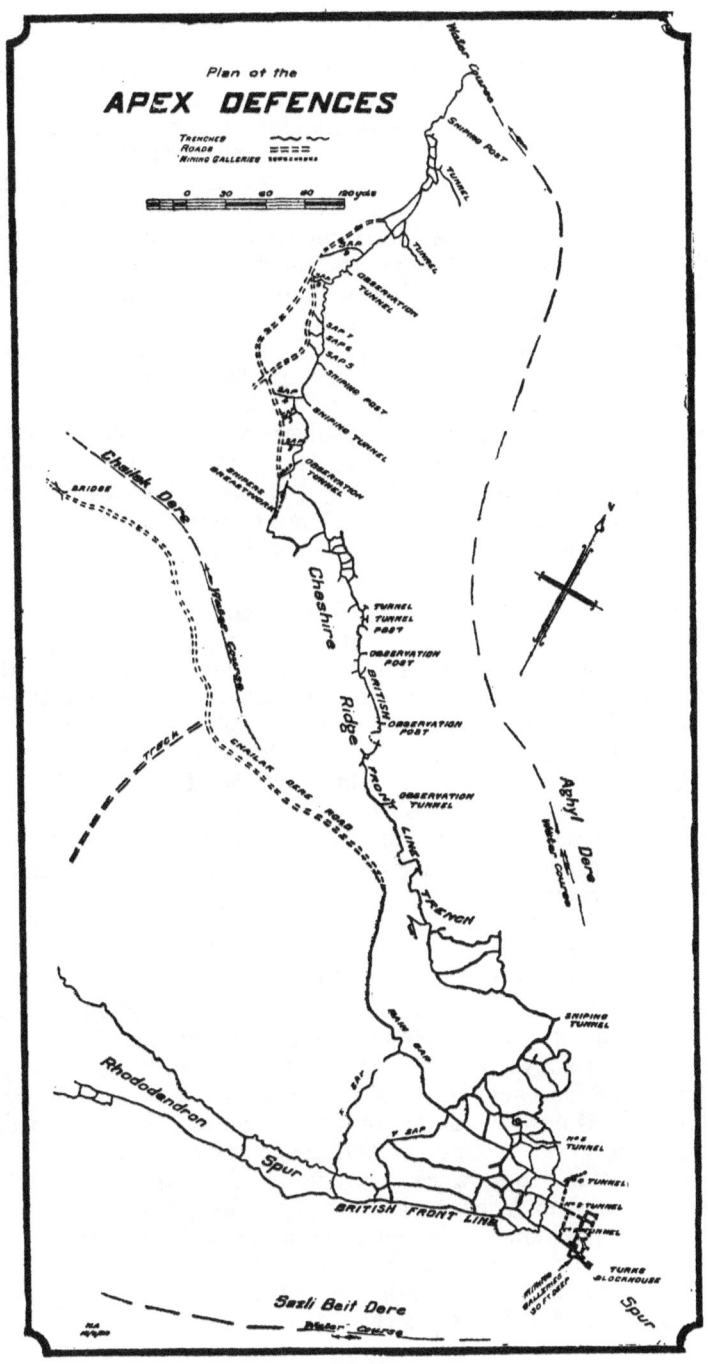

Field Companies and Field Troop.

the way of insufficient accommodation and bad weather, the general conditions obtaining were in extraordinary contrast with those on the Peninsula, and quickly worked wonders in the health and spirits of the gaunt, disease-weakened troops. Good fresh food was available in surprising quantities, men could sleep secure from the everlasting shells, recreational institutes sprang up, and even to walk abroad in the pleasant country-side, with women and children in the villages, and flocks and crops on the peaceful hills, was a certain tonic to minds overlong familiar with filth and slaughter. And to men who had not seen a hot bath for five months, the extremely good facilities existing at Thermos, some three miles away, were a boon beyond all price. Later on, the Field Troop, and even some of the 2nd Field Company, were given an opportunity of enjoying the attractions of Lemnos, and of sharpening their wits in contact with the eager banditti who masquerade as the normal inhabitants of that Grecian isle.

The 2nd Field Company, now numbering but some 75 fit men, received the balance of the new men available, and carried on with renewed energy. The main portion of the Company was attached to the 3rd Australian Light Horse in Sazli Beit Dere, where their especial cares were the trenches along the southern flanks of Rhododendron Spur and the defences at the Apex. Both fire and communication trenches were in poor condition here, and demanded much devoted labour. The difficulties of obtaining material for such an exposed spot were greatly lightened by the completion of a mule track graded by the sappers up the side slopes of Sazli Beit Dere. Ultimately all trenches were successfully completed, and the whole position in that locality was accurately surveyed. Malcolm Ross, the New Zealand Official War Correspondent, bore tribute to the Company's efforts in the following words:—"At Rhododendron Spur the Engineers were confronted with a very difficult position, being exposed in front and on each flank. The fire trenches were only two feet deep. On the right there was absolutely no protection. By dint of great ingenuity, and much hard work, both the Apex and the Spur were made secure, though the Turks, right, left, and in front, on the heights above, practically dominated the position." On completion of this job, the Company's energies were transferred to Chailak Dere, on the southern side of Cheshire Ridge, where a new road was formed right up from No. 2 Post to the Apex. While in this locality,

Horse Lines at Moascar Camp.

A Pontoon and Trestle Bridge erected by the Engineers at Moascar.

Engineers on Camels, returning to Moascar after constructing the Ballah Defences.

Photos by Major N. Annabell

The Attack on Sari Bair and The Evacuation.

Durrant's Post, in the front line at the head of the dere, was taken in hand, to the great satisfaction of the Australian Officer Commanding, who wrote a special letter of thanks and commendation to the C.R.E. The Field Troop, now pitifully few in numbers, was also with the Australians on Cheshire Ridge, where it was employed on wire entanglements and general trench improvement.

Engineers still remained at the Apex, which, by virtue of its location and of the activities there carried on, soon became on this new front much what Quinn's Post had been on the old; a stronghold whose safety was essential to the defence of the whole sector, but always commanded by the enemy and ever subject to hostile fire. Mining was carried on from the first, both by us and by the Turks, and despite the inevitable shortage of explosive, we gradually gained the upper hand by dint of unremitting toil and no mean skill. Lance-Corporal W. J. Riddell of the 2nd Company won distinction here for the gallant rescue of an injured comrade from No Man's Land under point-blank fire.

With October came cooler weather and a marked improvement in the general health of the troops in consequence, though all were sadly reduced by comparison with their original condition. With October also came the first storm of autumn—welcome rather than otherwise since the beach was strewn with wreckage, which was eagerly added to the depleted stores of the Engineer's Depot—but a disquieting indication of what might happen later on. Plans for winter accommodation were forthwith considered, but beyond making plans, what could be done? It was useless to decide on uniform methods of trench revetment, of drainage, or of shelter, when the materials essential to the fulfilment of any scheme however modest were not even within the range of possibility. The only decision possible was that each locality must do its best with the scraps available, and "the natural resources of the countryside." Steady inroads ever since the landing on that particular source of supply had long ago exhausted what had never been more than rock and clay and patches of twisted scrub. The report of the C.R.E. stated inter alia that "Corrugated iron in large quantities would solve all difficulties." Some time later 120 sheets arrived—not enough to make a large stable. There was no material, and would be none, and the knowledge of that bedrock fact of the situation was better than unfounded expectations. The shortage of course extended in every direction. The arrival of the 6th Reinforce-

Field Companies and Field Troop.

ments brought some fresh relief, but even after absorbing them the total number of sappers available did not bring the Companies up to half strength.

By this time the question of evacuation was prominent in the minds of the authorities in London, and doubtless had long disturbed the plans of Sir Ian Hamilton, since far from sending him reinforcements, they had already asked him to send three Divisions from Gallipoli to Salonika. Into the medley of conflicting facts and circumstances surrounding this point we need not attempt to enter here, but the fact noted above is pretty good evidence that the campaign had lost the wholehearted support of the responsible authorities and was doomed from that time onwards. Whether it could have succeeded under happier auspices, and just what degree of extra support would have been necessary, are points that will always be debated among military critics. Lord Kitchener and Sir Charles Munro recommended withdrawal; some time later Sir Ian Hamilton again referred to "the final folly of the evacuation."

No whisper of these momentous differences of opinion had yet reached the devoted garrisons of our hard held line on the Peninsula. What they had won they were still prepared to hold, and were still confident that the support necessary for final success would arrive at last. Then on November 27th came the great blizzard, with bitter, driving wind and heavy falls of snow. Within 24 hours the damage done was enormous. The floors and walls of the little clay dugouts became wet and greasy, and all tracks were rivers of mud and slush. All temporary shelters in the open collapsed under the weight of their snow mantle, and men were forced to shiver in any nook or cranny they could find unoccupied, while the carefully-cut trenches, destitute of all necessary revetment, showed sure signs of collapse. Many of the trenches became untenable owing to the flood waters draining down from the higher levels. Down in the Cove, all light craft were piled up on the beach, no very serious loss in themselves, but closely touching the question of future supplies.

On the 24th, mysterious orders had been given for 24 hours complete silence, probably to see what attitude the enemy was likely to adopt under circumstances approximating to those of the pending withdrawal. Any attempt to advance would have been dealt with, but apart from such precautions, no shovel was lifted and no shot fired. The Turk accepted the strange break in the proceedings with philosophic

The Attack on Sari Bair and The Evacuation.

calm, and employed the time in rebuilding his parapet and strengthening wire entanglements. The interlude was finally extended to 72 hours, when the blowing of a small mine was the signal to lay on afresh. The Turkish estimate of this manoeuvre, if any existed, has never been made public. With the frost following the blizzard came some relief in the way of drier tracks and trenches, but this advantage was quickly set off by the bursting of all water pipe lines. Sappers with large working parties were at once detailed for repair, and the renewed pipes were also placed underground. The water problem was as acute as ever, despite the streamlets now running freely in every dere, since they represented the drainage of the whole congested battlefield after many months of slaughter. Numerous wells came under the same disability, and the water barges, which were altogether dependent on the weather conditions along shore, became indispensable.

An extensive pumping plant had been landed early in November, along with a special pump expert sent out by the contractors to superintend its erection. However, the plant was relegated to the Engineers' Stores in the meantime, and the expert, a Mr. Bodman, was forced to employ his unexpected leisure in inspection of the other engineering marvels abounding all round him, and in the collection of souvenirs. He was housed with the 2nd Field Company, which provided him with an Australian hat and overcoat to minimise risk of accident. His performance at a coal-pinching expedition, where he took the part of an Australian Sergeant-Major at short notice, and as to the manner born, was the outstanding feature of the enterprise, and won him the hall-mark of approval from all his whilom hosts. Ultimately his pumping apparatus was urgently called for, but had only been in operation for a day or two, when it was dismantled and sent away prepartory to the final withdrawal.

Up to the middle of December Engineering activities to combat the approach of winter were carried on strenuously, though it was pretty generally understood long before that, that Christmas would never be spent on Gallipoli. Officially, of course, the word "evacuation" did not exist, but the instant removal to hospital ships of any man with the slightest disability, the open-handed attitude of ordnance and supply officials, and above all the number of troops who were sent away every night to an alleged rest camp at Imbros, convinced the most sceptical that something was in the wind. On December 16th further disguise was abandoned, and an Army Order informed all ranks of the decision to withdraw, and exhorted

Field Companies and Field Troop.

them to stand fast should any hitch occur during the operation. Many a time during that awful summer the troops had longed to see the end of the filth and hardships of Gallipoli, but not this kind of ending. Most of the garrison knew perfectly well that without reinforcements there was no reasonable course open but to withdraw, and were thankful that decision had been reached, but no sensation of relief could dispel the sense of failure, the feeling that the job was being left half-done, and that so many brave lads had died in vain. Sufficient indication of what might be expected during the winter had been afforded by the November blizzard, but it is perfectly certain that had official policy decided in favour of enduring the rigours of winter for the prospect of victory in the spring, there would have been no murmurings on Anzac.

The evacuation, in common with the landing, was a type of military enterprise unique in the annals of war. The numerous unfavourable circumstances which made it such a delicate operation, and so peculiarly liable to miscarry, are too well known to need further description. Knowledge of them serves to throw a vivid light on the skill and daring with which the arrangements were conceived and carried out. The sappers were directly concerned with the final measures undertaken. Reserve stocks of tools and stores were broken up and burnt or cast into the sea. In particular the beach entrances to the deres leading down from the trenches on the heights above were completely filled up with extensive wire entanglements, leaving only narrow means of exit for the retiring garrisons, which could be blocked up by dropping gates of wire already prepared. Similarly numerous blocks were prepared in the communication trenches, where the last men to leave could, if necessary, make a stand against the enemy sufficient to ensure the safety of the main body. Wire gates were placed in position to be closed as these last men came through on the final dash for the beach. Trip wires were also arranged so that interference therewith drew the safety-pin from Mills bombs, which by this time had made a belated appearance on the scene.

The final stage of the evacuation was conducted in two operations on the nights of the 18th and 19th December.

On the 19th there remained of the Engineers only the Acting C.R.E., the O's.C. of the Field Troop and the 2nd Field Company, and 13 other ranks, who spent the day in erecting two light jetties to assist in the evacuation of the Indian troops. All that day great efforts were made to induce the enemy to believe that everything was going on as

The Attack on Sari Bair and The Evacuation.

usual. Men with packs on their backs walked up the tracks leading to the trenches wherever they could be seen by the Turks. Fires were kept burning and blankets were spread in the sun round the areas that had usually been occupied by incoming troops, while in the front line a few men moved tirelessly up and down firing shots from all points from which fire had usually been prominent. Numerous mechanical contrivances were also in position ready to continue spasmodic fire long after the trenches were vacated by the garrison. These generally depended on a tin full of water with a gradual leak, or a time fuse which burnt through a string; in either case a weight being released which pulled a trigger.

The men of the Division remaining on Gallipoli on that last day, about 3000, were to be withdrawn in three parties known as A, B, and C, which would leave at varying intervals. Should the enemy attack at any stage of the proceedings, the great wire gates in the deres would be instantly closed and the deres themselves heavily bombarded by the warships. Whatever part of the garrison still remained in the trenches were to stand their ground till 2 a.m., and then to retire down the ridges to the sea, where some of them might possibly be picked up by the Navy. Virtually the arrangement meant the sacrifice of the rearguard to save the Army, but the ranks of the C party could have been filled many times over. Every man was a volunteer, though it was early decided by the wags that A stood for Alexandria and B for the Beach, while the best C could hope for was Constantinople.

Our last night on Gallipoli opened with a glorious peaceful sunset and not a ripple on the sea. As darkness finally settled down, intense activity broke out everywhere. The departure of each boatload of men was scheduled to a minute, and there was much to be done. The few remaining guns were hauled down to the beach, men went round lighting candles in the empty dugouts, while others maintained the faithful round of the front line and the intermittent rifle fire so essential to success. As the night wore on, nervous tension naturally increased, but the Turks remained quiet. Sappers remained at the Apex till the last moment in readiness to fire a prepared mine should such a proceeding become necessary, and as they left the enemy could be heard putting out fresh wire. The extra shipping on the coast had been interpreted as the forerunner of another grand attack. About 2.15 a.m. the last man in the trenches made for the main gate at the mouth of Chailak Dere, which was closed finally at 2.25 a.m. after numbers had been checked by a staff officer. The

Field Companies and Field Troop.

last definite action of the New Zealand Engineers on the Peninsula was the demolition of a Hotchkiss gun and a 5-inch Howitzer not considered worth removal. By 4 a.m. all troops were on board ship and bearing away for Lemnos. The fires along the beach were now in full blaze, and the lines of the Turkish trenches were picked out along the dark hillside by countless darts of flame as the occupants opened harmless fire. By dawn the sinister blood-soaked ridges of Gallipoli were but a smudge on the horizon.

No details of many individual acts of courage and resource by members of the 2nd Field Company are now available; possibly none were kept, since in those early days of the war, when every man put forth his utmost endeavours all day and every day, there was no careful organisation of distinctions and awards such as existed later on in France. In any case, no system of awards could possibly have arrived at complete justice in the matter, but the names of the following men are noted in the records for continuous faithful service in the front line throughout their stay on Gallipoli:—Sergeants C. E. Bradley and T. F. Rowe; Corporals W. J. Courtney, P. Scahill, and C. King; Lance-Corporals W. A. Laing and A. E. Gibb; and Sapper F. Drinkrow. Members of the Field Troop who achieved the same measure of distinction were:—Sergeant Brunsden; Corporals H. Dyson and K. Draffin; and Sappers C. Horne, W. Carter, G. Williamson, and H. Gray.

No reference to this aspect of the Engineers' experiences would be complete without some mention of Sergeants-Major T. W. Dollimore and J. J. Moore, who were later awarded commissions in the field. Both men were fully trained N.C.O.'s of the Royal Engineers, who had been selected for service in New Zealand as Instructors before the war, and had fortunately been sent to Gallipoli along with the 2nd Field Company. Their skill, resource and cheery courage made them towers of strength in the constant crises of the Peninsula campaign, and were a credit alike to themselves and to the best traditions of the fine Corps from which they sprang.

CHAPTER V.

REORGANISATION IN EGYPT.

From the period of reorganisation of the Australian and New Zealand Forces in Egypt after the abandonment of the Peninsula dates also the formation of the purely New Zealand Division.

As the scattered units arrived in Egypt the two purely Australian Divisions were sent to Tel-el-Kebir, while the Anzacs were concentrated at Moascar Camp, on the outskirts of Ismailia on the Suez Canal. The 7th and 8th Reinforcements from New Zealand had moved into the new camp a day or two beforehand, and had done what they could to prepare for the advent of the Gallipoli veterans. These came pouring in piecemeal with inevitable temporary confusion, but order and routine were soon established.

The intensive training at once put in hand seems to show that even at this stage it had been decided to send these Divisions to France in the spring, though no suggestion of the kind was made at the time. Day after day and often at night the troops were marched and exercised over the splendid natural testing ground of the Egyptian desert, till their physical fitness left little to be desired. The qualities of cohesion and steadiness which had been so little assisted by the almost guerilla conditions of warfare on the Peninsula were also markedly increased in all ranks during these days of trial. It must be admitted that in the general reaction following on relief from the strain of Gallipoli, there was a general tendency towards slackness in dress and deportment which threatened to extend from the old hands to the reinforcements newly arrived. With the reversion to regular duties and massed movements, this soon began to wear off, and finally disappeared in the fresh flush of enthusiasm which greeted the decision to form a New Zealand Division. In addition to technical training in their own special activities, the Engineers were engaged on camp improvements such as pipe laying and water supply, in building hutments, and in supervising native labour on the construction of tramways and light piers. Pontoon bridges were also constructed over the Sweet Water Canal near Ismailia.

Ismailia, though naturally not as interesting as Cairo, was quite an entertaining place in its own little way. The business

Field Companies and Field Troop.

portion of the town, as is so often the case in the East, was controlled by Greeks, whose highly inflated notions of the value of their wares were comparable only with those of their Egyptian fellows. Unlike the latter, however, the Greeks preserved a stolid indifference as to the success or otherwise of their efforts to ensnare a customer. Two large parks, with their ancient native stone work and beautiful palm trees, made a pleasant break in the monotony of the crowded houses; though most of the latter at this season were adorned with masses of trailing creeper. A canal traversing the centre of the town gave a splendid impression of cleanliness and beauty, until close investigation revealed its similarity to all other rivers and waterways in that part of the world. Lake Timsah, with its larger volume of water gleaming in the sun, and generally adorned by a battleship or two, was a much more inviting prospect, and as the warmer weather came on, the Ismailia shore was a general rendezvous for the troops, who came down in thousands to bathe and sport on the warm sands. Arabs were allowed to fish in Lake Timsah, under the eye of soldier guards, who went out in the boats with them to see that no floating mines or torpedoes came of the concession. Sappers told off to superintend these fishing excursions on a basis of a half share in the proceeds had rosy visions of fresh fish daily, until they saw the few miserable little sprats that were the only harvest gathered, and they were not sorry when their appointments were terminated. The subject of food recalls pleasant memories of the Christmas billies sent by the New Zealand Patriotic Societies, which were given out during January and February, and were most heartily appreciated by all hands.

While the Australians and New Zealanders were thus engaged training in reserve areas, extensive fortifications and defensive engineering works were going on out in the desert some seven to ten miles east of the Canal. Some quicker method of crossing the Canal than by the use of the cumbrous barges serving the purpose soon became essential, and the Engineers were called upon to construct floating bridges capable of being swung across the Canal when required. A mixed party of the 1st and 2nd Field Company men was detailed for this purpose. Floats were easily obtained from the Canal Company, which had large numbers of them always in use for carrying the discharge pipes which disposed of the spoil brought up by its dredges. On these floats suitable lengths of bridge decking and handrails were built, in such manner that two or more of the resulting bridge sections

Reorganisation in Egypt.

could be joined together by removable portions of decking and railing, thus enabling a bridge of any given length to be assembled in a short space of time. To prepare the floats and the wooden sections, which were put together on Lake Timsah, a special staff of Arab blacksmiths and carpenters was engaged, whereupon it transpired that in that favoured country no blacksmith or carpenter was ever called upon to work in the water, and a few fishermen were added to the pay roll to move round the floats and decking as required by the superior tradesmen. The tools of their crafts appeared to be contemporaneous with the pyramids, and were objects of great interest to the artisans among the sappers. Despite their ancient equipment and appearance, all these gentlemen had mastered the intricacies of modern methods of making a job spin out to the last half second. A side-line of theirs not yet introduced in less enlightened circles was the praying-mat. Now and again one or more of them would cease work and repair to a clear space, there to unroll their little mats and prepare for devotion. Rinsing their hands with cold water, they would wipe their fevered brows, and commence what was probably an appeal to Allah for more power to circumvent these energetic unbelievers. Back they would come in a few moments, seemingly greatly refreshed in body and spirit. In the course of time one unusually devout apostle of the true faith spoilt the whole arrangement by losing himself in meditation for half an hour, whereupon all praying activities were relegated to the smoke-oh interval, with an immediate marked decrease in the number of worshippers. To hear such names as Ahmed, Mahoud and Hassan, reeled off at morning roll-call, one could easily imagine himself in the presence of The Forty Thieves—the main difference in any case being purely numerical.

When a sufficient number of bridge lengths had been completed, they were formed into a raft and towed up or down the Canal to wherever the bridge was required, there to be put together finally by the Engineers. Three of these bridges, varying in length up to 400 feet, were erected at Ballah, El Ferdan and Serapeum. All shipping traffic was suspended during certain hours of the day while the bridges were swung, and the long columns of infantry, transport waggons, field artillery and camel trains poured over and pushed on into the desert. Camels move both legs on either side of their bodies together, and not alternately like a horse, and a line of them set up a tremendous swaying in the bridges to their own evident discomfiture.

Field Companies and Field Troop.

With the completion of the bridges, work on the desert defences went on with increased speed, and the Engineers were sent out there to supervise construction, a few of them being located at most of the Posts, which, in a series one to three miles apart, constituted the outer line of the defensive system. Here in March they were attached for rations and water to the New Zealand Mounted Rifles and English Regiments then in garrison, whose kindly treatment of their temporary guests will always be a pleasant recollection. All water out there was brought by the camel trains, each in charge of a ruffianly Arab, who was a past master in the gentle art of taking the last ounce out of his unfortunate charges. Camels have quite a reputation as "grousers," and invariably grunt and complain whatever load they are introduced to, but these particular animals in question, with 400 lbs. of water each to carry, probably had more ground than most for their querulous outlook on life.

The front line system at this time was still largely in process of construction. The Posts or fortified areas were much larger positions than are usually known by those terms, and were capable of accommodating a battalion, or even, in some cases, a brigade. Since difficulties of water and desert transport would effectually prevent the Turks from subjecting these positions to concentrated artillery fire for any length of time, more attention was paid to commanding position and to facilities for all-round fire than to concealment. Extensive belts of wire entanglement were laid out all round each Post, concealed where possible in folds of the ground, and arranged to lead attacking troops into narrow necks covered by concentrated machine-gun fire. Some three miles behind this front line of defence ran a second line, still far enough from the Canal to prevent any serious interference with traffic. The innermost line consisted of the positions occupied a year before at the time of the Turkish attack. The principal enemy to trench construction met with by the New Zealand sappers was the "Khamsin," an unreliable desert storm which constantly obliterated the work of days beneath clouds of drifting sand. Patient effort finally prevailed, and on relinquishing their du ies the Engineers received official commendation from Headquarters of both XV and II Anzac Corps.

Towards the end of March all New Zealand troops across the Canal, with the exception of the Mounted Rifles, were recalled to Moascar Camp. The usual vague rumours and peculiar mixtures of official frankness and reticence were again in evidence on every hand. Cryptic orders were read

Reorganisation in Egypt.

out about moving to another country, with weighty words as to the correct treatment of civilians in a strange land; followed by the advice of some less discreet or more sensible high official, who openly emphasised the importance of a gas helmet in France; and renewed again next day in terms which might have related to Timbuctoo or South America. That queer assumption of the old British Regular Army system that the rank and file has no native intelligence nor need of a mind of its own, and can be told any old fairy tale so long as it is hallowed by inclusion in an Army Order, never failed to interest and perchance irritate the civilian soldiers of the recent war, who, in the mass at least, had an uncanny power of detecting a bluff of whatsoever description.

On the 1st of March the New Zealand Division was definitely launched as a separate unit. For some time before, the arrival of the Reinforcements, added to the stream of men returning from hospitals, had made it quite apparent that there were many more men available than were necessary to bring the original Brigade up to full strength. But no casualties were occurring, and it was necessary to consider how the ranks of a full Division were to be maintained when the inevitable wastage of active warfare again set in. For those reasons considerable correspondence took place before the New Zealand Government finally agreed to the proposal to form a separate Division, though preliminary arrangements were put in hand pending receipt of their approval. To bring the Engineers up to full Divisional establishment, the Field Troop was disbanded and the remaining men were transferred to form the nucleus of a 3rd Field Company. With extra men coming in constantly from the sources already mentioned, all three companies were soon at full strength. Colonel Pridham received the appointment of C.R.E. to the new Division. The equipment of every man was now either renewed or brought completely up to date, and to be found with any unauthorised gear in valise or kit-bag was to run the risk of punishments ranging from being shot at dawn to being left behind in Egypt when the Division sailed for its mysterious destination. Definite orders a day or two later named France as the next scene of endeavour. On the 3rd April, a most vigorous and exacting inspection and review of the New Zealanders in full marching order was held by General Sir Archibald Murray, Commander-in-Chief of the Egyptian Expeditionary Force, when it may fairly be said that the new Division acquitted itself with distinction, and impressed him as a fine fighting unit. Thereafter sundry unauthorised articles of private gear

Field Companies and Field Troop.

were recovered from the kindly sands, and the troops were ready to take the trail once more.

The last night in Moascar Camp was marked by another slight demonstration against the general injustice the troops considered they had suffered in all dealings with the native shopkeepers who infested the neighbourhood of the Camp. Many of the battalions were already gone, but the remaining men decided to take their own line in the matter of winning the merchants from their evil ways, and also of exacting reprisals for the universal cheating and overcharging that had gone on; with the result that all huts in the occupation of the offending parasites were burnt down, and many of the unsavoury owners had a vision of swift and sudden demise which probably influenced the future course of their lives for at least a week. However, the path of virtue was beset with thorns, and every man in Camp on that particular night afterwards had his share of the cost of these vigorous improvements deducted from his pay by order of a prosaic Board of Enquiry.

On the 5th April, the Division had begun to move out. Some of the Engineers were detailed for certain duties in clearing up the camp, after which the three Companies travelled to Alexandria. During the next week or more the 1st and 3rd Companies' experiences were somewhat similar to those of the 2nd Company. After arrival in Alexandria in the early morning of the 8th, the 2nd Company embarked on the transports "Haverford" and "Ascania." Both ships lay in harbour that night, but with the early morning their heads were turned for the open sea and the stirring possibilities of the Western Front. No great regrets troubled any adventurous heart as the sands of Egypt faded slowly away astern.

The trip to Marseilles was not particularly enjoyable. Stiff uncomfortable lifebelts were worn day and night, quarters were necessarily restricted, and no lights were allowed after dark. Before leaving Egypt all troops had been inoculated once against typhoid, and most of them received a second dose on board, with the result that a large number felt more or less indisposed towards the end of the journey. All were heartily glad when, on Sunday morning, 16th April, the vessels reached Marseilles. The troops were allowed ashore, but their movements were restricted to the wharves near the disembarkation point, where arrangements were made to store all base kits, which were ultimately sent to England.

CHAPTER VI.

SUMMER AT ARMENTIERES.

At 9 p.m. on the evening of the 17th April, the 2nd Field Company left Marseilles behind and set forth on its long train journey to the British sector away in the North.

The charms of the South of France in spring have captivated the senses and excited the admiration of seasoned travellers since time immemorial. The Rhone Valley is not the least of its many attractions. To men straight from the filth and squalor of Gallipoli and the parched sands of the Egyptian desert, the pleasant farm houses tucked away among the trees, surounded with gay flowers and apple blossom, the broad green meadows and the miles of ordered cultivation, appealed with irresistible force, and every heart beat high with a joyous sense of adventurous anticipation. At wayside stations and at Lyons noteworthy attempts were made upon the language of the country, and bread, butter and other treasures were readily acquired by the optimistic spokesmen. Their success was attributed by unsympathetic comrades more to the intelligence of the natives than to the excellence of the idiom employed. Paris was not entered, though a glimpse of the Eiffel Tower was obtained from Versailles. After some 60 hours, the journey ended at Steenbecque, a small siding near Hazebrouck, where the tired men detrained in pouring rain. It is on record that the station estaminet there retailed beer at one halfpenny per glass, a blissful state of affairs never again experienced by the Division. A 10-mile march found the travellers in billets in stables round about Aire, and only too glad to lie peacefully on the straw. The mounted men of all three Companies detrained at Abbeville, about 50 miles south-west of Aire, where they received a pleasant first impression of British Army ordnance methods in France. On a given date, unfit horses were exchanged, and fresh ones provided up to the full establishment of a Field Company. A complete issue of gear and harness accompanied the horses. On reporting at a further given rendezvous, they received all wheeled transport and incidental equipment proper to their particular needs, with waggons ready stored with the necessary rations for man and beast. All that then remained was to satisfy themselves that their requirements were fully met,

Summer at Armentieres.

and to take the road for their several destinations. Within three days they were once more in the bosoms of their respective companies.

For about two weeks the Division lay about Aire, recovering from the fatigue of its recent journey in new and pleasant surroundings. The numerous small villages, each with its tall spire, surrounded by clusters of red brick houses straggling out towards the small farms where the whole homestead was built in a hollow square round a central courtyard filled with manure and every type of refuse, were to become common enough later on, but were fresh and interesting then. So were the kindly country folk, especially after the unattractive inhabitants of Egypt and Gallipoli. An occasional dull rumble to the eastward, and the faint flicker of far-off flares by night, were the only signs of strife, and even those belonged to a phase of war still new and untried. In view of the fresh experiences shortly to be faced, a portion of each day was devoted to training operations, particularly in the use and care of the previously unknown gas helmet; while to harden the troops after the voyage, and to accustom them to the hard paved roads of northern France, so different from the sands of the desert, many hours were spent in route-marching all over the pleasant countryside. The renewal of health and general morale induced by the exhilaration of fresh environment was given increased impetus by an allotment of leave to the United Kingdom. In connection with this privilege, opportunity was taken to emphasise the importance of personal cleanliness and general smartness. From this time forward renewals of uniform were so arranged that men going on leave were always able to show themselves in good order and condition.

On 1st May, the Division, now under command of I Anzac Corps, moved forward to the reserve area of that Corps, C.R.E. Headquarters, with 1st and 3rd Field Companies going to Estaires, and the 2nd Field Company to Doulieu. With the latter Company from Aire, or from the small village of Roquetoire to be exact, went a fox terrier dog who had attached himself to the strangers from the start. Henceforward he was known as "Jack," and right up to the end of hostilities, he was to all intents and purposes a soldier of the regiment, sharing good times and bad with perfect equanimity, and only in disgrace once, when he got among the legs of Brigadier-General Fulton's horse. While on the subject of company pets, mention may be made of the goat who joined the 2nd Company's drivers at Ismailia, without the

Field Companies and Field Troop.

written consent of his former owners. He went right through France and Flanders, living, on trek, in a special corner of one of the waggons. On the road to Germany he disappeared suddenly one night, probably the victim of some hungry Belgian. "Jack" disappeared about the same time, though no theories are advanced to account for him.

While the 1st and 3rd Companies were at Estaires, several small and unimportant constructional works were undertaken for Field Ambulances and other units. The 3rd Company also commenced work on the defensive systems covering the bridge heads at Maison Rouge, Brickfields and Factory Post, all situated on the river Lys between the villages of Estaires and Erquinghem. Within a week, however, they moved on to Armentieres.

On 12th and 13th May, the Division arrived in Armentieres, and began to take over the sector of the same name. At that time this sector extended from Pear Tree Farm, near the Armentieres-Lille Railway, to the river Lys in front of Houplines, a suburb of Armentieres. The C.R.E. and staff were quartered in the Rue Nationale, and the 1st and 3rd Companies in two near-by breweries; while the 2nd Company divided its favours between another brewery and the Armentieres Tram Barn. This apparent partiality for breweries is attributable solely to military exigencies, and to the sad fact that Armentieres drew much of its prosperity before the war from a thriving trade in beer. At this stage Armentieres was still full of civilians and largely intact. In the spring of the following year it was badly damaged by enemy artillery, but was only finally evacuated by the surviving civilians during the German offensive of 1918, when the town was bombarded with gas shells for 48 hours, and ultimately passed into German hands. Every kind of shop, estaminet and restaurant was in full play, and mention of, say, the "Au Boeuf," should still stir vagrant memories in staid civilian breasts of many a hearty jag sandwiched in between spells of war and muddy trenches. Other sources of entertainment included a fine theatre at the Ecole Professionale, a Y.M.C.A. Club, and a large and well-stocked British Expeditionary Force Canteen. In pre-war days Armentieres drew its electric power from Lille, and after the German occupation of that town, it was fully expected that power would be cut off. For some months, however, business went on as usual in that particular line, till at last the enemy discovered the true position of affairs, and Armentieres had to fall back on gas and candles. It was a New Zea-

A Trench near the Suez Canal.   A Street in Ismalia

The Canal at Ismalia.

Photos by Major N. Annabell

2nd Field Company Mascots.   *Official Photos.*

Summer at Armentieres.

land sapper who pointed out the possibility of the wires being still used for communication with the enemy, whereupon the cable was promptly unearthed and cut.

While the Engineers were settling down in their new quarters, selected officers and N.C.O.'s visited the front line area, and received all possible help and information from the R.E. Companies they were to relieve. The whole of this first trench system to be occupied by New Zealanders in France was composed of low-lying flats in the basin of the Lys, much cut up by the roads, canals and railways of a highly-developed manufacturing and agricultural region, with inhabitants still remaining in the numerous farms up to within two or three miles of the front line. After the hills and valleys of the Peninsula, this flat country seemed perilously insecure. The Germans, as usual, had appropriated the only ridge available, that of Perenchies, about a mile behind their front line, and completely dominated the whole trench area. Of natural cover there was none save trees and hedge rows, and traffic on the nearer roads was protected by the erection of long screens of hessian or scrim. In Gallipoli one moved about in narrow trenches cut deep in hard gravelly soil; here the trenches were wide open ways protected largely by built-up breast-works in country where the water was never more than a foot or so below the surface. However, it was soon realised that conditions were much the same on either side of No Man's Land, and for the moment at least Fritz was not in aggressive mood. Behind the actual front line, at a distance of generally 200 yards, ran a second or support line, with a third, called the subsidiary line, some 600 yards further in rear. In this particular sector, the defences of the town of Armentieres constituted a fourth defensive position, and south of that again, well behind the front area, a line from Armentieres to Fleurbaix was an additional safeguard against sudden enemy activity. This last line, with at least one further in the rear, was not controlled by troops in the front area, and need not be further considered here. For their first experience of trench warfare in France, the three Field Companies were located on the right, centre, and left subsectors respectively.

In the front line, in this as in all other stationary sectors, the first hasty breastworks, thrown up when the recurring clashes of the early skirmishing parties had given way to sustained hostilities by large bodies of men, had long since been extended into a comprehensive system of defence. The trace and profile of the breastworks followed much the same general

Field Companies and Field Troop.

rules as had been familiar in the trenches of Gallipoli. The parapet was at least 10 feet thick at the top, and 7 feet at a minimum above the ground level, while all occupants of the line were protected from the back blast of high explosive shells by another stout breastwork in rear called the parados, at least as high as the parapet and not less than 4 feet thick. Traverses, or strong buttresses of earth, jutted out from the front or occasionally the rear face of the trench, splitting it into a series of compartments. Strong and solid, and not less than 15 feet thick, their special function was to protect the garrison from enfilade fire, and to localise the effect of a shell or bomb bursting in the trench. The forward bays formed by each, long enough to hold five or six men, were known as the firebays, and were, or should have been, entirely for the use of the garrison in either defensive or offensive action. Here were located the firesteps, stores for ammunition and bombs, and such temporary shelters as could be arranged for the sentry groups always on duty. Too many traverses made for difficulties of supervision and control, and also facilitated bombing attacks along the trench, as grenades could be thrown from the cover of a traverse, generally into the next bay but one. This objectionable possibility was provided for by leaving occasional straight lengths of trench between adjacent traverses, long enough to defeat the best efforts of the German throwers, and commanded by protected loopholes in the end traverses. Some five yards in rear of the front fighting line and connected therewith at frequent intervals ran a continuous travel trench, enabling the whole or any part of the actual fighting line to be fully occupied without interference with, and unfettered by, the free use of this main artery of longitudinal communication. Needless to say, the sides of all trenches thus formed required substantial revetments, which are described later.

Communication trenches were occasionally formed provided with traverses as protection against shrapnel or enfilade fire, but such extras were of doubtful advantage, as they greatly impeded the movement of carrying parties and stretcher bearers. If they were essential, circular island traverses were the best, with the trench going round on both sides.

In one Flanders sector, the Division had a sentry post located in the communication trench immediately in front of one of these island traverses. On a certain cold wet morning two Engineer officers, one of senior rank and wearing very squeaky boots, were approaching this post from the rear. The sentry, all unconscious of danger, had set down his rifle and joined his companions round a small brazier, and had just fin-

Summer at Armentieres.

ished buttering a large round of hot toast. The squeak of the approaching boots just gave him time to jump to his stand before the eye of authority fell upon him. The rifle had to stay where it was, and after one hasty glance at his man, he decided to risk the lunch too, and stood solemnly to attention with the toast on his open palm, right side up. As the officers passed on round a bend his remarks to his mates were plainly audible. "Some sport, that old bloke! I wish they all had to wear squeaky boots and give a chap a chance."

At this period, the front line was not continuously occupied, the general practice inclining to a series of small garrisons about 200 yards apart. Though the gaps between these garrisoned localities were never held in any force, the parapet and travel track were necessarily kept in constant repair and patrolled at frequent intervals by the neighbouring garrisons. To ensure control of these areas in case of enemy attack, the parados and all intervening obstacles between it and the support line were levelled to the ground, and provision was also made for enfilade fire from wing trenches of the adjacent localities. To deceive enemy aeroplanes as to our actual position, without interfering with the fire of our own troops, dummy paradoses of netting and scrim on wooden frames were erected by the sappers. Dummy assembly trenches on the same pattern were also constructed quite early in our occupation of the sector, with a view to keeping the Boche in a pleasant state of uncertainty as to our ultimate intentions.

The support line was practically continuous, with complete parapet and parados unbroken by "gaps" such as existed in the front line. Though the whole line was maintained in a state of constant repair, series of fortified Posts were relied upon as the real centres of resistance in case of necessity. The subsidiary line also was maintained as a fighting trench, but as this was the location of the battalion in reserve, more attention was paid to shelters, headquarters dug-outs, field kitchens, etc., than was advisable nearer the front.

Access to the front line area was provided by long winding communication trenches, or C.T.'s, starting from the outskirts of the town. One commenced in the courtyard of a ruined house in Houplines, others led away from the actual streets. The method of communication trench construction followed here was practically the same on all the Flanders front. A shallow trench was cut, in which were erected wooden frames, known as "A" frames, at intervals of six feet. The "A"

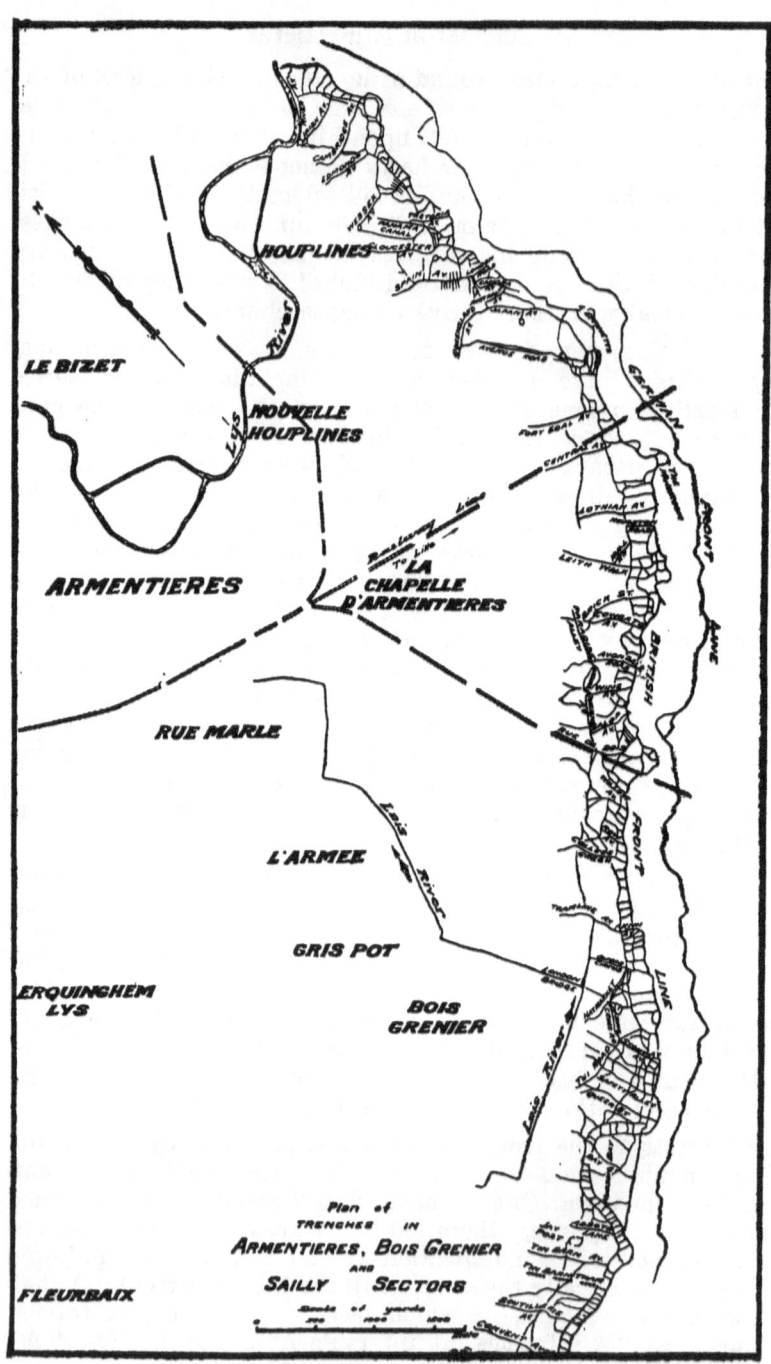

Summer at Armentieres.

frame, built of sawn green timber, and so called from its similarity in shape to the letter A inverted, required fairly solid beams for its construction, varying from 5in. by 2in. in the uprights to 3in. by 2in. in the bottom piece. Slight variations of size were obtainable to suit varying conditions, but the general type stood 5ft. high with a clear width between uprights of 1ft. 8in. at the bottom and 2ft. 11in. at the top. A larger size used only for very deep C.T.'s, and built of heavier timber, was 7ft. high and 3ft. 6in. wide at the top, and where the ground was largely built up, causing a heavy inward thrust on the uprights by the banks of wet earth, a strut was placed across the top to maintain the uprights at the correct distance apart. The particular advantage of the "A" frame was that it enabled new work to proceed from inside the trench without any necessity for exposing men to enemy fire while they constructed the outside anchorages necessary to any other form of wall revetment. If possible the banks were further supported by lengths of corrugated iron in wet country, or strips of expanded metal in dry, stretched from frame to frame. The height of the average frame above the cross piece being only 3ft. 9in., additional cover was provided by building up either side with sandbags, and occasionally extra ditches were cut outside and parallel with the trench, and the spoil was thrown up to increase the width and height of the walls. These ditches served an additional purpose in accommodating surplus storm-water. A smaller variety of the same frame, reaching some 2ft. above the cross piece, and known as a "U" frame, was largely employed in shallow trenches, or for keeping open important drains in soft difficult country. The cross pieces of all frames were about 15 inches above the bottom of the original cuts, and on them was laid a travel floor of duckboards, leaving the space beneath to act as a drain for the inevitable water.

To what circumstance or caprice the lowly duckboard owed its title has never been divulged. It consisted of a sort of rough ladder, the side pieces of 3in. by 2in. and about 7ft. long, with cross slats of 3in. by 1in., 18in. long, nailed transversely at intervals of about one inch. The side pieces were not parallel, a slight narrowing at one end enabling them to fit into the wider end of the next board, a succession of them thus forming a continuous board walk. Divisions especially favoured by Providence, or served by careful sappers of unusual skill in acquiring material, were further assisted in the uncertain pilgrimage to the front line by strips of wire netting nailed along the duckboards to ensure a firm foothold, but

Field Companies and Field Troop.

these were regarded as an extra by all right-minded soldiers. The duckboard is now known in military manuals as a trench board, but the use of such a term would only confuse any veteran who happens to read these pages.

The whole Armentieres sector when taken over by the Division was in a poor state of repair, and called for incessant labour with shovel and sandbag and every type of material. The existing breastworks were held up by all types of revetting, reminiscent of their various occupiers, but for new work and repairs the New Zealanders relied almost entirely on revetting hurdles, or trench frames and sandbags. These hurdles were composed of 3 uprights of 4in. by 2in. sawn timber, connected by 3 cross pieces of 3in. by 1in., one across the top of the uprights and the other two at intervals of 2ft. downwards. On this framework was nailed a sheet of expanded metal, which was found sufficiently strong to sustain any reasonable thrust by the imprisoned earth. Set on a vertical slope of about 4 in 1, lashed to one another, and anchored to pegs driven deep in the banks by ropes of twisted wire known as windles, these hurdles formed a ready and sufficient means of constructing the innumerable breastworks required. The traverses behind each fighting bay were simply provided by a series of these frames forming a kind of fenced enclosure, which could, if necessary, be erected first and filled with earth later. Damage was quickly repaired by the insertion of new frames where required. Apart from ordinary repair, a vigorous policy of improvement and reconstruction was carried out on all trenches, and these frames were used in thousands. Their manufacture was largely the work of civilians employed in the factories in the town under the control of the C.R.E. "A" frames had been used in many firebays, but as a general rule the New Zealander found himself cramped by the space afforded.

The Germans used brushwood revetting hurdles much more than we did. These are simply made of forest stakes interwoven with long thin saplings or flexible boughs in the manner of wickerwork, and are very strong and easily handled, lending themselves naturally to quick repair. Even where the British line lay through or near a large wood, such as Ploegsteert Wood, which we were to know well later on, there was very little use made of the material at hand. It may have been that the forests of France, which there, as everywhere else on the Continent, are looked upon as great national assets and most carefully tended and conserved, were being denuded of so many of their mature trees for war pur-

Summer at Armentieres.

poses that the authorities were particularly anxious to preserve the young shoots coming on for the future. That aspect of affairs of course did not worry the Boche, who had practically the whole of Belgium at his back to supply his brushwood requirements, and plenty of forced Belgian labour to make his hurdles. Forest timber of all sizes figured largely in German defensive works.

What the British armies in France and Flanders would have done during the four years of the war, had there been no sandbags to fill with dirt, is a subject which has not yet been given the attention it deserves by our imaginative writers. Next to the articles of intimate equipment that a man wore upon his person, the sandbag was probably the most general, as it was certainly one of the most useful, of all the varied munitions of war. Whatever work was going on in front, from building a wall to filling up a shell hole, the sandbag was indispensable; the last thing a man saw as he left his own trenches to attack was his sandbag parapet; included in his battle kit were more sandbags, and the first thing thought of to provide a little extra cover when consolidating his captured position was again the friendly sandbag. And for the carriage of rations, spare ammunition, sand or gravel, or any other burden of a suitable size, no other receptacle was ever thought of, while most men had one in similar commission for their private gear. As mattresses and extra blankets they were used in thousands, and as a type of rough legging in cold or muddy weather they were not despised.

The civilians remaining in the battle area lost no chance whatever of augmenting their supplies of bags, which were almost as popular tender in small deals as tins of bully beef. To outward appearance they made no great use of them, except as leggings or as waistcoats for the children, but there must have been some other cause to account for the avidity with which they seized upon every bag they could see. Quite likely they sold them back to the British Army along with large supplies made up at several local factories and small looms in the areas well behind the lines, for the Flanders residents are careful and thrifty souls. They probably boast more churches to the square mile than any other spot in Christendom, while wayside shrines, in continual use, and often simply festooned with the little wooden crosses the country folk brought along with their petitions for the safety of Jean or Henri, were almost as plentiful as estaminets; but the scriptural injunction against laying up treasure upon earth has either passed them by or left them very cold.

Field Companies and Field Troop.

The increased provision of fire steps was another matter taken definitely in hand by the sappers. These, as the name indicates, were stout planks fixed at such a height in the fire bays, that a man standing on them was about 4ft. 6in. below the top of the parapet, thus securing the maximum of cover consistent with full liberty of action. Many of the fire steps used by former occupiers had now to be lowered to suit their more lengthy successors. Fire steps were also fitted at suitable positions along the communication saps for use in defence against a possible flank attack.

All work in the actual front line was planned and carried out by the battalion in garrison, supervision only being provided by sappers. In support and subsidiary line work, however, all responsibility for plan and execution lay with the Engineers, the necessary working parties being drawn from the battalions in reserve. At first both day and night parties were employed; later on, in the less advanced positions, night work was abandoned except in special cases. In this quiet sector, no special advantage was gained by the added secrecy of night operations, and the amount of work done was naturally much less than in daylight. At this stage, the business of the day was very much of a routine nature. Even by the respective front line garrisons it seemed generally understood that no very desperate measures were to be expected from either side, and for hours together no sounds of war disturbed the serenity of the early summer days. Full advantage was taken of this opportunity to devote all available energies to the innumerable works requiring attention, and probably no period in the history of the Division, save the preparation for Messines, saw more solid work done than was performed at Armentieres.

By the middle of June, owing to redistribution of the Infantry Brigades, the disposition of the Field Companies was also altered, 1st and 3rd Companies remaining in front areas, while all engineering work in rear of subsidiary line was taken over by the 2nd Company. In addition to the routine works of this rear area, the defences of Armentieres town afforded a vast amount of work to the 2nd Company. These formed a series of defensive trenches and positions distinct from those of the regular lines in front, though necessarily constructed on the same general principles. Parties of civilians were employed on these rear defences and on drainage operations, under Engineer supervision, and rendered a good account of themselves. The river Lys running just in rear of Houplines and curving round Armentieres on the north and

Summer at Armentieres.

west was obviously a most important factor in the general strategic position. One of the first duties of the 3rd Field Company had been the preparation and placing of gun-cotton demolition charges on 12 bridges in and about the town, and these were now handed over to the 2nd Company. The charges were kept permanently in position, and were tested at regular intervals to ensure their efficiency in case of sudden emergency. On the Canal at the bend of the Lys just north of the town, two pontoon bridges were placed to provide alternative access to Houplines sub-sector, in case of heavy shelling along the usual road. A new communication trench was also constructed, its descriptive title of Lunatic Avenue being not so much a reflection on its users as a record of the fact that it ran past the Armentieres Asylum. During this period the town water supply system was also operated and maintained by the New Zealand sappers. Distribution pipes were run from a large central tank, which was supplied from a deep well by electrically-driven pumps, the necessary power being obtained from the plant of a disused factory.

Working parties from the battalions in reserve or support were met at appointed times and places by the sappers in charge of the respective jobs, served with tools and material, and piloted to the scene of operations. In general, at the appointed evening hour, activities were suspended with regularity and promptitude, and all working parties from the reserve battalion were able to return to their town billets Apart from the trifling details of periodic duties on guards and fatigues, they were then free to enjoy the amenities of civilisation for a few precious hours. This even temporary immunity from care had never been possible on Gallipoli, and was now of inestimable benefit to all concerned.

Material of all kinds was bountifully supplied and prodigally used. The main C.R.E. dump was situated on the bank of the Lys, and was supplied direct by numerous barges, and also by train. Three woodwork factories and a small sawmill in the town were operated by the Engineers, and here, with the aid of civilian labour, were constructed all the frames, duckboards, and other building requirements of the trenches. A small factory was also established for the manufacture of concrete bursters. These were reinforced slabs about 2ft. by 1ft. by 3in. thick, the principal use of which is explained later. The duckboards were the particular care of women workers, who became very expert at nailing them together, and relieved the tedium of the passing hours by what would now be called a community sing. Here, too, were pro-

Field Companies and Field Troop.

duced tables, chairs, desks, benches and stools for Headquarters, and any similar items needed by the various units of the Division.

Engineering circles at Chatham, the main R.E. Depot of England, are said to cherish very pleasant memories of an address delivered by a certain officer of the New Zealand Engineers, whose war services finally landed him in England, where he obtained permission to proceed to Chatham with the laudable intention of giving a few tips to the R.E. personnel of that ancient town. After stating his opinion that the main obstructionists in the way of free supplies of engineering material were undoubtedly Brigadier-Generals, of whom there were several present, he went on to state that the New Zealanders at Armentieres never ran short. The reason was that by a private system of intelligence he always knew when barges full of material were approaching up the Lys, and would then make it his business to board them some distance below the town, where he would amend the labels on the cargo in accordance with his requirements of the moment! This is obviously the solution of most supply problems, and even a Brigadier-General could hardly suggest a simpler method of stocking a Divisional dump.

All new dumps, trenches, posts or communications constructed by the New Zealanders were favoured with names reminiscent of home, and generally of Maori origin. One trench dug by Waikato men was forthwith labelled Ngaruawahia Avenue to the bewilderment of "Tommy" neighbours and relieving troops. At Houplines the 3rd Field Company established a dump which they christened "Waitangi Dump." An irate British Colonel attempted to pronounce the name with somewhat indifferent results, and then called upon a Sapper Sergeant to tell him what it was: "Waitangi, Sir!" "Waitangi! What the devil's that?" "It means weeping water, Sir, and is. . . ." "Then, why the hell don't you say weeping water instead of using that unpronounceable —— lingo."

While the sappers were busily engaged on their multifarious duties, the transport sections, both men and beasts, came in for a fair share of the prevailing activity. The requirements of the forward areas in the way of material were supplied from dumps established as close as possible to the scene of action. The replenishment of these dumps with every type of trench store was a heavy task calling for the nightly employment of all available transport. In addition to ordinary waggons and limbers, use was made of the pontoon

Summer at Armentieres.

and trestle waggons. These were relieved of the usual loading, and by an arrangement of the bridge decking to serve as a flooring, were converted into serviceable cartage vehicles. It may be noted here that a portion of the regulation equipment of a Field Company on active service is two double pontoons, each mounted on a special waggon, which also carries the necessary baulks and decking to form a span of bridging, while a third waggon carries two Weldon trestles and a further supply of decking timbers, the whole being sufficient to form a light bridge of 75ft. span suitable for traffic up to 18-pounder guns. In open warfare, when rapid movement is probable, and temporary bridging a necessity, this gear is indispensable, but for the first two or three years in France, when every Field Company in the land was trailing its pontoons about at every move, with great expenditure of energy in men and horseflesh, there was little prospect of any bridging. It was not till within a few months of the time when there really arose a definite call for the pontoons that they were all called into concentration parks, whence they were issued as required. However, as we have seen, the waggons served other purposes no less useful, if more lowly, than that for which they were originally designed. And on trek, the extra opportunities afforded for stowing spare kit sometimes prevailed over the regulations prohibiting any such misuse of the frail vessels.

From the forward dumps, tramways ran up to the actual line. Every night a working party under the control of two or three sappers took forward loads of material, and returned the empty trucks. The general movements of these parties and the position of the tramways were well known to the Boche, who was busily engaged in similar enterprises on his own side, and occasionally he caused considerable delay and annoyance to the tram parties, with damage both to track and personnel. Seldom, however, did they fail to deliver the goods.

In addition to the endless task of ordinary trench repair, a matter calling more for tools and labour than for any special skill, there were plenty of works to exercise the technical abilities of the Engineer Companies. The provision of new splinter-proof and high explosive-proof dug-outs was carried on steadily from the first. The general run of the existing shelters had been roughly constructed in the shape of a wooden box about 6ft. by 5ft. and 3ft. high. The vertical supports on either side were provided by pit-props. Fairly stout straight poles cut green from the young trees of the French forests,

Field Companies and Field Troop.

without trimming or dressing, were sent to the battle areas in great numbers. These were usually 6 to 10 feet long and 6 to 9 inches in diameter, though there was great variation in both dimensions. Everything up to 10 feet in length was called a pit-prop. Beams resting on the pit-prop supports carried a roofing of transverse boards, covered with such height of earth as might be available. Board flooring, and sides of timber or corrugated iron, completed the structure. Many of these existing shelters were in the front line, where their presence not only weakened the parapet, but created a certain amount of tension between sleepers and passers-by in the matter of protruding legs and feet.

New shelters were now constructed in front of the travel trench in rear, some of the old box type, but as many as possible of corrugated steel, the sides and roof being roughly on the curve of a small circle, with a board flooring as the diameter, so to speak, of the same circle. Instead of the row of pit-props, stout beams were laid on the ground on each side, to which the iron was securely fixed by means of bolts driven through holes in flanges turned for the purpose at the bottom edges of the steel sheets. Each semi-circle of steel was composed of two equal segments, which met and bolted at the top by means of flanges similar to those below. On this supporting arch was heaped a covering of loose earth, covered with packed sandbags. On these again were laid strong baulks, or pit-props, 2 feet apart, supporting a roofing of concrete bursters. The air space between the concrete slabs and the sandbags beneath was found to act as a protective cushion in the event of a direct hit by a shell, and the special function of the concrete was to ensure the bursting of the projectile before penetration, hence the term "burster." These small steel shelters, known as "baby elephants," were 5ft. 3in. wide and 3ft. 6in. high. Numbers of them were also erected in support and subsidiary lines. More ambitious shelters of the same shape, 6ft. 2in. high and 9ft. 6in. wide, capable of acting as company headquarters, or signallers' dug-outs, were also constructed of a heavier type of corrugated iron known as "English" pattern. For these, the arch was composed of two side pieces, with an overlapping centre piece, the whole being bolted securely together. The same system of cover was employed for protective purposes.

The idea of a "bursting course" in the cover provided against shell-fire was only evolved after some 18 months of sad experience of the results of enemy high-explosive shells. Of the materials available, the concrete slab was so

Summer at Armentieres.

much the simplest and easiest to handle that it practically appropriated sole rights in the name "burster," but failing the slabs, good results could be had from broken brick, or flint, or heavy baulks of timber, providing the air space existed underneath. Overhead cover, on a steel shelter, consisting of 2 feet depth of packed sandbags on top of 12 inches of solid concrete failed to avert destruction. Had the 2 feet of sandbagging given place to a row of large pit-props or iron girders spaced 2 feet apart and surmounted by sheets of iron upholding 1 foot of sandbags and 9 inches of broken brick, the result would have been less disastrous. It must not be inferred that no cover was safe which did not include air space. An arrangement of 9in. logs laid close together covered with corrugated iron, then with another row of logs, and finally surmounted by 6 feet of solid rammed earth came successfully through the ordeal of the "direct hit," but such a structure, in addition to requiring labour, was useless when head room was limited. Safe and shallow cover was well provided by the use of two layers of steel rails, the upper laid transversely on the lower, surmounted by walls formed by packed sandbags laid end on, one bag wide and three bags high, spaced at 2 feet centres apart. On these walls were laid the concrete slabs, painted on top in various colours to disguise the real facts of their existence. The total depth of this arrangement was but 2ft. 3in.

The first captured document which showed that the enemy had reached the same conclusions as ourselves with regard to an "arresting course" was taken in September, 1916, on the Somme. The diagram showed practically the same practice as our own, except that Fritz employed some 6 inches of solid concrete on top in place of the 3-inch slab used by us. He also introduced fascines about the middle of his protection courses, which being of a yielding, yet tough and springy consistency, served the purpose very well.

The foregoing may be taken to represent some indication of the principles underlying the construction of shelters in the battle area, though full treatment of even mere principles could be expanded indefinitely. Practice varied even more, according to the situation, the material available, and the individuals in charge of the work.

The construction of snipers' posts, almost always situated in the front line, was the particular care of selected sappers or N.C.O.'s who made a specialty of the work. This type of job invariably appealed to the sporting instincts of the aver-

Field Companies and Field Troop.

age New Zealand soldier, and was a veritable labour of love. On selection of a likely spot, a recess was dug into the parapet until the outside edge was almost reached. Thereafter operations became more secretive and every care was taken to avoid detection. First of all, a conveniently sized stand for the sniper was excavated, with the sides held up by hurdles or sandbagging. In front, at a suitable height, a ledge was cut out on which was placed a flat wooden box shaped like a trapezium, open back and front, with the smaller opening towards the enemy, and shielded by a trap-door when not in use. A wide field of fire was obtained by moving to either side of the larger opening in the rear. Before the final aperture was made in the parapet, some care was taken to attend to the ground outside. Loose earth or an old sandbag might move on discharge of a rifle and disclose the position. A favourite device was to surround the opening with old tins or similar trench rubbish of a safe nature. The hanging of a sack or blanket behind the sportsman to minimise the risk of discovery on opening the trap-door in front completed the preliminary arrangements, and the rest was a matter for the sniper and his quarry on the other side of the way. The above description merely represents the general conditions affecting the sniper, and all arrangements were capable of elaboration up to the point of a square steel structure to protect the head and shoulders of the operator, with a sliding steel plate to cover the shooting aperture when not in use. Under ordinary trench conditions such high-class articles were not generally available, nor was the average sniper in the least perturbed by their absence. So long as something in field grey passed his sights with reasonable frequency he was quite satisfied to carry on with or without mechanical assistance.

Along the low-lying flats of this trench area, destitute of all natural facilities for observation, recourse was had to artificial means of keeping a careful eye on the daily movements of the enemy. Several of the tall factory chimneys of Houplines and Armentieres were utilised for the purpose, and the preparation of these eyries afforded many opportunities to amateur steeplejacks among the Field Companies. An arrangement of alternate platforms and ladders inside the chimney, or, in some cases, spikes driven in the brickwork, usually enabled the observer's post to be located at a sufficiently commanding height. A narrow slit cut through the wall of the chimney afforded excellent observation, and was practically impossible to detect. Other posts nearer the line were located in tall leafy trees, and occasionally the remains

Summer at Armentieres.

of a farm building afforded a necessarily limited field of view. By each post was constructed a dug-out for telephone and personnel, as far as possible proof against enemy artillery. A clever idea used here right in the front area, and also met with in Fleurbaix later, was the artificial tree. This was a hollow steel replica of a tree trunk, which had been removed one night and replaced by the steel erection before daylight. A thin slit covered with gauze gave all necessary facility for observation. Later on, posts in the actual front line were fitted with steel protective sides and movable loophole plates. One peculiar aspect of observation posts or, in trench vernacular, O. Pips, was the number of units, to whom, on their own showing, an observation post was absolutely essential for the successful prosecution of the war.

The new conditions of warfare confronting the machine-gunners again often caused necessity for the services of the Engineers. The provision of accommodation in the vicinity of their posts was a constant routine job, usually satisfied by the erection of "baby elephants," but the construction of the actual posts was a more important work often undertaken. Open positions at the corners of hedgerows, or similar field sites, called for nothing much more than a little sandbagging and camouflage. Several covered positions in the Armentieres sector were put in at salient angles of the support line, or in convenient banks in the open fields. For these, a suitable hole was excavated in the bank, and provided with a low sandbag bench or mound in the centre, on which the gun was mounted. In some cases the opening towards the enemy was left wide and free, in others the opening was narrowed down towards the front by the use of sandbag walls. Across the top of the whole excavation was placed a heavy roofing of pit-props overlaid with concrete bursters, and the whole was surmounted by turf. Any type of erection with sharp angles which could throw a shadow in an aeroplane photograph was carefully avoided. A position frequently adopted was behind the remains of a brick wall of one of the ruined farmhouses dotted about the countryside. In these cases, shelter for the gunner was usually arranged by the erection of a "baby elephant" in the selected position hard against the wall. Broken brick piled round and on top of the steel arch afforded protection and concealment at the same time. A small sandbag mound inside the shelter gave a platform for the gun, and a horizontal slit cut out of the brick wall in front allowed for the necessary field of fire. This was the simplest, and probably the most effective type of the defensive positions pre-

Field Companies and Field Troop.

pared for the machine-guns, though here again it should be understood that only an outline of the general procedure has been attempted. In all engineering manuals or in Schools of Instruction the subject of machine-gun positions was elaborated in many forms, and with great attention to detail, measurements and so on, but in practice the sappers had to make use of what was available, and produce reasonably efficient results quickly.

Mention has already been made of the " Posts " which constituted the main centres of resistance in the support line. These Posts were a complete work in themselves, and the Field Companies in the line never had less than a full section constantly at work upon them. Occasionally the remains of an old farm, with its extensive walls and courtyard, formed a basis of operations, but more generally a site had been chosen in the open with due regard to field of fire, not only in front, but also covering the country between the Post and others on either side. Even command of country in the rear was an advantage, since the main principle underlying the whole scheme of these "islands of resistance" recognised nothing but a fight to a finish as the main object of their existence, should they ever be required to sustain enemy onslaught. Choice of ground, then, called for more than casual selection of a sunny patch. Other things being equal, the cover afforded by hedge-rows, or even a few tall trees, was a distinct advantage. The defensive walls were of the usual breastwork type, and faced at least three sides in a roughly circular form. A travel trench of duckboards ran right round the enclosure connected at either side with the general line of the support trench itself. Fire-bays were complete with fire-step and parados. Shelter for the garrison was provided at the most convenient spot, perhaps in the rear of the parados, or in some convenient mound in the centre of the enclosure, or possibly behind the broken trunks of a line of trees. Shelters were of the types already described. During our term in the Armentieres trenches all Posts were equipped with at least a proportion of steel shelters, properly protected by overhead cover. Most of the Posts, though workable, had been found in a poor state of repair. Damage done by enemy shelling had either been left alone altogether, or a makeshift substitute for a trench dug round it. In every case the New Zealand Field Companies, aided of course by their working parties, tackled the problem comprehensively, and by straightening trenches, laying tracks and strengthening and revetting all breastwork,

A TYPICAL BILLET IN FRANCE.

REMAINS OF A FARMHOUSE AT CHAPELLE D'ARMENTIERES.

BUTERNE LANE, NEAR HOUPLINES.

Photos by Major N. Annabell

Summer at Armentiers.

restored the Posts to perhaps a little more than their original splendour.

During the dry weather experienced in June, a shortage of water in some of the forward areas made it necessary to dig wells and instal pumps for their convenient working. To run short of water in Flanders of all places on the habitable globe seemed a queer vicissitude of fortune, when another month or so might easily see the same pumps busily occupied in assisting to keep the surplus surface water within reasonable bounds. Pumps were continually in use by the New Zealanders. Invariably a considerable proportion of the dug-outs taken over from their predecessors in any sector required the attentions of a pump to render them habitable, and the application of considerable concrete to keep them so. The probable reason is that these concrete jobs were generally done in summer, when the extreme rigours of the winter season were temporarily forgotten.

Towards the end of June much greater animation began to prevail on the whole northern front, and with the commencement of the Battle of the Somme on 1st July, a continuous activity of all arms set in, which lasted with slight respite until the Division was relieved in mid August. Wire cutting, bombardments of the front line, bursts of fire on billets, gas discharges or raids took place nightly. Not least in importance was the continuous series of raids now carried out with great skill and determination. The usual objects of a raid, to develop one's own offensive spirit, to secure identification of the enemy, to destroy garrisons and machine-guns and so on, were now reinforced by a necessity for assisting operations in the south, by keeping our northern opponents on the qui vive in their own trenches. Here, as elsewhere, raiding parties were accompanied by sappers, armed with mobile charges of guncotton, whose principle aim was the demolition of any important structure found.

The first raid attempted by the New Zealanders in France took place on the night of 16th-17th June, when a party of 4 officers and 83 other ranks of the 2nd Brigade raided a new enemy trench known as the "Breakwater" from its general shape and appearance. The construction of the "Breakwater" was not greatly advanced, and the raid yielded little in the way of Germans alive or dead. Four sappers of the 3rd Company accompanied the party, and blew up the only work of any magnitude they could discover, a listening post at the forward end of a German sap.

Field Companies and Field Troop.

On 25th June a highly successful effort was made by the 2nd Rifles on the enemy trenches opposite Pont Ballot salient. Some 30 Germans were killed in the open trench, and many more preferred to die in the seclusion of their dugouts by the agency of a Mills bomb, while 9 prisoners and much material accompanied their successful opponents back to our own line. Two sappers of the 1st Field Company took part in this raid. One blew up a gas engine used for pumping, while the other destroyed the enemy's main dugout, a commodious residence lit by electric light.

First Wellington took a hand in the game on 1st July, again with splendid results. One N.C.O. and a sapper of the 1st Field Company went over with the raiders, and contributed their share to the general performance. One of them discovered a large pump shaft leading from a deep well towards the German rear. A short excursion in search of the actual pump was cut short by the whistle signal for withdrawal, and he had to content himself with the destruction of the shaft. His partner attended to a large concrete emplacement provided with iron doors, and evidently used as a bomb store. With his charge laid and fuse already lit, he was ready to withdraw, when the doors were opened and four yelling Boches disclosed themselves within. Three were got out in time with the aid of an infantryman's bayonet, the fourth was slow and reluctant and shared the fate of his bomb store.

On the following night a raid by 2nd Wellington attacked the trenches near Frelinghien Brasserie. Four N.C.O.'s of the 3rd Field Company were included in this expedition. Owing to particularly prompt and vigorous shelling by the enemy artillery, and to poorly-cut access through his wire, the raid was not a success.

Two sappers from the 2nd Field Company took part in a further raid on 13th July. On this occasion 1st Otago had charge of the enterprise. Tremendous concentration of enemy fire seemed almost to argue fore-knowledge of the attack, and practically the whole of the raiders suffered injury. The sappers were both wounded severely. 2nd Field Company again sent 3 sappers with a 1st Auckland raid on the night of 19th-20th July. Nothing but dead and debris was found in the enemy trenches, and no subject for demolition presented itself.

Despite our raiding activity at this period, we enjoyed no monopoly of the pastime. The Boche made several notable efforts to return our attentions, including one particularly

Summer at Armentieres.

fierce attack on 8th July on the Mushroom, an undesirable salient in our lines. The hasty lines of trenches thrown up under fire in 1914 approached one another more closely here than at any other point within miles. The flooding of one of his mine tunnels by our Engineers early in July may have inspired more than usual resentment. An intense bombardment completely destroyed the trenches and most of the garrison, and the enemy gained temporary possession of his objective. Sappers of the 1st Field Company were included in a mixed party, which immediately counter-attacked and successfully evicted the invaders. The rest of the night was fully occupied in repairing our front parapet, complete restoration of the locality occupying several days of unremitting toil. Several Engineers distinguished themselves in these numerous raids, and some at least received awards, but unfortunately no satisfactory records of their exploits are now available, and they cannot be given the attention they undoubtedly earned.

One natural result of our increased activity was a disposition to retaliation on the part of the enemy. This generally resulted in a bombardment of Armentieres, which gradually began to wear a battered appearance. On one occasion a shell in the 1st Company's billets caused 14 casualties, and on another, the 2nd Company's brewery was set on fire. Assistance rendered by the warrior inmates placed the brewer under a heavy debt of gratitude, which he cheerfully liquidated with a good spirit. Two nearby houses were slightly affected by the conflagration, and the inhabitants, all asleep in the cellar, had to be roused to a sense of their danger by eager sappers. Meanwhile two of their brethren, more far-sighted in emergency, had seized the opportunity to effect a perfectly unnecessary rescue of two much-sought-after demoiselles in a neighbouring estaminet, and thereby established a lead that was never seriously threatened as long as the Company remained in Armentieres. This enemy activity naturally led to considerable damage to the trenches and other works in our area, now beginning to show unmistakable signs of the energies lavished upon them. The daily shelling effectually removed all haunting fears that work on the sector would fail from lack of suitable objects to engage our workmanlike attentions. Owing to the increasing risks in the town, all Engineer transport and mounted personnel were sent into camp on the outskirts. Most of the horses were sent for a spell to Hayes' Farm, near Pont de Nieppe, and civilian transport was hired for supplying requirements of the moment.

Field Companies and Field Troop.

On 3rd July the 2nd Field Company moved out to Bois Grenier with the 3rd Rifles, and took over from the 7th Field Company, Australian Engineers. Here they were employed on works similar to those already handled in the main sector. More than passing interest attaches to Bois Grenier from the fact that that area was the one occupied by the heroes of Ian Hay's "The First Hundred Thousand," and here were seen in radiant glory those blood-red fields of poppies which are now so intimately associated with all memories of Flanders.

With the Field Companies, as with the rest of the Division, life went on along these comparatively peaceful lines until the 13th August, when the New Zealanders marched out of Armentieres en route for an unannounced destination. As they left the town they passed through the 51st Division, which was waiting to march in and take over the recently vacated billets. The war-scarred ranks of the famous Highlanders, all clad in the romantic garb of old Gaul, and straight from fresh glories earned on the bloody fields of the Somme, were an inspiring and never-to-be-forgotten sight to the young battalions from overseas. And the Highland battalions, between whom and all colonials a cheering spirit of understanding cameraderie always existed on whatever front throughout the war, were not slow to show their appreciation of the brave show made by the marching columns. Waving bonnets lined the roadside, while the skirl of the pibroch and the roll of the drums rose above the tumult to cheer the New Zealanders on their way, and to stir the breasts, not only of those whose ancestry hailed from old Scotia, but of all privileged to enjoy the experience.

Temporary billets were now occupied in the Hazebrouck area, the 1st Company being located at Racquinghem, the 2nd at Wallon Cappel, and the 3rd and Headquarters at Blaringhem. Route-marching and general training were indulged in till the 21st August, when entrainment took place at Arques near St. Omer, for a training area in the Abbeville district at the mouth of the Somme. This finally settled all question as to the ultimate destination of the Division. Detraining at Pont Remy and Longpre, a short march found the three companies finally located at Hocquincourt, Limercourt, and Allery respectively, with C.R.E.'s headquarters at Hallencourt.

CHAPTER VII.

THE BATTLE OF THE SOMME, 1916.

After 18 months of patient preparation, the British Armies in France were at last able, in the summer of 1916, to undertake an offensive campaign on a large scale. The Valley of the Somme was selected as the scene of operations most likely to yield success, and here, in conjunction with our French Allies, a grand attack was launched on 1st July. In his despatch of 23rd December, 1916, the three main objects of the offensive were clearly set forth by the British Commander-in-Chief: to relieve the increasing pressure on Verdun; to stop further transfers of German troops from the Western Front to other theatres of war; and to wear down the strength of the enemy forces.

To General Rawlinson of the Fourth Army, assisted on his northern flank by troops of the Third Army, was entrusted the task of directing the destinies of the British troops engaged in the combined enterprise. The initial result, particularly in the northern sector of attack, fell far short of expectation, but by steady persistent effort against great odds, an advance of about a mile was achieved in the southern area by the middle of July. A further grim struggle of a month or more saw the enemy now in the last line of his original system of defences, and the main objects of the undertaking successfully achieved. By the end of August it was considered that a further attack in force had every chance of finally dislodging the Boche from his carefully prepared trenches. Once in the open, and shorn of the tremendous advantages borne of his first choice of position and months of energetic and skilful fortification, it was felt that he could be engaged on an equal footing with results entirely favourable to his confident assailants. The New Zealanders were honoured by inclusion in the ranks of the selected British forces detailed for this final grand assault.

In the meantime, in preparation for the coming ordeal, the Division was resting in the brooding peace of late summer among the sequestered villages of the lower Somme. The peasants here seemed curiously out of touch with the stirring march of events; their only visible emotion, even at the advent of the troops, found expression in the billeting of large dogs beneath their apples trees, the removal of pump handles, and

Field Companies and Field Troop.

in similar small courtesies not fully appreciated by their guests. A strain of subdued excitement, due to the certainty of stern work ahead, gave an extra fillip to training operations. In view of the services most likely to be required of them, the Engineers concentrated on the speedy laying out of trenches, the handling of working parties, rapid wiring, and consolidation of captured positions. Constant route marching hardened the men after their recent spell of trench warfare.

It may easily be seen that Engineers faced with the job of providing trenches at a certain spot, and strictly limited as to both time and labour, must work on some definite plan if the necessary results are to be achieved, and the services of each man fully utilised. With this end in view all sappers were instructed how to mark out various types of trench according to the demands of the situation, and how to estimate accurately and quickly how much of the work could be performed by the average soldier in the time available. The amount of digging laid down by British Army Manuals as a fair thing to expect from the ordinary soldier was 80 cubic feet in 4 hours. There were times when this amount was not achieved in a long day, but under good conditions and pressed by motives of personal safety or by a desire to be somewhere else, the New Zealander could cut it out in half the time, or less, and very often did.

By the 27th August, the sappers were on the move again, and proceeded by road and train via Mericourt L'Abbe to a point on the Fricourt-Mametz Road, between Fricourt and Becordel. Here was found the Transport, which had come by road the preceding day, and the whole Engineer establishment went into bivouac on the roadside, with the Pioneer Battalion alongside. The first autumn rains had now set in, and the only shelters available, roughly constructed of pontoon decking, were urgently required. On the evening of arrival, ration arrangements were not all that they might have been, and a temporary shack just opened by the Y.M.C.A. suffered a tremendous onslaught from wet and weary men. An extract from a sapper's letter shows how misfortunes heighten one's sympathy with the sufferings of others:—

"Another long march to-day in mud and rain, with the cursed pack weighing a ton long before night. We stuck it out, but were mighty glad to see the sign of the old Y.M. and to get a warm drink and some grub. As I came out of the shed, I saw Captain ―― with his boot off examining a blister on his foot, and that was as good as another cup of hot coffee!"

The Battle of The Somme.

All around were signs of a most intense activity. The roads were one solid mass of ordered traffic, waggons, guns, limbers, tractors, lorries, and flashing in and out among them all the motor cycles of the incomparable despatch riders. Mile after mile, ridge upon ridge, lay the congested bivouacs of the British Army. The morning sun could scarcely penetrate the smoke of the myriad fires that hung like a grey pall in the calm air, and by night a thousand camps were pricked out on the dark fields by clusters of twinkling lights. The sound of the guns ran the whole gamut of intensity from the harsh crash of our own heavies, down through the bark and swish of the lighter field pieces, to the far-off throb of the German artillery beating like a pulse in the murky atmosphere. Always the guns, never idle, never silent, roaring like savage animals eager for their prey. All early impressions of the scale of artillery in modern war, begotten of the now insignificant experiences of the Armentieres sector, were swept away by the mighty flood of continual gun-fire. Nor was any very accurate readjustment possible for some time. The mind was enveloped by the wonder and immensity of the crowded events. Above the chequered scene hundreds of British 'planes flew hither and thither at their own sweet will, and long lines of observation balloons strung out against the hazy sky. A few German balloons were faintly visible, and an occasional enemy aviator made a hasty reconnaisance from a safe height.

The first work undertaken by the Field Companies was the consolidation of the old German Second Line on the Bazentin Ridge. The trenches here were naturally in a broken and battered state, and appeared worse by contrast with recent scenes of endeavour. The whole countryside was sodden with rain, the bottoms of the trenches, destitute of duckboards, were simply a slough of mud and water; the sides, unsupported by any revetment, fell in at a touch, and the whole was soon trampled into a viscous mass of tenacious bog that made all travel a laborious and exasperating pilgrimage of woe.

Engineers and Pioneers were immediately set to the repairing of two trenches known as the Savoy and Carlton. The reconstruction and revetment of selected fire bays was put in hand at once, and valiant efforts were made to improve the existing communication saps. In the prevailing scarcity of all material, particularly revetting hurdles and "A" frames. these saps were almost a hopeless task. The unfortunate digger, bogged to the knees in slush, managed to heave a certain amount out of the trench during the day, only to find that it slithered in again over night. A certain amount of wiring

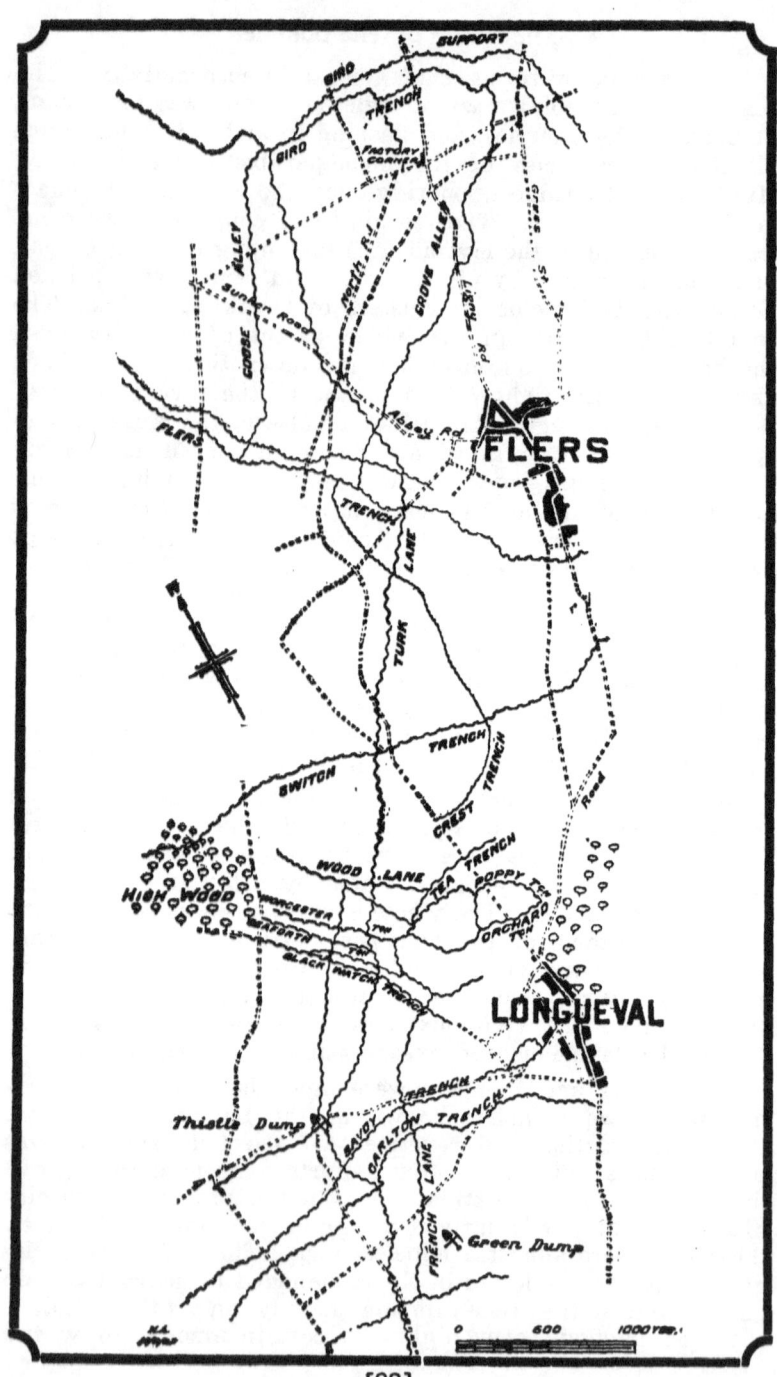

The Battle of The Somme.

was done in front of the new trenches, and several deep dugouts were commenced pending the arrival of the main body of the Division. The first issue of that comforting beverage known as rum took place in these early days on the Somme, and cannot be allowed to pass unrecorded by any account which professes an interest in the simple pleasures of the hardy soldiery.

While the sappers cleared and drained these works, the transport drivers were fully employed in carting material from a regimental dump at Mametz siding to two dumps in the forward area known as Green and Thistle dumps. In these dumps were placed large supplies of all material likely to be required in the consolidation and defence of ground won from the enemy, notably wire, sandbags, picks and shovels. Duckboards, revetting hurdles and other more elaborate articles of trench equipment belong rather to later days, when a hold on the captured territory had been definitely asserted.

All dumps belonging to a Division are controlled by the Divisional C.R.E., who obtains his supplies through the Chief Engineer of the Corps to which his Division belongs, with the exception of a limited amount that may be purchased locally if circumstances are so favourable as to admit of local supplies of anything required. Aladdin would have been hard pressed to provide local supplies on the Somme. Each dump is always guarded and controlled by a Sapper or N.C.O., who builds himself a kennel from the materials at his disposal and settles down to await what the Fates may send. Since a dump is always easily picked up by enemy aviators, and is moreover a point frequently visited by parties of troops, the gifts of fortune generally take the form of enemy shells, and the apparently simple calling of a dump keeper is an appointment of considerable uncertainty.

Early in September, the efforts of the Engineers were transferred to the more congenial task of preparing particularly for the advent of their own Infantry. A day or two were spent by all available units on the road from Mametz to Montauban. The surface mud was shovelled off, and a layer of brick rubble put on to give a firm foothold. Side drains and large sump pits to control surface water materially improved the road. Thereafter, in company with the Pioneers, the sappers set about the construction of two new communication trenches for up and down traffic. These were known as Turk Lane and French Lane, and ran from the dumps to the advanced areas. The Pioneers worked on Turk Lane, the

Field Companies and Field Troop.

Engineers on French Lane. For the first time in France, the sappers were working with their own job all to themselves, spurred on by this fact, and by a friendly rivalry with those redoubtable warriors, the Pioneers, they made a great effort. The two saps were dug throughout to a depth of 3 feet, and by a second operation were lowered to a depth of 5 feet, and provided with duckboards. It was here that the first real bombardment with gas shells was experienced, one Company losing 2 officers and 20 men in one night. Heavy rain hindered the work throughout. Night after night the men came home soaked with rain and mud, with no prospect of drying their clothes, and the morrow saw but repetition of the same conditions. However, on arrival of the Infantry battalions on the 11th, two splendid communication trenches, each some 4000 yards in length, duckboarded and revetted throughout, lay ready to conduct them from the dumps right to the advanced line of posts in Black Watch Trench. Runner posts were provided in both saps. In an area pitifully ill supplied with such advantages, these two saps became quite famous, and were known by envious neighbours far and wide. In fact, they set a new standard for the area, and the increased endeavour consequent upon an effort to live up to them was of great benefit all round.

By the 10th September, the assembly trenches necessary for the assaulting battalions in the coming attack were already under way in rear of the occupied shell holes between Tea and Orchard Trenches. Up to this date, with the exception of two advanced sections, the Field Companies had remained in their original camps, and had overcome the long distances to the various jobs by using the pontoon wagons to give the men a lift. Continuous wet weather had made this proceeding at last impossible, and on the 13th, preparatory to the day of attack, the whole of the 1st and 2nd Companies moved up and joined the advanced sections in dugouts in Montauban. The 3rd Company remained at Fricourt in reserve.

The Tanks, concerning which so many wild rumours were current, that they might have been anything from subterraneans to flying machines, now made their appearance, and while not quite up to extreme anticipation, were a sufficiently diverting spectacle as they lumbered solemnly over or through every species of obstacle. Despite their sloth and clumsiness, they were to prove highly effective on the morrow, when positions which might ordinarily have held up an advance for hours, fell to their insidious assault in a few minutes. Later on, when the Germans took special measures to

The Battle of The Somme.

combat them, they were less successful, and lost much of their initial prestige until 1918, when their greatly increased speed restored them to favour with the fighting men.

During the 14th, in broken weather, final preparations were made for the great assault, practically unimpeded by enemy attentions of any kind. On this day, all Engineer transport, which had already been strenuously engaged in carting material over the heavy roads, moved into a fresh camp at Mametz. Advanced dumps of all materials had been established ere this, and parties were now detailed to carry up on the morrow whatever stores might be called for by the fortunes of the battle. The main duty of the Engineers was to be the immediate construction of Strong Points in ground won from the enemy. The approximate location of these Points, with reference to the several objectives of the attacking infantry, was fixed by the C.R.E. before the advance, both to save time, and possibly to obviate the risk of a faulty choice of position due to a hasty decision on the field during the strain and stress of the engagement.

By the time of the Somme battle the experiences of modern warfare had firmly established the Strong Point as a definite feature of all operations in attack. It was recognised that trenches won by assault, especially when the lines were of value and importance, were certain to be subject to counter-attack just as soon as the enemy could rally his forces or employ his reserves. In the time available, it was impossible to convert the whole captured trench into a position suitable to withstand attack from its previous rear, where wire and cover were absent and numerous saps afforded hidden means of approach. Nor were men likely to be available to defend the whole length of line. Hence a break through in the centre, for example, would mean divided forces taken separately, and rolled up from the flanks, with disaster as the only end to a promising venture. To meet this type of contingency the Strong Point was evolved, a more or less circular trench system, complete in itself with firebays and sandbag parapets, capable of accommodating up to 40 or 50 men. Two or three hastily sandbagged emplacements for machine-gunners, sited at salient points, were additional items of equipment. Properly selected on commanding positions at convenient intervals apart, these Strong Points constitute a miniature series of minor forts very like the "posts" and "localities" of the established defensive lines of stationary trench warfare, and

Field Companies and Field Troop.

form an exceedingly powerful nucleus for any system of defence. A further development is the use of enveloping wire entanglement, but since the wire catches the eye of the enemy aviator, who invariably passes on the good news to his artillery, the advantages accruing are questionable.

Though trenches dug on a circular pattern generally provide the easiest means of securing fire command in all directions, it does not follow that the lie of the country is always suitable for that class of Strong Point. Another type of construction often in use was the cruciform system, based on a central length of traversed trench cut towards the enemy with two smaller lengths, running off on either side, approximately at right angles in the shape of a rough cross. Fire from trenches laid out in this form can be trained in any desired direction, and machine-guns placed at the ends of the intersecting lengths ensure cross-fire on the attacker wherever he may be.

The cruciform system of construction was particularly well adapted to circumstances which called for the immediate provision of defensible positions capable of holding back enemy attacks for the time that had necessarily to elapse before a complete trench line could be dug. The side lengths prolonged and joined up became the main trench line, while the central stem could be extended to the rear to act as a communication sap. In such a case as this, the Strong Points were always maintained as such after the completion of the through trench, and the hasty work of the first few hours was gradually improved and amended with more and better machine-gun positions until the post had attained full development as a centre of resistance. Such points are harder for enemy artillery to range on, and easier to conceal from the sky than closed circular works. Having in view the ultimate purpose of their existence, their final equipment should include stores of bombs, ammunition, food, water, wire and sandbags with the provision of Headquarters, telephone, and other dugouts necessary for a continued and successful defence. It will easily be seen that the general principles underlying the existence of the "Strong Point" remain the same in all cases, and so long as these are satisfied, minor questions of size and shape may be safely governed by the exigencies of each particular situation.

By midnight of the 14th all troops were in position. Each man was supplied with two gas helmets, extra ammunition, a filled water bottle, and extra rations in addition to the "iron" ration. Enemy artillery was curiously silent, and the splendid fitness and zest for battle of the waiting men were not

The Battle of The Somme.

diminished by exposure to the nervous strain of a heavy bombardment passively endured in crowded assembly trenches. Most of them even slept a little, but by 6 a.m. the first faint promise of a fine day found them calm and ready, keen to put their fortune to the test.

At 6.20 a.m. the peaceful air was shattered by an intensity of British fire never before experienced or imagined. The struggling light of the dawn, imperfectly assisted by the stabbing flashes of the belching guns, was almost powerless to contend with the dense clouds of smoke and dust, and in a few moments the shadowy line of steadily advancing figures had vanished into the unknown. As usual, the objectives set for the various assaults of the day were shown on the maps in different colours, and were known by those colours to those concerned. The first objective was the Switch Trench (or Green Line), a powerfully defended line connecting the German Second and Third Systems. Behind that lay a Brown line on the farther slopes, with a Blue Line on the German side of Flers village and a Red Line beyond Gueudecourt.

Within half an hour the 2nd Brigade had captured the Switch Trench and intermediate defences on the crest. Following them the 2nd Field Company passed through the enemy barrage with little casualty and commenced to construct a new line of trench with a Strong Point at either end. As a result of previous experience this line was placed some 70 yards in advance of the Switch, and the wisdom of this proceeding was fully appreciated when the German shells began to rain upon the trench they had just lost, the position of which was known of course to a yard. All day and night the bombardment of the Switch continued, and aided by this incentive to action, the new trench sank rapidly. By the time it was noticed and bombarded, it was practically complete, and though there was much redigging and numerous casualties occurred, these were far less severe than would inevitably have followed from any attempt at permanent occupation of the Switch itself. On three separate occasions during the day, Lance-Corporal H. J. Mascall passed through the heavy barrage with wounded men, returning to his work immediately. He remained on the job all night, then, since several senior N.C.O.'s had been wounded, he continued at work all next day in order to complete the post. For this and previous good work under fire he was awarded the French Military Medal.

Second Lieutenant C. W. Chilcott, who had previously served with distinction on Gallipoli, was conspicuous here for gallantry and coolness under fire, and ultimately received a

Field Companies and Field Troop.

well-earned Military Cross. Sapper D. R. Campbell, of the 2nd Field Company, also came under official notice for his display of coolness, energy and courage during these operations.

By 8 a.m. the Brown Line was in the hands of the 4th Rifles. General consolidation and the construction of Strong Points were immediately put in hand by the 1st Field Company. Aided by strong working parties from the battalions in reserve, they soon made an improvement in their allotted position. The machine-gun emplacements were at once utilised, and had a satisfactory opportunity of proving their worth during the German counter-attack in the afternoon. By next day all Strong Points and as many other positions as possible were wired, but this appeared to give away the position to the enemy. Thereafter they were subjected to intense bombardment at short intervals—fortunately with high-explosive shells, which sank deep in the soft earth and had a very local effect. Shrapnel would have been much more effective.

Though the Red Line was not finally won on the first day of assault, our position as far as this was established beyond doubt by the evening of the 16th, and the Engineers were transferred from defensive works to tackle the problems of water, shelter, and communications. These problems were rendered more acute by the pronounced break in the weather which occurred on the 17th September. Now, as happened so often again later on, the unfavourable elements caused serious delays in the British plans of attack, and gave so much more time to the harassed enemy to repair the breaches in his broken defences and to bring up fresh defenders. No experience of the fortunes of war on French battlefields was as exasperating as this. To spend weeks of toiling preparation, followed by the heavy losses inseparable from the preliminary assaults, and then to have all prospect of a final smashing blow washed away by circumstances over which there was no control, was an experience which called for all the fortitude inherent in the British soldier.

Notwithstanding the pouring rain with the consequent superfluity of surface water in every direction, there was little enough suitable for the use of the troops. The village of Flers was known to have contained many wells, but was being so vigorously bombarded by the enemy as to put occupation of the area quite out of the question. However, water was essential at once, and the 2nd Field Company was detailed to explore the resources of the village and to render avail-

The Battle of The Somme.

able whatever supplies of water might be found. The wells were not hard to discover, but practically every one had been more or less destroyed or filled up with filth and refuse. The work of restoring them was greatly hindered by the heavy shelling experienced, but within a short period sufficient numbers were in working order, complete with pumps or windlasses, to ensure a steady and expeditious supply.

A series of deep dugouts for the use of Headquarters of Brigades, Machine-Gunners, Signallers, and similar units, was commenced in Montauban, and completed by the end of our period of occupation. One large deep shell-proof dugout, which served as Advanced Brigade Headquarters till the close of our operations on the Somme, was constructed in Ferret trench between the Switch and Flers. Several Dressing Stations were urgently required at suitable positions in the captured area, and the construction of these was naturally given preference. The miserable weather conditions, combined with an absolute lack of shelter in the shell-torn countryside, caused a tremendous call for temporary accommodation, such as steel shelters for battery signallers, company headquarters, machine-gun posts, and so on. This call was satisfied as fast as the limits of time, material, and human endeavour would allow. Not that they represented the only pressing needs of the moment. Thousands of men were living the daily round in constant rain, and sleeping under the flimsy shelter of a waterproof sheet or a length of corrugated iron, and for these there was no relief possible. The opportunity for drying clothes afforded by the first fine day was so generally made use of that it is questionable whether as many men in a state of nature had ever been seen in those parts since the Stone Age.

For the whole of the front area occupied by the New Zealand Division, there was but one line of approach for wheeled traffic, up the Longueval-Flers Valley. By day it lay open to enemy observation, and by night it was never neglected by his artillerymen. The question of Engineering supply alone became extraordinarily acute. Construction of a new road from Thistle Dump up to High Wood by the 3rd Field Company gave some slight measure of relief, and a line of Decauville Railway from Longueval to Delville Wood was put down by the 2nd Company for the purpose of running up shells for the heavy artillery. Ordinary transport was quite unable to deal with these weighty masses of metal in the existing state of the roads. Delville Wood at that moment was fully justifying the sinister reputation associated with it throughout the Somme operations, and 2nd Company men

Field Companies and Field Troop.

engaged in putting up Regimental Aid Posts and other urgently needed shelters suffered numerous severe casualties.

Decauville Railway, so called from the name of its inventor, consisted of light steel rails laid on a gauge of 60 centimetres. The sleepers were flattish thin steel plates, about 6 inches across. Rails and sleepers were bolted together, and supplied ready for laying in lengths of 5 metres. A fairly level bed was easily prepared for such a narrow gauge article, and the line could be quickly taken up at any time and removed to another locality. For meeting the problem of immediate supply in the early days of an advance before more permanent arrangements could be made, this type of light line was wonderfully successful, and was in use by hundreds of miles.

With an improvement in the weather on 20th September came further opportunities for offensive action. Our initial successes had not been won without heavy losses, but the New Zealanders were far from done with, as the Boche was to learn to his cost before we finally left the Somme. At mid-day on the 25th, in beautiful weather, the attack was renewed. A strong position known as Factory Corner, about 1500 yards due north of Flers, was the first objective, and was carried without serious difficulty. During the next few days, a constant series of attacks was maintained on the strong German positions at The Circus, Gird Trench, and Gird Support, on the higher ground beyond Factory Corner. Determined opposition from the enemy and execrable weather conditions made the work of consolidation particularly strenuous. Gueudecourt had fallen into the hands of our right flank neighbours on the 26th.

During these operations the 3rd Field Company, which had been engaged on reconstruction of the Bazentin-le-Grand-Longueval Road, was detailed for the consolidation of newly-won ground, the construction of covering Strong Points, and to assist the Pioneers in the extension of the existing communications.

By the time a definite hold had been established on the forward positions, Turk Lane and Fish Alley had been pushed forward as far as the Abbey Road. At Factory Corner were found a splendid deep well containing 75 feet depth of good water and a large dump of German engineering material, both of which materially assisted the progress of the offensive in that particular locality.

Second Lieutenant A. O. Glasse showed high qualities of skill and endurance during this period, and his consistent

Major D. J. Gibbs, D.S.O.

The Battle of The Somme.

good work was finally recognised by an award of the Military Cross.

This class of work continued in bad weather, in a waste of mud and water, till the 3rd of October, when the sector was taken over by the 41st Division, and the sorely tried but undismayed New Zealanders trudged heavily back to concentration camps behind the lines preparatory to moving northward once more. Covered with the mire of a six weeks' sojourn in filthy trenches permeated by the sickening stench of putrefying bodies, with the ceaseless roar of the guns still ringing in their ears, and the sight of death in a dozen forms still hovering before their eyes, most of them were insensible to any particular sensation save one of relief that it was over for the time being. But all were uplifted and sustained by a sense of a good job well done, and faced the future with the serene fatalism which marks the seasoned soldier. It is later on, when the numbness of fatigue has worn off, and an increased mental activity accompanies renewed physical well-being, that the absence of familiar forms and faces sends regretful memories back to some corner of the stark field they will never leave again. But there is little room for emotion in the soldier's life; yesterday is gone for ever, to-day there is much to do, and to-morrow—who can tell?

The general health of the Field Companies, in common with the rest of the Division, had been considerably lowered by the trying conditions experienced, and in the last few days, sick parades had been largely attended. Dozens of men were casualties in various hospitals, and many more lay buried in the cemeteries of the battlefield. It may be noted here that no grave of any sapper or N.C.O. of the Field Companies, with the exception of those who fell in raids behind the enemies' lines, was ever left unmarked by a reliable record.

A day's rest, with the inexpressible luxury of a hot bath, combined with change of scene, soon put fresh heart into the jaded sappers, but they were weary men who marched away from the Somme to entrain at Albert. The section cyclists and transport did not entrain, but returned to the Abbeville area by road as they had come. Passing through Amiens, the train ran as far as Longpre, still far from the destined billeting area. Here in the dusk of a cold wet evening, the inscrutable ways of Providence and British Armies decreed that the men should march the remaining 10 or 12 miles, much of it alongside the railway line, to their respective villages. In heavy silence the tired sections took the road, but if the sad truth must be told, very few men reached their destination

Field Companies and Field Troop.

that night. A few hardy spirits, thereafter known ironically as the "Main Body," managed to complete the trek, but a great number fell out by the wayside, and sought such shelter as they could find. Morning showed them that theirs was no peculiar state. Men of almost every unit in the Division were to be seen on the road, some engaged in cooking a wayside meal, others emerging from the shelter of hedge or hayrick, while others again were holding high festival among the blackberries growing all along the road. By night all were safely within the fold once more. The transport sections came in on the same afternoon, with horses completely knocked up. For two days the horse lines were an unusual sight, with horses lying down in all directions.

The erstwhile cold-hearted inhabitants now suffered a complete reversal of form, and could not do enough to show their appreciation of the heroes in their midst; a commendable attitude of mind of which the heroes took full advantage. But the constant drain of the Somme battle on the strength of the British Armies was still going on, and no Division could be left long in idle seclusion.

On the 10th October C.R.E. Headquarters entrained at Pont Remy, and proceeded north to Merris near Bailleul. Next day the 1st Field Company entrained at the same place, and finally landed at Estaires. The 2nd and 3rd Companies entrained at Abbeville, and found temporary resting places at Bleu and Strazeele respectively, all Companies being now in reserve areas of the Sailly sector on the Lys.

CHAPTER VIII.

WINTER ON THE LYS.

By the 14th October the Division had taken over the sector it was to occupy during the winter. This new territory, lying to the immediate south of Armentieres, and extending from Bois Grenier as far down as Laventie, was officially known as the Sailly sector, though more associated in the mind of the average soldier with Fleurbaix, the name of the village immediately in rear of the front area. The 2nd Brigade returned temporarily to Armentieres, and came under the command of General Franks, who was then holding that sector with two brigades. The 3rd Field Company accompanied them to the old sector, and Major Gibbs received a temporary appointment as C.R.E. of "Franks' Force," as the garrison was then called. In the new area, Colonel Pridham's headquarters were located at Sailly Sur-la-Lys, a small village five miles up the river from and west of Armentieres. 1st Field Company was located at Sailly also, while the 2nd Company found itself quartered in two fine farms just outside the village of Fleurbaix, three miles south-west of Armentieres on the road to Neuve Chapelle.

From the Aubers Ridge, in front of Lille, the whole countryside in this locality falls gently towards the Lys, with innumerable small streams and drains running down along the hedgerows into that sluggish stream. In the area occupied by the front line trenches, the fall in these streams, now swollen with rain, had become practically imperceptible, and the whole length of the line was intersected by a succession of shallow waterways liable to become broad stretches of morass. However, the front line itself and the saps leading up to it, notably Tin Barn Avenue, all of the breastwork type familiar to Armentieres veterans, were in exceptionally good order, practically revetted and duckboarded throughout. The front line in this Sailly sector was unquestionably the most comfortable and best equipped of all the many occupied by the Division in France or Flanders. The parapet was sufficiently high and of surprising width, the whole line was duckboarded, and the communications rearward were sufficient. About 70 yards behind the front line ran an old disused support line, where fires were occasionally lit and various aspects of constant occupation simulated in order to draw German shelling where it was least inconvenient. Further

Field Companies and Field Troop.

back lay the real support line, a continuous fire trench, broken at suitable intervals by a series of fortified Posts, which held the garrison. A third or subsidiary line well in the rear of the first two was a continuous trench also, but in much poorer condition, with selected lengths only kept in a fortified state. A further series of somewhat larger Posts at greater distances apart was located along the subsidiary line. Several of them were well provided with accommodation, and the remains of scattered farmhouses sheltered many of the garrisons, but here, too, shelter was generally insufficient for the coming winter months.

During the previous summer much work had been done in clearing and lowering the Lys, and in opening up some of the larger streams, principally the Laies, but with the winter coming on, drainage was still of the utmost importance. The problem of dealing effectively and comprehensively with this constant menace of surplus water was met by the Field Companies by the appointment of skilled N.C.O.'s to the charge of definite sectors. By constant inspection and patrol obstacles were detected and the possibilities of the situation determined, and the provision of large working parties achieved the necessary result. Flooding did occur on a mild scale, but in no case were dugouts or sleeping quarters in the line affected. For a considerable distance in the front line, a broad open drain flowed along just behind the travel trench and was ultimately diverted down one of the communication saps, where it found a convenient stream bed beneath the duckboard track. Constant cleaning of the ditch below the duckboards was necessary in all communication saps if dry passage was to be expected. Working parties were issued with gumboots for this task, sometimes as many as 3000 pairs in a day, and were provided with dry socks at night, but despite large drying sheds erected by the sappers at the sap entrances, the problem of drying the gumboots was never satisfactorily solved, and the draining remained a wet and dirty job to the last. Free issues of Y.M.C.A. cocoa and biscuits were always available at the drying sheds, as one small gleam of sunshine in a cheerless existence, and gentlemen who had never seen a drain congregated there in great numbers at the appointed hour.

Of only less importance than drainage was the provision of adequate shelter for all front line garrisons. Many small concrete dugouts already in existence were found not to be waterproof. These were drained and properly finished off by the Engineers, and a few similar ones put in, but the usual type of accommodation erected took the form of steel or iron

Winter on the Lys.

shelters made with "baby elephant" or English pattern. The "baby elephant," capable of housing two men comfortably, or three at a pinch, was most in demand in the front line, where the unusually ample parapet made its construction a simple matter. Advantage was occasionally taken of the extra cover available to construct larger shelters than usual by raising the steel structures up on the pit-prop supports used for the walls of the primitive wooden shelters. The English pattern dugouts demanding 6 feet of headroom, exclusive of overhead cover, was unsuitable for the front line, but numbers of them were constructed in the "posts" and "localities" of the rear lines.

In the support line were several deep dugouts electrically ventilated and lighted, and each able to accommodate a company. At Cellar Farm and Wye Farm additional dugouts of this description were put in hand, and a special working party of 2 officers and 120 men was attached to the Engineers for the purpose.

The "deep" dugouts of the battlefront varied considerably in dimensions according to the needs of the situation. The main characteristic shared by all was a sufficient depth below ground to ensure protection from heavy shell fire without any extra provision in the way of overhead cover. Naturally these were never constructed in very forward positions. The entrance shafts, starting from small wooden chambers, level with the trench floor, and furnished with gas-proof doorways, were driven downward on an inclined plane provided with stairways, and with walls and roof sustained by strong timbers, to a depth of about 20 feet below the ground line. Here a small level landing or platform about 2ft. 6in. wide was provided, from which the entrance stair turned at right angles and sank another 3ft. or more to the level of the dugout floor. From the landing, in addition to the second stairway at right angles, a continuation of the first flight of steps was carried on a short distance dropping suddenly into a square pit about 3ft. deep. This was provided to accommodate German bombs, should a hostile raiding party be moved to use such means of attacking a trapped garrison. Two entrance shafts were always provided for each dugout, not only on account of trouble from the source just suggested, or from the blocking of one entrance by shell fire, but also to ensure fresh air. The dugout itself in the primitive form in which it was most frequently used was a restricted cavern, generally about 20ft. long, 7ft. wide and 6ft. high, with walls and roof strongly supported by heavy frames made of pit-props or stout beams. In areas at all subject to sudden attack

Field Companies and Field Troop.

a series of caverns of about this size was preferred to one or two large chambers, and was much easier to construct and maintain. In a series, of course, each entrance shaft served two dugouts, one on each side, and the frequency of the shafts was an added measure of protection for those below. Expansion of this general idea of underground shelter was limited only by the nature of the soil, or by the ideas and abilities of the constructors. In the chalk country of Picardy, for example, the Germans had underground systems almost akin to small villages, lighted, warmed, and ventilated by electricity, where whole battalions were able to shelter and carry on their numerous daily activities. In 1918, on our second visit to the Somme, we were to have intimate experience of this type of shelter.

For some weeks after arrival in this sector, the general policy of the Division, with numerous raw levies among the battalions was constructional rather than aggressive, an attitude which seemed to win the complete approval of our opponents of the moment. The system of working was the same as had previously been employed in Armentieres. The front line work was executed by the Brigade in garrison under sapper supervision; all other works were designed and carried out by the Field Companies with the aid of working parties drawn from the Brigades in reserve. At no period were engineering activities less subject to enemy interference. Large main dumps had been established in Sailly, Bac St. Maur, and Armentieres, and were constantly being replenished both by rail and by river barges. The transport lines were situated as close as possible to these main dumps, and material flowed up to the trenches in a constant stream. Forward dumps were soon well equipped, some within 500 yards of the front line, and the clatter of the waggons on the frozen roads could have been heard miles away in the calm misty atmosphere. From these forward dumps tramlines ran right up to the front line and even along behind the foremost breastwork. The sound of corrugated iron and rails being thrown about on a frosty evening must surely have aroused the German sentries, but they rarely showed any sign of real interest. There were times when the almost total lack of sound or movement immediately opposite lent some colour to the firm conviction of a large number of the "boys" that the sole occupants of the opposing front line were the flare-boys, unfortunate youths whose job was to wander up and down the line at night, firing an occasional rifle and shooting off the innumerable flares with which all German garrisons invariably enlivened every evening.

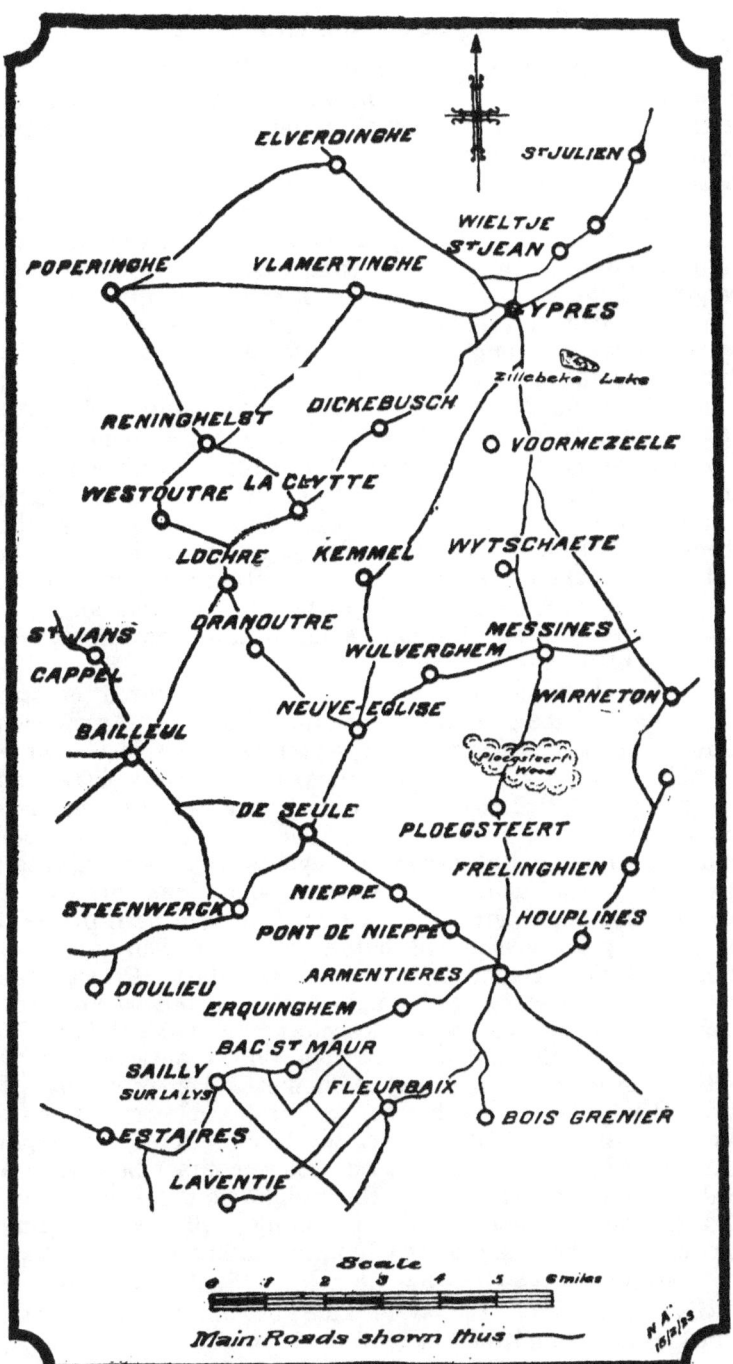

Field Companies and Field Troop.

The organisation of general supply had reached such a pitch at this time that special material urgently required on a certain day could be "ordered" as late as 5 p.m. on the preceding evening. Every evening a runner took lists of required material, made up by the Engineer subalterns in charge of the various works, and delivered them to the officer in charge of the horse lines who thereupon obtained the material from the main dump, and sent it up the same evening by the transport waggons belonging to the section in charge of the particular work. On delivery at the forward dumps it was received by a trucking party belonging to this same section, and taken up during the night to the site of next day's operations. Supplies of ordinary material always in use were maintained at the forward dumps and drawn from there as required.

The heavy rains experienced during November put the maximum strain on all types of trench revetment, in addition to the shelters and drainage systems. Sandbags not more than three months old broke away altogether, proving themselves but a temporary expedient. The "A" frames showed the best results, but owing to gradual weakening by time and occasional shell splinters, the long side uprights showed signs of needing anchorage outwards.

All trench and communication ways required constant attention and absorbed a vast amount of labour. At the same time other requirements of the sector were not lost sight of. Trench kitchens and sentries' and runners' posts were made proof against the advent of winter, several M.G. emplacements were built, tramlines and trucks were kept in repair, and all dressing stations and dugouts were systematically provided with doorways proof against gas attack. A wet blanket hung across an open doorway had been proved to be fairly good protection, but a gas-proof doorway was a more ambitious structure than that makeshift. Outside each entrance now treated was built a kind of small wooden antechamber, about large enough to hold a man comfortably. The side walls of the outside entrance sloped outwards at the bottom, in such manner that a blanket screen provided with a wooden roller at the bottom and fastened over the top of the doorway in rolled-up form would roll down the sloping wall immediately it was released. Close contact between wall and blanket was ensured by the weight of the bottom roller and the slight slope of the sustaining wall. At the inner entrance another blanket was hung as an extra precaution.

In Armentieres sector the 3rd Field Company was busily engaged on the same kind of work. One section renewed all demolition charges on the bridges across the Lys

Winter on the Lys.

at Armentieres and included in this operation those at Erquinghem and Fort Rompu. An endeavour to enlist the assistance of the elements against the foe met with much success. It has already been noted that the country was very flat and also that the Boche occupied an area slightly higher than our own. The numerous small streams running from his country down through ours to the Lys were now in full spate. On a wet and windy evening, with the assistance of 300 infantrymen and much timber and sandbagging, 12 dams were erected in selected streams with the object of forcing back the water and flooding the German trenches. From the appearance of the lakes which resulted from this undertaking, it must have given the German drainage experts some food for bitter thought. So bitter indeed, that the dams were made the objective of German raiders some days later, when they blew up one dam without materially improving their unfortunate condition.

Another small enterprise run by the 3rd Company in Armentieres deserves a line or two. This was a full-sized smoke concert held in their own particular brewery with real cakes and ham sandwiches and other local products of a cheering nature. During a temporary lull in the proceedings Colonel Pridham presented Corporal K. Watson with the D.C.M. he had won a year before as a sapper on the Peninsula.

Early in December the 3rd Company returned from Armentieres and went into billets in Sailly village, with its transport located at Bac St. Maur. It thereupon became the Company in reserve and was employed on baths, stables, and similar works in rear, in addition to taking charge of all work on the reserve system of trenches. In view of the rapid approach of winter, attention to back areas had been constantly given since the taking over of the Sailly sector. Baths, laundries, and drying rooms had been established and were constantly being extended and repaired. During the cold weather which followed in January, all water pipes at the Baths burst, and caused a mild crisis in the domestic affairs of the Division. Every effort was made to render all rear billets waterproof and sanitary, and duckboard tracks were put down to prevent the fouling of the floors by the inevitable mud and straw. A special work of great magnitude had been the provision of proper stabling accommodation for all the horses connected with Divisional transport. Overhead cover was not as difficult to provide as decent flooring. Ordinary ground in that soft country was trampled into a bog within two days. This trouble was overcome by a liberal use of concrete slabs, ashes, and broken bricks. Despite

Field Companies and Field Troop.

the prevalence of that particular article around the shelled areas, not a particle of brick was to be touched until proper arrangements for amount and payment were made with the French civic authorities. It has been stated that one or two bricks got past the barrier occasionally. In any case, before the real rigours of winter set in, all horses were comfortably installed in satisfactory quarters.

At irregular intervals of ten days or so the troops in line were relieved, and on such change-over days, owing to congestion in the front area, work in the trenches was seldom attempted. A visit to the Divisional Baths at Sailly consumed at least a portion of the sappers' leisure moments. This entertainment was probably followed by a football match, or perchance a visit to one of the larger villages in rear. Some revisited the scenes of former triumphs in Armentieres, generally with disappointing results. Either the house was bare and empty, or the accustomed corner by the fire was filled by some strange and assertive brother-in-arms, usually from Scotland.

It was not that attractions were entirely lacking in the immediate vicinity. Fleurbaix, for example, was a maze of small shops, with an especial penchant for coloured silk postcards; and cosy estaminets and egg-and-chip kitchens were filled to overflowing every evening. In addition, the ever solicitous Y.M.C.A. erected permanent institutions per medium of the ubiquitous sapper, and there provided nightly entertainment of a high order.

One attractive young demoiselle who was laying up a tremendous "dot" from a steady trade in eggs and chips had no doubts as to the class of client Fortune had favoured her with during that winter. "Ah! these New Zealanders," said she, "very good! but" with uplifted hands and eyebrows, "What pigs. Always say six eggs Mamselle! Last year we had Scottish, not much money, though very nice, too. But Mon Dieu!" she added with a sorrowful smile, "Beaucoup pinch! beaucoup pinch!" For the probity of Scotland it is to be hoped no one will understand what she meant.

Considering the water supplies of many of these small estaminets it is a wonder that more sickness was not caused. Plenty of the wayside farmhouses, where the thrifty inhabitants were always ready to supply coffee to the troops, had no water supply at all other than the deep roadside ditch, which in many parts of low-lying Flanders is filled with water all the year round. Opposite the door could be seen the watering place, in which an expanse of water about a yard wide clear of the prevailing green weed showed where the kettles and buc-

Winter on the Lys.

kets were constantly being dipped and withdrawn. One prominent resident in this area gave permission for the Engineers to pump out and fill up an offensive cesspit in his grounds, but complained bitterly later when the water level of his well, a chain or so away, was found to have sunk during the process. The native of the region is of course so impregnated with germs from birth that nothing can disturb his internal economy; officially, no troops were allowed to touch water which had not been tested and treated by the sanitary experts.

At this time also, between Sailly and Bac-St.-Maur, the Divisional Entertainers came into being and had their first performance in a large malthoid theatre erected by the Engineers. This building was used for cinema shows, instructive lectures, and once was the scene of festivities when Divisional Headquarters essayed to provide the children of the surrounding district with a Christmas tree. But the ability to command and direct the destinies of 20,000 soldiers was powerless when faced with a crowd of children excited to frenzy by the unaccustomed display of toys and sweets, and casualties were many and severe. By far the most popular form of amusement with the men of the New Zealand Division during these winter months was their national game of football. Even those who did not play found great pleasure and excitement in watching the struggles, and large crowds could be seen almost any afternoon gathered about some frozen field, crying hoarsely on their chosen fancies. War or no war, mud, snow, or frozen ground nothwithstanding, on went the good old game. The Field Companies were no exception to the general rule. The sections played each other, the drivers played the sappers, the Companies played one another and whenever occasion offered tried conclusions with outside units. When no matches were toward, all hands were always ready to punt a ball about, including officers of years and discretion. On one historic occasion, a prominent captain was well in the rush for a soaring ball, which finally landed in a pool of mud and slime sufficient to abate the speed of the accompanying lesser fry. But nothing could halt the gallant captain. In he went, shiny leggings and all, in a smother of mud and foam. The writer was privileged to overhear the bitter cry of his watching batman:—"Now, isn't that a fair —— I'll have to clean those —— boots in the morning!"

By the middle of November the pressure of urgent preparation for the coming winter had somewhat abated. Our opponents still carefully refrained from any serious aggressive tactics, but if by so doing they hoped to ensure for themselves a peaceful and friendly sector, they were doomed to dis-

Field Companies and Field Troop.

appointment. With rested troops at full numerical strength again available, Headquarters decided to resume hostile activities, thus maintaining the fighting spirit of the Division and giving the new men a chance of putting a finish on their warlike education. Medium and heavy trench mortars largely increased their previous efforts, and raids were taken up again with renewed enthusiasm.

On 16th November a raiding party from 1st Rifles accompanied by six sappers of the 3rd Field Company attacked Turks' Point. Everything in the German front line was found flooded, and no signs of a garrison were to be seen. Five days later six sappers from the 1st Company took part in a 1st Canterbury raid on the trenches opposite the Cordonnerie. A pair of rotting human legs projecting from a mound of earth was the only sign of the enemy encountered. A concrete wall 9ft. high, strongly protected by barbed wire, and thought to conceal a mine shaft, was blown up by some of the sappers, while the remainder demolished a large concrete dugout.

A more ambitious enterprise was attempted by the 4th Rifles on 17th December, when twelve sappers were selected to accompany a large party of 5 officers and 170 other ranks, who went across to attack Corner Fort. While the Infantry was engaged in its usual activities in the presence of the enemy, the sappers searched for suitable subjects for demolition. The only object of importance appeared to be a large pumping plant which was effectually destroyed, while a long section of tramway was given the benefit of the remaining explosive.

During December the first machine-gun "tubs" were installed, generally about the support line. These were more or less a new departure, and unfortunately no real opportunity was given of proving their efficiency or otherwise. The "tubs" were ordinary round wooden contrivances large enough to hold a machine-gunner and his gun, or two men at a pinch. A lid or cover of steel was provided coming well down over the sides all round. At one place on the circumference of the steel circle, a suitable aperture for the use of the gun was arranged. By a ratchet system worked from inside the lid could be made to revolve, giving a field of fire in any direction, while the occupants of the "tub" were protected from any attack save through the aperture in front of them.

Just before Christmas, 6 officers and 200 other ranks of the New Zealand Engineers paraded for a Divisional inspection by Sir Douglas Haig. Christmas Day was observed as a holiday as far as possible, and in each of the three Companies all officers and men available sat down together to a well-spread

Winter on the Lys.

board. General Godley, accompanied by General Russell and Colonel Pridham, visited the 2nd Company's temporary banquet hall, and spoke a few seasonable words. Needless to say, he hoped and believed that next Christmas would be spent far from the fogs and snows of Flanders, with which pious wishes his hearers were evidently in hearty accord.

Two days later, at the Headquarters of II Anzac Corps in Bailleul, in the presence of the staffs of the Corps and of the Divisions comprising it, General Godley, at the request of the King of Montenegro, invested Major G. V. Barclay, V.D., with the Montenegrin Order of Danilo recently conferred upon him.

On the 2nd of January, further satisfaction was given to all members of the New Zealand Engineers by the news that Colonel Pridham had been awarded the D.S.O.

Throughout the month of January the Field Companies took advantage of the comparative lull in general activity to detach a section at a time from front line works and to devote a week or so to training operations in rear. In addition to the regulation brush-up gone through on such occasions, one company at least devoted much time and energy to a skating slide on a convenient small pond. Demolition experiments conducted by another led to various shattered windows and broken roof tiles on the adjacent farm billets, and very nearly spoilt the entente cordiale prevailing between the farmer and his New Zealand guests. After Christmas, the ground had become too hard for any serious attempt at ordinary trench work. While the heavy frosts continued, the incessant labours of drainage were more or less unnecessary, and in any case work under such conditions gave results so meagre that working parties could not be induced to consider them worth striving for. No suggestion to reduce or "washout" working parties was ever acceptable to the authorities, and day after day large bodies of men wended their way to the trenches, there to amuse themselves as best they could till it was time to go home again. Sliding on the frozen drains was a favourite form of relaxation from the horrors of war—and work. And they were there in case of a German attack, which is about the best that can be said for the state of affairs then prevailing. In any case, owing to heavy demands elsewhere, a great shortage of material was now in evidence.

Though not conducive to great achievement with pick and shovel, and in spite of certain discomfort from the cold nights, this succession of clear bracing days raised the spirits of the troops and greatly improved the general health. All

Field Companies and Field Troop.

tanks and water pipes in the front areas were quickly affected by the severe cold, and it was early found necessary to protect them with covering of straw and sandbags. By mid-January, the prolonged frost made it certain that "Thaw restrictions" would follow its natural end, and supplies of R.E. material were accumulated in the forward dumps, to be reserved for use during the first days of the thaw. Thaw restrictions were a natural outcome of the enormous cost of maintenance of all roads in the battle zones. By these regulations, no wheeled transport, except ration carts and a few other special vehicles, were allowed to use the roads at all until the restrictions were removed by a general order from Headquarters.

On 26th January the Division extended its front to the left and took over the Right Brigade area of the 3rd Division. The 3rd Field Company was allotted to this new sub-sector and moved up to Gris Pot. A large draft of reinforcements had recently been absorbed by the Companies.

Considerable time and labour were spent in January and February in erecting successive swathes of barbed wire entanglements behind the support line as far back as Fleurbaix village. All were not erected on lines parallel with the front. Several lines embracing wide strips of country in the front area ran convergently towards the rear, with the hope of ultimately drawing possible attackers into a narrow neck where they could be profitably engaged by previously sited machine-guns. Many of these swathes were 10 yards wide, one dense mass of stout stakes and tangled wire, and it was a matter of considerable annoyance to the New Zealanders to read of the comparative ease with which the Germans were allowed to side-step these obstacles in their attack of March 1918.

The 2nd Rifles undertook the first raiding activity of the New Year on 7th January. Two officers and 80 men accompanied by four sappers of the 2nd Field Company made a successful attack on a strongly garrisoned point in the enemy's line known from its apparent shape as the Lozenge. A large portable bridge specially prepared for the event by the sappers assisted them across a considerable stream in No Man's Land, whence they rushed the enemy trenches.

Our final and biggest enterprise in the raiding line in the Fleurbaix area took place just before relief. 500 men of the 2nd Auckland Battalion were detailed to attack both front and support lines of the enemy's system over a length of front which gave the operation more the air of a minor assault than of a mere raid. Very careful preparation

Winter on the Lys.

was made, and the whole plan of attack was worked out in detail over an exact replica of the enemy's trenches. This was laid out in rear, from aeroplane photographs, by the 2nd Field Company, the lines of trenches being marked by shallow cuts in the frozen ground, filled with straw to avoid enemy observation. A mass of artillery supported the raid.

At 5.45 a.m. on the morning of 21st February in unusually heavy mist the attack was launched. Sixteen sappers, eight from 1st Field Company, and eight from 2nd, accompanied the raid, fully equipped with explosives. Lack of daylight was a severe handicap to the raiders. Many parties failed to distinguish their objectives, others went too far and were cut off. Many Germans were reported killed, and a considerable number were taken prisoner. Our own casualties were by no means light; of the sixteen sappers, only six were uninjured and few of them found any opportunity of dealing with their explosive owing to the number of their own troops about. At the time the attack was hailed as a great success, in retrospect it wears more the air of a costly experiment.

Corporal L. G. Pope, of the 2nd Field Company, was prominent on this occasion, showing great dash and enterprise in pushing forward into enemy country, where he succeeded in blowing up several dugouts before being finally disabled by two severe wounds.

The thaw was just commencing when the Division received orders to take over the Le Touquet-Ploegsteert sector, and this was finally completed by the 25th February, after relief by the 57th Division. C.R.E.'s new Headquarters were now at Steenwerck. The 1st Field Company marched out to Bleu and thence moved up to billets at Dou Dou Farm, and took over the left sub-sector from the 25th Divisional R.E.'s. The 2nd Company marched to Pont de Nieppe and took over the right sub-sector from another R.E. Company of the same Division. The 3rd Company found its destination at Le Don Camp, when it remained Company in reserve, employed on usual back area requirements.

In the eyes of men used to keeping their sector in reasonable order, the Le Touquet trenches now occupied were in a disgraceful condition. The fervour and poignancy of the remarks passed by the unfortunate individuals allotted to some of the alleged shelters will never be forgotten by any of those privileged to hear their views. By all appearances, nothing had been done to the earthworks since they were first thrown up by the original defenders, and the thaw did not improve matters. Duckboards lay at all and any angles up to the vertical, with little paths round them now feet deep

Field Companies and Field Troop.

in mud. Parapets, held up only by a kindly frost, and protected by a few strands of broken wire, were now crumbling to pieces, and in some places afforded no cover whatever. The German sniper was in a 'state of bold and enterprising activity quite unacceptable to the New Zealand Brigades now in line, who speedily put an end to his sporting proclivities. Communication saps were narrow and knee deep in mud. Long stretches of trench, even in the firing line, were completely under rising water, dugouts were either falling to pieces or being quietly filled with surplus slush from the trenches. All ranks accepted the challenge of the untoward conditions with energy and enterprise. The 2nd Field Company soon discovered that the lie of the country in its area and the proximity of the Warnave stream combined to render drainage a feasible proposition; working parties threw the mud about with apparent enthusiasm; dugouts were cleaned and drained, tracks laid, and parapets repaired; and when the sub-sector was handed over to the 3rd Australians on 13th March, it bore at least some aspects of a soldierly appearance. Much that might have been done could not be attempted owing to lack of necessary material.

The Division now moved northward once again, and took up the position it was to occupy with minor modifications until the Battle of Messines. The left flank of the Divisional area now lay just beyond the village of Wulverghem; the right was bounded by a line running from Ontario Avenue in the front line near St. Yves back through Suicide Corner, as the cross roads in the centre of Ploegsteert Village were known. The whole sector was divided into two Brigade fronts, north and south of the river Douve. The northern portion of Ploegsteert Wood still remained in our lines.

C.R.E.'s Headquarters remained at Steenwerck. The 1st Company, operating from the same billets as before, took over from the 121st R.E.'s a sub-sector extending from Ontario Avenue to the Douve; from the Douve to the left flank was in charge of the 2nd Company, now billeted in the partially destroyed village of Neuve Eglise. Its predecessors were the 122nd R.E.'s. The 3rd Company, still in Le Don Camp, took over works in back areas from the 150th R.E.'s. On 24th March owing to heavy shelling the 3rd Company vacated this camp and moved to fresh quarters in the Weka Lines near Romarin.

The country now occupied by the New Zealanders was in complete and welcome contrast with the low-lying flats of the Lys. In front, on the southern tip of the broad low ridge bearing the same name, the shattered houses of the village of Messines lay clustered about the more massive ruins of the

A SHRINE AND RUINED CHURCH AT NOUVELLE HOUPLINES.
Photos by Major N. Annabell

REMAINS OF THE YPRES CATHEDRAL. A PORTION OF THE CLOTH HALL IS SHOWN IN THE BACKGROUND.

FORMING A PLANK ROAD NEAR YPRES. *Official Photo*

Winter on the Lys.

medieval church and the Institution Royal, a large R.C. Orphanage for girls. The extensive cellars known to exist in this stout old building were expected to provide serious opposition later on. The ridge ran in a northerly direction past Wytschaete, Zonnebeke and Hooge right through Passchendaele, where we were to meet it later under less fortunate auspices, and away to the far north at Dixmude. Though only some 210 feet in height, this long ridge had furnished unrivalled observation for the Boche since 1914. At Wytschaete a low saddle connected it with Mont Kemmel, quite the most dominant feature in the plain of Flanders. South of Messines the German lines fell away abruptly into the valley of the Douve. Rising in the hills behind Kemmel and flowing between the southern slopes of that mount and a chain of lower hills, of which Neuve Eglise and Hill 63 are the most eastern points, the Douve meandered down a wide valley, and after entering the German Lines at La Petite Douve Farme, finally emptied its sluggish waters into the Lys near Warneton.

Our right sub-sector was largely covered by the forest of Ploegsteert, affording splendid cover and easily traversed by infantry. The small hill of St. Yves at the north-eastern corner of the forest was the salient feature of this portion of our line. In the central area, a mile or so behind our front line, rose the beautiful rounded hill of Rossignol, called Hill 63 from its height in metres, whence the southern slopes of Messines Ridge and enemy territory right down the valley of the Douve lay open to splendid observation. Behind lay miles of rolling wooded country and, half hidden in the haze to the north-west, the line of wind-mill crowned heights stretching from Kemmel to the distant spires of Mont des Cats made irresistible appeal to men far from the hills of home. Almost due north of Hill 63 and east across the Douve from Wulverghem, lay another important rise, screening Wulverghem from observation, and crowned by heavily fortified positions, known as Midland Farm.

Several good road lines led in from the rear areas. Hyde Park corner, at the southern end of Hill 63, on the old main road from Ploegsteert to Messines, was also accessible by an alternative route leading in from Romarin past Red Lodge and along the foot of the rearward slopes of the hill. Here were situated several log houses and Catacombs, deep tunnelled shelters capable of accommodating a brigade. Forward of Hyde Park Corner the road to Messines mounted the hill, and, coming under direct observation, ceased to have any attraction for either transport or pedestrians. Just before reaching Red Lodge, the road from Romarin turned to the

Field Companies and Field Troop.

left, and running up past one of the wayside Shrines with which rural Belgium is so plenteously endowed, crossed the hill crest near the "White Gates." There it joined a country road running westward from the former hamlet of Le Rossignol on the forward slopes of Hill 63 to join up with the Neuve Eglise-Wulverghem road about half way between those two villages. The left sector deepened on the Neuve Eglise-Messines road running through Wulverghem. Just eastward of the road intersection at "White Gates," now the sole remaining relics of a former magnificent chateau, a tree-lined roadway ran down the hill to Ration Farm, just in rear of the extensive remains of La Plus Douve Farm on the Douve Stream. Here Battalion Headquarters and Advanced Dressing Stations were established in fine concrete shelters built inside the old farm walls. Alongside the road down the hill ran a deep communication trench, sharing indiscriminately with the roadway the euphonious title of Plum Duff Avenue.

Scattered here and there in quiet corners of the wayside fields and up and down the winding Douve, isolated graves of French artillerymen, Scottish clansmen, and yeomanry of the English shires furnished grim evidence of earlier struggles for the shell-scarred ridge and mute appeal for further effort.

The whole countryside, covered with woods and hedgerows, and dotted with the now battered and deserted farmhouses of the unfortunate Belgian peasants, was soon to burst forth into the delicate glory of early spring with a sudden magnificence strange to Antipodan eyes.

CHAPTER IX.

THE BATTLE OF MESSINES

Ever since the early months of the war, when the German thrusts on the Channel Ports had been barely stemmed by the blood and heroism of the British Regular Army, the menace of a third and possibly successful attack was an ever-present spectre shadowing all deliberations of those responsible for Allied, and particularly British, war policy. The urgency of removing this danger at the first possible moment was keenly realised. But the perils of failure were fraught with possibilities not less serious, and during the initial stages of our war preparations the matter remained in abeyance. With the growth of our Armies in men and experience, however, the unattainable hopes of earlier days passed into the realms of possibility, and in November 1916 an Allied Conference decided upon a British offensive in Flanders during 1917.

In accordance with sound military policy a preliminary attack on the salient south of Arras would endeavour to engage the enemy's attention, and distract him from consideration of our preparations further north until it was too late to interfere with them. Success in the north meant the security of the Channel Ports and the safety of our main lines of communication, with a tremendous corresponding increase in our freedom of action. Additional important aspects of the main operation were the extinction of enemy submarine bases at Zeebrugge and Ostend, and the disorganisation of the whole right flank of the enemy position. The latter, in particular, presented attractive possibilities of further achievement. All these fair hopes were to fade unrealised. The tremendous increase in enemy man-power on the Western Front, due to the Russian revolution, aided by delays due to a change in the Allied plans put an entirely different complexion on the attack when it finally materialised.

Early in 1917, the French Commander-in-Chief, General Nivelle, brought forward fresh plans embodying a grand French offensive on the Aisne. This scheme now took pride of place amongst the offensive proposals of the Allies, and a consequent shortage of labour and material in the north somewhat compromised our later efforts in that area. Had success attended Nivelle, a vigorous exploitation of his opening would have followed, to the probable abandonment of the Flanders enterprise altogether.

Field Companies and Field Troop.

In April, after a British feint at Arras, the French sent four armies against the southern end of the Hindenburg Line, opposite Laon. Wave after wave, the blue lines were shattered and dispersed by the machine-guns of the strongly entrenched enemy; the offensive was a failure; and Nivelle was succeeded by Petain.

The stage was now cleared for the British performance in the northern theatre, the fateful Third Battle of Ypres. Prior to this conflict, and essential to its success, was the capture of the redoubtable ridge which marked the line of the invading armies from the Ypres salient down past Wytschaete and Messines to the valley of the Douve. Its possession assured to the enemy not only incomparable observation of all our movements in the salient about Ypres, but also exceptional opportunities for neutralising, by means of a flank attack, any advantages we might gain in projected operations in that sector.

Of all engagements fought by the British Armies in France, this Battle of Messines stands pre-eminent alike for the careful, detailed and methodical preparations undertaken to reach a pre-defined goal, and for the speed and certainty of the success which crowned those efforts. A source of tremendous satisfaction to the New Zealanders was the fact that, with full realisation of the importance of the coming struggle, they were allotted the task of preparing for their own attack with ample time to make suitable arrangements. The enemy likewise could not possibly have remained ignorant of our intentions; with his opportunities for observation, the ever-increasing scale of our activities left no room for doubt. Presumably he took steps to improve his defences, though his unusually strong position may have lulled him into a false sense of security. In either case, it was a soldiers' challenge of the most direct description, to be driven home later with a vim and celerity unfortunately rare. The varied aspects of the vast enterprise now in hand allowed full scope to the abilities of the Engineer companies.

The first concern of the C.R.E. in forecasting the very large share in the Divisional preparations that would inevitably fall to his lot, was the provision of material. Unfortunately this was still in very short supply, and it was not until May, when other Allied enterprises further south had subsided, that our requirements in that line received anything like full satisfaction. Failing adequate supplies through the usual Army channels, recourse was made to local manufacture in Divisional workshops. In pursuance of this policy, works situated at De Seule, where the road to Neuve Eglise left the

The Battle of Messines.

main Bailleul-Armentieres highway, were gradually put into full running order with extra engines, breaking-down saws, benches, and all other appliances of a well-equipped mill and factory. A force of 115 men and 25 women civilians was employed by the C.R.E. to cope with the increased output. In addition, 12 sappers and 25 Pioneers were detailed for work in the shops in various mechanical capacities. In the first month more than £30,000 worth of material went out from these workshops at De Seule, and right up to the day of attack they furnished the great bulk of all Divisional supplies in the way of R.E. material capable of local manufacture.

In the initial stages of our preparations, Engineer attention was largely given to the screening and improvement of the means of access, both road and tramway. On the left the main road of approach from Neuve Eglise to Wulverghem was open to Boche observers in Messines for its whole length, and all troops proceeded in single file down on one side of the road close against a continuous band of hessian stretched from tree to tree. In addition, where the road descended from the village of Neuve Eglise, transverse streamers spanned the way, and fluttered in the breeze like a series of triumphal arches. The approaches to the right and centre portions of the Divisional area, via Red Lodge and Hyde Park corner, were effectively screened from all but aeroplane observation by Hill 63. All roads of course were subject to periodic shell fire, and the consequent damage, augmented by the unusually heavy traffic, kept large parties constantly employed on repair and reconstruction. To form a circuit and join up existing roads, a new corduroy road of heavy planking was constructed from Wulverghem down the valley of the Douve to Ration Farm, with considerable relief to the congested traffic.

At every important cross roads, deviation ways were cut across the corners, both to assist traffic and to avoid probable enemy shell fire on these attractive targets. As time wore on, all Infantry and horsemen were forbidden the use of the main roads altogether. Overland routes, marked on either side with stakes, painted white at the top and provided with direction boards where necessary, were laid out across the fields between all localities frequently in use. Quicker movement and fewer casualties were the result, both to the troops on the tracks and to the transport on the roads.

The main New Zealand Divisional dump for the Messines operations was situated at De Seule along with the mill and factory. This was supplied by a broad gauge railway line direct from base areas via Steenwerck and Bailleul. The latter place was quite the most promising of the towns within

Field Companies and Field Troop.

reasonable reach behind the Messines sector, and boasted clubs and canteens in addition to numerous shops and restaurants. This country is reported to have been once the seat of John Balliol, a Scot who took service with the French King in days gone by, and ultimately became a Constable of France. This early start in the country may explain the ease with which the kilts could still make hacks of all other competitors for local favours anywhere in France during the war.

The heavy line from Steenwerck ran on up the hill to Neuve Eglise village, whence a light tramline ran down the old Kemmel road as far as the crossing of the Douve, where a subsidiary dump was located at De Kennebak cabaret. From De Kennebak the tramway ran on down the leafy valley of the Douve, past the remains of Wulverghem village, where another subsidiary dump was located at Souvenir Farm, and on to Ration Farm, which was the main forward dump for all the preliminary operations just in front of Messines Village. A second tramline from De Seule coming up past Romarin led to the large Canpac (Canadian-Pacific) dump near Hyde Park Corner, and a branch line from this feeder ran northward to a small dump established at the Shrine behind Red Lodge already mentioned. From here material was nightly carted across the hill and down Plum Duff Avenue to Ration Farm. Ration Farm about 9 p.m., on any of the fine warm evenings preceding the battle, presented a scene of most intense activity. By road and tramway, troops, horses, and material commenced to flow out and in as soon as ever the kindly shades of evening fell down between us and the German observers on Messines. Ration carts, water carts, mail carriers, trucking parties; all made the place a common rendezvous, and hundreds of men en route for the night's work in the forward trenches passed through the Dump in search of tools and to carry up material. In general, hostile shelling was astonishingly slight. But on a morning in April, a heap of trench mortar bombs which should have been moved forward the night before, was struck by a lucky 5.9 shell. The resulting explosion tore a tremendous hole in the road, and wrecked all shelters at the Dump, causing heavy casualties among the sappers and working party employed there at the moment.

From all these advanced dumps, trench tramways ran forward into the front line areas, but large trucking parties working every night for weeks before the battle could not fully cope with the tremendous daily demand for material. Large carrying parties, both by day and by night, were freely used to augment the supplies. All tramways, though under

The Battle of Messines.

control by the C.R.E., were run and maintained by the Pioneers.

The existing communications, particularly in the Wulverghem sub-sector on the left, were fortunately in a very fair state of repair. The communication trenches known as Calgary Avenue and Medicine Hat Trail were especially enduring monuments to the skill of their evident constructors. Both these avenues started in the vicinity of Ration Farm Dump, and feeding as they did the front line area immediately beneath the village of Messines, their condition was a very vital factor in the success of the preliminary preparations now undertaken.

Accommodation for Brigade and other Headquarters during the coming attack was put in hand early. The original intention was that the 3rd Canadian Tunnelling Company should construct deep dugouts in each sector, but owing to unsuitable ground, tunnelling was not attempted in the right sector.

By the end of March three entrance shafts to lead into a dugout 25 feet below ground were being sunk in the left sector. The three shafts were to be connected underground by 6ft. by 3ft. passages, off which eleven chambers 12ft. by 8ft. were to be constructed. Two Brigade and one Battalion Headquarters were to be accommodated in these chambers. This dugout was situated in Calgary Avenue about 120 yards behind our front line. The spoil from the underground workings was brought to the surface in sandbags, which was officially earmarked for raising the side walls of Calgary Avenue. Great numbers of these bags failed to reach the side walls, and their greasy clayey contents did not endear the tunnellers to passing wayfarers. In the right sector, in lieu of tunnels, three concrete shelters were constructed by the 1st Field Company, one each for Brigade, Signals and Wireless Headquarters.

For the safe housing of other Battalion, Signals and Wireless Headquarters during the attack, thirteen concrete dugouts were constructed, six in the actual front line and the remainder according to the proposed disposition of the battalions at zero hour.

The dugouts in the front line were rather a problem. When completed with shell-proof cover such dugouts were about 12 feet high. To excavate more than a foot or two was not impossible, but highly inconvenient, owing to the waterlogged subsoil. However, by the accumulation of years, the parapet in places had been built up at least 10 feet high, and a little judicious nocturnal raising of the crest in the selected

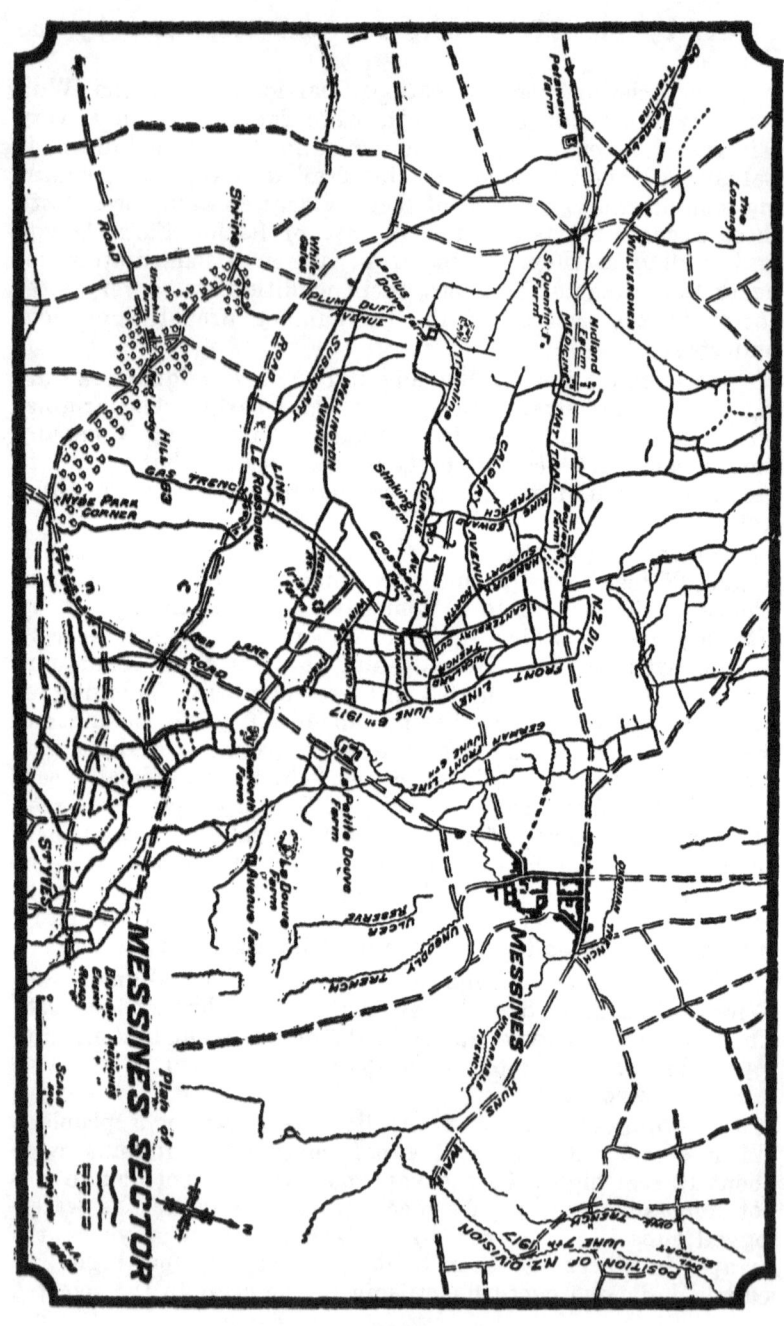

The Battle of Messines.

positions passed unnoticed by the enemy. Three special parties of eight men working continuous eight-hour shifts, under two experienced Engineer corporals, were put on to each dugout. Excavation to within a few inches of water level was soon completed. On this soft and uncertain floor were laid sheets of iron, crossed angle irons, sandbags of gravel and cement, paving stones from the adjacent Wulverghem-Messines Road, anything strong and solid, and the whole was enveloped and filled in with six to nine inches of concrete. Reinforcing rods, such as were used extensively by the Germans, were unavailable for our work, and we had to fall back upon angle irons and long screw pickets, which were set cross-wise and also vertically in the floor during construction, and served as reinforcement for the walls when erected.. On this now stable foundation was generally placed one of the large types of curved iron shelters, though lacking these, the dugout was often completed of concrete alone. Above and on either side of the iron roof and walls was placed concrete, frequently interlaid with bent angle irons or screw pickets, to a thickness of at least 12 inches. The side walls of concrete were run up straight, the one furthest from the enemy to a height of five feet or so forming a ledge on which were erected a number of short stout pit-props to act as columns supporting a strong longitudinal beam. The other side wall was built up solid to such a height that steel rails set transversely, resting on this wall and the aforesaid beam, cleared the arch comfortably. The steel rails were laid at intervals of about two feet, and on them again was deposited a complete flooring of "bursters," concrete slabs 12in. by 24in. by 3in., and the whole finished off with further layers of sandbags and dirt as high as the safe limit of cover. Any space left between the finished outside walls and the parapet was filled solid with rammed sandbags. During construction the whole was protected by a canopy of hessian or some similar camouflage. This type of shelter was considered safe against any but the heaviest shells. Each of those constructed for the Messines offensive sustained several 5.9 shells with only temporary damage.

In addition to the new structures built for the attack, great numbers of old dugouts were strengthened and renovated. Some of these earlier erections had evidently been a source of great pride and joy to their original constructors, who had often left complete evidence of their identity on properly painted signboards. One decrepit ruin had a long record of vicissitude preserved on a large board let in above the

Field Companies and Field Troop.

entrance:—
    Constructed by the 1st .... February, 1915.
    Improved by the 2nd .... June, 1916.
    Further improved by the 5th .... January, 1917.

Heartily condemned by the New Zealanders, May, 1917, was the last entry on the slate—a pleasant break in the monotony of the previous efforts, and a more accurate comment on its condition.

The amount of sand and gravel required for all these structures was enormous, and had to be carried up in sandbags from Ration Farm Dump, necessitating the employment of large special parties daily. The average soldier, doubtless with a strong suspicion that dugouts were not for him, had a great aversion from this gravel carrying, and a tremendous amount was unavoidably spilt on the journey. An attempt to solve the problem by instituting a task of three bags per man for the day's work was a great success, until the sight of long lines of coatless men tearing energetically up the sap laden with gravel was so unfamiliar to the suspicious gaze of one sophisticated Brigadier, that he made enquiries and promptly forbade the employment of such devices. Thereafter the parties worked twice as long and brought half as much gravel.

Existing communications, though good as has been noted, were insufficient for the final purpose in view, particularly as all ground within a mile of the front line lay under direct observation from Messines. More saps were necessary in order to expedite and distribute the inevitable excessive movement of troops, working and carrying parties. When this work was finally completed we had five main communications, and also four short avenues between front and support lines. Practically every battalion in the Division had its turn on the new saps laid out by the Field Companies, and such names as Waikato and Taranaki took their places in a crowded nomenclature significant of the scattered units of the British Empire. To avoid congestion certain saps were for OUT traffic only and others reserved for IN traffic only. During bombardment all these approaches were patrolled and any blockage immediately removed. Directly beneath Messines, any new work in progress had to be protected by camouflage of whatever description was available.

Extra attention was also brought to bear on the question of the relief and speedy evacuation of all who might be wounded in the coming operations. Special parties of sappers were employed for weeks in removing all corners in the com-

The Battle of Messines.

munication saps which could hinder the free passage of stretcher cases. Advanced sites for Regimental Aid Posts were carefully selected in each sector, and no stone was left unturned to ensure the safety and comfort of those requiring them. Situated just in rear of the support line, and adjacent to OUT saps, these Posts were constructed of English pattern iron shelters, set in a bank or well protected by earth walls on either side. Steel rails and concrete bursters were laid overhead, "in" and "out" connections were provided with the main outward communication trench, and as a final precaution, the stations were provided with gas-proof doors. Several direct hits failed to put these shelters out of action, and the medical personnel were able to work freely through the offensive operations ensuing. Once clear of the rearward ends of the main OUT trenches, specially marked routes directed stretcher bearers back to the Advanced Dressing Stations on main roads, whence motor ambulances evacuated stretcher cases, and special overland routes guided walking wounded back to the Casualty Clearing Stations. The main dressing stations in rear, such as were situated at Red Lodge and Kandahar Farm, were prepared for all emergencies with a detailed thoroughness previously unknown. By the day of attack, these were impervious to any ordinary shelling. Located as most of them were in the rooms and cellars of old brick farmhouses on the side away from the enemy, they were already safe from anything but a direct hit. The roofs were now given extra support by stout pit-props at regular intervals, then overlaid with rows of steel rails, upon which was spread a complete covering of "bursters" and the whole piled up with sandbags full of broken brick. The walls on the enemy side were also protected by sandbags full of brick built up as high as the roof in a wide solid mass. No bunks were used, but extra stretcher rests were fitted up in such a manner that stretcher cases could be treated and put straight into the ambulance without removal from the original stretcher. Tables, benches, water supply and gas-proof doors were all attended to, and in many cases extra motor roads were made to provide a continuous circuit for the ambulances.. This road work also made heavy calls on the broken brick, of which fortunately the Boche maintained a continuous supply amongst the farms of the neighbourhood. Nor was the question of cover confined to the needs of the wounded, and the staffs of the various Headquarters. At convenient intervals along the communication saps and in other suitable spots, shelters were provided for use as relay-posts, both by runners and stretcher-bearers. These were not very grand, but they serve as an illustration of the completeness of the preparations made.

Field Companies and Field Troop.

On the 6th of April, the 3rd Australian Division extended northward and took over our right sub-sector as far as Winter Trench. At the same time the 25th Division on our left took over an area extending to the Wulverghem-Messines Road. The contracted front now held by the New Zealand Division corresponded roughly with the area defined as the Divisional assembly position for the coming assault. The 1st and 2nd Field Companies retained their respective positions on the right and left of the new sector, the line between their operation-areas being marked by Currie Avenue.

No mention has so far been made of any work undertaken on the actual trenches of the area, as distinct from communications. On the most peaceful and well-built sector in France, the ordinary routine of trench improvement and repair was more than sufficient to keep every available man employed. Here, with definite engagements daily looming nearer fraught with unknown possibilities of weal or woe, in the face of a foeman looking down from a vastly superior position on every movement made, the whole question of trench construction assumed a special significance. One particular aspect of the preparation for offensive can never be lost sight of by the prudent commander. It is always open to enterprising troops, especially when strongly posted, seeing an opponent engrossed in the multitudinous affairs of his own contemplated attack, to seize that very moment for a sudden counter-stroke. Such sallies, over and above the prospect of upsetting the attackers' plans, may possibly reveal unexpected joints in his armour resulting in his serious discomfiture.

In view of such contingencies, one of the earliest trench works undertaken at Messines was the construction of a new reserve line running from Plum Duff Avenue on the upper slopes of Hill 63 across to the Petawawa Farm on the Wulverghem-Messines Road. This was surveyed and taped by the 2nd Field Company during 22nd March, while at the same time sufficient tools were collected on a country road behind "White Gates" just out of sight of Messines. In the evening 10 companies of Infantry parading at the same spot were supplied with tools, and led on to various sectors of the new line already marked out in company tasks. By midnight the job was completed satisfactorily. On later evenings this line was continued right across to the Divisional left flank, and was finally connected by a Switch line to a strong new defensive position created round the small hill by the remains of Wulverghem Church. This again was joined up to a strong fortified post further to the left known as the Lozenge.

The Battle of Messines.

In the more advanced areas the work of construction and renewal went on without cessation day and night. The problem of assembling a large body of troops on the restricted battle front allotted to the Division was early in the minds of the responsible authorities. Obviously additional assembly trenches were required, and just as certainly it was folly to leave their construction till the last minute. Better to have them ready and allow the Boche to expend his destructive energies upon them, if so minded, while they were yet empty of men.

The possibilities of the unusually wide No Man's Land on our left front appealed to the imagination of the Divisional Commander with great force, particularly since our existing front line in that sector lay at an awkward angle with the direct line of assault on the hillside village. Between us and the German line some 200-300 yards up the slope to Messines ran the valley of a small sluggish stream known as the Steenebeek. And here in this valley, under the very noses of the German garrison, our new assembly trench was now to be dug. This task, under the circumstances one of extreme delicacy, calling for unusual skill in organisation and a perfect discipline in all ranks, was carried through without a hitch. Just after dusk on the evening of the 13th, Lieutenant Keilar of the 2nd Field Company and four sappers slipped over the parapet and proceeded to stake out and tape the line of the new work. With them were two officers of the 2nd Brigade whose knowledge of the ground gained on constant patrol was of great assistance. By 9 p.m. their task was completed, and 500 men of 2nd Otago were filing out on to the job, shovel in hand. Working with great energy and under splendid control, they had finished the new line and left for camp again by 3 a.m. without casualty. On the following evening this new line was connected with the old front line and drained into the Steenebeek, and subsequent operations saw it finally completed with travel and support trenches in rear. By the actual day of assault, the front area was supplied with successive lines of assembly trenches sufficient for all requirements.

On the 15th April, the sappers of the 1st and 2nd Field Companies and half of the 3rd Company moved into huts among the trees at Red Lodge corner. These billets were much nearer to the scene of the works now in hand, and were pleasantly situated on the outskirts of the Wood, which had not yet lost all the attractions formerly surrounding the hunting box of the Belgian King. About the end of the month, consequent upon a temporary withdrawal of the 25th Division, the 2nd Field Company was ordered to relieve the 106th Company R.E., and took up new quarters between Neuve Eglise

Field Companies and Field Troop.

and Dranoutre, working on the immediate left of their previous sub-sector at Wulverghem. The duties here set them were mainly the provision of shell-proof dugouts for the Headquarters personnel of the batteries detailed for that sector of the coming offensive. These shelters were located in various localities from the open fields to the cellars of occupied farmhouses. It was here that one conscientious officer, on proposing to erect structures in a certain barn, was invited by the daughter of the manor to delay his operations "but five days" for the sake of a speckled hen who had selected the same barn as a suitable place in which to hatch a brood. Monsieur waited, nor did the speckled hen fail in her appointed mission, but all to no purpose. A German battery wiped out the whole farm three days before the grand attack. Such are the uncertainties of war!

On 10th May the 2nd Company returned to Red Lodge and resumed its former activities on the left of the Divisional sector. During its absence, its sector of the Divisional front area had been run by the 1st Field Company.

An adequate supply of water both during and after the offensive was a further objective of Engineering activities. Existing sources of supply were four in number. Two pipe lines came from back areas, where they were fed by existing lakes, catchments on Kemmel and neighbouring hills, and even from sterilising barges on the Lys. Another line led from a deep bore on Hill 63, and shallow wells throughout the area contributed the fourth quota. The three pipe lines were continued forward to the farthest limit of safety, and just in rear of the actual trench area four extra water points holding 4000 gallons each were constructed. Each of these consisted of large square tanks brought up in sections, and put together on a stout stand high enough from the ground to enable a passing file of men to use the tap in turn without delay. The main water pipe was tapped, and a line of pipe run underground as far as the tank stand, where a vertical supply pipe fitted with controlling mechanism led the water finally into the tank. No direct hit was required to damage this type of structure, any shell splinter or shrapnel bullet was sufficient to destroy its utility. To ensure safety as far as possible, the sites were carefully selected, and the finished article was heavily fortified with sandbagged walls and top, which were then camouflaged to nullify or minimise the shadow always thrown by such an erection on an aeroplane photograph. Local reserves of water, in large barrels or in petrol tins, were formed in the trench area, some as far forward as the support line. One trench tramway truck, fitted with 20-gallon tanks, was allotted

The Battle of Messines.

to each Brigade for general water supply purposes. Large numbers of wooden troughs were also provided in all transport concentration areas.

One regimental officer, on inspecting the proposed assembly position of his battalion, some days before the attack, decided that he was about to be overlooked as regards water, and sent down a special party to the nearest Field Company Headquarters with a special request that he should be allowed four barrels, and that they should be delivered to his own messengers forthwith. The barrels destined for his particular area had not at the moment come to hand, but his men were ultimately supplied with four barrels. A barrel is not a convenient article to carry far, especially in crowded saps, and his enterprising party finally solved its problem by knocking out the ends of the offending articles, and carrying them up slung on poles. The commotion caused by their arrival is beyond the scope of this story.

Side by side with this amazing welter of preparation in the trench areas went a steady increase in all classes of British artillery. Night after night long lines of weary gun teams rumbled through the rear villages, day after day another obscure hedgerow of leafy copse was found bristling with the sinister black muzzles. Not all were able to find suitable natural cover. The open fields behind Hill 63 were dotted everywhere with the parti-coloured erections of netting, scrim or hessian which concealed additional batteries from enemy aeroplanes, while ammunition dumps of varying size were all over the countryside, and were frequently struck by enemy shells, despite all attempts at camouflage.

The process of camouflage is another of the numerous devices called into existence by the Great War, at first in a crude form, but later developed into a highly complicated organisation strictly based on the scientific properties of light and shade. The primary object of it is not concealment from view in the ordinary sense, but concealment of the fact that something is being hidden; in other words, deception.

The principal risk of detection run by any gun or other position of importance was from the air, but the chief opponent to be overcome was not the enemy aviator; the expert who interpreted the meaning of his photographic records was far more dangerous. Every variation of colour, texture, or shape in a natural landscape is recorded on a photograph in terms of light and shade as a pattern of black and white intermingling in varying intensities of grey. These patterns run from the simple monotones of regular unbroken fields. to the highly complex variations produced by ruined villages,

Field Companies and Field Troop.

shelled areas, or devastated woods, and variations in colour are much less marked than variations of texture. Long standing grass shows dark on account of the shadow thrown by each erect blade; the same grass pressed down throws less shadow and consequently appears lighter. This explains the ease with which slight tracks can be detected on a photograph, which are almost invisible on the ground. Earth contains little texture, especially if long exposed, and never shows even dark on a photograph. The basis of successful camouflage therefore is to regard any position from the point of view of the pattern it will present on a photograph, and then to select cover that will reproduce a similar pattern, or one that will combine inconspicuously with the original.

The more usual clues by which positions were betrayed to the enemy were disturbed soil, tracks, shadows, blast marks of guns, and regularity of constructional design.

Disturbed soil, especially among vegetation, would obviously show a distinct photographic tone. Tracks in the open were impossible to conceal, since any covering substance opaque enough to hide them would itself throw a dense and conspicuous shadow. The only remedy lay in keeping all tracks along hedges or beneath trees where natural cover was easily augmented, or by disguising the real destination of "open" tracks by the provision of additional conspicuous "dummy" tracks. Shadows were a prolific source of betrayal. A mound-shaped camouflage on a flat surface, for example, might be perfect concealment at midday, but if of any opacity would be certain to throw a tell-tale shadow as evening drew on. However the fact that shadows must always throw in the same direction was some help in devising means to overcome their dangerous tendencies. Advantage might be taken of some definite existing shadow, or cover could be erected that would throw a shadow so irregular and fantastic as not to be thought the result of human agency, or else an attempt could be made to eliminate shadow altogether. This was best attained by using a flat cover with no sides, the centre of sufficient capacity to conceal material or spoil, while towards the edges the opacity diminished sufficiently to blur the shadow cast by the opaque centre without being of sufficient intensity to cast a definite shadow itself. Further, the increasing transparency towards the edges allowed the camouflage to blend gradually with the ground showing through it.

Sagging of any portion of the cover would at once have thrown a distinctive shadow and had to be carefully guarded against. Blast marks could only be attended to by the gunners themselves, by using removable camouflage or by firing

Lieut. Colonel H. L. Bingay, D.S.O.

The Battle of Messines.

over distorted fixed shapes of expanded metal, which would disguise the blast marks on the ground beneath. Any aspect of regularity of design was to be avoided, since regularity in nature is unknown. Straight lines or rectangular shapes required distortion, and this principle of irregular shape was also applied to the opaque centres of the flat covers already mentioned. Regular spacing in the position of guns was likewise to be avoided; unusual marking on a photograph might escape notice once, but could hardly hope to do so if repeated several times at regular intervals.

Before proceeding to camouflage positions of importance, great assistance was often gained from inspection of a photograph taken by our own aircraft. With this knowledge of the appearance of the selected spot from the air, facilities for concealment were more easily determined, and the requisite character of camouflage selected. Though special circumstances could be catered for by the Corps Camouflage officers, given reasonable time for manufacture at the special factories, the usual material on issue was composed of fish netting, wire netting, or sheets of scrim, more or less garnished with raffia, painted canvas knots, or islands of painted, variegated, or plain scrim, made up in different sized squares and rolls. Additions and alterations were easily made on the site by the aid of grass or boughs and so on, and it was generally understood that the material issued was not suited to every locality, but was the basis from which could be completed the type of cover suitable to the particular needs of the individual position.

Many varying devices were adopted by different operators, and doubtless many more might have been thought of. A note or two on the particular systems usually adopted in specific cases will round off the foregoing general description of principles. Railway guns were easily disguised as ordinary railway trucks. One 12-inch howitzer spent many useful months masquerading as a dump of R.E. material. A scheme often adopted to cover an important position in open fields, always a difficult problem, was to create a large structure of very regular shape in strict uniformity with adjacent strips of cultivation, and throwing no shadow. This entailed considerable material and labour, but the result showed merely as an alteration in the landscape due to some normal agricultural operation. Blast marks on snow were covered up with fresh snow, or crushed chalk, and occasionally a sloping platform was placed under the muzzle to deflect the blast off the ground. Artificial camouflage would not hold snow, each

Field Companies and Field Troop.

erection showing up as a dark square, necessitating the use of large islands of white calico.

Actual guns were always painted in green, cream, and brown, with a strong line of black between each colour, on the principle that while frequent changes of position made it impossible to harmonise exactly with the varying surroundings each time, one or more of the adopted colours would blend with any landscape, leaving the visible remainder in a broken series of patches effectually disguising the form of the gun.

Long trenches were impossible to conceal effectually for any time, though short lengths could be well treated with painted scrim. Camps likewise could not be hidden, though hut surfaces could be treated to minimise moonlight reflection. Dummy trenches or other works painted on canvas failed under expert investigation, since the painted shadows would not move with the sun. A good deal of quite effective camouflage was effected by local garrisons or machine-gun teams without special material at all, using grass, sods, boughs, and derelict rubbish of the battlefield.

A great number of gun positions were prepared by the Engineers, mainly the 3rd Company. Shallow pits about two feet deep were dug for each gun, covered with a type of arched iron shelter known as "large elephant." These "large elephants" were similar in size and shape to the English pattern iron shelters already mentioned, but were of much stronger design. Covered with packed sandbags all round the arch, and protected by sandbag walls in front, they furnished the gunners with comparatively good shelter. Gradually, as battery after battery came into position and began to register, the weight of metal on the enemy position increased, though never at any time was indication given of the full strength of our impending blow. However, quite a sufficient demonstration was made to arouse Fritz's antagonism, and though he paid no special attention to our front line area, an increasing activity was brought to bear on all rear areas where villages, dumps, transport lines and battery positions afforded an increasing variety of targets.

On the night of 6th May he opened up a particularly heavy bombardment, during which many casualties were caused, especially in the village of Neuve Eglise. On the western edge of Ploegsteert Wood near Red Lodge the 1st Field Company experienced a full share of the vicissitudes of the night. Five of their huts were fired by a direct hit, and the resulting casualties were intensified by the flames

The Battle of Messines.

which immediately enveloped the flimsy tinderbox structures. Most of the Company records were burnt. For weeks the comparative immunity from German shell fire of Ploegsteert Wood behind Hill 63 had been a source of wonder and satisfaction to those most concerned. Thousands of men were packed among the trees, and scarce one with any cover that a shotgun could not have destroyed. Now apparently conditions were to alter, and immediate steps were taken to provide increased protection. The few dugouts already in existence were strengthened by a liberal use of forest timber and sandbags, new ones were built where the configuration of the hill afforded most protection, and in particular several tunnels provided with alternative exits were driven far into the hillside.

But no such protection was possible for the occupants of the crowded horse lines further back. The 2nd Field Companies in particular, whose transport was located just below Neuve Eglise on the road to De Seule, suffered severe casualties during the bombardment of May 6th. No less than 20 horses were either killed or wounded, and of the drivers, all of whom stuck gallantly to their charges during the shelling, eight were severely wounded. On the 7th all horses and transport personnel were removed to fresh positions near the Nieppe-Bailleul road, where they escaped further molestation.

In order to provide a small permanent body of labour, always available when required, a carrying and working party of 1 officer and 100 infantrymen was attached to each Field Company on the 18th May. This arrangement was continued right through to the completion of the Messines operation and worked exceedingly well. Its permanent adoption would seem to be the solution of some aspects of a troublesome question.

Officially speaking, each sapper is a trained man in some particular trade, and his time is being wasted whenever he is not supplied with adequate labour to carry out his job. On the other hand, it is a source of annoyance to infantry units to be constantly called upon for all kinds of working parties, and the men themselves, classing a job they will probably never see again as simply one more fatigue of no particular moment, are not likely to put forth any very enthusiastic efforts unless tempted by a set "task" to get work finished quickly and get away again. And the "task" was seldom looked upon favourably by the authorities except in special cases. The permanent man does twice the work, because he sees enough of what is in hand to take an interest in it. No one would claim that every individual sapper was actually a highly

Field Companies and Field Troop.

trained man whose time was of great value. But he should have been, and the system of working had to be arranged on the basis that he was. Whether engaged in defensive or offensive operations, a Field Company must have labour, and the provision of even the small permanent nucleus mentioned was a decided step in the right direction.

On the 19th May, the 3rd Company took over the works of the 1st Company, which forthwith became Company in reserve, and by the end of the month moved out into fresh billets at De Seule. At the same time all Engineer transport was concentrated in the area just south-east of Steenwerck. On the 20th, in anticipation of the exigencies of the supply situation on the days immediately preceding and following zero hour, the Divisional Pack Transport Unit was formed. All pack-horses and attendant personnel of the three Field Companies forthwith became part of this force.

About the same time two Field Company dumps were established, one in each sector, adjacent to the tramways, at Boyle's Farm and Gooseberry Farm. These were stocked with a view to operations after the attack only, and pending that event their supplies were rigorously conserved. No battalion dumps were established and no necessity for them arose. A multiplicity of scattered dumps is no advantage. All cannot be kept stocked, and troops finding one dump exhausted do not know where to look for another. Attacking troops were fully equipped with tools and sandbags before their final parade in battle kit.

On the night of 22nd May, four sappers of the 3rd Company accompanied a raiding party of 2nd Rifles to enemy territory near La Petite Douve Farm. The German trenches were found in a very poor condition with dugouts damaged and blocked up with debris. Further demolition appeared unnecessary and was not attempted.

By the end of May the 4th Infantry Brigade, recruited from surplus reinforcements in the camps in England, made its appearance in France, and after inspection by General Godley at Bailleul became part of the New Zealand Division. With the new Brigade came the 4th Field Company under the command of Major Skelsey. About the end of March arrangements had been made by the C.R.E. with a view to an exchange of officers and N.C.O.'s from the Field Companies with those in the Reserve Depot in England, to take effect every two months. Men with long service in the trenches would thus obtain some short respite from the daily round of shelling, and their experiences would assist in the training of

The Battle of Messines.

the men in the Depot. On the other hand, reinforcement N.C.O.'s would gain valuable experience of trench warfare before being called upon to assume full responsibility in the field. Accordingly, on 21st March two officers and eight N.C.O.'s from the Field Companies had been sent over to England, a like number arriving from base to take their places.

One of the last tasks assigned to the Engineers was the provision of bridges across the Douve capable of supporting tanks. Search along the banks revealed the existence of the remains of old cart-road bridges and culverts in several places, the brick abutments of which were still usable, and with the aid of steel girders and heavy decking, four bridges, which safely fulfilled their purpose later, were erected by the 1st and 3rd Companies.

By the beginning of June, all major preparations were complete, and a few days were available for the perfecting of minor details. On the 2nd, 50 reinforcements arrived from base and were allocated to the various companies.

On the afternoon of 5th June, eight sappers from 1st Field Company, armed with 20lb charges of guncotton, accompanied a raid on La Petite Douve Farm, where three heavily fortified concrete dugouts had been found to exist. Two were destroyed, but the charge laid on the third failed to explode, and was recovered on the 8th. Sapper H. J. Tuck was conspicuous in this operation, laying his charge and waiting till the whole of the raiding party was clear before firing it, though subject to both machine-gun and shrapnel fire all the time. He would probably have won the Military Medal had not delay been caused in presenting his case owing to the wounding of the infantry officer in charge of the raid.

For a week or more before the attack, the enemy deluged Hill 63 every night with gas shells, and though the Field Companies suffered few casualties, the constant alarms of the gas sentries, combined with the continual disturbance caused by the gunners, both friend and foe, made it extremely difficult to obtain any proper sleep. The evening of 6th June was cool and sweet after a sharp thunderstorm. Special parties of sappers were on duty all night patrolling the communication saps, ready to remove any obstacle to the free passage of the incoming assault battalions. By every available route across the dark countryside, these now came marching up from the concentration areas to take post in their assembly trenches. At 3.10 a.m. on a dark, misty morning the famous mines were blown simultaneously.

Field Companies and Field Troop.

"The inception of a deep mining offensive on the Second Army front dated from July, 1915, but the proposal to conduct offensive mining on a grand scale was not definitely adopted till January, 1916. From that date onwards, as the necessary labour became available, deep mining for offensive purposes gradually developed, in spite of great difficulties from water-bearing strata and active counter-mining by the enemy. In all, 24 mines were constructed, four of which were outside the front ultimately selected for our offensive, while one other was lost as the result of a mine blown up by the enemy. Many of these mines had been completed for 12 months prior to our offensive, and constant and anxious work was needed to ensure their safety. The enemy also had a deep mining system, and was aware of his danger."

Comparatively little sound was caused by the explosions, but, before the red flash had faded from the sky, the thundering roar of the British artillery rent the heavens with a deafening crash. The great assault was launched.

The initial task of the Engineers was to be the usual construction of Strong Points in positions selected beforehand to accord with the possible variations of fortune on the morning of attack. The various objectives were known as usual as Blue, Brown, Yellow, Black and Green Lines. The Black Line, well in front of Messines Village, was to be the limit of the New Zealand effort, the capture of the Green Line farther on being assigned to the 4th Australians. Within an hour prisoners commenced to flow back. In a shade over two hours the final New Zealand objective was won. The 2nd and 3rd Field Companies thereupon moved up to the positions selected for the construction of Strong Points in support of the Black Line, viz., abreast and in front of Messines Village. The infantry was found well dug in, and any movement on the surface drew German fire at once. In most cases it was inexpedient to commence work on the Strong Points till the middle of the afternoon. By late evening four were completed and occupied by the neighbouring garrisons. The remaining four were completed on the following evening, and all those likely to avoid direct observation were wired. These works were small, to contain a platoon and two machine-guns each, and were placed to give flanking fire and mutual support in case of successful counter-attack. During the progress of this consolidation work, enemy shelling was heavy and continuous. Outstanding examples of determined courage and devotion to duty were shown by numerous Engineers, notably Sergeant H. E. Fricker, Corporal D. A. Kennedy, Lance-Corporal A. P. Mackie, and Sapper J. Tindall of the 3rd Company, and Lance-

The Battle of Messines.

Corporal M. G. Easton of the 2nd Company. Each of these men had set a high standard of soldierly conduct under fire, and was given an immediate reward of the Military Medal.

Other men conspicuous for their courage and skill while engaged on general consolidation work during the progress of the Messines offensive and after, were Sergeant C. King of the 2nd Field Company, Sapper L. Robinson of the 3rd, and Sergeant A. M. Oliver of the 4th.

Early on the morning of the 7th a small reconnoitring party from the 2nd Field Company went into Messines Village in search of water. All wells were found blown in and filled with rubbish, but the important discovery was made that at least one well was poisoned with arsenic. All water from Messines was accordingly banned. In any case, owing to intensity of German fire, little use could have been made of any water that had been available in the village. Parties were thereupon set to work on shallow wells outside Messines in places where good indications existed. Within two days an estimated daily supply of 10,000 gallons of tested water was available. Corporal J. H. Anderson was awarded the Military Medal for coolness and courage during the exploration of Messines Village.

As soon as our line had cleared Messines Village, the work of constructing new roads and communication trenches went on apace. This work was largely undertaken by the Pioneers, but the 1st Field Company, being in reserve, was called upon to form an urgent track for mule traffic from the head of the tramway at Medicine Hat Trail past the forward dump at Boyle's Farm and on to the Wulverghem-Messines Road. A fair amount of clearing wire and filling in old trenches was necessary, and a bridge across the Steenebeek occupied one party for several hours, but by evening the track was complete and well marked with white stakes. Heavy shelling was experienced during the middle of the day. During the evening of the 7th a heavy sterilizing plant was installed at La Plus Douve Farm for the utilisation of the Douve for water service, and one section from the same Company was fully employed on the 7th and immediately succeeding days in clearing and maintaining all communication trenches for the rapid passage of stretcher bearers. Several urgent lengths of light tramline were laid to new battery positions. In addition, all available transport was utilised to maintain supplies in the dumps at Boyle's Farm and Gooseberry Farm, now meeting a heavy demand from advanced areas.

Field Companies and Field Troop.

The recently constituted 4th Field Company had its first experience as a front-line unit on the evening of the 7th, when it commenced to repair and reconstruct the old road running from Hyde Park Corner across the right flank of Hill 63 and to Messines. Hyde Park Corner was never among the health resorts of the Messines sector, and the new company was well broken in ere sunrise. One section was detailed for preparation of Heavy Artillery positions in Armentieres during this evening, and found that the job offered no attractions other than those being enjoyed by the men on the road. Succeeding days were spent by the whole Company in repairing the Wulverghem-Messines Road.

On the 10th June the sector was handed over to the 4th Australian Division, and the Field Companies, along with the rest of the New Zealand Division, moved out for a brief spell in rear areas. Headquarters moved to Rue de la Gare, Bailleul, 1st Company remained at De Seule, 2nd Company moved to Watts' Lines near De Seule, and 3rd Company to Hillside Camp, Neuve Eglise. Engineer casualties during the attack had fortunately been comparatively light.

The 4th Field Company, having only just entered the arena, was not withdrawn from line with the others, but continued its road-mending activities in front of Wulverghem. On the 10th June, one section was despatched to Pont de Nieppe to take over work on the Le Touquet sector, so well and unfavourably known to the other companies in the preceding March. Here it was joined by the remainder of the Company on the 15th. Working sections bivouacked in the region of the support line, Headquarters remaining in Pont de Nieppe.

From all reports of the 4th Company's experiences at Le Touquet, in common with all predecessors, it found the sector in such a frightful condition that evidently little or no work whatever had been done on it for years. The war diary, sweet fountain of truth and accuracy, (all war diaries share these characteristics), shows that when they left the sector at the end of August it had been overhauled and refitted. It is certain that a vast improvement was effected.

The Company included a considerable leavening of "old hands," and the remainder of the men, who had been condemned to a long stay in England through no fault of their own, were more than keen for work when their opportunity at last arrived. As a mild set-off against the disadvantages of the area, the orchards round Le Bizet were well stocked with fruit, and many of the fields, graced by wild flowers and pop-

The Battle of Messines.

pies, were further adorned with temporarily forsaken crops of potatoes, peas, and beans. These would have formed a welcome addition to the army rations, had there been no regulations prohibiting their use. Base rumours were current of hoarded sugar rations, and supplies of home-made jam, but such stories lack official confirmation, and need not be repeated here.

On 12th June the Division re-entered the scene of activity, taking over the Ploegsteert sector from the 3rd Australians. C.R.E. Headquarters moved once more to Steenwerck, the first three Field Companies being located at Weka Lines, Romarin; Stuff Camp, Pont de Nieppe; and Nieppe Village respectively. The 2nd Company now exchanged positions with the 1st Company and became Company in reserve, all works in rear areas coming under its charge.

The whole front of this formerly familiar sector now comprised ground recently won from the enemy, and work of every kind was waiting on all sides. Tracks, tramlines, water supply and concentration of stores and material were the most urgent requirements of the situation. At the same time, Engineer personnel was made available for the supervision of large working parties on trenches and communications. Several miles of new track were soon ready for mule traffic, and the former roads of the area were put on something like a working basis. Existing tramlines were extended and large quantities of stores were collected at Prouse Point, Maison 1875, and Divisional dumps further forward. Several wells were discovered in the advanced areas, others were dug and put in working order. From the Douve to the Warnave, two miles each of new front and support lines were traced out and dug, and south of the latter stream the old German line was converted into a new front line, with our former line as a support line behind it.

The main strength of the Company in reserve during the latter half of June was employed on the electric lighting system of the Catacombs on Hill 63, on the water supply system in Ploegsteert Wood, and on a series of Strong Points in the subsidiary line. A splendid well was discovered beneath one of the old buildings in Ploegsteert Village of sufficient depth to justify the rehabilitation of an ancient pumping engine. From this supply pipes were laid right up through the Wood to the large storage tanks at Can-Pac Dump, feeding on the way two smaller open tanks used for local needs at the Strand and Regent Street, two well-known communication tracks leading through the Wood to the front line. The weather was very warm, but water was none too plentiful,

Field Companies and Field Troop.

owing to constant breaks in the line, and to periodic crises arising out of the dilapidated state of the pumping engine. Consequently, when it was found that the Strand tank was empty every morning, a night water-guard was posted. Still the supply was extraordinarily low in the morning. Some time elapsed before it was discovered that an old sap near the tank afforded cover to thirsty marauders with a perverted sense of right and wrong and a length of stolen hose, with which they took turns at siphoning the water out of the tank into dixies in the sap below. All pipes were laid on the surface as it was found that burying them did not afford sufficient added security to compensate for the time lost in locating and mending a break when one occurred. Patrols were maintained on the line night and day, and found the work sufficiently arduous, especially as the Germans kept the famous Wood in a constant reek of phosgene and mustard gas. The mustard gas, now encountered for the first time, had an unmistakable odour of wet mustard and was particularly pungent. Patrols mending breaks in the pipe line caused by mustard gas shells found that the water which collected in the small shell hole beneath each break was sufficiently impregnated with the mustard to cause swelling and blisters to appear on the arms some hours later. Sapper T. Drummond, of the 2nd Company, was indefatigable in his efforts to maintain the pipe lines, working all hours frequently under shell fire, and it was largely due to his exertions that the supply of water was so well maintained.

On 28th and 29th June the Division was again relieved by the 4th Australians. The short tour in the line had been more than usually trying. A constant series of minor attacks had been carried out nightly by all battalions in line with a view to improving and rounding off the splendid victory gained on the 7th. These had kept the enemy in a constant state of irritated uncertainty, and his shelling had been heavy and continuous in consequence, while shelter and means of communication were very far from adequate.

C.R.E.'s Headquarters were now removed to Vieux Berquin. By the end of the month, 1st, 2nd, and 3rd Companies were located in rest billets in pleasant farm buildings round about Doulieu. The 4th Company still remained in line with the 4th Brigade, under the tactical command of the Australians.

The endurance and determined fighting spirit shown by the New Zealand infantry throughout the whole of the great enterprise just concluded were beyond all praise. Once again

The Battle of Messines.

all ranks in the Division had very special reason to feel proud of those among them on whose devoted shoulders the main burden of the day fell with the greatest weight and frequency. Along with whole-hearted admiration of the powers of their fighting comrades, the Engineering units felt a quiet glow of satisfaction in the undeniable fact that all their weeks of special preparations had materially lightened the final task of their own Division, and assisted in a glorious triumph of the British arms.

No facts are strained by a plain statement that the men of the Field Companies were always conscious of a feeling of keen disappointment that, in the hour of the final call, the technical nature of their job forced them to remain in at least comparative security, while the men beside whom they had worked for weeks for a common object went forward to the death-grip alone. In the Army every man's opportunity comes in good time, but when one is young and fit, the red blood runs fast, and it takes more than a grain of philosophy to realise the truth that "they also serve who only stand and wait."

Well quartered, and favoured by beautiful summer weather, the Companies settled down to enjoy their brief spell of rest and quietness. Leave was plentiful, parades were few and short. On the first Sunday, a massed church parade was held, one of the very few occasions on which all three companies were on parade together in the presence of the C.R.E.

The 2nd Field Company at this stage had a unique opportunity of extending its war experience. In company with the Rifle Brigade and the Pioneer Battalion it was ordered to the Woesten area in Belgium, there to assist the 1st French Army in the construction of gun pits and roads and other measures incidental to its co-operation with the British attack about to develop. In that peaceful sector, the preparations for the impending offensive were the only visible signs of war. No shelling marred the green expanse of the smiling fields, no shattered trees and broken roads dispelled the mid-summer charms of the ripening countryside.

Work was conducted in two shifts on the task system, and went on swiftly with practically no interruption. The French soldier, as we saw him there, loves to linger at his toil. With frequent pauses for a yarn and a smoke, he jogs along contentedly till the evening meal about 3.30 p.m. calls him to rest from his labours. The mental attitude of the New Zealander, stripped to the waist, grimly intent on cutting out his job in the shortest possible time in order to get back to

Field Companies and Field Troop.

camp to the enjoyment of his own devices, filled our Allies with audible amazement. Admiring poilus thronged each gunpit, and but for the fearful imprecations of their own sergeants would have made that pastime the business of the day. Two official meals, the first about 9 a.m., are the rule of the French Army. Breakfast consists mainly of brown bread and coffee, and by contrast with the hearty rations of the Britishers, the general fare seemed both hard and scanty. A standing joke of the lesser French comic papers hinged on their assertion that the British Army would greatly increase its successes if it could be induced to move even half a day in advance of its ration supplies.

The French Army treated the New Zealanders as honoured guests, entertaining them with band concerts and supplying a daily issue of wine, while the proximity of the camps and the long summer days gave every opportunity for individual personal contact between the soldiers of the respective armies. Several New Zealand reputations for linguistic ability went utterly by the board or were badly shaken during these encounters. "I say, Jack!" one Rifleman was overheard to remark, "I thought Bill could do a bit at this Francais." "Well, he can, can't he?" replied Jack. "Damned if I know," continued the former speaker. "He tried to get the time from one of 'em this morning, and the old —— gave him a match!" Obviously these good times could not last, and by the 14th July, the French National Fete day, the works were complete. In an atmosphere of general festivity, somewhat heightened by a free issue of champagne, cigars, and extra wine, the working parties prepared to return to their own Division. By midnight they were on the march in pouring rain sustained by the happiest recollections of their short experience of their gallant allies. On the 16th, the 2nd Field Company returned to the billets they had recently vacated near Doulieu.

Both going to Woesten and returning, the Company passed close beneath the foot of the hill, Mont des Cats, crowned by the Trappist monastery whose spires had been visible alike from Hill 63 in front of Messines, and from the country round Fleurbaix. The hill-top was additionally interesting as the spot where the German Prince Max of Hesse was killed by the British cavalry patrols early in the war. Several monks were still in residence, marching to work in the fields every day several paces apart, since one of their vows is silence. Two only among them hold converse with outsiders, the Abbot and the Sacristan—called by the Tommies in garrison the O.C. and the Quartermaster. If the Abbey's vocal efforts had de-

The Battle of Messines.

pended on the Quartermaster alone, it had still been fairly well represented. The hill and adjacent ridges are said to have harboured certain of the wilder tribes that troubled Caesar long ago; certainly the site of one of his main camps was at Cassel, some 10 miles to the westward, from whose church spire the radiating lines of the old Roman roads can be seen to this day.

During the absence of the 2nd Field Company the 1st and 3rd Companies, with Headquarters, had leavened a little training with a good deal of sport and amusement. On the 4th July, in preparation for the Divisional gymkana which followed on the 8th, they held a very successful sports meeting of their own. The rival claims of would-be representatives were tried out, and not a few of the many aspirants found themselves a trifle "short of a gallop." However, those selected for the more important contests on the 8th did very well, and many sappers' names figured in the prize lists.

On the 18th July the Division moved back into the line again, re-occupying its old position in the Ploegsteert sector. The Engineers were disposed as follows:—C.R.E. at Steenwerck, 1st Company to Weka Lines taking over the left sector, 2nd Company to Watts' Lines in reserve, 3rd to Watts' Lines taking over the centre sector, while the 4th Company remained on the right sector. The commencement of the long-delayed attack in the Ypres salient was now rapidly approaching. In other sectors, a series of feints was continued, particularly from Lens, threatening Lille from the south, not with any vain hope of deceiving the enemy as to our ultimate intentions in Flanders, but to dissipate his reserves and artillery over as large a front as possible.

To the New Zealanders on the extreme right flank of the Second Army was allotted the task of a demonstration against the Warneton Line. An advance here, in addition to threatening a passage of the Lys, with possibilities of enveloping Lille in the background, would effectively secure the right flank of our major operation. The centre-piece of the New Zealand enterprise was the capture and retention of the village of La Basseville. To further the illusion with regard to our crossing of the Lys, a series of dummy assembly trenches was dug on the bank of the river with conspicuous guiding tapes leading back toward our lines. Generally speaking, work in the forward areas was along routine lines. In pursuance of the policy so successfully employed at Messines, both 1st and 3rd Companies were supplied with 100 attached infantry to enable them to handle urgent calls with adequate despatch and efficiency. On the evening of the 29th

Field Companies and Field Troop.

July two sappers from 1st Company accompanied a raid with the intention of demolishing some troublesome M.G. emplacements, but the party failed to reach its objective. At dawn on the 31st July the roar of the guns to the northward told of the commencement of the attack at Ypres. At the same time the New Zealanders attacked La Basseville, and established themselves firmly beyond the village.

On 1st August, 3rd Field Company assumed charge of a large portion of the left sector from the 1st Company, which forthwith moved northward and took over the sector immediately beyond the Douve from the 9th, 10th, and 11th Field Companies of the 5th Australians. Heavy German shelling marked the continuance of our minor operations beyond La Basseville, and a new C.T. was dug from the top entrance of the Catacombs in Hill 63 to St. Yves. By the 6th, our offensive posts had been advanced as far as seemed necessary for the moment, and new permanent systems of front and support lines were put in hand. Continued bad weather and the low-lying nature of the country made this work a wet and dirty job, especially as material was extremely difficult to bring up over the broken country. A special salvage party, and the use of abandoned German stores went some way towards assisting the difficulty. Both heavy and light lines of railway were now up as far as La Petite Douve Farm, our original front line, but advanced tramways were only in course of construction. For a considerable period all trenches and communications were simply ditches knee deep in mud, and except under exceptional circumstances travellers preferred to risk their luck and take to the open. North of the Douve conditions were especially bad, with no defined lines whatever, and the 1st Company was not sorry to see the last of this area on the 23rd, when 4th Australians took over the pleasant task of converting it into a habitable locality.

During the whole of this period German shelling was continuous and very severe. Sergeant John McKay, of the 1st Field Company, whose fine work at Messines had brought him under official notice, was again conspicuous for his energy and courage under fire. Corporal A. H. Loke and 2nd Corporal S. Forsyth of the 3rd Field Company, both of whom were Gallipoli men, also added to their records of devoted service during these operations.

Rear areas were in no better case than the front line. For a comparatively inactive front it is doubtful whether the Boche at any time bestowed more attention on our back villages and camps than he did during the month of August. Continuous shelling by day gave place to the ominous drone

The Battle of Messines.

of his bombing planes by night, and the sharp crash of his heavy bombs was heard every evening over an increasing radius of unpleasantness. So active did he finally become that all iron-roofed huts in the Divisional area were given a coat of tar, and sprinkled with sand. Without some such arrangement, dew or rain, especially on moonlit nights, furnished a glistening beacon for the enterprising bombers. The Divisional baths at Pont de Nieppe were a favourite target with the German gunners, and after numerous attempts at repairs, during one of which a valuable N.C.O. of the 2nd Company fell into a huge vat of dirty water coincident with the arrival of a big shell, new baths were erected on a smaller scale at Papot, Pont d'Achelles, Kortepyp, and Romarin. Laundries were also renewed at this stage.

On relief north of the Douve, the 1st Field Company moved out to La Motte for a few days, and finally went on to Wizernes, whence it was transported in motor lorries to Bainghem le Comte, in the Aa Valley west of Lumbres. There it was joined by its transport, which arrived by road via Wallon Cappel. On the 29th, 3rd Field Company sappers reached Wizernes and went on to Longueville, where they also were joined by their transport via Arques. C.R.E. with Headquarters had handed over to 8th Division on the 27th and removed to Caestre. By the 30th he had arrived at Colembert. On 2nd September the 4th Company had also arrived in the Lumbres area at Alincthun.

Here, along with the rest of the Division, the Field Companies enjoyed some weeks of comparative rest. Training was carried out along the usual lines, varied by occasional jobs required about the training area. Several ordinary huts and baths were given to the 3rd and 4th Companies; to the 1st Company, probably in recognition of its long service and experience in delicate situations, fell the onerous task of repairing and enlarging the W.A.A.C.'s camp at Wisques. No details are now available, but it is understood that the job was carried through with satisfaction to all concerned. A further opportunity of extending its circle of acquaintances was allowed this Company a few days later, when the necessary labour for constructing a rifle range was provided by a Chinese Labour Corps. The 3rd and 4th Companies also figured in reviews held on 10th and 14th, the latter a Divisional review by the Commander-in-Chief at Harlettes.

On the 11th the Divisional Horse Show was held to decide on New Zealand's Divisional representatives for the forthcoming Corps Show. Captain Annabell's charger "Leo," which had won 1st prize at the previous Divisional Horse

Field Companies and Field Troop.

Show, was again too good for its opponents, and secured two first prizes, one for "Best charger in the New Zealand Division." Later on, it was successful in further competitions. This horse was originally sent from New Zealand with the Field Troop attached to the Main Body, and remained with the Engineers till the date of demobilisation in Germany.

The 2nd Company had moved out to Pradelles on the 30th August and by 4th September was settled at Morbecque with its transport on the work of converting the II Anzac Corps School into a New Zealand Reinforcement Camp. The work was mostly a good clean building job with good weather and plenty of material to ease the strain. An interesting feature of the work here was the erection of 40 Nissen Bow huts, which, though quite familiar and largely used in all rear areas, had not so far come under the hands of the Company. The Nissen hut, so called from the name of the Canadian officer who designed it, was distinctly one of the discoveries of the war. The never satisfied demand for shelter was a constant problem on every portion of the front, and this hut, with its simplicity of construction, lightness and portability, met the needs of the situation with marked success. All material used was prepared at the Base and sent forward in standard bundles, sufficient for 1 hut or 20. The flooring, of light 1-inch boarding, was supplied in made-up segments which only required fitting together on the supporting joists. The sides and roof were composed of corrugated iron sheets, forming an arch, much after the style of the English pattern iron used for front area shelters, and bolted together on the same principle. The ends, complete with windows and door, were likewise supplied in prepared sections, which could be erected in a few minutes. Stoves, shelves, bunks or tables could be added as desired, but without any accessories the hut could supply 40 men with a dry place to sleep in, and as such was a welcome institution in any area. In crowded camps some small measure of protection against bomb splinters was afforded by the erection of encircling banks of earth; against anything in the nature of a direct hit, of course, the cover provided by the huts was of no more use than brown paper.

Football matches at Morbecque were of daily occurrence, and inter-sectional rivalry was keen. On Sundays a Company team was wont to scour the countryside for fresh scalps, and scored many a glorious victory.

On July 27th Lieutenant-Colonel Pridham, D.S.O., R.E., had relinquished command of the New Zealand Engineers, and

The Ypres Cloth Hall Before The Great War. *Photo lent by Major N. Annabell*

The Ypres Cloth Hall after nearly Two Years Bombardment by the Enemy.
Photo sent by Major N. Annabell

The Battle of Messines.

under instruction from a Medical Board, had left for England to take a few weeks very necessary rest. From the formation of the 1st Field Company in Egypt right through the stern days of the Peninsula, and for 15 months in France, he had occupied the position of C.R.E. to the New Zealand Division, and as such had been Officer Commanding New Zealand Engineers. A man of ripe experience in his chosen profession, and highly trained in the best traditions of the British Regular Army, he was a source of inestimable benefit to the force of raw civilian soldiers fortuitously thrown under his hand. Possessed of a naturally simple and sincere disposition, with plenty of quiet force and none of the frill and bluff so objectionable to the colonial mind, he had a knowledge of men and affairs that enabled him to handle his unfamiliar command with a sure touch. No man was ever heard to question the wisdom or justice of "the Colonel's" decisions. An English gentleman and a pukka soldier, Colonel Pridham has no need of further enconium from us. Of our constant regard we like to feel he was sufficiently assured long since. His place was taken by Lieutenant-Colonel H. L. Bingay.

CHAPTER X.

PASSCHENDAELE.

For some weeks the Field Companies enjoyed a spell of comparative rest, working or training in their back areas. During the whole of this period the rumble of the distant guns about Ypres was ever in the air, now rising to a definite staccato, now falling to a subdued throb only noticeable to one in some confined space, according to the vagaries of the breeze, or to the changing conditions of the battlefield.

The grand offensive, successfully opened by the Fifth Army on 31st July, was not so auspiciously prosecuted during the succeeding phases, and by September it was clearly seen that additional forces must be employed. General Plumer and the Second Army were called upon for the necessary effort. By an attack on 20th September, augmented by further successes on 26th September, fair progress was made, and the final capture of the main ridge looked like a feasible proposition. At the same time, no strategic positions of real value had yet fallen into our hands. The new policy of defence adopted by the German High Command was already proving its sterling worth.

The bitter experiences, gained on the Somme and at Messines, of the possible effects of concentrated artillery fire on fixed trench lines had caused the enemy to modify his views regarding defensive measures, and his continuous lines of trenches formerly relied upon had now given place to a system of small, closely distributed machine-gun posts, all mutually supporting, and each well protected by its own system of wire entanglements. Generally only about 10 feet square, built of solid reinforced concrete, with walls and overhead cover up to six feet in thickness, these posts were almost indestructible except by the direct hit of our heaviest shells, while the handicaps of poor observation facilities and unstable foundations laboured under by our Artillery were increased by the very skilful manner in which the enemy had sited and concealed his structures.

Once among the "pill-boxes," as these posts were christened by some inevitable Tommy humourist, all attempted advances to date had been at once held up, since the ordinary creeping barrage had little or no effect on the machine-gunners securely sheltered in each stronghold. However, though prospects of achieving the results first aimed at were now

Passchendaele.

extremely dim, there was still time before the winter to take the main ridge, which, in addition to a dominating position, and relatively good winter quarters, would afford us a good starting place for renewed operations in the spring.

By September 24th came the expected orders to the New Zealand Division, and the 25th saw them on the road to Ypres. C.R.E. Headquarters, 1st, 3rd, and 4th Field Companies marched up to staging billets in Hazebrouck, Renescure, Campagne and Sart respectively. Next day found the three Companies again on the road, putting in the night at St. Marie Cappel, Wallen Cappel, and Campagne. On the 27th the Belgian border was crossed once more, and passing via Watou and adjacent camps, the sappers took up final quarters on the Yser Canal bank on the outskirts of Ypres. All transport was concentrated near Vlamertinghe.

The trek had been commenced in sweltering weather and concluded in heavy rain, and the heavy packs and crowded roads did not improve either situation. However, the long spell in back areas had wonderfully improved the health and condition of the Companies, which were providentially in fine fettle for the work and weather that lay ahead. The 2nd Company came up from Morbecque to Poperinghe by rail a day or two later, and after a night spent on the roadside at Goldfish Chateau, went into bivouac in a sodden field at Salvation Corner, just in rear of the other Companies. The new month found the New Zealand Infantry established in strange country in trenches some four miles in front of the old British Front Line. Little time was to be allowed them to familiarise themselves with their new positions. The lateness of the season and the urgency of the operations in hand combined to insist upon a speedy climax. New Zealand's share in the coming attack was to be the capture of the Gravenstafel Spur.

Lines of communication in the new sector were particularly inadequate. The whole of the traffic from the battle front was forced to pass through Ypres, and, from there to the rear, the main road through Vlamertinghe to Poperinghe formed the only available outlet.

Once forward of Ypres, road conditions became worse and worse until the area of recent fighting was reached. There the roads ceased to exist. Long stretches of greasy gleaming slush, interspersed with small islands of firm ground, still capped with a yard or two of paved road, amid pools of slimy knee-deep water, showed where they once had been. Choked with the debris of broken waggons, abandoned guns, ammunition boxes, shells, accoutrements, and, nearer to the front, the decaying remains of dead animals, they needed but

Field Companies and Field Troop.

the lines of twisted and distorted trees standing as in mute despair at solemn intervals along the shattered roadsides to complete the ruin and desolation of the scene.

Even foot traffic across the broken country, now saturated by constant rain, was strenuous labour to an unburdened man. To the early carrying parties, toiling hour after hour over the endless morass, the work was heartbreaking and the results negligible. The 1st and 4th Field Companies, with parties of 100 Infantry attached, were each immediately ordered to construct a forward mule track and a double duckboard track.

These tracks, known as No. 5 and No. 6 Tracks, ran forward on either side of the old Wieltje-Passchendaele Road, starting respectively at Oxford and Admiral Roads in the vicinity of Wieltje, where an advanced Divisional Dump was now established at Bilge, supplies coming by motor lorry from Vlamertinghe and Poperinghe. The mule tracks were provided with planking or road mats in the worst places, and a pathway was formed for the drivers. At first these mule tracks were located near the duckboard tracks, which, with the natural perversity of human nature, the drivers immediately proceeded to use in preference to their own. The mules essayed to follow the bad example, with poor results to the duckboards, and thenceforward the two tracks were constructed at a more discreet distance apart.

Double duckboards allowed of up and down traffic on each track and the free passage of stretcher-bearers. The 3rd Field Company took over the work of maintaining both existing and newly formed tracks, and since before the end of the Divisional operations these attained a total length of 20 miles, some idea will be gained of their extensive charge. More than usual damage was done to the tracks, as the German observers were quick to notice the unusually intense traffic thereon due to difficulties of travel elsewhere. Several miles of dry weather tracks were also formed and staked with painted pickets, but since there was no dry weather after the 4th, they were practically useless.

The ground then became so sodden with rain, and was so cut up by the recent firing, that any attempt to travel at random across country was simply floundering from one shell-hole into another. These lay for miles with scarce a yard between, all filled to the brim with dark slimy water and the scattered debris of the battlefield, mingled all too often with the grisly remains of the poor wretches who had gone under in the preceding weeks.

Passchendaele.

At no period in the Divisional experience on the Western Front was material more urgently required, or more difficult to come by, than during these first weeks in October. The one road forward of Wieltje, still in a precarious condition of hasty repair, was jammed solid with guns vainly endeavouring to get up to more advanced positions. Horsed transport was out of the question. Stray vehicles might have got forward in the course of time, but there would have been no return. Consequently all material required in the advanced area had to be transported on the shoulders of carrying parties. Their performances reached about the limit of human endurance, and all available packhorses in the Engineers' transport sections were used to supplement the supply of duckboards, but the full needs of the situation were never satisfied.

Unfortunately no assistance was received from the Light Railways. A light 9lb. tramline would have been invaluable, both for preparatory work and for evacuation of wounded during the offensive, but material was nowhere available. Arrangements were made to lay a 20lb. line, for which materials were available in the rear dumps. However, to cart these forward by horsed transport or motor lorry in the time available was an absolute impossibility. Had Light Railways been able to deliver the gear at their terminus, all had been well; but even this proved beyond accomplishment. There may have been good and sufficient reason for this disregard of merely Divisional requirements, but the truth may well be stated here that on numberless occasions, happily less serious than the present one, there had been a curious difficulty in procuring necessary material by the Light Railways for work in forward areas.

As September gave way to October and the day of New Zealand's entry into the battle lists came nearer, there was no cessation of effort either at front or rear, but still the results in terms of solid advance were extremely meagre. The far crest of the main ridge, crowned with the battered remains of Passchendaele Village, where ever and again the burst of a heavy shell temporarily shut out the misty picture, still lay well beyond our reach.

This main ridge, running due north from Polygon Wood, of our later acquaintance, to about the point where the Ypres-Roulers railway crosses the hills, there turns in a north-easterly direction for Passchendaele, and at the same time breaks in a north-westerly direction into a low broad outline running down to within a mile of St. Julien Village. Known as Gravenstafel Spur, from the name of the village situated

Field Companies and Field Troop.

half way down its length, this elevation lay almost square to the line of the New Zealanders' advance, close beyond a flooded marshy watercourse known as the Hanebeek. Not far from its junction with the main ridge, the easy outline of the spur was surmounted by a small isolated crest known as Abraham Heights, so called by the Canadians in the Second Battle of Ypres. Further on again, and separated from Gravenstafel Spur by another small stream known as the Ravebeek, which merged later into the Stroombeek, lay the Bellevue Spur. Both these formidable obstacles, with every approach guarded, and every fold in the ground lashed by the machine-gun fire of cleverly hidden "pillboxes," had to be surmounted before the final assault on Passchendaele could be thought of.

During the night of 3rd October special efforts were made by the sappers to assist the movements of the assaulting battalions, and to prepare for the inevitable rush of work on the morrow. Lance-Corporal Dunbar Gunn of the 3rd Field Company was conspicuous for gallantry and determination under heavy shelling and bombing, and was awarded the Military Medal. Gravenstafel Village, and the whole spur including Abraham Heights, lay within the objectives set for the New Zealand attack on 4th October. The sinister Bellevue Spur was to come later.

At 6 a.m. in a cold windy drizzle, the British guns opened the account. To surprise the enemy, no preliminary bombardment had been carried out, and Fritz on his part had been particularly quiet for reasons of his own. Down along the dark foggy marshes of the Hanebeek a German Reserve Division was silently coming into position for an attack at dawn. Our barrage anticipated their proposed attentions by about 10 minutes,, and, in addition to cutting the unfortunate Reserves to pieces, it disarranged the German organisation all day with results entirely favourable to our own enterprise. All objectives and a large number of prisoners were taken well up to time-table. By evening the Spur was held from end to end by a well-dug line of continuous trench some 400 yards down the further slopes. A support line of posts nearer the top, and a further continuous line just behind the crest, provided additional security and good observation. Within a short period communication trenches were established over the crest and down to the foremost line. Though won at some cost, the day's victory was undoubtedly complete in the New Zealand sector, an experience which was happily repeated on either side of them. The capture of Otto Farm, a former German dump well stored with fascines, brushwood and timber, furnished a welcome addition to available supplies, with-

Passchendaele.

out which the sappers could not possibly have compassed the results achieved. By mid-day on the 5th, heavy rain set in once more, and the whole sodden area became a precarious slough of mud and water.

This pronounced break in the weather, coming as it did at the most inopportune moment possible, from the point of view of the British Armies, and no less therefore of our own Division, so intensified the difficulties of travel and transport that the question of tracks and roads became the paramount consideration of the hour; so much so that, during the whole period of this Divisional occupation of the front line, the principal energies of the three Field Companies engaged in the line were absorbed by that work alone. As has been noted, the enemy was fully aware of all that was going on in this particular direction, and time and again shrapnel crashed down among the working parties, while occasionally bursts of concentrated heavy fire forced them to withdraw temporarily. No incentive to persevere was more potent than the sight of the weary men returning from further forward, sometimes wounded and scarcely able to crawl, or even whole men with mud to the thighs, and utterly fagged out by the struggle across the broken wastes.

Since dawn on the 4th the 1st Field Company, along with the Pioneers, had been concentrated on the work of repairing the one main road, and by 8 p.m. some field guns were already on the way to more forward positions. Next day more still were brought up, but with the rain came inevitable delay and almost a stoppage of movement. Several guns were hauled through somehow by main strength and determination, but the road soon became impassable, and the road workers were fully employed in pulling out bogged guns and helping them to the nearest few feet of comparatively firm ground on either side of the slushy canal that marked the line of the former roadway.

Lieutenant G. V. Russell of the 1st Field Company was awarded the Military Cross for good work and gallant conduct on this occasion. No less admirable in their own spheres of action were the achievements of Sergeants B. V. Cooksley and C. H. Elsom, Lance-Corporal J. R. Gilbert, and Sapper A. T. Brokenshire of the same Company, each of whom received an immediate reward of the Military Medal.

Immediately the advance had gone forward, extension and maintenance of the duckboard and mule tracks were pushed on with all speed. By nightfall the 3rd Field Company had reached Dump House, level with Gravenstafel Village. Gallant conduct and coolness under heavy shell fire

Field Companies and Field Troop.

while engaged on this important work brought Military Medals to Sergeant W. J. Brown, Corporal D. W. Stronach, and Lance-Corporal T. Hatful.

Of cover in the forward area there was none, and could be none, save the captured German dugouts. Even Dressing Stations were dependent on that uncertain source of shelter. Most of the concrete pillboxes were small, and many had been more or less damaged by our artillery. Parties from the 3rd and 4th Field Companies were continuously occupied in pumping out and generally patching up these captured dugouts, but had all been in first-class order, there had still been no prospect of weather protection for 90 per cent. of the unfortunate garrisons.

At the same time other sections from the same Field Companies continued the duckboard and mule tracks, but naturally under still further difficulties of supply and construction, owing to the increased demand for other stores consequent upon the advance, the constant passage of troops and wounded, and the pitiless opposition of the elements. Beyond the limits of the tracks the sappers erected numerous guiding stakes and notice boards containing full directions to various destinations, without which accurate movement in the featureless wastes would have been impossible.

Meanwhile the 2nd Field Company had not been idle. While the more extreme needs of the Divisional routine had been imperfectly satisfied by the provision of the various tracks, it was quite evident that, for any successful prosecution of the main advance, a road that could cope with wheeled transport and heavy guns was an absolute necessity. No style of earth or stone construction available was of the least use in dealing with the torn and waterlogged terrain. Timber was the only solution of the difficulty. This was a Corps job and was tackled by the 2nd Field Company along with the Engineering troops from the 49th Division. Train load after train load of heavy beams, green and rough cut straight from the saw, was landed at the railhead near Wieltje and thence carted out in lorries, waggons, limbers, cooks' carts, anything that would carry a load and help to relieve the pressing need of the moment.

From Wieltje towards Gravenstafel the road led down a long easy slope to the stream crossing at the bottom marked by Spree Farm, where German dugouts had now been converted into a Dressing Station, and the block of traffic on that road is still something to remember. Lying open to direct observation from Passchendaele, it was always a stand-

Passchendaele.

ing marvel that enemy artillery did not shell it out of existence. Even moderate efforts would have completely disorganised at least two of our Divisions. Not that it was altogether exempt by any means. Taking one thing with another, to get a load of material up the road in day time was a day's work. The conflicting claims of those anxious to extend the road itself and of those who wanted the sole use of what road already existed, led to an impasse which reacted most unfavourably on the progress of the extension. The 2nd Field Company adopted the method of concentrating all available transport efforts on the hours between midnight and dawn, and thereby managed to supply approximately the needs of their daylight building gangs. Both by the carters at night and the builders by day an enormous amount of time was consumed in patching the holes constantly torn by the German shells, or in extricating the vehicle of some careless or unfortunate Tommy lorry driver.

The method of road construction adopted was to lay on an approximately level prepared bed four or five lengthwise stringers, to which were spiked broad stout beams making a continuous decking. Rough planks at either side operated as wheel guards and held many a crazy side-slipping lorry on the uncertain way. Forward of Spree Farm the old road-line was abandoned altogether, and a new road bed was prepared through the shell holes to the foot of Gravenstafel Spur. Any length of bed that was prepared ahead of the decking invariably attracted some unfortunate mule driver forcing his way up to the forward guns with his few shells, and it was a common experience to have to excavate three or four bogged mules before going on with the roadway. As time wore on, the field guns got up by degrees, till the area anywhere near the road just behind Gravenstafel Spur was set thick with them, and their casualties must have been severe.

Heavier guns also essayed the passage, but few got past Spree Farm, and not many as far. Their struggle generally ended in setting up within a few yards of the roadside, and making the best of a poor situation. The shelling attracted by the increasing congestion of guns made actual work on the road a perpetual task, as the broken timbers consequent upon a direct hit were harder to remove and renew than they had been to lay in the first place. All stores of heavy ammunition brought forward had perforce to be dumped at the end of the road, where on several occasions German shells found them out, the result being great craters torn in the road bed, and the destruction of all in the vicinity. Corporal A. E. Gibb

Field Companies and Field Troop.

and Lance-Corporal G. H. Shelley were awarded the Military Medal for gallant conduct and devotion to duty during the progress of this work.

The difficulties and bitter discomfort experienced in the front area were faithfully reflected even in rear. Men paraded in wind and rain in the early dawn, trudged wearily over the broken wastes to a day's work in mud and slush, and returned later in more rain to flimsy bivouacs on open ground that was practically a pond, where they lay down in clothes and blankets that had not been dry for days. And then not to sleep save when exhausted Nature asserted herself. With the first watches of the night came the detestable penetrating double-stroke whirr of the large German bombing 'planes. The silver streak picked out on the dark countryside by the Canal served them well as a landmark, and not a night passed without several casualties among the occupants of the crowded camps along the banks. On the first evening spent in the locality Engineer transport lost five men and four horses; on another occasion a hutment occupied by 2nd Company officers had the roof blown off, fortunately with only one casualty. He was a highly philosophical or a very weary man who could rest peacefully with nothing between him and those prowling night birds but a sheet of tin or a waterproof sheet. So long as the brutes were in the sky, there was always a chance of trouble, and the tension was prolonged in a manner quite distinct from even heavy shell fire.

On the 6th, the New Zealand Infantry were relieved by the 49th Division, and passed back into reserve areas behind Ypres. The Engineers and Pioneers were left in the battle area, owing to the extreme necessity for the tracks and roads upon which they were engaged. Until the 11th they worked under the control of the 49th Division, whose G.O.C. called personally later at New Zealand Headquarters to express to the C.R.E. his appreciation of the work done for his Division.

During one particularly cold wet dawn the sappers found themselves alongside West Riding Pioneers, one of whom was none too clear as to their identity. "Say, choom!" said he to a gaunt New Zealander, "what do them letters N.Z.E. stand for?" "New Zealand Esquimaux!" was the expressive reply.

During the attack on the 9th the New Zealand Engineers had further opportunities for distinguished service, and several of them were recommended for immediate rewards by the G.O.C. 49th Division. Sapper J. K. Ramsay, of the 1st Company, in addition to fine work on road reconnaissance, volunteered to assist in bringing in a wounded officer of the

Passchendaele.

Y.L.I. and succeeded in his task despite heavy machine-gun fire. Corporal J. W. Duggan, 2nd Corporal W. D. McKinley, and Sapper J. Walker of the same Company, and Sapper H. McMillan from the 3rd, all showed outstanding qualities of courage and determination while engaged on roads and tracks. Each of them received the Military Medal.

By this time it had become a matter of serious question whether the attack should be gone on with. All prospect of achieving the original objects of the offensive had admittedly vanished. The extremely skilful disposition of the German defences, and the atrocious weather experienced, had proved to be obstacles against which unremitting effort and dauntless valour had alike been vain. It is no secret that the cessation of hostilities at this comparatively favourable stage was definitely contemplated. It is probable that those saddled with the responsibility of decision were forced to weigh many other issues beside that of purely military expediency; in any case it was decided to persevere.

The 9th of October was the date set for the next blow, and arrangements were even made for reserve troops to be brought up at short notice to press a possible German retreat. However, the weather continued unsuitable, no guns could advance, and finally the exploitation proposals were dropped in favour of a further deliberate attack on the 12th. For this second effort, the 49th Division, now about to take part in the assault on the 9th, would be again relieved by the New Zealanders. Unfortunately for themselves and all concerned, the 49th were able to make but little impression on the German defences confronting them, and by nightfall lay on the line of their first objective only. The 3rd and 4th Field Companies had been on hand to assist in consolidation, and in cleaning up captured pill boxes, but the German machine-guns on Bellevue Spur were so active that movement was impossible, and the Companies were recalled to repair tracks further in rear.

Although arrangements were considerably upset by this failure on the 9th, plans were nevertheless completed to carry on the attack on the 12th. The Second Army effort on this day was to be confined to New Zealand and Australian troops only, the objectives being the capture of Passchendaele Village and the Goudberg spur to the north.

On the 10th the New Zealand Infantry began to relieve the troops of the 49th Division, who were found badly disorganised by their recent failure, and in no position to supply any reliable information to the incoming battalions. Little

Field Companies and Field Troop.

assurance was needed of the grim fact that the enemy's wire entanglements and concrete shelters were practically intact. The evidence of patrols immediately sent out, supporting the results of direct observation from Gravenstafel, left no room for doubt as to the well-nigh impregnable positions in front, and confirmed the worst suspicions of the unfavourable nature of the country to be crossed. Under these conditions a postponement of the attack would have been welcomed till the wire at least had been dealt with, but Army orders had already gone forth and the die was cast. Under the circumstances there remained for each man but the grim determination to go forward and do his duty. Everything now depended on the measure of artillery support accorded. That this was fully realised by the artillerymen themselves was best evidenced by the superhuman efforts put forth to get the guns and ammunition forward. Unfortunately there are limits to human endeavour. Even the few guns that were pulled through the morass were forced to fire from unstable foundations, with trails sinking in the mud every few rounds, thus affecting alike the speed and accuracy of the shooting.

Low over all hung the leaden sky, with cold winds sweeping the forlorn wastes and a constant succession of bitter rain storms thrashing the Flemish swamps. In knee-deep mud on the night of the 11th the Infantry struggled forward to the assembly positions. Down in the swollen Ravebeek the whole of the 1st and 3rd Field Companies were busily constructing stream crossings, eight of which were completed during the evening. Covered with cocoanut matting, these ensured a firm-footed passage of the obstacle, and the attackers were lined up well on time. Later on, when the duckboard tracks were brought forward, the best of these crossings were converted into more or less permanent foot-bridges. In connection with this operation, 2nd Corporal A. A. Howard and Sapper J. Houston, both of 3rd Field Company, received well-merited awards of the Military Medal.

At 5.25 a.m. on the 12th the attack opened, but where was the heavy barrage that alone could have mended the fortunes of that stricken day? Practically unsupported, the infantry struggled across the lead-swept slopes with a pluck and devotion never surpassed in war, only to find as they came within striking distance of the foe that the way was barred with double belts of wide unbroken entanglements, against which both skill and fortitude could only beat in vain. Dozens of men deliberately sacrificed themselves in an endeavour to cut through by hand, some even reached the

Passchendaele.

second belt before they fell and hung among the pitiless wires; others rushed the few gaps left open, only to find a certain bullet from machine-guns carefully sited for that very purpose.

Not till every battalion involved had poured out its blood like water, and had strewn the stark slopes with swathes of gallant dead, were the few survivors forced to break off the impossible struggle. Where they failed, no men could have succeeded. It is questionable whether the authorities knew exactly how much they had asked. Exhausted men struggling through mud and water in pouring rain cannot well compete against a skilled enemy waiting in concrete shelters armed with machine-guns. But weather and machine-guns and lack of supporting artillery notwithstanding, the Boche could never have stopped them had the wire been cut. That impregnable barrier was the main cause of failure at Bellevue, as it had been the reason for almost every British failure since the Highlanders came to grief at Loos in 1915. No more need be said here of what was a bad day for New Zealand, save that no sense of chagrin or dissatisfaction with the results achieved could have equalled the anger and disappointment of the gallant survivors.

The sappers held ready for the usual consolidation duties following a successful advance were not to be called upon that day, and were at once thrown into the work of extending and improving communications, now even more important owing to the failure of the attack, with consequent slight disorganisation, and to the tremendous congestion of wounded men.

Bold reconnaissance of tracks, water, and dugout facilities, under exceptionally heavy fire, by 2nd Corporals G. H. Thorpe and F. G. Taylor, and Sappers J. W. McKay and A. Springall, all of the 3rd Company, brought each of them a Military Medal. Sapper F. Smyth of the same Company was also conspicuous on this occasion.

On the 13th, in company with every free man in the Division, the Engineers assisted to carry in the wounded. The regimental stretcher bearers were quite unable to cope with the terrible task; over some of the country six and eight men were required to carry out a single case to the ambulance at Spree Farm. To add to the difficulties, the outgoing 49th Division on the 10th had left the battlefield and Aid Posts strewn with their wounded, all of whom received succour and attention without distinction. Despite all efforts, dozens of wounded men were doomed to lie for hours and even days in

Field Companies and Field Troop.

the cold rain and hail, and many must have perished who might have been saved under more favourable conditions. It was afternoon on the 14th before all surviving wounded were finally clear of the battlefield. It is pleasant to be able to record that, in general, stretcher bearers were able to work right up to the wire entanglements without interference by the Germans, while such places as Waterloo Farm, where as many as 200 stretcher cases were massed at once, in full view of German observers, were free of hostile shell fire.

Back at Spree Farm, congestion of traffic was now attracting intense shelling with constant heavy damage to the road. For outstanding energy and bravery while engaged in this vicinity, Lance-Corporals D. McM. Fullarton and A. W. Danby and Sapper J. W. Garnett of the 1st Field Company were awarded the Military Medal. A similar distinction, awarded to Driver A. Johnstone for exceptional coolness and resource in the control of his team under concentrated shell fire, was timely recognition of the unobtrusive but none the less sterling work continually being performed by all transport drivers.

By this time stores were coming forward more freely, and a dump established at Spree Farm enabled better progress to to be made with the plank road, which 2nd Field Company were still advancing in the neighbourhood of Gravenstafel. But this improvement was too late to affect Divisional activities to any extent.

The construction of baths near the Dead End of the Canal by the 1st Field Company marked the first opportunity for attending to needs other than those of the immediate battle front, but those also were to serve the needs of other Divisions. On the 18th the Canadian Corps took over the sector, and on the 21st all Engineer works and dumps were handed over to 3rd Canadian Divisional Engineers. It is interesting to note that the front line handed over to the Canadians was in much the same position as the line occupied at the time of the German gas attack in the Second Battle of Ypres, when Canadian troops made such a gallant stand before being overwhelmed. Many of the Canadians were not in the line at the actual moment of the attack, but were rushed from Ypres to replace French colonial coloured troops, who had stampeded before the gas, and by all accounts were then half way to the coast.

C.R.E. Headquarters, 1st, 3rd and 4th Field Companies now entrained at Ypres and returned to the respective billets occupied in the Aa Valley before the battle, and there the remainder of the month passed in rest and light training operations; 2nd Company returned soon after to Morbecque and resumed its labours at the Corps School.

Passchendaele.

In common with all ranks of the Division, the horses of the various transport units had found the last few weeks sufficiently trying. Those belonging to the Field Companies were in very poor shape after the constant packing in the heavy mud, and stood in urgent need of the rest now given them. It may be noted that some horses are very much affected by shell fire. Many of those which happened to suffer actual injury, or only shock, from a too intimate acquaintance with a bursting shell, were never the same again. In some extreme cases, twitching limbs and other signs of collapse followed even the scream of a projectile passing overhead.

Three weeks operations by the redoubtable Canadians saw the fall of Passchendaele and the occupation of country which had been included in the objective set for the New Zealanders in one day.

And there one of the grimmest and bloodiest struggles of the whole war came to a conclusion. The British casualties had been enormous, and the results by contrast with the original aspirations poor in the extreme. The New Zealanders took consolation from the fact that their morale was not seriously impaired by the recent severe ordeal, and looked forward to another day with Fritz, when the chances of war should be on a more even footing.

CHAPTER XI.

WINTER IN YPRES.

For some three weeks the Field Companies occupied rear areas, engaged in light work of training and recreational sports. These last were run by a committee set up in each Company to organise amusements, both indoor and out, during the coming winter months. In due course, on the 12th November, came the call to move. By the 17th, after the usual temporary stoppages en route, C.R.E. Headquarters with 1st, 3rd, and 4th Companies, were established round and about Chateau Segard Camp between Ypres and Dickebusch. A week later the 2nd Company relinquished Corps work at Morbecque and moved up into billets in the ramparts of Ypres near the Lille Gate. The 3rd and 4th Companies joined it in the same locality on the 25th, and 1st Company moved at the same time to Belgian Battery Corner in the vicinity of Kruisstraat, south-west of Ypres. Corps was now taking over from 1st Anzac in the area south of the Ypres-Roulers railway. The portion of the Corps front to be occupied by the New Zealand Division, known as the Becelaere sector, lay immediately in front of the famous Polygon Wood, so called from its shape lying between four bounding roads, and extended from the ruins of the hamlet of Molenaarelsthoek generally south-westward towards the sinister Menin Road. Enveloping part of Reutel, our line fell away into the marshy valley of the Polygonebeek, flowing from Polygon Wood to join the Reutelbeek in the German Lines; thence, mounting the easy slopes crowned by Cameron Covert, it fell again into the Reutelbeek, and rose once more across the base of a high tongue of land on which stood Polderhoek Chateau. Our responsibility ceased at the Reutelbeek. The Chateau had been taken by the Australians on 4th October, but was recaptured by the enemy shortly after, and owing to its extensive command over a large portion of our front line system, became the objective of a local Divisional attack some time later. Half a mile behind the front line, and towards the northern boundary of the Divisional area, stood a high artificial mound known as the Butte de Polygon. Popular opinion in the Division could not be induced to regard this as anything but a grandstand for the racecourse visible amid the remains of Polygon Wood lying south-west of it. In reality the mound had been constructed to facilitate the musketry training of the Belgian soldiers

Sergt. Samuel Forsyth, V.C.

Winter in Ypres.

formerly quartered in Ypres barracks. It was now a maze of underground tunnels and shelters, constructed by the Germans, and used as Brigade and Battalion Headquarters for our garrison in line. Further back towards Ypres the smaller woods of Glencorse and Nonnebischen were separated from the Westhoek ridge by a low-lying area drained by sister branches of that same Hanebeek crossed at Gravenstafel. South of Westhoek, at about the same elevation, lay Clapham Junction on the Menin Road just in front of Hooge. From the Junction an old road led directly into our right sector past Black Watch Corner.

Behind Westhoek again nothing broke the level expanse of repellent desolation till the eye rested on the walls of Ypres. The remains of the glorious tower of the famous Cloth Hall still rose proudly over the shattered remnants of the ancient and mighty city, which had formerly boasted its own trained soldiery, and had once defied the passage of an English army in the good old days when English kings were wont to make periodic forays on their Continental neighbours.

Surrounded by a deep moat, the sturdy ramparts, monuments to the 17th century genius of Vauban, still stood largely intact. Three main gates pierced the walls, the Lille Gate, the Dixmude Gate, and the Menin Gate; the last leading out eastward along that Via Dolorosa, the Menin Road, by which so many British soldiers had passed to return no more.

With temporary modification in the disposal of working sections, Lille Gate remained the virtual centre of Engineering activities during the coming winter, especially when the C.R.E. occupied quarters later on in the same locality. In course of time the homes under the ramparts became extremely comfortable. Every shelter, from little one-man cuddies to elaborate excavations holding 40 men, had bunks and a stove, and later many of them were lit electrically from the Corps system. The broken remnants of the former buildings supplied plenty of fuel.

No written words could ever convey a true sense of the awful state of this last poor corner of unconquered Belgium. Former roads, hedgerows, farmhouses, all had long since disappeared, no green leaf appeared on the broken tree stumps, not a bird disturbed the silence of outraged nature. The very streamlets had ceased to flow, and were merely a succession of festering shell-churned pools choked with the poisoned remains of dead mules. Miles of such transport roads as existed about Westhoek were piled high on either side for their whole length with the shattered remains of every con-

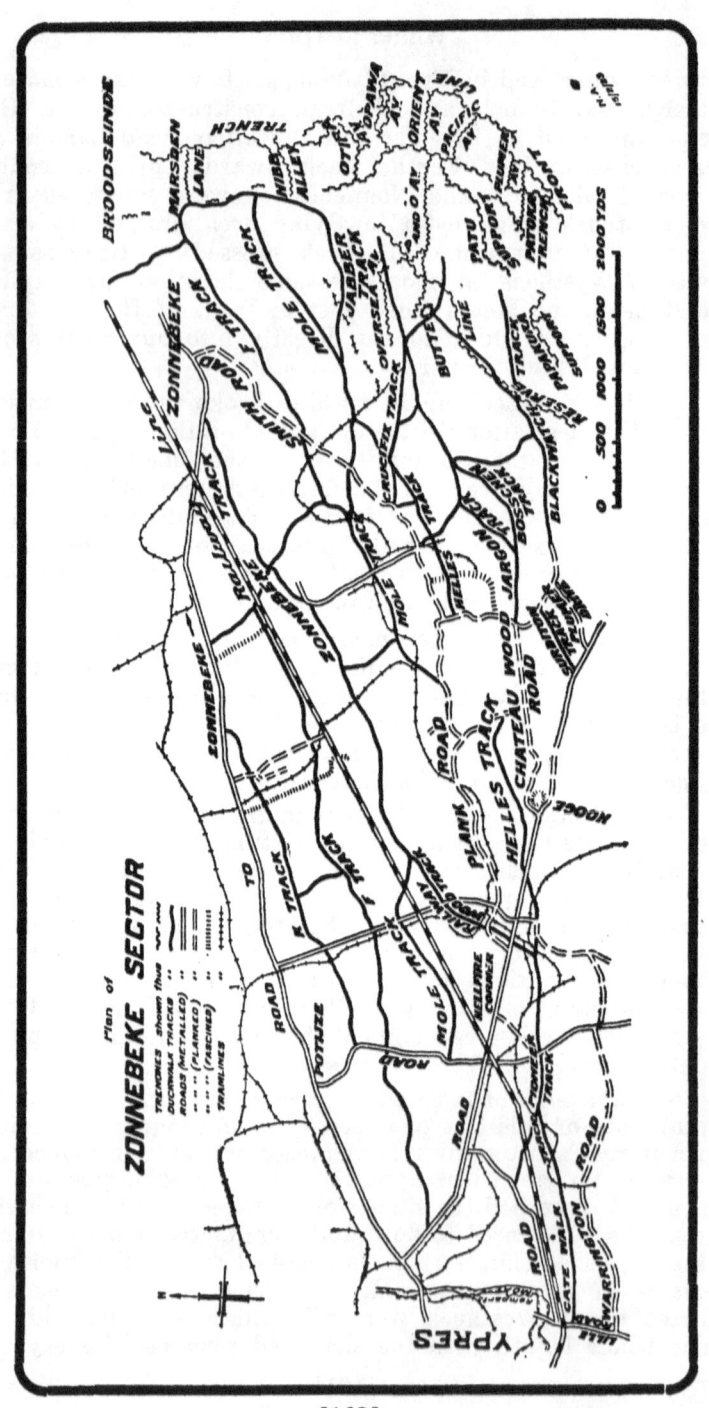

Winter in Ypres.

ceivable article used in war. And over all the sickening stench of death in many forms, perhaps buried only to be thrown once more abroad by the unrelenting shells.

The front line area when taken over consisted largely of the scattered posts and unconnected lengths of local trenches inseparable from the changing fortunes of the recent severe fighting. The enemy was still well entrenched, with adequate artillery in position, and plenty of ground suitable for hidden assembly. Vigorous measures were at once taken therefore to build suitable systems of trenches and wire entanglements, capable of ensuring a successful defence against any hostile enterprise that might be in view.

Three lines of trenches were now to be constructed. In the meantime, the first would still remain a system of posts in selected shell holes, to be joined up later; the second, or support line, was to be a continuous trench, with fortified localities covering the gaps in front; while the third would be maintained as a reserve position, gradually equipped with shelters and conveniences impossible further forward.

Decent communications were again a prime consideration, from motives both of travel and supply. One of the sappers' first jobs was the re-laying, straightening, and extension of all duckboard tracks. These were taken in hand right from Ypres forward, though the principal work in the way of new construction naturally lay in front of Westhoek. The importance of other trench work, and the shortage of material, combined to force a decision not to dig communication saps in the meantime anywhere short of the immediate front. Overland tracks had to suffice elsewhere, with alternative routes for use in case of heavy bombardment. In the course of time it was hoped to sink the tracks, and thus provide them with at least splinter proof cover in the shape of earthen side walls. For some weeks, while the ground remained like a muddy sponge, enemy shells buried themselves deeply before explosion, resulting in very local effect, and the side walls were not particularly required. Later on, when the frosts laid an iron crust over the whole countryside, shells exploded instantly and sent their jagged splinters in all directions, causing casualties even 200 yards away. Once forward of Glencorse Wood and the crossing of the Hanebeek, an unsavoury spot known as Dead Mule Gully for obvious reasons, all movement came under direct observation from Polderhoek Chateau, whence the German garrison was never slow to enliven the traveller with a burst of fire. All forward track work was accordingly done at night, still with numerous

Field Companies and Field Troop.

delays and inevitable casualties due to the constant spray of machine-gun bullets.

During the whole of December, the laying of new forward tracks and the maintenance of existing ones went on without a break. Ultimately, this sector was probably better supplied with overland trails than any other in which the Division operated. "F" track in the left sector, for example, ran without a break from just outside the Menin Gate right through to the front line on the ridge at Broodseinde. Similarly one could travel direct from the Lille Gate to Reutel in the right sector, though the track went by various names at different stages of the journey. The last stretch on Black Watch Track, with Polderhoek so close that the Boche could almost see if one's boots were clean or not, was a journey to be undertaken swiftly, and large parties of fellow travellers were to be avoided. In addition to the main through lines, cross trails ran wherever there was any necessity for lateral communication. So numerous did the tracks become, that a complete survey was made by the 2nd and 4th Field Companies in order to place them all correctly on the map for the information and use of Divisional Headquarters. The provision of authentic direction boards at all doubtful points was a considerable job in itself.

Already on the 3rd December, the constant annoyance suffered from the machine-gunners of Polderhoek Chateau had inspired a special attack on their stronghold by two battalions of the 2nd Brigade. The Chateau was really opposite the area occupied by the IX Corps, but, if a desire to see it put out of action was any criterion, there was no doubt as to which Division should have the honour of making the attempt. Heavy bombardments were laid on the easy target for several days before the assault, and clouds of red brick dust testified to accurate shooting, but apparently no serious damage was being done to the well-protected personnel. The 3rd Field Company sent up parties from reserve, who laid special tracks through the neighbouring Corps area to the selected assembly positions. On the day of assault, a heavy weight of artillery supported the direct attack, and also endeavoured to neutralise enfilade fire from the German supports, but all to no purpose. The garrison was very much on the alert, and a storm of machine-gun bullets completely baffled the storming troops. Insufficient training and the marked preponderance of inexperienced reinforcements among the companies were considered to be the causes of failure. Thereafter Polderhoek remained in German hands, a perpetual irritation to all and sundry.

Winter in Ypres.

The Field Companies were now disposed as follows:—2nd on Right Brigade sector, 4th on Left Brigade sector, and 3rd on Reserve area works, while the 1st Company, after a week or so spent in the forward area, was now employed on works for II Anzac Corps. To each of the three Companies on Divisional work was allotted the now usual special infantry working party of 100 men. Three small reinforcement drafts also arrived during the month.

Owing to the pronounced hiatus in our front line caused by the valley of Polygonebeek, and to the constant menace of a flank attack from Polderhoek Chateau should the weather harden, the distribution of Brigades in line after early December was a little contrary to usual practice. The length of line was divided into Brigade sectors as usual, but one held the southern sub-sector between the Polygonebeek and the Reutelbeek with only one battalion in line, whereas the Brigade to the north was forced to employ three battalions in line to garrison its long stretch. The 4th Field Company, operating on the northern sub-sector, was hard pressed to cope with all the demands upon its services entailed by the large area in its care.

Corporal A. C. Ford and 2nd-Corporal J. S. Strawbridge of this Company came under official notice here for their personal courage and resource, and for determination in rallying working parties dispersed by heavy shell fire.

Though the immediate provision of proper tracks had been made an urgent work in the new sector, work on the trench systems had been no less energetically carried on. The positions of both support and reserve lines had been traced out by the Engineers in the first few days of the occupation, and strong working parties were busy every night, digging and draining, while duck-boarding and revetting followed as fast as time and material allowed. Drainage as a general thing presented no difficulties in the 2nd Company sector, save that of labour. The small gullies already mentioned were easily utilised to dispose of surplus water. In the left sector, the 4th Company was not so fortunate, and drainage problems caused much greater expenditure of energy. The front line, except in the area in front of Cameron Covert, where the marshes of the Reutelbeek caused a stretch of untenable ground half a mile wide, was quickly in process of conversion from its original state of detached shell holes into a continuous line. Here also the work of the garrison was assisted by the proximity of several small depressions falling away towards the front, without which their efforts to ensure

Field Companies and Field Troop.

a dry trench would have been largely abortive. The gap caused by the Reutelbeek itself was well covered by the strong position of the well-wired support line on the high ground behind it. The names given to the new trenches, such as Papakura Support, Patoka Trench, Papanui Switch, had a pleasant and familiar ring to New Zealand ears after such atrocities as Molenaarelsthoek or Polygonebeek. As soon as the defensive trenches in support and reserve lines showed signs of definite progress, sections of the Field Companies were put on to revet, to build fire bays, to lay duckboards, and particularly to establish well-wired fortified "localities" on suitable positions.

The Light Railway and tramway systems were steadily creeping forward all the time. Sidings were put in by the sappers at Wattle and Crucifix Dumps, and material commenced to come forward, though never in sufficient quantity. Concentration of traffic round these dumps was very soon marked by the enemy, who shelled them heavily and repeatedly. On Boxing Day Wattle Dump was treated to a particularly violent burst which killed and wounded several men of a working party and disorganised the remainder. Corporal A. R. Penman of the 4th Field Company showed fine courage and contempt of personal danger in attending to the wounded under fire, and was awarded a Military Medal.

A vast amount of the work going on both in front and support lines was being executed with material salvaged from the old German lines. Great hauls were made in the neighbourhood of Glencorse Wood, where a special dump was established at the rear end of Black Watch Track. This was also fed by wheeled transport from Clapham Junction, or from Hooge by Chateau Wood Road. The latter enjoyed a particularly sinister reputation with all transport drivers, and the number of derelict waggons and dead mules piled on either side of it seemed to lend some colour to their statements. The Field Companies' drivers were up at the furthest limit of possible wheeled activity every night in an effort to keep pace with the demands for material, both special and general.

Anything brought forward by them was drawn from a large main dump on the Menin Road at Birr Cross Roads, through which ran the Light Railway from Ypres which ultimately served Wattle and Crucifix Dumps. All night, at uncertain intervals, but especially just before dawn, when the general need for retirement before daylight caused a slight congestion of traffic, the enemy lashed all roads vigorously with shrapnel and H.E.

Winter in Ypres.

In general, Engineer transport was extremely fortunate, but on the 3rd of January, the 2nd Company teams were caught in a fierce bombardment on the Westhoek Road. Several shells dropped right among the horses, killing and wounding several. Three drivers were also severely wounded. 2nd-Corporal F. G. Gleeson, who was in charge of the party, exhibited great coolness and gallantry under heavy fire in extricating the remainder of his horses and waggons, thus obviating a block on the road which would inevitably have caused further serious losses. One of his loading party, Rifleman W. E. Hallam, assisted him in his dangerous work, and stood by the wounded though run over by a passing waggon. Both men received the Military Medal.

It was on this same road a week or two later that Lance-Corporal H. Fake of the 2nd Company earned a Military Medal under similar conditions. The road was badly damaged and impassable and still under heavy shelling. Ambulances with wounded men were portion of the held-up traffic. Fake was the mainstay of the repair gang who mended the gap, under fire, and he thoroughly deserved the reward which followed.

Following hard on the provision of trenches and tracks came the question of wire entanglements. In many places it was quite possible to pass between posts on a dark night and wander into the opposing lines. Stray Germans, by accident or design, achieved the performance regularly. It was inadvisable to wait till the work could be undertaken in force on an organised footing. Any considerable advance by the opposing armies here in front of Westhoek would also have entailed the immediate vacation of our recent hard-won gains about Passchendaele. Both catastrophes were to occur with the German drive in the coming spring, but for the moment we were in possession and intended to remain so. And night after night the wiring parties were out among the shellholes, till the protecting "aprons" lay right across the front.

For the more intimate control of this and other problems in actual front line defence, small parties from both 2nd and 4th Field Companies were permanently stationed at the Butte to assist the efforts of the garrison in a technical capacity. The working and carrying parties sent forward each evening by the rear battalions had a particularly long, trying journey in country little known at first to most of them, and were wont to arrive at Crucifix Dump, near the Butte, in a pretty fatigued condition. They had then to be guided over another waste to the scene of the evening's employment, cheered on by

Field Companies and Field Troop.

frequent bursts of fire from the accursed Polderhoek Chateau half a mile to the southward. Constant attention from that quarter was a certainty, whatever the luck of the night in the way of ordinary shelling.

Proper daylight exploration of the ground by the Engineers was an utter impossibility. A little reconnaissance work could be effected by moving about the few existing trenches or crawling among the crowded shell holes. Even that was done at imminent risk from snipers. Most of the day was taken up in that manner and by investigation of the drainage possibilities of the area. As soon as the dusk made movement possible, new drains and barbed-wire lines were sited and marked out before the little parties hastened back to the Butte to act as guides to the arriving working parties. When these would arrive no man knew, and dawn was often close at hand ere the night's work was complete.

The enemy was quick to note the increasing lines of wire. Ranging on them accurately with artillery by day, he not only caused immediate damage, but was able to ensure considerable casualty amongst the workers in the evening. His machine-gunners needed no ranging, they could sweep the whole line near Reutel without any trouble whatever. And wherever the two or three small gullies of the sector afforded some extent of dead ground, the time of the year and the continued heavy shelling had combined to form a wide and treacherous morass, though this particular aspect of affairs was not entirely unfavourable. The extensive marshes caused by the overflowing Reutelbeek and Polygonebeek south of Cameron Covert formed an impassable barrier to any German attack from that quarter, and before the frosts ensured a firm passage wire entanglements were in position.

The principle of barbed-wire entanglements used as a protective measure in war was known long before 1914, but, as with every other warlike device and expedient, new ideas were constantly evolved and put into practice as the long struggle drew on. By 1917, though the wide belts of stout stakes laced and interlaced with random coils of wire were still in use in their proper setting, there was only one type of wiring used to any extent when rapidity of construction was the principal consideration. This was technically known as "double-apron," and the more usual term of "rapid wiring" always meant that type of construction. In addition to wire, the only materials involved were screw pickets, long and short. These were steel rods, about half an inch in diameter, shaped exactly like a corkscrew, with a small loop at the top of the shaft, and smaller eyelets or loops formed by a twist in the

Winter in Ypres.

rod at intervals of about a foot down the shaft. Penetration of hard or frozen ground was assisted by means of the sharp point on the screw's end. The pickets were screwed into the ground by the aid of a short stick placed through the loop on top acting like the handle of a corkscrew. The handle of the infantryman's entrenching tool was ideal for this purpose. In position, the long shaft stood some 4 feet out of the ground, while the buried screw end was sunk about 18 inches. A line of these driven 6 to 8 feet apart formed the main basis of the "fence." Six feet away, both in front and rear and situated opposite the gaps between these main uprights, were placed lines of short pickets, screwed 18 inches with only the steel loop and a projecting spike left above ground.

Several leads of wire were then run out along the fence, again by means of the entrenching handle thrust through the centre of each coil, one man to a lead. Some three or four strands were secured continuously from post to post by means of the eyelets noted; others were woven diagonally from the eyelets on the long pickets down to the loops on the short, and back to the next long one, and so on. Following the diagonal bracing, continuous lines were again run lengthwise from diagonal to diagonal. Contact was secured where no eyelets existed by a twist with the invaluable entrenching handle. Wiring gloves and cutters were an item of supply, but were never much in evidence. This type of construction was soon reduced to a definite drill movement, involving 10 or 12 men to a party, and for speed and utility far surpassed any other known method.

Further protection could be arranged by the erection of additional lines behind the first. Occasionally "single apron" only was employed; the name explains itself. One great advantage attached to the use of the double-apron system was that any experienced sapper, knowing the extent of his proposed job, could estimate beforehand exactly how much material would be required for its performance.

The belts of wire put up in the support and reserve line areas were erected by special sections of the 2nd and 4th Field Companies, aided by working parties, and were distinct from purely front line work done by garrisons with the assistance of the small parties lodged in the Butte. The rear lines of wire were not arranged uniformly in lines straight across the front, but were sited to take full advantage of the marshy streams and gullies, to help to break up and deflect the line of advancing enemy parties, and to prevent them from making use of any dead ground. Defensive machine-gun positions were chosen to accord as far as possible with this idea.

Field Companies and Field Troop.

Several other types of wire entanglement were in occasional use, either in the absence of "double-apron" material, or used in conjunction therewith. "French wire" or "gooseberries," made of plain wire, and concertina wire, using the barbed species, both depended on the idea of hasty balls of wire rolled loose and laid in rows, staked down with pickets, and connected right along the tops with a horizontal wire, and protected again by a low trip wire in front. These were more effective when used between two fences of double-apron than when relied upon alone.

Low wire entanglement consisted of a series of rows of pickets, about 2ft. 6in. high, with horizontal and diagonal wires tightly strung from picket to picket, and coils of loose wire thrown into each bay. This system required to be at least 30 feet in width, and, though less conspicuous than any other type of wire erection, was very difficult to handle at night. It was seldom used in France.

Shelter was very unsatisfactory in the first weeks of the Divisional occupation. To begin with, there had been none existent, and though small parties were put on the work at once, very slow progress was made owing to lack of material. A few small steel shelters were established in support and reserve lines, but they were very few. One section of the 2nd Company was detailed to assist the N.Z. Artillery with O. Pips and shelter for the forward gun crews, but here, again, the material was sadly to seek.

Such German pill boxes as existed had all been cleaned, pumped out, and fitted up for our own use, but Dressing Stations and various Headquarters commandeered the great majority of them. Where a concrete dugout had been acquired by ordinary troops, there were so many aspirants for a corner that a man was almost as comfortable in the holes cut in the bank of the open trench, lined with a waterproof sheet and covered with a sheet of iron, which were fair samples of the general accommodation available about Reutel during this winter. All pill boxes by whomsoever occupied were well wired to act as Strong Points in case of enemy attack.

The 3rd Field Company in the reserve area had more opportunity as regards material, but the calls made on its services were necessarily many and urgent. Several new camps were built complete. One, consisting of 40 huts to hold a battalion, was erected outside Lille Gate in a trifle over three weeks.

The baths at Cafe Belge were in great need of attention and were put in good working order, and new baths were

Winter in Ypres.

erected at Birr Cross Roads. Horse-standings were again in strong demand, as were new stables. The same strict regulations existed here with regard to the removal of broken brick, of which thousands of tons lay piled about the ruins of Ypres. Probably the same regrettable breaches of the regulations were committed by thoughtless and energetic gentlemen with horses standing in 12 inches of mud. Such notices as "Bricks must not be removed without authority" are proverbially subject to destruction by enemy gun fire.

Christmas Day was spent as a holiday as far as possible. By the end of the year, a pleasing transformation had been effected in the Divisional area. The trench systems, of course, still required much attention, but the fact that three lines of trenches actually existed where none had lain before was fair ground for satisfaction; and in addition, several new avenues and short switches materially strengthened the general position. The front line was practically wired throughout, and before support and reserve lines the protecting screens of "double-apron" were well in hand. The former shell holes of the front line were now a continuous trench, and good progress had been made with fire-bays, revetting, and drainage. Several "localities" both in front and support lines lay ready to dispute the passage with any hostile invader. The work had all been carried out under adverse conditions, both as regards weather and enemy shelling. The frosts and snows experienced all through December made occupation of the trenches a comfortless and fatiguing duty, and materially increased the labours of all working parties.

One section of the 3rd Company was detailed for work among the camps round Dickebusch, a particularly low-lying and cheerless locality south-west of Ypres, where the few scattered civilians seemed to be constitutionally affected by their surroundings. Here they used broken brick by the ton, but without much effect on the oceans of slush existing everywhere. A sapper, who had made commendable progress in acquiring a knowledge of the French language, for military purposes only of course, was one day engaged in sweet dalliance with a maiden of the country near Ouderdom; how romance clings to the very name! Their artless prattle had reached the critical stage, as the warrior was due on a working party that evening., "Well, where do you go on Sundays?" he inquired. "Oh, Sunday is our day of amusement. I go to see my friends on Sundays," she replied. "Ah! Yes! but where?" persisted the ardent wooer. "Dickebusch!" she murmured.

Field Companies and Field Troop.

"Dickebusch!" echoed the gallant lover, relapsing into his native tongue with a crash. "Well, I'll be ——!" All was over.

Corps policy, by mid December, under pressure of the unwelcome fact that the enemy now enjoyed numerical preponderance on the Western Front, was definitely committed to defence. This was the first occasion in France on which the New Zealand Division had been committed to a passive role, and the unusual proceeding was as a fleeting breath of disquietude before the storm of the desperate German drive in the following spring. All defensive works were to be enlarged and strengthened, and necessary amendments, if any, made to conform with the expectation of a determined enemy attack in large numbers. A Corps line of resistance well in rear of the front area, which had previously existed only on paper, now took definite shape, and effectively absorbed the energies of all labour that could be spared from the forward lines.

Early January was still very cold. A mantle of snow somewhat alleviated the unredeemed ugliness of the devastated landscape, but ere long the good progress noted on the tracks and trenches "in front" received a decided set-back. With the thaw about the middle of the month came the usual collapse of all unsustained earthwork, with its natural sequence in blocked drains and flooded trenches: salutary evidence that the sappers' insistence on berms and slopes in all trench construction was not entirely due to technical idiosyncrasy. The energies which the Field Companies had begun to divert from purely trench and track works to the improvement of accommodation were transferred back again. Great efforts were necessary to keep the trenches inhabitable at all. Fortunately material was now brought up as far as Crucifix Dump at the Butte by Light Railway, and supplies were much more plentiful. "A" frames and revetting hurdles were used in numbers reminiscent of old times, and by concentration on the "localities" and selected positions, some improvement was effected in the lot of the unfortunate garrisons.

A gum-boot store and drying shed became a necessity. Quite an extensive institution was erected by the 2nd Company at Westhoek, boasting a store, two drying rooms, a room each for issue and for changing boots, and—not the least of its many attractions—a free coffee stall, run by the ubiquitous Y.M.C.A. Despite camphor treatment and all precautions, "trench feet" were becoming common, and the gum-boots arrived none too soon. The water literally poured down some of the trenches, and in one stretch 800 yards were silted up.

Winter in Ypres.

Even back in Ypres life was not entirely free from the uncertainties of the season. Some enterprising sappers of the 4th Company, who had built themselves a home on one of the small islands at the edge of the frozen moat, awoke one morning to find themselves cut off by deep and perilous waters. However, their rescue afforded the pontoons a Heaven-sent opportunity of vindicating their right to be regarded as essential munitions of war. The Ypres Moat was still inhabited by a pair of beautiful white swans, which had survived all the piled misfortunes of this unhappy city. Their safety and rights as original inhabitants were guarded by an Army order, and they were still there late in 1918, and may even yet be paddling round lamenting the absence of the stir of bygone days.

Tram lines and tracks suffered along with the trenches from the break in the frosty weather. In many places they had been unavoidably constructed over filled-in shell holes, which, subsiding with the thaw, upset all calculations as to grades and security. Most of the forward tram lines were ultimately provided with duckboards. No amount of official displeasure was sufficient to keep pedestrians from utilising the tram track as a highway, hence to guard against complete removal of all ballasting on the boots of the trespassers, duckboards were laid between the rails, and "no thoroughfare" restrictions were removed.

By February, weather conditions took an improved turn, and the work of steadily improving the Divisional sector went on with increased speed. Accommodation schemes were again revived. Gas proofing of all important shelters and of the deep concrete dugouts and dressing stations at Hooge and Birr Cross Roads had been carried out long since. The Butte was finally put out of commission as a shelter by a gas bombardment on the evening of 18th-19th February. In common with all other well-used points of the front area, it had successfully weathered many previous bombardments with gas shells. On this occasion the usual precautions were at once taken, and the night passed without casualty. Next morning, however, when the heat of the sun commenced to thaw the frozen ground, polluted air rose all round and gradually filled the Butte before it was noticed. Every man of the two Headquarters in residence was evacuated, more or less poisoned. Since no serious results finally eventuated, the incident caused little unhappiness to the battalions in line, who still cherished memories of a severe "strafe" delivered a few evenings earlier on the subject of laxity in the matter of precautions taken against gas attacks.

Field Companies and Field Troop.

Great activity in Artillery circles had necessarily prevailed following the decision to adopt a defensive policy on the British Front. Since the New Year the 2nd Field Company had kept men constantly at the disposal of the N.Z. Artillery, who were now fairly well equipped with all "O Pips" and gun positions necessary to their work.

In rear areas, the 1st Field Company in reserve was completely engaged in the extensive Heavy Artillery preparations occasioned by the new policy. Not only was each battery on the front to be provided with a well-equipped permanent position, but, in the case of the heavy guns, reserve positions also were constructed in rear, in case adverse attack should render the idea of permanence illusory. These artillery positions were made a very urgent charge, and to a permanent party of attached infantry, aided by 50 men from artillery brigades, was added an additional 400 men from the Reserve battalion giving the 1st Field Company a daily labour strength of 1500 men. In a single fortnight nearly 800 truckloads of material were used, including fascines, sleepers, concrete slabs and blocks, cement, shingle, sand, reinforcing rods, sandbags, duckboards, and iron shelters. To these were added the daily loads of all available Company transport, while a small force of Corps lorries and waggons was called in to transport the various parties to the scattered scenes of their labours. The digging of pits and approach roads thereto, even the heavy plank platforms of the gun mountings, were matters of no great intricacy. The shelters for crews and battery command posts took longer. The latter in particular were of concrete and secure against ordinary shelling.

In some instances captured pill boxes were utilised, in which case the former rear walls and overhead cover were increased to a thickness of 5ft. 6in. In other cases new concrete dugouts were built, with requisite reinforcement. A special forge and smithy were established to handle the necessary work. Observation posts were not forgotten. On completion of the work, the Company enjoyed the hearty commendation of both Army and Corps Commanders.

Many of the Heavy Artillery brigades had a number of West Indian Bermudans on their strength, who acted more or less as general labourers, handling the heavy shells and digging pits. Each man was as black as the proverbial coal, and not altogether a Georges Carpentier as regards facial contour. Several of them were going homewards one evening, when a mixed party of New Zealanders and Australians loomed up out of the fog. "Hullo," cried one New Zealander, "here

Winter in Ypres.

come some more Aussies!" "Oh no, Sir!" replied the leading darkie, "we are all New Zealanders!"

On the 8th February, owing to an extension of the Corps front Northward, the 2nd Field Company took over work in the Zonnebeek sub-sector from 66th Divisional Engineers. Tracks here were in a very poor state and totally unprovided with notice boards. In addition to the improvement of these defects, work was along the usual routine lines till the relief shortly afterwards.

On 23rd February, all work in the Divisional area was handed over to the R.E. companies of the 49th Division. The 2nd and 3rd Field Companies were relieved by 456th and 458th Field Companies, while the 57th Field Company replaced the 4th Field Company.

On the 7th February, owing to the steady thinning of the Divisional ranks, the 4th Brigade, as such, had ceased to exist. With its disestablishment died the hopes of the 4th Field Company, which was now earmarked for reinforcement to the other three companies until the passage of time brought about its final absorption. For some weeks, however, the Company remained as a complete unit, working on the Corps defence line. A further step towards dissolution came on 21st March, when the Company ranks and equipment were liberally drawn upon to supply deficiencies in the other three Companies prior to their move southward. The depleted Company was then attached as Engineer unit to the New Zealand Entrenching Group, composed of surplus infantry units from 4th Brigade, with whom it worked until the passage of time finally brought about its complete absorption in the three older Companies.

The 4th Company had enjoyed only 10 months of existence as a complete unit, but during that time had borne a full share of the fortunes of war, and had grown into a first-class Company, with the happy experience that increasing efficiency had kept pace with a steady growth of esprit de corps and mutual friendship and respect among all ranks.

On relinquishing work in the front line area, the whole strength of the N.Z. Engineers, with the exception of the 2nd Field Company, was employed on the Corps defence system. Their work consisted almost entirely of constructing concrete dugouts and erecting barbed-wire entanglements. Everything could be done in daylight, with the added advantage that Corps jobs had first call on any facilities in existence, such as light railways and extra motor lorries. Material was always on hand in requisite quantities, and the working

Field Companies and Field Troop.

parties rode to and from their work on the railway tracks in most unusual comfort. Over 1500 tons of concrete were used on this job.

The 1st Brigade now remained in the area for work on the same Corps line. The 2nd Brigade entrained at Ypres on 23rd February, and proceeded to the Corps reserve area round about Staple, a small village west of Hazebrouck. With it went the 2nd Field Company, which was finally located near Hondeghem. All ranks now in the rest area had passed some strenuous weeks in the notorious Salient, and the good quarters and fine weather experienced heightened the sense of freedom and relief. Each morning was devoted to various training exercises and to lectures, but in the afternoon, sports, cross-country running and football held sway with at least an equal expenditure of energy and ardour.

On the 15th March, the 2nd and 3rd Field Companies exchanged areas and duties. Ever since Christmas, an invariable accompaniment of all clear frosty nights round Ypres had been the ominous drone of the German Gothas, punctuated by the vicious cracks of their exploding bombs. Apart from the inevitable uneasiness caused in crowded open camps and horse lines, the amount of damage done was inconsiderable when compared with the experience of the autumn. The majority of the sappers were housed in the ramparts, and no casualties were sustained, though several bombs fell among the unprotected shacks that ultimately congregated round the Lille Gate. A Y.M.C.A. hut, built mostly of tarred paper, survived without a scratch. Divisional Baths, a bare hundred yards away, were temporarily closed down on several occasions. But new and, if possible, more unwelcome agents of destruction made their appearance in January and both then and in March caused heavy damage in many forms. These were the long-range high velocity guns, thought to have been borrowed from the German Navy, which certainly at that time can have had singularly little use for them.

The 2nd Company had returned from rest areas only four days when the transport lines came in for their share of the attentions bestowed on back areas by the naval gunners. Eleven horses were killed outright, and twelve others seriously wounded, fortunately without injury to transport personnel.

The weather had remained exceptionally good ever since withdrawal from the front trenches, and work on the Corps line, no less than the training at Hondeghem, went on smoothly under almost ideal conditions. But not for long were the

Lieut. Colonel L. M. Sheera, C.B.E., M.C.

Winter in Ypres.

Companies to be left in enjoyment of these peaceful occupations. Ominous rumours began to creep up from the South. Ere long these gave place to the grim certainty that the expected German attack had broken out on the Somme, and that Ludendorff's hordes, pressing forward vigorously in great numbers, were meeting with quite unexpected success.

Day by day a further substantial advance was credited to the enemy. He was nearing Flers and Guedecourt. When and where would he be stopped? This matter assumed an intensely personal significance with the New Zealanders, and as a means of putting an extra finish on the great increase in health, morale, and fighting form due to the recent rest and relief from the strains of the severe winter, could hardly have been excelled. That territory so intimately bound up with the grim experiences of their first great effort on the battlefields of France, captured from the enemy in close fight after so many weary days, and soaked with the blood of such numbers of their bravest and best, should fall back into German hands like this, practically without a struggle, seemed almost an unconsidered trifle in a daily advance. The whole idea was preposterous. But Flers was left far behind, and still the relentless march rolled on. On the 21st March, instructions to be ready for the road at short notice reached all units of the Division. The 1st, 2nd, and 3rd Field Companies profited by the warning to bring their establishments up to full strength in men, material, and horseflesh by drawing on the now finally doomed 4th or Reinforcement Company. 23rd March saw the 1st and 2nd Companies at Ouderdom, handy to the railhead. By the afternoon of the 24th advance parties of the Divisional units, including C.R.E.'s Headquarters, had said good-bye to Flanders flats for ever, and a steady succession of troop trains was pulling out from Hazebrouck, Caestre, and Hopoutre near Poperinghe. The usual practice of sending Engineer transport by road was abandoned this time, and after some strenuous loading of horses and vehicles, the 1st and 2nd Companies left Hopoutre on the 25th. The 3rd Company marched from the rest area to Caestre, and entrained there on the same day. No announcements were made as to destination; none were required.

CHAPTER XII.

GERMAN OFFENSIVE, 1918.

It is not to be assumed that the success attending the opening stages of the German drive in March, 1918, was due to the fact that the Allies had not foreseen that such an attack was practically a certainty, or that they had taken no steps to withstand the onslaught when it should eventuate. As early as the previous December the inevitable result of the Russian collapse in reinforcing the German Divisions on the Western Front with hundreds of fresh battalions had caused a definite change of Allied policy from attack to defence. It was fully realised that, until the arrival of the American Armies, the initiative must pass once more to the enemy, and that the German War Lords were not the men to neglect any means of improving their unexpected opportunity.

That Ludendorff would strike hard and strike soon was a foregone conclusion; where the blow would fall was the unknown crux of the situation. The point of junction of the French and British Armies on the Cambrai front, though by no means the only spot suitable for attack, seemed to present the most attractive possibilities for the definite success so essential to the "strong peace" overtures which would assuredly follow from the time-pressed leaders of the Central States. British military opinion determined on Cambrai as the most probable danger point, but was equally decided that a temporary loss of ground there was fraught with less serious possibilities than at Ypres or at any other point of the British line likely to be selected by the enemy. The whole front was in progress of energetic fortification, but in view of the foregoing conclusion the Cambrai area was not especially strengthened until February, either by material means or by large reserves of troops.

Three defensive zones were contemplated, of which the third was only a skeleton at the moment of attack. These lines were confidently expected to hold up any assault long enough to enable adequate reinforcements to arrive. Special defensive measures had been undertaken at Peronne to guard the crossings of the Somme.

During the winter, while the British Armies laboured on their fortifications, the very number of the German Divisions had ensured quick reliefs and long periods of rest and training in the special methods devised by Ludendorff for this, his last

German Offensive, 1918.

desperate throw for victory. On the eve of attack, more than 70 German Divisions, every man fresh and rested, lay over against the British Third and Fifth Armies. Even the uncertain chances of the weather favoured the enemy. A particularly heavy fog on the morning of 21st March covered the advance of the van battalions until they were almost upon our front line. S.O.S. signals, obscured by the mist, brought no assistance in time, communications were cut and, before the waiting batteries had any clear knowledge of the position in front, they too were enveloped by the overwhelming rush of the massed hordes of the enemy. By evening on the 21st, the remnants of the British garrisons and all local reserves on the greater part of this front were struggling desperately to preserve a footing in their second zone of defence; on the extreme right of General Gough's Fifth Army south-west of St. Quentin, the Boches were already clear of all obstacles.

The 22nd was another day of fierce fighting against hopeless odds, marked by several forced withdrawals further north to conform to the increasing German success in the extreme south. On the 23rd General Gough abandoned the Peronne bridgehead, and withdrew the whole remainder of his Fifth Army across the Somme, leaving the V Corps, on the extreme right of the Third Army, more or less in the air. The Germans drove through the gap thus created between the Armies with great energy and skill, the ensuing compulsory retirements in the Third Army in the next two days causing further inevitable loss of touch and co-ordination between the IV and V Corps.

Meanwhile the New Zealanders formed one of the reserve Divisions which were being hurried to the scene from less active fronts as soon as the weight of the German thrust made it apparent that their main enterprise had been definitely launched. The first destination proposed for the Division was on the left of the Third Army, but the constant changes in the situation altered this to the Bray area on the Somme, where Divisional Headquarters came under VII Corps at Corbie on the 24th. A further change on the 25th occasioned removal to Ribemont in the Ancre Valley, where Divisional Headquarters arrived the same night, the Division being now under Third Army control.

German pressure was still being maintained with extreme vigour and a good deal of success, notably as regards the gap existing between the IV and V Corps already mentioned. At 10 p.m. on the 25th, General Russell received orders to move by way of Hedauville to establish a line between Hamel and

Field Companies and Field Troop.

Puisieux, with the object of closing this highly dangerous and still widening gap between the Corps. At 1.30 a.m. on the 26th, Divisional Headquarters, including C.R.E., were established at Hedauville. While these preliminary arrangements for their reception were going on in the south, the scattered units of the Division were losing no time on the road. The speed and skill with which the administrative staffs pushed them through to the new front left little to be desired.

Beyond Amiens, the railway line was already cut by hostile bombers, and the majority of the New Zealanders, including 1st and 3rd Field Companies, detrained at St. Roche Station on the outskirts of the town. The 2nd Company detrained at Ailly-sur-Somme. In all cases the orders were to leave all baggage at the detraining stations under guard, and to move independently in the order of arrival, making all possible speed to Hedauville. After a short halt and a meal, the Field Companies, among many others, took the road eastward under full packs on the morning of the 26th. Some of the earlier units had been pushed forward in motor lorries, but the supply of those conveyances soon broke down under the extraordinary demands of the moment and the difficulties presented by the congested roads.

From every farmhouse by-way and country lane, streams of unfortunate refugees were debouching on to the main roads, causing an unimaginable tangle of bewildered traffic. Here would be the gigantic waggon of a more prosperous farmer drawn by the splendid staunch horses of the French agricultural districts, and laden with a mountainous pile of household gear; there some poor labourer was dragging his miserable store of scanty possessions in a hand-cart, aided perhaps by a large dog harnessed underneath and pulling like a demon, or by the less vigorous efforts of wife or daughter. Numerous children complicated matters, save when too young to run beside the caravan. In that case they were slung precariously on top, along with aged relations, the household cat, or a few stray fowls. One cart passed with two babies swinging in an old bath beneath one corner of the tailboard, while the family coffee pot and a broken lantern clinked cheerfully on the other side. The large mattress surmounting another wobbly erection was shared by a grandmother, a babe and a goat, not equally by any means—the goat was securely settled in the centre. Occasionally some crazy load would collapse, causing a temporary stoppage of the whole procession, when the shrill cries of the women and children and the violent altercations of the old men made up a scene that might have been sufficiently amusing had not tragedy brooded so darkly

German Offensive, 1918.

over the whole occasion. The prevailing expression on each face, especially the old people, was one of bewildered despair; that this thing could happen to them after passing them by for three years seemed quite unbelievable. The fact that it had happened to thousands of others made no difference. At such times each individual family appropriated the whole pathetic burden of misery and sorrow to itself.

The extraordinary tenacity of affection with which the French peasant clings to his poor little patch never failed to excite the sympathy of the troops, but could hardly strike any chord of complete understanding in the mind of the average colonial, well used, in many cases, to seeing the "old home" sold once a year, and not in the least dismayed by change of scene, often electing in fact to carve out a new home from the inhospitable bush, with the nearest neighbour 10 miles away.

In France estates descend equally to all children and not to the eldest son, which partly accounts for the extreme smallness of the farms, and the poverty of the peasant class, whose piece of land is virtually their all. By nature and tradition their whole life is bound up with the soil they are reared on, and the passage of centuries has made little change in either their customs or surroundings. At Messines and in many other parts of the Front Line the numerous hedges of the countryside had to be trimmed and passages cut through them to facilitate the free movement of attacking troops. It is on record that Caesar's legions in Gaul found in the same hedges or their predecessors a similar difficulty and overcame them in the same way.

Meanwhile, hour after hour, with no sign of a halt, the long columns pushed steadily forward. At the village of Pont Noyelles, the C.R.E. was awaiting the arrival of the Field Companies and, during a short conference of the commanding officers, the jaded sappers threw themselves down by the wayside, hoping the end of the march had come. However, there were still many weary miles to Hedauville, which was finally reached the same evening. The diary of the 2nd Company records the fact that, during the whole long trek of 24 miles under heavy packs, not a straggler had left the ranks.

From dawn on the 26th such units as were then on the spot had been sent on to check the advancing enemy in front of Englebelmer, securing the right flank of a further main advance on Hamel and Serre which was to be made as soon as ever sufficient men arrived on the scene. The 1st Rifles successfully achieved the first requirements of the situation, and by noon a considerable number of additional troops had arrived at Hedauville, as expected. After a hasty meal and the inevitable small delays consequent on preparation for

Field Companies and Field Troop.

battle, a composite brigade of various battalions moved off under General Young, and after numerous encounters of more or less magnitude with scattered bodies of the advancing enemy, were able to establish themselves just short of Beaumont-Hamel, in what had been the original British front line before the Battle of the Somme in 1916. Northward of this satisfactory position the situation wore a much less favourable appearance. No troops had become available for the attack towards Serre until evening, and by that time the Germans were established in force as far westward as La Signy Farm, half way between Colincamps and Serre. Despite small local successes, our main line of defence was forced to establish itself still west of that position, and with a gap of a mile or more still existing between our northernmost troops and the 4th Australians at Hebuterne, who were fulfilling the same mission as ourselves in trying to close the gap from the northern side.

All the evening up to 9 p.m. belated battalions were still concluding their long march at Hedauville. At midnight a further composite brigade under Lieutenant-Colonel A. E. Stewart moved out to close this gap. Forgetting natural fatigue under the stimulus of a clear call to immediate action, this force was in position to make the final dash at dawn on the 27th. The enemy, evidently unprepared by their recent successes for such decisive opposition, though in superior numbers, fell back at once, abandoning both personal gear and material, and by early morning touch was established with the Australian flank, and the gap between the IV and V Corps was definitely closed. Executed by men who had suffered the fatigues of no sleep for two nights, with makeshift arrangements as to food, and who in every case had come weary and footsore straight from a forced march, these exploits were sufficient tribute to the spirit of the Infantry, and an earnest of their sound physical condition.

In spite of the comparative ease with which the Division had completed this important first commission on the new field, it was quite obvious that the German troops, still in large numbers, and all flushed with the exhilaration of a successful advance and the promise of speedy victory, could not in any way be considered as finally held. Even before the inevitable commencement of the hostile attacks which continued all day on the 27th, Corps had decided on the location of a reserve position which, under the name of the Purple Line, ran in rear of Mailly-Maillet, Colincamps, and Hebuterne. To this urgent work, at daybreak on the 27th, the energies of the three Engineer companies were directed, accompanied by the Pioneer Battalion and by all three Light

German Offensive, 1918.

Trench Mortar batteries, who were debarred from their share of the more interesting events further forward by the non-arrival of their special Stokes ammunition.

A continuous line of defence was of course impossible, and the proposal aimed at was the establishment of a series of strong supporting posts. Marching by Forceville, the working parties moved northward, and reached their allotted positions about midday. The afternoon and night were spent on constructing posts, a sufficient number of which were ready towards dawn, and were then manned by the tired constructors in view of a possible enemy attack early on the 28th. This failed to materialise, though heavy fighting took place during the day, and on relief by infantry garrisons later in the morning, the Field Companies moved on northward to billets in the region of Sailly-au-Bois. The transport and headquarters sections of each company had moved up to Sailly-au-Bois during the preceding day, and were now ready with such food and accommodation as the circumstances permitted. By evening the sappers were once more at work on the posts, and after a night's toil the same routine as before was carried out, Engineers remaining in garrison until their completed posts were taken over by Infantry. Each post was built to hold a platoon of 40 men, with at least six firebays in each, properly revetted and duckboarded. Drainage and wiring were completed on succeeding evenings. By the end of the month the Purple Line could count on some 60 posts, mutually supporting, and together capable of putting up a stiff resistance to any further enemy enterprise in that locality.

Till the afternoon of the 28th, right from the hour of entrainment in Flanders, the weather had been perfect, and the fact that both contending parties were far in advance of their artillery and forced to rely on their own efforts, had given a pleasant personal turn to the proceedings which, at least on our side, was a very welcome change to men straight from the stagnation and restriction of trench warfare. It was not that our men considered themselves at a disadvantage when both sides had their artillery in support, but the open style of warfare, with its greater opportunities for individual enterprise and dash, seemed to place a higher premium at once on the personal element, and for that reason alone was entirely acceptable to the New Zealanders, who had come to regard themselves as quite able to take care of any Boche on fair man-to-man terms. That they were not alone in this comfortable opinion, somewhat inflated though it may appear, is witnessed by the following translation of a French Army Order, issued shortly after the Armistice in November, 1918.

Field Companies and Field Troop.

Portion of the Order deals particularly with the part taken by the Division in holding up the German offensive of 1918.

"Minister's Office, Paris, 28th November, 1918. The President of the Council of the Ministry of War mentions in Army Orders the name of the following English officer: Major-General Sir A. H. Russell, New Zealand Division. Has led to countless victories a splendid Division, whose exploits had not been equalled, and whose reputation was such that on the arrival of the Division on the Somme Battlefield during the critical days of March, 1918, the departure of the inhabitants was stopped immediately. The Division covered itself with fresh glory during the Battle of the Ancre a la Sambre, at Puisieux-au-Mont, Bapaume, Crevecoeur, and Le Quesnoy. For and by the order of the President of the War Council of the Ministry of War.—Boeker, Colonel, Adjutant-General to the Cabinet."

Meanwhile, by the evening of the 28th, rain had set in heavily, which, with the increasing arrival of artillery, the inevitable mud, and considerable shortcomings in the way of rations and dry quarters due to the rush and bustle of the last few days, combined to invest proceedings with more of an air of the usual dull and hard routine associated with trench warfare in country ill-supplied with the necessary trenches and attendant conveniences. Continued heavy fighting marked the close of the month, but the German efforts to advance were everywhere successfully held up in or about the front line, without any recourse to the emergency positions now standing ready in the support area.

On the 28th, C.R.E.'s Headquarters moved up from Hedauville to Bus-les-Artois, where they were more in touch with operations in front. On the 30th all front line transport was ordered to the rear, and the Engineer sections bivouacked in the fields round Coigneux and Louvencourt. At the same time the sappers were forced to withdraw from Sailly-au-Bois, which was now out of the Corps Area. 1st and 2nd Companies moved to Bertrancourt, the 3rd to Louvencourt.

Material at this stage was naturally very hard to obtain, supplies being sent for as far as Doullens and Arras. A Divisional dump was gradually being established at Bertrancourt, and a fortunate find of considerable R.E. stores at Euston, east of Colincamps, formed the basis of a very useful local supply in that area.

The Divisional sector was by this time definitely fixed, which enabled an allotment of ground to be made among the Field Companies. A further line of defence forward of the Purple Line had been mooted as soon as the results of the German attacks on the 28th to 30th made it apparent that

German Offensive, 1918.

the Division had their measure, at any rate for the time being. By the 3rd April, the line was traced out, running from Hebuterne to Englebelmer, passing eastward of Colincamps and Maillet-Mailly, and the three Field Companies were placed on the job forthwith, operating on right, centre, and left sub-sectors respectively. In addition to this new line of defence, parties were continually at work joining up the separated posts of the Purple Line and converting the whole into a continuous fortified line. Trench labour here was considerably lightened by the fortunate fact that the Divisional front area included many lines of the original British systems of 1916, many of which required little attention to enable them to be incorporated with the new systems.

An important concession to the urgency of the trench needs of the moment was allowed by an alteration in design. Instead of right angled traverses as heretofore, an oblique layout was now adopted, thus securing an additional 30 per cent. of length in the trench for the same outlay of time and labour. Furthermore no trench was dug lower than the depth of a convenient firing stand at the first operation, leaving further improvements to a later stage if conditions remained favourable. A greatly increased width of trench was a special feature of the new design, and was intended to hold up enemy tanks. Whether it would have succeeded in that worthy purpose we cannot say, but, from the ease and frequency with which British tanks crushed many of the new lines, it seems highly uncertain.

Reconnaissance had been a feature of the Engineering measures taken ever since arrival in the area, and this was systematically continued on allotment of definite sub-sectors. Search for suitable dugouts was carried on and revealed a great scarcity of any that were at all shell-proof, but the principal object in view was the location and survey of all objects likely to assist a German advance which could be destroyed by us before withdrawal, if such became necessary. Roads and railway lines obviously came under that category, but, in addition, arrangements were made by which convenient buildings could be blown down and utilised to block thoroughfares and cause delay; while note was also made of the possibilities for defence of all commanding points, and such outstanding features of the landscape as the tall chimney at Acheux cross roads, now used as an Artillery O.P., were marked for immediate destruction should need arise.

Apart from shells only two types of explosive material were used to any extent on the British front in France—guncotton and ammonal. For sudden and severe shattering action, nothing could compete with guncotton, but the regular

Field Companies and Field Troop.

shape of the rectangular block in which it was made often acted against complete contact with the object sought to be destroyed, and without close contact much of the power of this explosive is wasted. No such handicap was met with in the case of iron rails, steel bridge girders, iron doors of dugouts, water pipes, and so on, and with them guncotton could be absolutely relied upon for a faithful job. Ammonal, compounded principally of nitrate of ammonia and aluminium, has a somewhat slower explosive action and therefore exerts a better lifting effect than guncotton, and was always used in mining operations and to blow up buildings or tall chimneys or for similar purposes. Dynamite is more powerful than either of the two explosives mentioned, but is not so safe to handle or store, and was seldom used.

The prudence of the defensive measures which had been undertaken was unquestionable, but it soon became increasingly evident that the Division was firmly established on the line held, with little risk of very summary ejection. It appears now, from sources of German information available since the war, that Ludendorff definitely abandoned serious aggressive action on the Somme in April in favour of other attempts further north at Arras and in Flanders.

Be that as it may, while his attacking battalions were yet in the first flush of their victorious march, the New Zealanders, brought to the scene piecemeal and pushed into battle within an hour or two of arrival, had stopped them in their tracks from the outset of the fight. Not content with that achievement, they had turned the tables on their opponents and taken back sufficient of their newly-won gains to ensure a strong position overlooking much of the remainder, while reserve positions heavily wired lay ready, quite competent to deal with anything short of a grand assault. To crown all, a distinct feeling of confidence and exhilaration was most noticeable in all units; fatigue and discomfort were overshadowed by a pleasing presentiment that in the class of fighting now in evidence the Boche was due for some long unpaid scores. Numerous congratulatory messages from past and present Corps commanders expressed high commendation of the Divisional exploits.

As the stability of the position increased, so the energies of the technical troops were more distributed to works other than those of pure defence. From the 9th April, the Divisional sector was held by two Brigades in line and one in reserve, the C.R.E. conforming to this arrangement by employing 1st and 3rd Field Companies on right and left brigade sectors respectively, with the 2nd Company in reserve employed on the hitherto neglected requirements of the rear areas.

German Offensive, 1918.

Such dugouts as existed in the area were now furnished with gas-proof doors, water supplies were investigated, and all roads were repaired and drained. It seemed probable that the coming summer would disclose a serious shortage of water facilities, and considerable time was spent in selecting new water points for men and animals and in installing the necessary conveniences. The scarcity of accommodation and the obvious character of the country, combined with persistent vague rumours of the existence of old chalk workings underground, quickened a general search for ancient galleries. Success at Louvencourt, where some 50 caves were found at a depth of 50 feet, and also at Bus-les-Artois, where shafts were driven into old workings from two wells in the very grounds of Divisional Headquarters, made it almost certain that good shelter was only awaiting discovery in the more forward villages. The 1st Field Company, guided by records discovered in the parish church at Maillet-Mailly, and by the excellence of its chalk construction, concentrated on that locality. Various unfortunate inhabitants were put through a mild species of third degree, but all were unanimous that no caves existed. At this point in the explorations, information was received that a Frenchman had been seen to disappear suddenly in a certain locality. That was the end of the secret of the good staunch folk of Maillet-Mailly. An inclined stairway 2ft. 6in. wide was discovered running down to a depth of some 60 feet below the surface, where a large dry catacomb was found cut out of clean chalk. A vertical shaft discovered later provided perfect ventilation. Larger entrance shafts were immediately driven and gas-proofed by the 1st Company, and accommodation was forthwith available for about 1000 men.

A day or so later on an aged civilian was found, who, for various minor considerations, consented to point out the entrance to another old well, with shaft and cave, which had stood him and other villagers in good stead in 1870. Situated under the floor of an old building, the opening had been well concealed and was finally discovered bricked up. The air in the shaft when opened was found quite impossible, and lighted candles or paraffin torches were extinguished immediately on entry. Soundings showed the well to be 150 feet deep with 4 feet of water. Mirrors salved from nearby houses were used to deflect sunlight down the well, and a shaft was clearly seen leading off at a depth of 60 feet.

Eventually the well was cleared of foul air by means of a blacksmith's blower and a long length of rubber hose. Investigation then disclosed several galleries 15 feet high and 12 feet wide, most of which had fallen in. The best remaining

Field Companies and Field Troop.

chamber was effectually blocked by a built-up brick wall, and speculation as to the possible nature of the concealed wealth ran rife. However, some treacherous villager visited the scene of operations on the night preceding the projected opening of the treasure chamber, and removed every stick of the ventilating and elevating tackle. Two days later the sector passed to an English Division, and the secrets of 1870 remained undisturbed.

Other underground caverns were discovered later, but many of them were in poor repair and of no use as accommodation. Several dugouts for battalion and other headquarters required in and about the Purple Line were now dug into the chalk in preference to the system necessary in Flanders, and mining became such an every day job in this area that tunnelling officers from the N.Z. Tunnelling Company at Arras were attached to the Engineers for expert supervision. Sets were manufactured by the Company carpenters from salvaged material in the villages, and the ordinary pick cut down and re-pointed made an excellent substitute for proper mining tools. In general about 30 feet of head cover was allowed, which was quite safe from ordinary shelling, though the Tunnellers at Arras could remember a 17in. shell which came through 40 feet of cover, and then went some distance into the floor of an unlucky dugout.

As the new works and other features of the Divisional sector increased in number and complexity, it became increasingly difficult to move about with speed or certainty. Numerous overland tracks and communication trenches were in existence by this time, and the Field Companies carried out a comprehensive scheme of local survey and marking with notice boards. The maps thus obtained gave complete information of each sub-sector, and were of great assistance to the brigades concerned. From this time onwards, the frequent changes of the situation made it necessary to revise these local detail maps continually, and each Field Company kept one or more surveyors continually at work.

A noteworthy feature of Army organisation was the fine supply of maps of any sector of the front continually available any time after the first year of the war. Originally great difficulties were experienced on this score, because none of the great military powers had foreseen the need of large scale trench maps, nor had entertained the possibility of making them while hostilities were in progress. Pre-war policy in Britain and the Continent was to maintain a stock supply of maps of likely theatres of war, drawn on a scale of about half an inch to the mile. The British Expeditionary Force went to France armed with one of these maps and was promptly

German Offensive, 1918.

driven off it. Similar small scale maps were then borrowed from the French Army. Belgium was better off than any other belligerent, having recently completed a fine series of maps of her territory on a 1/20,000 scale. After the battle of the Aisne, with the advent of stationary warfare, large scale maps became an absolute necessity, and an enlargement of the somewhat out-of-date French 1/80,000 was tried with poor success.

The map makers were now faced with an unprecedented problem—how to make accurate maps on a large scale showing all local detail without going on the ground. The only possible groundwork available for such maps was the records of the cadastral surveys of each Commune, done in Napoleon's time, which had been lodged in the principal towns of the Communes, such as Cambrai, and had been in enemy hands since the early days of the war. Fortunately, copies of these cadastral maps were discovered in Paris, and from them the war maps were built up, and were surprisingly accurate. As time went on, of course, they were amended and improved as the result of further local surveys, of aeroplane photographs, and of constant topographical interpolation, all of which work constituted a great separate enterprise conducted by special Field Survey Battalions of the Royal Engineers, and cannot receive more than passing mention here.

Mention of Napoleon recalls the fact that he was primarily responsible for the paved roads which abound all along the north-east frontier of France, and without which extensive military movement in that low-lying and often waterlogged area would have been impossible. There can be little doubt that the military aspect of affairs was more in his mind than the mere provision of good roads, and it seems to suggest that there were some far-sighted military experts in the world even before 1914.

In rear areas work of every kind was plentiful, though the unsettled conditions were not rendered worse by approaching winter, as had so often been the case on former occasions. Many men, nevertheless, especially in the early days of April, were still short of blankets and extra clothing, due to misadventure to the kits stacked at Amiens on the road in, and there were few of the small amenities generally in evidence under a more organised state of affairs. The Y.M.C.A., well to the front now as ever, did its utmost to provide small comforts for the troops, and before long the Divisional Entertainers resumed their wonted role on numerous improvised stages erected by the sappers according to programme.

Field Companies and Field Troop.

Bath-houses at Bertrancourt and Louvencourt absorbed a fair amount of technical labour, and were erected on an extensive and detailed scale hitherto unapproached. Timber, with many other appliances, was mostly salvaged from the ruined villages round about. These baths were able to deal with 100 men an hour, including the issue of clean clothing. Very few new dugouts were urgently required in rear; large numbers of men were housed in catacombs, and, for smaller units and Headquarters, slight repairs and gas-proofing were generally sufficient to enable some former building to be inhabited. Deep shell-proof quarters were provided later as time and labour permitted.

About the middle of April the three Field Companies were at last relieved of their pontoons and other special bridging equipment, which were parked at Rosel, and later transferred to a Pontoon Park near Abbeville until necessity arose for their use, when they would be returned by motor transport. The waggons and horses remained with their units to assist in supplying the heavy daily cartage demands, due both to great need of material and the fact that much of it was unobtainable from adjacent dumps and had to be salvaged over a wide area. Road needs in particular were causing great demands on the transport at this stage, and no less than 34 extra Corps lorries and waggons were engaged on carting R.E. stores and road metal for use on the various highways of the Divisional area.

On the 22nd all transport was again moved to a new camp close to Bus-les-Artois. Next day the Division side-stepped northward, taking over the Hebuterne sector from the 42nd Division. The 3rd Company remained on its present sub-sector, now on the right, while the 1st transferred its energies to the area taken over from the 42nd Division, and established new headquarters and billets near Sailly-au-Bois. The 2nd and 3rd Companies were still camped about Bertrancourt.

During the whole of May, work in the Divisional area, extending now from One Tree Hill north-west of Beaumont Hamel to east of Hebuterne, varied only in location from what had gone before. Front and reserve lines were in constant process of improvement, extension and wiring, and far behind, outside the sphere of Divisional influence, were supported by line upon line of carefully selected trenches, which, well wired and provided with numerous posts, lay ready for any possible renewal of enemy operations.

After many rebuffs and false scents, the patient searchers at Sailly-au-Bois were at least rewarded by the discovery of excellent caves at a depth of some 72 feet. The entrance, as usual, led in from an old disused well. On completion of a

German Offensive, 1918.

new inclined drive for more convenient access, very slight repairs were necessary to render the caves suitable for habitation, the available accommodation being sufficient for 2000 men. Underground workings of more or less magnitude were also discovered at Hebuterne and Bertrancourt.

During May, the number of American officers and N.C.Os. attached to the Division for first-hand experience of the art of war was a good indication of the efforts being put forth by our latest Allies to place their men in the field as soon as possible. The Engineering units received their quota of the visitors, whose invariable good spirits and keenness to share the fortunes of the day, combined with a modesty of demeanour not previously considered typical of the average American, made very favourable impression on their hosts. Certainly their experiences were not so severe at the moment as those of their comrades fighting further south. A member of one of the coloured regiments there was asked by a new chum friend to tell him what an attack was like. "Well," said he, "it's like dis. De guns start, an de officer says, 'Come on!' an you jus' climb outer de trench an say, 'Good mornin' Jesus!'"

On the 21st, the 152nd Company R.E. from 37th Division also came under the New Zealand C.R.E. as a reserve unit, and was allotted all work on the Purple Line. The 2nd Field Company was thus free to devote more time to Divisional requirements in rear, of which deep dugouts still formed the principal item. Despite the number of catacombs now available, a register of all deep dugouts required for the Division, compiled in order to arrive at an order of precedence in construction, disclosed the fact that 122 of these structures were either completed or in course of excavation. From these and other sources great quantities of chalk were now available, and were freely used to provide clean, hard flooring for all horse standings of the Divisional transport.

By the end of May a tremendous transformation had been effected in the whole area. The Front and Support System now consisted of series of posts practically joined up by continuous lines of trenches, well wired and in good fighting trim. Communication trenches were numerous and generally in good order, though there was room for more clearing and duckboarding, while the addition of fire steps to facilitate flanking fire had been noted for early attention. The ultimate aim was to render all communication trenches capable of defence in the event of attack from either flank, and to this end they were wired both sides, and frequently made the sides of fortified localities. Behind lay the Maillet-Mailly—Colincamps—Hebuterne Switch, a system of posts in depth

Field Companies and Field Troop.

except at Hebuterne, where it was a continuous trench. The whole of this Switch was well wired and practically completed, save in the town of Hebuterne, where measures had still to be taken to improve the field of fire. Many buildings had been demolished, and long swathes or rides cut through the woods in front, to provide for intersecting streams of fire from the Switch and the forts established on the outskirts of the village. The original Purple Line, greatly extended and improved, had by this time expanded into a Purple System of Front, Support and Reserve lines, all based on the original posts, and with numerous connecting trenches since cut to join them up. The whole of the Purple Reserve was a continuous line of trench, dug to a depth of 3 feet 9 inches. More wiring still remained to be done here. The Beaussart-Colincamps Switch was an additional short defensive length lying between the two villages named, running somewhat obliquely to the Purple Front and immediately in front of it.

The forts already mentioned on the outskirts of Hebuterne were yet another expansion of the defensive policy of the time. Where the ground was suitable for a prolonged stand, series of posts and communication saps were amalgamated into fortified areas of considerable size, ready to meet attack from any quarter, well wired all round, and provided with machine-gun emplacements, cross communications, and at least some degree of internal shelter and other conveniences. So numerous had the various posts and forts now become that confusion was only averted by a scheme of numbering, which was forthwith shown on all local trench maps, and carried into practical operation by numerous painted signboards and notices erected by the sappers.

Of the large programme of dugout construction in hand, an appreciable portion was complete and the remainder well in hand. Search for underground workings at Colincamps and Courcelles had proved vain. Dry weather tracks were all pegged and named and in constant use, roads were in fair repair, wells and waterpoints were well up to requirements, while further in rear, camps, baths, transport lines, and other phases of Divisional requirements had all received a fair share of attention. Reference in one works diary of this period to oven doors and fly-proof meat safes indicates an attention to detail which would suggest that all was well with the domestic economy of the Division, unless these contrivances were merely noteworthy on account of their rarity.

Enemy artillery, save for periodic bursts of fire of short duration, had now become surprisingly quiet, a state of mind faithfully reflected by the Boche front line garrisons, which were showing none of the dash exhibited a month earlier. No

Major N. Annabell, M.C.

German Offensive, 1918.

Man's Land was practically a British preserve, while the few hostile raids attempted were either repulsed with heavy losses or abandoned by the attackers after a very half-hearted showing. As enemy morale appeared to wane, so did that of the New Zealand infantry increase. The class of country occupied, no less than the general conditions obtaining, lent itself easily to offensive enterprise. The welter of old trenches and broken shell holes, overgrown with the luxuriant vegetation of another summer, furnished excellent cover and supplied opportunities for individual effort which appealed irresistibly to the sporting instincts so strongly developed in the colonial troops. Before long, forays, ranging from organised raids down to a silent swoop by one or two bold adventurers, were taking place daily, and always with marked success. The entertainment of watching German sentries caught and hustled across to our lines was constantly enjoyed by our Front Line garrisons in broad daylight. The atmosphere of conscious superiority thus engendered had marked effect on the spirits of the whole Division, whose cheerful outlook of life was further enhanced by the removal of certain leave restrictions.

An increased allotment of leave was now granted to Paris and other French centres, and compensated in some part for the continued cancellation of all leave across the Channel. Numbers of men were also sent to military rest camps established on the coast at Wimereux and other places round Boulogne. Apart from the exciting presence of numerous W.A.A.Cs, there was nothing here to disturb the peaceful round of ten summer days by the sea, and the fortunate travellers derived great benefit from the change of scene.

On 7th June, some six weeks after arrival on the Somme for the second time, the New Zealand Division was relieved by the 42nd Division and withdrawn to Corps reserve area, taking over there from 37th and 42nd Divisions. The C.R.E. was established at Pas-en-Artois, the 1st and 3rd Field Companies at Couin and Henu respectively, while the 2nd Company remained in the same billets and took over work on the Purple system under control of C.R.E. 42nd Division.

Any delusion laboured under by the companies in Corps reserve as to the amount of rest involved was soon dissipated by the discovery of numerous jobs awaiting improvement and completion, though a fair amount of sport and amusement was squeezed into the programme withal. On the 20th, the Engineering units, including the New Zealand Tunnellers, held a most successful military tournament and gymkhana, a secondary motive being the "spotting" of likely representative talent to compete in the Divisional sports a few days later.

Field Companies and Field Troop.

The talent was there all right and in surprising quantity, but there is no record of the Divisional prizes being scooped entirely by sappers.

On the 21st, a further short move found the C.R.E. at Authie, with the 1st and 3rd Companies in the Bois du Warnimont, where various small works of no particular importance were carried out. At the end of June, a party of 20 other ranks per Company left for a course of exchange duties at the Reserve Depot in England. At the same time, the Engineers among other units were honoured by a visit of inspection from Mr. Massey and Sir Joseph Ward. The familiar sight of these intrepid statesmen, now visiting the very battlefields to assure themselves that all went well with the brave boys of their island Dominion, was a tremendous solace to many a home-sick warrior. The general appropriate atmosphere of affection and esteem was further heightened by the many expressions of genuine approval which were bestowed on the troops, who might have been a trifle less fractious, and more attentive, had not most of them put in a long march to attend this compulsory parade. However, in reality, all were pleased to see "Bill" and "Joe" in tin hats, and to hear that on the home front, anyway, the fires were still burning merrily.

CHAPTER XIII.

THE FINAL ADVANCE.

On the 2nd July the New Zealand Division returned to the line, holding this time the centre of the Corps front, from the south-east tip of Biez Wood, which lay south-west of Bucquoy, to east of Hebuterne, running along the north of Rossignol Wood. C.R.E.'s headquarters were now established at Couin. The 1st Field Company, in billets just north of Coigneux, took over reserve area works from 421st (Wessex) Field Company. The 2nd and 3rd Companies, located at Sailly-au-Bois and Chateau de la Haie, took over work on right and left Brigade sectors respectively, relieving the 502nd and 505th (Wessex) Field Companies.

Within the Divisional area now lay the ruins of the village of Gommecourt, where the Germans had successfully held up the first British attacks in July, 1916. The famous Park and the woods surrounding the village still lay as the march of war had left them, in accordance with proposals of the French Government to form the area into a National Park, as a permanent record of the devastation of war. The maze of old German dugouts still remained intact, and the trenches lay practically as they were vacated when the British advanced in 1916. The dugouts were particularly welcome, but, owing to the north-eastern trend of our line, all former trenches were now running more or less at right angles to the front, and had perforce to be utilised as communication trenches, while those old communication trenches which were in a suitable position for use as firing lines required considerable attention before they could be fully occupied. The whole Gommecourt Ridge, whence one could gaze eastward over miles of desolated Somme country almost as far as the former Divisional goals at Flers and Factory Corner, was of great defensive importance, as its capture by the enemy would have placed the New Zealanders and the left flank of the Corps in a dangerous salient. The network of old German and British trenches, covered with acres of rusty wire and numerous shattered remains of former woods, had formed a good nucleus for the extensive protective works which were found already well in hand when the Division took over the new sector.

An epidemic of influenza early in the month caught the Engineers along with the rest of mankind, and numerous evacuations to isolation camps followed. Fortunately serious

Field Companies and Field Troop.

cases were few in number, and the majority of the invalids were back with their respective companies within a short period.

Engineering activities at this stage were practically identical with those performed during the preceding Divisional occupation of the front line. The desperate necessity for urgent defensive measures had passed by some time since, but there was still room for any amount of work on the numerous trenches and communications now in existence all along the line. Even in a comparatively quiet sector, the ordinary wear and tear of the day meant constant attention and repair, if trenches were to remain habitable. However, fresh fields of endeavour were shortly to be made available by the ever aggressive infantry.

The left of the Divisional front about Rossignol Wood was by long odds the least satisfactory portion of our occupied trench area. Here one battalion occupied such a pronounced salient between Rossignol and Biez Woods that the two front line companies lay facing different fronts at right angles to one another. Furthermore, our extreme left flank lay on a narrow valley which prohibited suitable contact with our neighbouring Division, the 37th, and gave the enemy an opportunity of driving through at the point of junction. Rossignol Wood itself was a sufficient menace. Covering 20 acres or more right against our front, and free from all observation from our lines, it offered the Boche exceptional opportunities for massing his forces for a substantial attack at the very point where we were least prepared to withstand it. These facts were all sized up by the garrisons concerned within a few hours of occupation, and before ten days had passed vigorous measures were in progress for amending the unsatisfactory state of affairs. Partly by minor assaults, partly by steady pressure of insidious penetration wherever an opportunity of gaining a few yards presented itself, the enemy was gradually forced back. This was a continuation of the undisguised daylight tactics of individual scouts and small patrol parties in constantly harassing the enemy which so appealed to the particular warlike genius of the colonial troops and was of such great value in establishing ascendancy over the less enterprising Boche.

By the 15th the situation was considered propitious for a minor attack in some force that should finally clear Rossignol Wood and establish a new front line all along the left flank, free from the disabilities now sought to be adjusted. To say that success was gained lightly would do full justice neither to the fighting abilities of our own troops, nor to the defensive efforts of the enemy; but by this time the

The Final Advance.

Divisional infantry had reached such a pitch of confidence and aggressive enthusiasm that there could be but one result to their efforts, and in due course the enemy was driven clear of the Wood.

As the advance pressed on, the newly-won territory came under the hands of the sappers, who toiled unremittingly to provide the necessary new trenches, and to open up adequate communications. Great assistance in the field, and much good fellowship on less stern occasions, was enjoyed from a party of American soldiers of the 2nd Battalion 305th Regiment U.S.A. Engineers, who were attached to the New Zealand Field Companies at this time to assimilate knowledge and experience.

That the fighting spirit of the German soldier was not yet quenched by his reverses was shown on the 25th. In the latter stages of the fight for Rossignol Wood, the enemy had appeared to withdraw voluntarily to higher and safer ground, but since then the pressure had continued relentlessly till he was finally pushed off the ridge crowned by two fine trenches known as Moa and Shag. Here, in addition to a number of good shelters and dugouts, our troops enjoyed direct observation over the enemy lines and had forced themselves into a salient threatening both his flanks. Spurred on by these considerations, the Boche decided to contest our tenure forthwith. After fairly heavy bombardment all day on the 25th, the enemy attacked at evening. In several parties over about half a mile of front the attackers came on in determined style, leaving their cover as they neared their destination, and making a bold final dash covered by a shower of stick bombs. But all to no purpose. The machine-gunners caught them before they were more than clear of their protecting saps, and as they broke and ran the barrage crashed down among the survivors. One strong party succeeded in effecting temporary occupation of our "post" opposing it, but even that success was of short duration. Reserves were immediately at hand, which worked round the occupied post from each flank, and those of the victorious Germans who were not killed became inmates of the prisoner's cage. Within half an hour of the commencement of the attack our line was completely re-established, and during the evening the garrison was relieved by fresh troops.

With this confident re-assertion of our hold on the coveted high ground, our aggressive efforts were temporarily relaxed. An unduly exposed outlying post at Chasseur Hedge was in fact withdrawn on the evening of the 27th to Jean Bart trench to ensure a more compact line of resistance. With the capture of Chasseur Hedge had come into our hands two deep concrete dugouts crammed with enemy trench mortar ammunition. On

Field Companies and Field Troop.

withdrawal these were marked for destruction. During the afternoon supplies of ammonal had been carried forward by a party from 2nd Field Company, which now arranged its explosive among the German shells and totally destroyed both shelters under cover of a heavy artillery crash. The trenches now occupied as our front line were destitute of wire entanglement protection and, though in fair order when captured from the Boche, required considerable alteration to make them effective against attack from their previous rear. The efforts of the sappers to improve the situation were minimised by the difficulty of getting up material, by continual hostile shelling, and by the torrents of rain which now drenched the whole countryside for three days, and turned all the newly-won territory into a knee-deep bog.

Hebuterne village in particular was conscientiously bombarded by the German gunners, and carrying and transport parties were forced to run the gauntlet every night. Corporal J. Q. Adams of the 2nd Field Company was in charge of one party which was struck by a shell, which destroyed the waggon, and wounded horses and driver and three of the accompanying sappers. The horses thereupon bolted and eventually became entangled in a belt of barbed wire. Adams succeeded in extricating them, still under fire, and ultimately managed to deliver his material in the forward line. For his coolness and courage, which had been marked on many other occasions, he was awarded the Military Medal. Experiences of this kind were by no means uncommon among the transport sections. Driver A. J. McLean of the 1st Field Company won the same decoration a few weeks earlier near the same spot. With urgent material to deliver he pushed through a heavy barrage, only to run into concentrated fire at his destination, where he personally unloaded his waggon and returned safely with his team.

The new reserve line, now in course of construction to meet the needs of our considerably advanced occupation, was employing the energies of large parties from the Field Companies in line, and this turn of the weather brought drainage problems to the fore once more in a manner reminiscent of the best Flanders traditions.

In rear areas the 1st Company had almost completed the construction of the Chateau de la Haie line, and was giving additional, and now much-needed, attention to the provision of dugouts, gas-proofing, baths, wells, horse standings and road repairs, and was continually altering and improving the numerous more or less temporary camps which press steadily on the heels of an advancing army. Here again difficulties of material and hostile shelling somewhat hindered

The Final Advance.

progress, though for every shell received by us the unfortunate Boche had overflowing measure in return. The British Heavy Artillery, now at a supreme pitch of organisation, bombarded his lines front and rear with a frequency and intensity which alone would have been some intimation that the scales were slowly turning at last.

As early as the first week of August, enemy withdrawals on various portions of the front, notably in the north, in the Lys country so well known to the Division, indicated that the German High Command had realised the failure of its recent offensive, and was now preparing to shorten sail wherever it could give ground without serious dislocation of its main lines of defence.

These laudable intentions were not unexpected by the British, and the first signs of any attempt to carry them out were eagerly watched for on the Divisional front. Constant patrols by day and night maintained steady touch with the enemy, determined not to be left too far behind should his modesty induce him to essay an unobtrusive retirement. An unoccupied post, discovered in the early morning of 14th August, was the first sign that the birds had flown. Immediate investigation proved that such was the case along the whole front of the Division. Patrols, followed by stronger parties, were immediately on the trail. Divisional orders were definitely against any wild advances by isolated parties, regardless of support and of contact with the troops on either flank, but by evening New Zealanders were in the fringe of Fork Wood and on the outskirts of Puisieux. Strong opposition by extensive enemy forces north of them, round Bucquoy, made further advance impossible in the meantime.

This welcome change in the situation was at once reflected in the operations of the Field Companies. All hands were long since heartily tired of the constant round of digging and maintenance inseparable from the stagnation of trench warfare. Now the first call of the situation was the provision of roads and communications to enable the advance to proceed, with the problem of water supply coming next in importance on a long programme of new activities. The former roads leading forward of Hebuterne and Gommecourt were taken in hand with vigorous enthusiasm. By the 18th, Field Artillery had moved forward and was already in position to support a fresh advance.

Definite offensive operations by the British Third Army commenced at 4.55 a.m. on 21st August, though the main call on the New Zealand Division was reserved for the 23rd. For an adequate conception of the true position it is necessary to

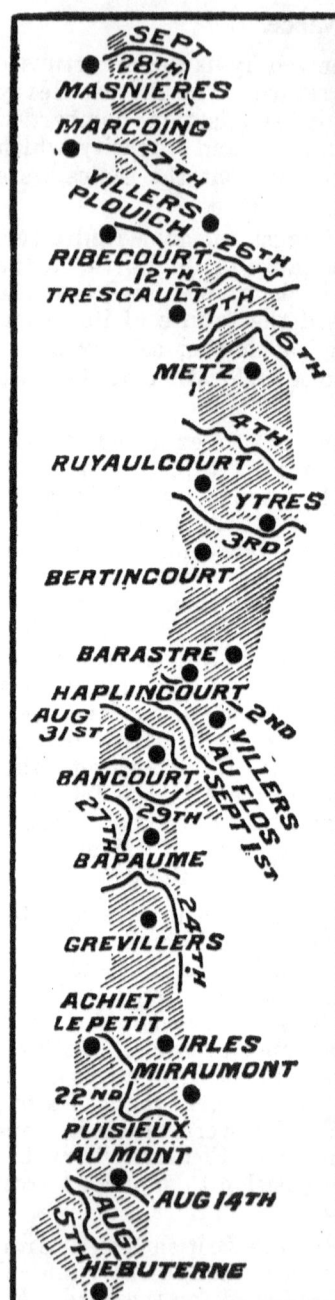
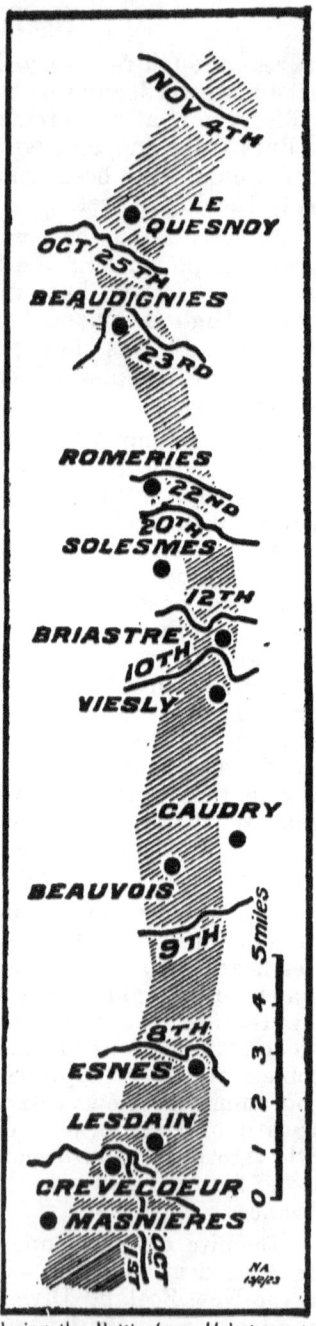

Plan of area captured by the N.Z. Division during the Battle from Hebuterne to Le Quesnoy, showing the dates the various objectives were gained.

The Final Advance.

take some brief notice of the numerous factors leading up to this consummation.

Once the great German attack launched in March had been definitely stemmed, it was quite apparent that all hope of victory in the field had passed from them for ever. The advent of American troops now made it absolutely certain that the initiative must pass once more to the Allies, whose recent exploits augured well for their ability to make the most of it. The best Ludendorff could hope for was peace based on the exhaustion of both sides, with a possible advantage to Germany from her successes on the Eastern Front. As early as the 8th August, Foch's first tentative efforts to test the strength of the enemy in an attack by the British Fourth and French First Armies, on the Paris-Amiens railway, had met with such unexpected good fortune that further French successes on the Oise deepened his opinion that the time for a general counter-attack had indeed at last arrived. The same facts quickened the Boche's intention to withdraw. North of the Somme, on the Third Army front, this course of action was doubly pressing, since our recent advance south of the River now accentuated the salient in which the enemy forces round Puisieux had found themselves when stopped in their onward march.

That withdrawal on Bapaume would take place was therefore a practical certainty; that it would be as leisured and orderly as the Allies cared to permit, with every attention to detail in the way of devastation and obstruction, was also sure. But this time we were to have more to say in the matter than on previous occasions. We had the advantages of observation, also of taking the enemy lines in enfilade instead of by frontal assault, and last, but by no means least, the spirit of aggressive confidence in his individual or collective superiority over the enemy had never been more marked in the Allied soldier. The New Zealanders, with memories of Passchendaele still rankling in their breasts, were simply spoiling for close quarters, and in the immediate as well as the more distant future were to be under constant reprimand from Corps Headquarters for an excess of zeal and impetuosity in a campaign where those qualities were rated as cardinal virtues. Influenced by these favourable auspices, the Allied Commanders decided to advance at once, not only with the hope of disorganising the inevitable Boche retreat, but also to minimise as far as possible the amount of damage inflicted on the unfortunate countryside. Heavy German reinforcements south of the Somme shifted the scene of the British effort to the Third Army front, where the Albert-Arras railway was fixed as the first objective, to be taken on the 21st. By

Field Companies and Field Troop.

the 23rd it was hoped that events would be sufficiently forward to enable the New Zealanders to come in on that day, and make a bold push for Bapaume.

For once even the elements were on the side of long-suffering Britain. At the hour of attack a heavy fog blanketed the fields and hedgerows, and saved many a lucky soldier during that fateful dash across the open that must be endured before the opposing machine-gunners could be reached and dealt with. Puisieux fell at once, and by nightfall British field guns were up in the outskirts of the town ready for further action. Heavy fighting followed all day on the 22nd, during which the important spur north of Miraumont, marked by the Beauregard Dovecot, was taken and retaken more than once. In plain justice to the German rearguards, it must be stated that their skill and tenacity were alike above reproach, though of but temporary avail. By afternoon of the 23rd the attack was astride the Arras Road, and menacing Bapaume from the north-west. Just beyond the Dovecot, a huge dump of Engineer stores was captured, including a great amount of explosive already prepared for use in small road mines and in many other varieties of trap calculated to snare the unwary —sure evidence that our advance had been too speedy for enemy expectations.

The advantages expected from the south-easterly direction of the attack, taking the very heavily defended lines in front of Bapaume from the flank, were more than realised, and no effort was spared to make the most of the favourable opportunities for exploitation. Experience derived from Ludendorff's own methods in March was not disdained. Particular stress was laid on the importance of each unit striving to reach and hold its allotted objective, irrespective of the success or otherwise obtaining on either flank.

In a fresh assault launched at 4.15 a.m. on 24th August the New Zealanders were allotted the capture of Loupart Wood and Grevillers, with Bapaume as an enticing ultimate goal if all went well in the earlier stages. A good start was made in the semi-darkness, but later on the trees and wire in the Wood, aided by the extremely strong posts and defences in front of Grevillers, neutralised the efforts of our tanks and held up the advance.

Conspicuously fine work had already in the course of the 2nd Auckland advance been done by Sergeant Samuel Forsyth, New Zealand Engineers, who was attached in accordance with the prevailing custom to an infantry battalion on probation for a commission. His magnificent efforts now to overcome the check were to win him a Victoria Cross. The official record runs as follows:—

The Final Advance.

* "On nearing the objective his company came under heavy machine-gun fire. Through Sergeant Forsyth's dashing leadership and total disregard of danger, three machine-gun positions were rushed and the crews taken prisoners before they could inflict many casualties on our troops.

During subsequent advance his company came under heavy fire from several machine-guns, two of which he located by a daring reconnaissance. In his endeavour to gain support from a tank he was wounded, but after having his wound bandaged he again got in touch with the tank, which in the face of very heavy fire from machine-guns and anti-tank guns he endeavoured to lead with magnificent coolness to a favourable position. The tank, however, was put out of action.

Sergeant Forsyth then organised the tank crew and several of his men into a section and led them to a position where the machine-guns could be outflanked. Always under heavy fire, he directed them into positions which brought about a retirement of the enemy machine-guns and enabled the advance to continue. This gallant N.C.O. was at that moment killed by a sniper.

From the commencement of the attack until the time of his death, Sergeant Forsyth's courage and coolness, combined with great power of initiative, proved an invaluable incentive to all who were with him, and he undoubtedly saved many casualties among his comrades."

Again, on the 25th, Bapaume was placed in front of the New Zealanders as a trophy worthy of their best endeavours. No encouragement was required to ensure a gallant effort. An early morning mist was again helpful, but with full day came once more the grim check from well-concealed machine-gunners. The tanks allotted for the day's enterprise were late at the rendezvous, and when they did arrive a vigorous temporary engagement of our own rear did little to assist the tide of battle. However, by late afternoon distinct progress had been achieved, and the smoke of burning dumps behind Bapaume afforded some slight satisfaction as evidence of increasing concern on the part of the enemy. In pouring rain all that night energetic patrols pushed on and gave the foe no respite.

But by the 26th the German defence had so stiffened that, despite vigorous efforts then and on the two succeeding days, progress was practically impossible. By evening of the 28th, Corps orders were to keep a keen lookout for evidence of enemy withdrawal, as it was felt that his supreme efforts of the last two days had been expended to gain time to arrange

---

*Extract from Col. H. Stewart's History of the N.Z. Division.

Field Companies and Field Troop.

the details of a further retreat elsewhere, and that once that was satisfactorily accomplished he would abandon Bapaume to its fate. Events proved this to be an accurate forecast. In the early hours of the 29th, diminishing signs of enemy activity encouraged the ever active patrols, which by 10 a.m. were through the town and hard on the heels of the retiring enemy. That night a line of trenches was laid down in front of Bancourt to provide cover for the forward troops in case of counter-attack. A section from the 3rd Field Company with 500 men of the reserve brigade stuck to the job all night under heavy gas shelling and rifle fire, but before daylight our forward patrols had again moved the enemy on, and the trenches were never used. Similar unavoidable sacrifices of time and labour were of constant occurrence all through these days of rapid movement.

The events of the next day or two were repetitions of what had gone before, marked by ceaseless gallant effort on the part of the attackers, and by a stubborn defence no less admirable on the part of the hard-pressed German rearguards. Steady progress was maintained, and by the night of the 1st September the line lay in front of Villers-au-Flos, where especially violent machine-gun fire was experienced. Events on other fronts combine to cause this to be regarded as the close of the Battle of Bapaume.

The success of the Third Army had been unquestionable, but by no means lightly purchased. All authorities agree in according due deference to the skilled tactics and marked bravery which distinguished the German retirement. The New Zealanders' share of the prisoners taken amounted to 47 officers and over 1600 men. That these results were not recorded without ceaseless effort on the part of the attacking troops goes without saying. To the Engineers, though not included in the more stirring adventures of the forward fighting line, fell a heavy share of the labours and technical difficulties, of which the speedy and effective handling was such a necessary factor to success.

Among the sappers' manifold duties, the repair of roads was naturally an ever present item. Their prototypes among the enemy had expended great energy and no little skill in the mining of all important cross roads, and many other positions calculated to cause a maximum of delay. In most cases, time was too precious to attempt final repair, and the obstacles were side-stepped by the provision of new temporary roadways of timber or of brick around them. Apart from the extensive and well-organised general schemes of destruction carried out on roads, railways, and bridges, with which, as a definite factor in war, no one can have any reasonable

The Final Advance.

complaint, the retreating Germans appeared to have spent an enormous amount of time and ingenuity on all kinds of petty traps and devices of a malignant nature. The inconsiderable amount of damage likely to result from many of their bright ideas made them of no real avail as warlike expedients, and one is driven to the conclusion that the average German soldier found his simple pleasure in the performance of these queer little tricks.

Who can imagine a British soldier, for example, if forced to abandon a dressing station full of wounded men to the mercies of the enemy, arranging first a dead body in such a way that, after evacuation of the wounded, any removal of the corpse would fire a charge? Trip wires were placed in every variety of position, likely and unlikely, all arranged on the simple principle that removal of the wire fired a charge, to the probable extinction of the curious wire-puller. Doors and entrances of shelters, dugouts and houses all were liable to be fitted with some type of friction or percussion device calculated to surprise if not delight the intruder. Books and other articles left on tables, even pictures and mirrors hung on the walls, required careful inspection before being touched. Lumps of explosive were mixed with the coal dumps, or hidden carefully in fireplaces and chimneys with a view to ignition when a fire was lighted. All souvenirs such as helmets, shellcases, badges and bayonets, left in conspicuous positions, or articles left sticking in the ground such as stick grenades or shovels, could safely be labelled dangerous till their bona fides was investigated.

Dugouts, as the home and dwelling place of these humourists, were especially dangerous. If there was no charge concealed beneath the entrance step so that the first pressure of an entering footstep caused an explosion, the furniture was almost certain to be well equipped with explosive, or the bunk only required occupation to betray the full extent of their hospitable preparations. In one house, a grandfather's clock was so equipped that the running down of the weight would complete an electrical circuit and demolish the whole building. Bathing places were fully provided with pointed stakes and barbed wire arranged below water level.

The above probably represent only the amusements of the private soldier in his leisure moments, though during the German retirement circumstances over which he had little control must have seriously curtailed his periods of relaxation. There were numerous instances of larger and more organised traps. Of these the principal were delay-action mines. All these mines, of whatever size and composition, were fired by a fuse containing a detonator and exploder charge, the action

Field Companies and Field Troop.

of which depended on a corrosive liquid eating through a wire, the length of the required delay being determined by the strength of the corrosive liquid.

In many cases these traps and mines were rendered harmless by the mere cutting of a wire, which could be done by anyone, but the whole matter of dealing with enemy explosive devices was rightly considered a technical work, and as such came within the scope of the Engineers' duties. For handling some of the larger mines beneath roads and railways, several experienced miners were attached to the New Zealand Engineers from the New Zealand Tunnellers, and they fully maintained the high reputation gained by their unit in France. A spear fashioned out of a long steel rod and a spade handle, very similar to the weapon employed by the kauri gum-diggers of North Auckland, was much used by the prospectors for probing areas where mines were thought to exist, and saved a large amount of otherwise unavoidable digging.

An adequate supply of water was expected to be a considerable difficulty before the British advance commenced, and events justified the premonition. Even in front of Rossignol Wood, all supplies were being brought forward from rear areas. With the constant movement of the advance, the problem of supply became quite acute. Numerous parties of sappers were constantly employed on water service alone, prospecting for wells, clearing and purifying such as were found not entirely destroyed, and providing the necessary gear for convenient usage. The general enemy procedure as regards wells had been to smash both engine and pump at each one, and then to throw the pieces down the shaft along with any filth or rubbish readily available. To clear the accumulation from a depth of 60 to 80 feet was quite a task, and consumed much valuable time.

Storage troughs, horse watering points, suitable arrangements for rapid filling of water-carts, and in many cases the installation of hand or power-driven pumps, all came under the charge of these water patrols. No water of any kind was used before investigations were made as to its purity, and the erection of proper notices at each supply point was a further duty of the parties in charge. In the strange country occupied daily by the advancing troops there was a tremendous call for notice boards of all descriptions, and a busy time was spent by the Field Companies' signwriters.

Ordinary trench construction, despite the changed conditions of warfare, was very far from falling into the general disuse that would have been perfectly acceptable to the majority of the optimistic fighting troops. To break the pleasant exhilaration of some days' successful advancing by

The Final Advance.

a return to the dull routine of trench digging was not at all in accordance with their views of the proper conduct of war. However, the more prudent authorities decreed otherwise, and the provision of reserve posts and defensive lines, often abandoned the next day in favour of similar positions further forward, was an inevitable accompaniment of each successful advance, and absorbed the energies of many sappers.

The 1st Field Company, for the moment in reserve, had a similar experience with regard to the works usually required in rear areas. Erection of hutments, gas-proofing of dugouts, provision of bath and laundry facilities, and the hundred and one small requirements of the supply and administration branches of Divisional activities were no sooner completed than the exigencies of a changed situation necessitated a renewal of the same activities elsewhere. But no one heeded that small fly in the ointment, either in front or in rear. After so many months and months of stagnation in weary trench lines, or of painful advance under conditions of such peril and travail that success was almost too dearly won to possess many attractions, the armies of Britain were properly on the move. We had the Boche going home at last and almost on the run. Every man privileged to be there felt it in his bones and exulted, not least of his satisfaction being a comfortable conviction that the Hun was likewise fully aware of his changed fortunes. What mattered the long day, or the tedious task, with fresh success waiting in the morning?

The more important of the immediate obstacles now confronting the advance of the Third Army were the extensive Havrincourt Wood and the strongly-defended Trescault Spur immediately behind it. On 2nd September the advance was renewed, the New Zealanders proposed share in the day's exploits being the capture of Haplincourt. It is inexpedient to follow here the operation of the next few days in detail, since they presented no particular features of importance, and the activities of the sappers were confined to the ordinary duties consequent upon advance, already described and now probably more or less familiar to the reader. The time had not yet come for the bridging exploits which were to be a notable feature of later stages of this campaign.

By evening of the 8th, after continuous but not especially heavy fighting, the tide of advance was through the Wood and washing against the lower slopes of Trescault Spur. This ridge, whose crest was fortified by old British trenches, was now to be defended with a determined valour which was a fair indication of the German desire to maintain a wide defensive zone in front of the famous Hindenburg Line, at last within striking distance some three miles further on.

Field Companies and Field Troop.

Amongst other fresh Divisions placed to dispute the passage of this important outlying stronghold were the famous Jagers, seasoned veterans of the first class of German manhood. However, despite the natural strength of the position and the valiant efforts of the redoubtable Jagers, the Spur lay in our hands by the evening of the 12th. Next day was cold and stormy, but was marked by constant conflict along the ridge, honours finally resting to a large extent with the Jagers, who succeeded in forcing us to abandon the crest in several places and were not finally dislodged till some days later. Notwithstanding this slight local check, the general stage was now well set for an assault on the Hindenburg Line.

On the 14th, in company with the bulk of the New Zealand Division, the Field Companies passed back into rear areas for a brief period of rest and recreation. During the next 10 days various odd jobs were performed in rear areas, between periods of training and sport, and considerable time was taken up in drawing complete pontoon equipment at Avesnes-les-Bapaume.

In view of the probability of considerable bridging being required to cross the Escaut Canal and River, all ranks were put through a brief course of training in the service likely to be required of them. While the Division remained in rest areas many men revisited the scenes of former experiences at Flers. Some 160 crosses were made by the sappers, and were erected over New Zealanders' graves on the old Somme battlefield; and a large wooden cross 16 feet high was also erected at Flers by order of Divisional Headquarters.

By the evening of the 28th the New Zealanders were once more in the line, which had been considerably advanced during their absence, and in the early morning of the 29th they again attacked the enemy with marked success. By this time the whole of the main defences of the allegedly impregnable Hindenburg Line, with its hundreds of concrete posts and huge dugouts built into the earth beyond all possible reach by hostile artillery, and all protected by acres of massed barbed wire, had fallen to the armies of Britain. We now lay along the high ground of Bonavis Ridge, overlooking the deep Canal, with no further prepared obstacles of great importance in front save the last strong system of the Hindenburg support lines, known as the Masnieres-Beaurevoir Line, and now clearly visible across the valley beyond the line of the Canal.

Further beyond again, the eye dwelt longingly on green fields and wooded slopes, untouched by the devastation of war, with villages nestling amid the trees, and the peaceful smoke of civilian firesides rising on the calm air. Away to the north lay the towers and spires of Cambrai. In the immediate fore-

The Final Advance.

ground, on the near side of the poplar-bordered Canal and River, was the long straggling village of Rue des Vignes. Across the Canal, half a mile northward, Crevecoeur lay on a sharp bend, while possibilities of crossing further south were menaced by German rearguards in the village of Vaucelles. The whole countryside across the Canal was alive with enemy movement. Even guns were plainly visible still in process of removal, and the sight intensified the general eagerness to press on. However, patrols pushing aggressively down the forward slopes of the ridge were soon hampered by increasing German gunfire, and the sight of numerous parties of the enemy taking up position on the further bank made it plain that the crossing was to be warmly contested.

During the evening full preparations were made for an attack at dawn, while patrols tested the German defences all night in hopes of reaching the shelter of the Canal bank before daylight. The Germans remaining on our side of the Canal opposite Crevecoeur fell back on the village during the hours of darkness, but further upstream in front of Vaucelles no progress could be made till daylight, when advance was rendered singularly difficult by the numerous well-posted machine-guns on the enemy's bank. Plans for the attack proved that Vaucelles would be a tough nut to crack, but no special trouble at Crevecoeur was anticipated, despite the fact that the Canal cuts across a sharp bend of the River at that point, leaving the village protected not only by the Canal, but also by the River, while a small branch stream intersecting the island lying between River and Canal afforded yet another obstacle to the advance.

At Vaucelles the bridge was discovered with the centre span blown up and the remainder of the edifice rendered quite unapproachable by the German rearguards in the village. A small party from the 2nd Field Company essayed to reconnoitre the position more closely, but were forced to retire without success. Their leader, Lieutenant F. K. Broadgate, was killed by a German sniper as soon as he raised his head from the shelter of an old sap in which the party had wormed its way forward. Nor was much better result achieved at Crevecoeur. One attacking party managed to reach the island, and one of their number even succeeded in removing the demolition charges from the stone bridge spanning the further stream but, with dozens of machine-guns filling the narrow passage with a perfect storm of lead, no attempt to reach the village had even a remote prospect of success. In fact, as far as the New Zealand front was concerned, the attack was definitely held up. The Field Companies lying ready with their pontoons and other bridging apparatus were forced to content them-

Field Companies and Field Troop.

selves with overhauling their gear and with making further exhaustive searches to increase their available supplies of suitable materials for the heavier bridges that would be necessary before guns and vehicular traffic could continue the advance.

On 1st October, a further attack was made on Crevecoeur by crossing lower down the Canal, where a passage had been forced on the previous day, and by coming at the village from the north-west. Against these fresh tactics the place fell quickly, but even then no progress was possible higher up the Canal on the remainder of the New Zealand Front. A party of Engineers from the 1st Field Company under Lieutenant A. W. Thomas, who had been attached to the 1st Brigade throughout its operations, and had been of great assistance in removing demolition charges and delay-action mines from bridges and dugouts, now further distinguished itself by building under fire a footbridge across the river to the island, and by repairing a traffic bridge for horses and transport. For gallant individual efforts here, and in reconnaissance work under heavy fire later, Lt. Thomas received the Military Cross. Corporal A. T. Brokenshire, who had won the Military Medal at Passchendaele, showed that his prowess on that occasion had not exhausted his qualities of skill and courage. For his excellent work on these Crevecoeur bridges, both on 1st and 2nd October, he was awarded the D.C.M. Lance-Corporal D. D. Rennie and Sapper R. W. Adams further swelled the list of Military Medal winners belonging to the 1st Field Company by their gallant conduct at Crevecoeur. The former worked continuously on the bridges under fire until they were completed, while Adams, in addition to his labours on the actual bridges, made constant excursions into territory occupied by the enemy to collect bridging material from a small enemy dump fortunately undestroyed.

Other Engineers were by no means idle and had already succeeded in placing two pontoon bridges down on the bank of the Canal ready for use as soon as circumstances would permit. This was not yet however; until the evening of the 4th, heavy bombardment and ceaseless machine-gun fire were maintained both on the captured village of Crevecoeur and on the whole length of the Escaut Canal as far as Vaucelles. On the 1st October, our right flank had side-stepped northward, and was now more in the locality of Rue des Vignes, but with even less prospect of crossing there than Vaucelles had offered.

But further south events were moving and, during the night of the 4th-5th October, the enemy fell back on his Masnieres-Beaurevoir Line, fortunately sufficiently far from the Canal to leave room for the following battalions to make

The Final Advance.

suitable dispositions for the continued attack soon to follow. No sooner did hostile shells falling on Vaucelles and the immediate neighbourhood announce the fact of the enemy retirement, than there was a rush of our waiting infantry to cross the Canal and get after them. Some companies were diverted south and crossed on the Vaucelles bridge, others were accommodated by hasty temporary repairs to the demolished bridge on the Tordoir Lock at the southern end of Rue des Vignes, but the majority crossed on rafts hurriedly thrown together by the waiting Field Companies.

This retirement of the enemy had not been unexpected, and on the evening of the 4th Sergeant A. Ward of the 2nd Field Company had been detailed to prepare a raft ready for possible use at dawn. Despite heavy shelling and machine-gun fire on the village and canal bank, Ward and his men carried forward their material some 2000 yards, in several trips, and constructed their raft at the selected point. The first signs of daylight found the attacking infantry on the further bank. An award of the Military Medal was immediate recognition of Sergeant Ward's tenacity and devotion to duty. As soon as these preliminary needs of the immediate pursuers were satisfied, the whole energies of the 1st and 2nd Field Companies were bent on the construction of heavy traffic bridges, with sufficient success to make possible a continuation of the attack on the 8th October.

By the evening of the 7th some bridges were still incomplete and the bridging parties were subject to constant shelling. At Tordoir Lock, where 2nd-Lieutenant D. Doake of the 2nd Field Company was in charge of bridge construction, conditions were unusually severe, a bombardment of gas shells, lending additional emphasis to the heavy gunfire, being concentrated on his locality. However, Field Artillery were to cross that bridge at dawn, and Doake and his men worked on steadily all night. When the guns arrived in the morning they crossed without mishap or delay. Doake's cool courage placed him forthwith among the wearers of the Military Cross. 2nd-Corporal A. M. Heath and Sapper A. C. Schioler of the 2nd Company also rendered yeoman service throughout this period.

During the night of the 7th October and all day on the 8th, Sergeant D. McLaren of the 1st Field Company had also been engaged on repairing these bridges. It was largely owing to his energy and disregard of personal danger, working at times with the bridge in flames, that all crossings had been kept open both before and during the operations, and his efforts were also rewarded with the Military Medal.

Field Companies and Field Troop.

The German lines now fronting the Third Army represented the very last of his definitely prepared positions, and were naturally expected to provide a mighty obstacle. With unshaken faith in the prowess of its attacking Divisions, IV Corps set an objective which included the whole of this strong system, with instructions which pointed to an expectation that the close of the day would see our new line beyond the village of Esnes. On the New Zealanders, by virtue of their position on the Corps Front, fell the brunt of the fighting, and by night the line lay beyond Esnes as anticipated. The sappers were still busy on the Canal, where further pontoon bridges were being put in position, and all bridges were maintained in good order. German shelling continued very heavy, and the constant repairs rendered necessary would have been a hard task even in undisturbed surroundings. However their efforts were not in vain. All Divisional and attached Artillery were safely across the Canal soon after mid-day. As evening fell enemy bombing planes were particularly active, while a heavy bombardment drenched our rear areas with gas.

A cold dawn on the 9th was heralded once again by the crash of the New Zealand barrage and the advance of the indefatigable infantry. But on this occasion their opponents were missing, nor was touch again established till the afternoon, when machine-gun fire was encountered from the village of Fontaine-au-Pire. As darkness fell, patrols pushed on and found both it and Beauvois evacuated. On went the leading battalions forthwith, and before daylight had reached the Le Cateau-Cambrai Road. Beauvois still sheltered a few civilians, and was practically unscathed, though astonishing scenes of filth and desecration marked the close of the German occupation.

Throughout the war, with perhaps special emphasis on their voluntary retreat to the Hindenburg Line in 1917, wherever and whenever the Boche vacated French territory, the recovered lands and villages returned to their distracted owners in a condition that will attach a sinister stain to the name of the German for generations. Thousands of French farms and hundreds of towns and villages, when not completely destroyed, received the almost indelible imprint of a calculated devastation such as no country in Europe had ever experienced before this war. In place of the smiling fields and prosperous homes of pre-war days, France recovered but a wilderness of terrible desolation. Churches, schools, public buildings and private dwellings, works of art, historical monuments and records—all had shared the same fate of ruthless destruction. The valuable possessions of the wealthier people were stolen and taken away; the few poor sticks and worthless little house-

The Final Advance.

hold treasures of the peasants were broken or burnt; wells were filled with dung; every garden and bush was uprooted; and as a crowning infamy every fruit tree was sawn off at the stump. There can be no doubt of the official intention to leave these fertile lands blasted and barren for a decade, and the thorough manner in which the work had been executed is another illuminating sidelight on the curious mentality of the German species. No one who has not seen this thing can understand how deeply the bitterness of it has eaten into the soul of France; those who did see it were looking on at the misery of others, not their own; but even so they do not find it hard to sympathise with the present day attitude of stricken France, however impossible of fulfilment her aspirations may appear to minds less influenced by searing memories or perchance more anxious to see the evil-doer once again on a sound commercial basis.

By 1 a.m. on the 11th, our leading battalions had cleared Briastre, and reached the banks of the River Selle. Though but a tributary of the Scheldt, the Selle flows in a deep valley, with a fair depth of water and an average width of some 30 feet, while high slopes on either side completely dominate the actual line of the stream. Here, taking full advantage of a naturally strong position, the over-taxed rearguards of the harassed enemy were bidden to make another stand.

During the evening of the 10th, the 37th Divisional Engineers had managed to bridge the stream some half-a-mile above the New Zealanders, but all bridges on our own front were found destroyed, nor was it possible to provide more before daylight. In the hour or two available, however, some parties of our infantry crossed on the 37th Divisional front, and working back along the opposite bank were in process of disposition for a further advance when the dawn disclosed them to the enemy, who lined all the eastern slopes of the valley in strength. At once heavy fire compelled them to take shelter, and they remained all day under cover of a large factory. Here Lieutenant A. W. Thomas and his men of the 1st Field Company again rendered yeoman service in pushing across the stream a temporary bridge of trees and rails which maintained some touch with the main body. Night had fallen on the 12th before our various attacks ultimately triumphed over exceeding stout opposition, leaving us consolidated along the railway line at Belle Vue. With this establishment of a bridgehead covering the Briastre crossings, the advance was temporarily discontinued, and the New Zealanders passed into reserve.

After the constant progress of the last few days, the time was ripe to devote extra attention to the problems of rear roads

Field Companies and Field Troop.

and railway communications. The energies of all three Field Companies were fully absorbed by reconnaissance of the captured territory, and by the familiar tasks connected with water supply, baths, laundries, hutments, repair of craters, plank roads, provision of signboards, the erection of a Divisional theatre, and so on ad infinitum. Even as the advance went on from day to day, sections of the Field Companies, especially the Company in reserve, had been forced to find time for a certain amount of this routine work, particularly as regards supplies of water. Thus in Beauvois on the 10th, 2nd-Corporal F. S. Wilkinson of the 2nd Company had been engaged on urgent water operations under circumstances of great danger from violent shell fire, which resulted in several casualties to his party. Wilkinson was not to be diverted from his purpose, and carried his job to completion with a courage and determination that won him a Military Medal.

The 1st Field Company were now notified that their services would be required by the Chief Engineer, IV Corps, to erect a tank bridge over the Selle River following a further attack set down for the 20th, and they devoted some time to preparation of gear and material. Colonel H. Stewart, in his History of the New Zealand Division, thus describes their efforts:—

"The heavy shelling on the river had barely abated when the Engineers were hard at work on the bridge. By extraordinary exertions it was completed in 13 hours. This rapidity of construction no less than the skilful and thorough nature of the workmanship elicited warm congratulations from General Harper and his Chief Engineer, who on the 21st personally witnessed the heaviest class of tank pass safely over. On the following day the same company constructed a heavy traffic bridge in 15 hours."

These two bridges were constructed side by side in the gap left by the destruction of the former brick arch bridge. The maintenance of pontoon and foot bridges across the Selle was entrusted at the same time to the 2nd Field Company. The 3rd Company, who had been Company in reserve, were to have their special opportunity without delay. On the 22nd this Company moved to an assembly area south-east of Solesmes, where they joined the 2nd Brigade, who were to carry the St. Georges River crossings on the 23rd. The now usual success attended the day's advance; so much so that the leading troops were able to cross the St. Georges River without much difficulty, and by most commendable enterprise pushed on into the village of Beaudignies and secured two bridges across the Ecaillon still intact. Meanwhile the 3rd

The Final Advance.

Field Company was busily erecting a bridge at Pont a Pierres to enable the Artillery to continue the advance. The enemy was already shelling heavily all possible bridge sites, and it was with great difficulty that the 3rd Company was able to complete its job by daylight.

Next day three Weldon trestle bridges were thrown across the river in this same locality. The 1st Field Company had been instructed to repeat its performance of the 20th by erecting another tank bridge at Pont a Pierres. Investigation of the situation disclosed an immense crater 80 feet wide and 20 feet deep which had been blown in the road by the departing Boches, and had involved the former bridge abutments in the general ruin. To repair this damage was impossible at the moment, but the erection of a fine double-way heavy bridge of two 20-feet spans supported by a massive trestle pier, quickly reopened the road to Beaudignies for the passage of guns and waggons. The new bridge was approached by a short deviation on either side of the stream. Heavy planks on one side and broken brick on the other furnished a temporary roadbed that successfully carried the weightiest traffic.

Constant violent shelling of the area immediately surrounding these bridges caused repeated damage to the structure, to say nothing of the personnel employed. Colonel Stewart may be fairly quoted once more:—

"No unit, however, can boast of a higher standard of duty or hardier fortitude than the Engineers, who, making light of difficulties, dangers and disappointments, persevered with, completed and maintained their work."

Conspicuous gallantry and devotion to duty were shown by 2nd-Lieutenant D. R. Mansfield, and Lance-Corporal E. R. W. Pledger, of the 1st Field Company, the latter's efforts being rewarded with the Military Medal. Sappers G. M. Bennett and A. Newport of the 1st Field Company also came under official notice for their qualities of skill and courage shown under heavy fire during the bridging operations at Pont a Pierres. Both had also been prominent in the erection of bridges at Briastre a few days earlier.

The 3rd Company were no less assiduous in their efforts, nor less steadfast in maintaining a high standard of efficiency and cool bearing. 2nd-Lieutenant E. W. George was particularly prominent in the operations at Pont a Pierres and won the Military Cross, while a Military Medal was awarded to 2nd-Corporal George Campbell, whose performances on the 4th set the seal on a long period of courageous service.

Meanwhile the scene of conflict lay in front of Beaudignies, where the determined opposition met with pointed to a

Field Companies and Field Troop.

desperate stand before the famous old fortress of Le Quesnoy, now less than a mile to the eastward. So vigorous and numerous indeed were the enemy troops, and so heavy the increased fire of his artillery and trench mortars, that the plan of advance was broken off on the 25th to allow of very necessary reorganisation. The numerous re-adjustments from a moving to a stationary warfare which followed brought the Engineers once more in touch with the details of trenches, posts, elephant shelters, and gas-proof protection, which they had fondly hoped were left behind for ever. The erection of 3 artillery bridges and 14 foot bridges across the Ecaillon, however, all cut from the trees growing along the banks, was some earnest of the temporary nature of the change of policy. Constant attention was also necessary at Pont a Pierres, where the bridges still remained the storm-centre of continuous German bombardments.

A welcome draft of 54 reinforcements, mostly "old hands," joined the Field Companies at the end of the month, replacing some 60 men sent to the Depot in England in due rotation, 10 days earlier.

The ancient fortress of Le Quesnoy, soon to become so intimately associated with the military exploits of one of the youngest and smallest countries in history, had many a time stood in the forefront of the conflicts of the Old World. Its very existence is due to the fact that in that region no topographical obstacles protect France from invasion from the north-east, and the military experts of mediaeval France had been forced to rear their own barriers against outside aggression, since Nature had been remiss. The extensive ramparts of former days, however, though maintained and improved by the great Vauban, whose skill had provided the stubborn walls of Ypres, were even before the war considered obsolete. Three gates entered the town, now boasting little more than 5000 inhabitants.

Some eight miles to the south-east of Le Quesnoy, beyond the great Forest of Mormal, now largely destroyed by the Boche, lay the most important feature of the strategic situation, the Aulnoye Junction. This and other centres of communication about Maubeuge, only 15 miles due east of Le Quesnoy, were of the utmost importance to the demoralised Huns, since their fall would probably involve the cutting of the main line of retreat for the extensive German forces now falling back before the French and Americans. The wording of the official despatch clearly defines the position at the end of October.

"By this time the rapid succession of heavy blows dealt by the British forces had had a cumulative effect, both moral

The Final Advance.

and material, upon the German Armies. The difficulty of replacing the enemy's enormous losses in guns, machine-guns and ammunition had increased with every fresh attack, and his reserves of men were exhausted.

"The capitulation of Turkey and Bulgaria and the imminent collapse of Austria—consequent upon Allied successes which the desperate position of her own armies on the Western Front had rendered her powerless to prevent—had made Germany's military situation ultimately impossible. If her armies were allowed to withdraw undisturbed to shorter lines, the struggle might still be protracted over the winter. The British Armies, however, were now in a position to prevent this by a direct attack upon a vital centre, which should anticipate the enemy's withdrawal and force an immediate conclusion."

This attack was set down for the morning of the 4th November. The New Zealanders were to establish a new line on the further side of Herbignies village, a total advance of about four miles.

Despite their lack of modern finish, the ramparts of Le Quesnoy still presented far too serious an obstacle to be attacked frontally with inevitable heavy loss of life, when other methods of subjugation lay open to the attacking troops. Intense bombardment might have hastened matters, but then only at the expense of civilian lives, and of the destruction of historic monuments and private property. Plans were accordingly laid to envelop the town from both flanks, eventually surrounding it without unduly delaying the progress of the advance on Herbignies. To the Rifle Brigade, which was to conduct the preliminary stages of the advance, was left the honour of mopping up Le Quesnoy.

During the night of the 3rd-4th November there were no signs that the German garrisons in and about Le Quesnoy were expecting an attack. Desultory shelling was maintained on our positions, and at 5.20 a.m. a double orange flare, denoting all clear, was seen to rise above the town.

Ten minutes later the operator must have had a suspicion that his signal was premature. A tremendous bombardment fell on the German positions, while drums of burning oil were hurled on the ramparts with a view to concealing the enveloping movement of our troops now about to take place. After a hard struggle in the immediate environs of Le Quesnoy, the attacking battalions swept forward without any particular resistance, and by mid-day had reached the final objective about Herbignies on the outskirts of the Forest of Mormal.

Field Companies and Field Troop.

To the 3rd Field Company had been allotted the work of clearing artillery tracks right through the double railway lines north of the town within two hours of zero—fixed on this occasion at 5.30 a.m.—and of assisting the endeavour to find a way into the fortress. The section detailed for the tracks followed the infantry at the beginning of the attack and reached its objective without casualty. The rails were immediately blown out with guncotton charges, when passable roadways were easily dug through the embankment. An enemy machine-gun not far distant was enfilading the line of railway, but fortunately the gunner was prevented by mist from any accuracy of aim, which alone enabled the work to be completed in the specified time.

Meanwhile the battalions of the Rifle Brigade, to each of which was attached a party from the 3rd Field Company, who withdrew numerous demolition charges from bridges and road crossings, were encircling the walls of Le Quesnoy, each intent on securing the honour of first entry into the fortress. Strong defence was encountered from the garrison, which increased the natural difficulties of the position.

The Moat, instead of a single wide ditch, was found divided into an outer and inner moat by a series of disconnected fortifications, some 20 to 30 feet high, with brick or sandstone sides, acting as an extra rampart and known as "demilunes." Trees and undergrowth grew in and around these outlying bastions, which together with the varying direction of the walls rendered it difficult to preserve a sense of direction, and furnished excellent cover for the German snipers and machine-gunners now holding each position in considerable force. Beyond them lay the inner moat before the final rampart, watered by a small tributary of the Rhonelle, which, entering the fortress through a sluice gate on the south-east side, flows along the moat in a stream about seven feet wide and leaves the walls by another sluice on the north. West of the town this stream runs generally underground. With expectation of finding the inner moat flooded, the attackers were provided with cork mats, but only the normal amount of water was found in the stream. The final rampart showed a 60 feet wall of solid brick.

In expectation of a final assault on the walls 10 ladders had been prepared by the Engineers, and placed overnight at the shrine on the Ruesnes road west of the fortress. When the barrage opened in the morning, these ladders were carried forward by sappers attached to the 4th Rifles attacking in that area. After considerable difficulties, these parties succeeded in scaling one of the outer bastions, and, emboldened by success, endeavoured to rear their ladder against the inner

The Final Advance.

wall. They were immediately discovered, and the infantry officer in charge was shot down. One of the sappers in charge of the ladder was also killed and two others were wounded, and the attempt was seen to be hopeless.

Up till 9 a.m. various other attempts to approach the inner moat failed, though some more of the outer bastions had been occupied by enterprising platoons of the 4th Rifles. The final capture was only a matter of time and, rather than sacrifice lives unnecessarily, recourse was had to propaganda. However, no reply to the various messages inviting surrender was received, and by mid-day many enquiries as to the prospects of the town's early fall began to arrive both from the Artillery officers anxious to move forward without making a long detour, and from numerous working parties and others on the flanks of the town who were subject to periodic bursts of fire from its commanding walls.

In the early afternoon, another attempt was made on the walls. This time the attacking party was able to reach the western bank of the inner moat without opposition, with the final wall towering above them. By a fortunate chance a narrow stone bridge spanned the moat, and offered some prospect of reaching the top of the wall with the 30ft. ladder available. At the first attempt a German post on the walls above drove the party back at once. A light trench mortar and several Lewis guns were brought forward in support and, under their covering fire, a final attempt was made. This time the ladder was safely reared, and a moment later a New Zealand officer stood on the ramparts, where he was soon joined by eager Riflemen, and the town was ours. For conspicuous gallantry and devotion to duty while carrying and controlling the indispensable ladders, Lance-Corporal A. J. Randall received the D.C.M. and Sapper J. Hodgson the Military Medal.

During the night of the 3rd, 2nd-Corporal T. MacLennan of the 3rd Field Company had been occupied under heavy shell fire in erecting a road screen to hide the advance of our assaulting troops to their jumping off positions. In the morning he repaired and maintained his work till it was no longer required, when he was prominent in work on the roads round Le Quesnoy, though still under machine-gun fire from the ramparts. He showed coolness and skill of a high order, and received the Military Medal for his exploits. For similar work in constructing an avoiding road near Le Quesnoy, while under heavy fire from the walls of the town, Sergeant W. J. Fix of the same Company, who had been prominent on numerous other occasions during the preceding three months, received the same decoration. Sapper J. E. Foster was another member

Field Companies and Field Troop.

of the 3rd Company who was conspicuous for devoted service under heavy fire during this momentous day.

While the 3rd Company had been engaged on the special preparation for its share in the Le Quesnoy assault, the 1st Company had been still actively engaged on the never ending requirements of roads and bridges. A heavy lorry bridge at Mesnil Farm was completed prior to the fresh attack, and numerous log bridges to facilitate the rapid advance of our artillery were run up at various selected crossings on the Ecaillon. By this stage in the campaign, the energies of at least one section were always employed on the work of dismantling temporary trestle bridges in rear as these were replaced by the erection of more solid structures, and in bringing forward the retrieved bridging with a view to its employment in the new advanced areas constantly falling to our arms. Searching for additional material, either in abandoned German dumps or in destroyed buildings, filling up small craters, or constructing road deviations round larger ones, were practically the only calls allowed to compete with this constant demand for bridges, at which the sappers were becoming highly efficient. With the increasing dexterity born of continual practice came a pardonable pride in the reputation their good work undoubtedly achieved. Small parties were kept constantly on the move after each fresh advance, examining the state of captured roads and bridges, locating German dumps and reconnoitring the possibilities of the captured area with regard to water, the shelter of troops, supplies of timber, and similar considerations. The actual work connected with water supply, billeting areas, baths, laundries, and other rear requirements was for the moment in the hands of the 2nd Company, now taking its turn of duty as company in reserve.

Meanwhile, the fall of Le Quesnoy was already but an item in the day's work to the troops round Herbignies. The Rifles were scarcely in the town ere the 2nd Brigade was on the road forward to take up the attack on the Mormal Forest on the 5th. Though German depredations had cleared large tracts of the original wooded area, the debris left by their operations and the jungle of dense undergrowth which had followed, made the Forest even less open to the passage of troops than had been the case formerly. Altogether, these 20,000 acres of bush, marsh, and stream, with innumerable opportunities for enemy posts, and with little or no facility for the passage of guns and transport, were expected to provide a serious delay. Nor were these expectations unrealised, though the numbers of great trees which had been felled across the roads were not the obstacle they might have

The Final Advance.

been to men less accustomed to axe and saw than the New Zealanders were. A champion axeman among the sappers found great opportunities of displaying his skill, and the speed with which he went through his blocks completely fascinated passing Tommies. Pouring rain added to the difficulties of an arduous day. However, conscious of the fact that they were to be relieved on the morrow, the battalions of Otago and Canterbury were not to be denied, and, when Lancashire troops of the 42nd Division arrived to continue the advance, they were able to form up on the Bavai road, with the line of the Sambre clearly visible across easy rolling fields.

The New Zealand Artillery were in action again on the 6th and their resolute efforts to traverse the mined and boggy tracks through the Forest called for assistance from the Engineers. A bridge on the only serviceable road had naturally been demolished, and the state of all approaches was so bad that only temporary material was available to cross the stream. A section of the 2nd Field Company was on the spot, and forthwith constructed an improvised bridge of branches and pick handles, which saw the majority of the guns over the obstacle before a clumsily driven waggon capsized into the stream, and wrecked the makeshift crossing.

In succeeding days, several more bridges were erected, notably at Le Quesnoy and at Pont Billon, where a lengthy structure occupied both 1st and 2nd Field Companies for several days. Following the capture of Le Quesnoy, the 3rd Company had assisted in the general rehabilitation of the town, many of whose buildings were left in filth and confusion by the Germans, according to their peculiar custom, and had also erected bridges at the Valenciennes Gate and in the Rue Victor Hugo. They also removed objectionable German street signs, such as Hindenburgh Strasse, and restored the original French names. It is pleasing to record that much of the labour necessary for cleaning up the town, and for removing the numerous booby-traps and mines installed by the enterprising Boche, was supplied by the 700 prisoners who were taken with the fortress.

The scenes of joyful welcome which had met the victorious troops within the walls of the old city beggar description. Every able-bodied soul in the place turned out to wave and cheer. Many of the older people stood inarticulate, with tears streaming down their faces, while the younger and especially the fairer members of the community, as one remembers with regret, showered flowers and caresses upon the unfortunate soldiers with undreamt-of profusion. For once in a long performance the stage bore some resemblance to the glorious scenes which make war in the story books such a noble and

Field Companies and Field Troop.

exhilarating pastime. Here, as elsewhere in liberated territory, the French flag appeared so quickly and so generally as to lend some colour to the base report that certain canny Germans, who had foreseen the triumph of our arms, had ordered up a supply of cheap flags from the Fatherland to sell to the French civilians, in readiness for the great day.

On the 10th, President Poincare paid Le Quesnoy an official visit when, in the presence of a New Zealand guard of honour on the Place d' Armes, the town was welcomed back to the bosom of France, while the bugles blew and the strains of the "Marseillaise" once more rose free upon the breeze.

At midnight on 5th-6th November the New Zealanders in line began to be relieved and, since the Armistice followed within a week, the capture of the Mormal Forest was the last of the long list of Divisional exploits in the war. That this last appearance had been well up to previous high standards was a matter of keen satisfaction to all concerned. As one evidence of that waning strength and diminishing morale of the British arms, in which the German staff professed such comfortable belief, it must have appeared somewhat lacking in essentials, even to those skilled and critical judges. The words of General Russell's order, issued on the 8th in Le Quesnoy, may well mark the conclusion of this chapter:

"The Divisional Commander wishes to express to all ranks his appreciation of their work during the past fortnight's operations. At no time has the Division fought with more spirit and determination, nor have its efforts at any time been crowned with greater success. The Divisional Commander is convinced that the results achieved are due to the determination of every individual to do his utmost towards the common end."

The hour of the Armistice, 11 a.m. on the 11th November, found the Field Companies still in the forward areas about Le Quesnoy, engaged on roads and bridges, and the usual lesser structures incidental to all periods in reserve. The news was received by the Division, as by all other troops on the spot, with a total absence of that excitement and hysterical display of emotion which were such features of the celebrations in London and other great centres of the Empire. A disposition to take things as they come is soon one of the most fortunate possessions of the soldier, and possibly army atmosphere is not conducive to excessive freedom in thought or action. Troops on leave were not proof against the contagion of civilian rejoicing. A hearty Australian accosted a New Zealand officer in Trafalgar Square with a surprisingly complete salute and a generous invitation. "Look here, sir, a few of us boys are

The Final Advance.

going to knock old Nelson off his perch. Will you take charge?" The latter portion of November was spent by all Units of the Division in reserve about Beauvois, where the Field Companies occupied their time with light training and recreation, and in overhauling all gear and equipment. An inspection of each company was carried out by Brigadier-General Carpenter, Chief Engineer to the IV Corps, accompanied by Lieutenant-Colonel L.M. Shera, C.R.E. N.Z. Division.

The IV Corps, with which the New Zealanders fought so long, was not selected for the march into Germany, but, probably in order to give the New Zealand Division the privilege of entering Germany, the New Zealanders were eventually transferred to the II Corps, and began their long march from Beauvois on the 28th November. Passing through Caudry and adjacent villages, the Division received a splendid send-off from the 37th Division, whose battalions lined the roads while their bands played the New Zealanders through. Coming from the tried companions of many a hard day, this kindly feeling was greatly appreciated and heartily reciprocated.

Thereafter the long march proceeded by regular stages right across Belgium in fairly good weather, though rain and mud hindered progress occasionally. No special incidents marked the unbroken series of triumphal entries into villages and towns, where the whole population appeared to vie one with another in expressing hearty welcome, and in speeding the troops on their way, laden with flowers and flags and other gifts of a more material nature. Many opinions of the Belgians, based on long experience of the dour Flemish peasantry of Flanders, were amended on closer acquaintance with the warm-hearted and vivacious Walloons of the central districts. Verviers, near the German frontier, occupies a special niche in the memories of those privileged to experience its enthusiastic reception. This town is the centre of the Belgian woollen trade, and, since many of the prominent business men had been in the Southern Hemisphere on wool-buying excursions, they knew New Zealand well and had a special interest in her soldiers. The constant change of scene and the historical interest attaching to such towns as Liege and Charleroi also helped to sustain the tedium of the long journey, which was completed by the Field Companies without losing a man.

On 20th December the German frontier was crossed, and the Field Companies entrained at Herbesthal for Ehrenfeld, near Cologne, whence a short march brought them into billets

Field Companies and Field Troop.

round about Leverkusen. Here the companies were employed in the various brigade areas, reporting on roads, bridges, buildings, water and power supplies, traffic circuits, bathing and laundry facilities and so on. Dumps were established in connection with the defences of Cologne Bridgehead, and large parties were employed in the forests cutting pickets for our barbed wire entanglements.

Sightseeing was encouraged and, early in the new year, educational classes were commenced to prepare all men for their return to civil life. These classes, which were continued on board each returning troopship, might have had more success had they not been forced to contend with the constant disorganisation inseparable from gradual demobilisation, and with the natural reluctance of war-weary men to assume studious responsibilities.

As early as the middle of January, the first draft of 1914-15 men had left the Engineers for England and demobilisation. Thereafter the process of disbandment continued with regularity, and with quite unexpected celerity. On 4th February the 3rd Field Company ceased to exist, personnel being absorbed into the remaining two Companies. Horses of all three Companies were handed over to the Army authorities, mainly for despatch to England. Some of these animals had been with their respective companies throughout the war, and were as highly prized as all other good soldiers. However, for them, return to New Zealand was out of the question. All vehicles, with special gear and equipment, were absorbed into the Ordnance stores of the occupying Army. Throughout February drafts of men were despatched to England. By the 2nd of March, the hour of the 2nd Field Company had struck also, and all remaining men on its strength were absorbed into the waning ranks of the 1st Company. The few remaining sappers were now employed on the old familiar job of erecting notice boards and directions about the villages of their immediate area, and this was the last noble task of the N.Z. Engineers in the Great War.

By the 25th March, all was over with the N.Z. Division, and 30 men were all that remained of the N.Z. Engineers at the final moment of dissolution. These departed for England next day, along with the C.R.E., Lieutenant-Colonel L. M. Shera.

The internal relationships of the New Zealand Engineers throughout the war were singularly free from incident of an unpleasant nature. Time and space have prohibited detailed description of the lighter aspects of military life, of the extraordinarily good feeling and genial cameraderie which in

The Final Advance.

retrospect stand out as the brightest spots in the whole tremendous medley of experiences. While the sappers were not alone in possession of these virtues, no account of their war performances would be complete which did not refer to the extremely happy conditions existing throughout the Engineering Unit. The absence of serious crime was doubtless due, to some extent, to the fact that most of the men were of the trained artisan class, with a responsible outlook on life well established long before they were caught up in the vortex of war. To the same training may be attributed that high degree of technical ability which was undoubtedly possessed by the great majority of the Unit, and which was never long found wanting in dealing with the innumerable calls on their skill and ingenuity furnished by the ever changing crises of the great struggle. Not that any close monopoly of skill and energy lay with the highly trained men; each Company included many sappers who had previously found a living as bushmen or farmhands, or in the variegated school of general back-country labour, and these were noticeably not the least of their fellows in an emergency. With the stern challenge of untoward circumstance to native resource and grim determination they were already quite familiar, and thus equipped were well able to bear their share of an enterprise where those qualities had full play.

The Unit was entirely fortunate again in its supreme control. Lieutenant-Colonels Pridham and Bingay, as successive C.R.E., set a particularly fine standard of loyal and devoted service, not only to the Division, but to their own immediate charge, a tradition which was ably carried on by Lieutenant-Colonel Shera when his turn came towards the end of the campaign. The respective commanding officers were actuated throughout by the same lofty motives of duty and efficiency. Many of the junior officers were highly trained men; others had won their spurs on the field by virtue of practical experience and the possession of outstanding personality. Of the majority of the non-commissioned officers it would be difficult to speak too highly. Among the number of trained and intelligent men in a technical unit, where casualties are comparatively few, stripes are hard to win; those men who did achieve the distinction, particularly in the higher grades, were a splendid example of courage, resource and unflagging energy, through, in many cases, the whole course of the war.

None of these facts and circumstances would have been of great avail in supporting the Unit through its trials and achievements without the wonderfully high standard of duty and good-humoured endurance shown by the average sapper. It is true that he was seldom allowed to fire a shot in France,

Field Companies and Field Troop.

though called upon to carry and clean a rifle, to his frequent disgust, over hundreds of weary miles, but every soldier knows that the strain of war is by no means confined to the actual clash of assault. In trench warfare the area immediately behind the front line is much more subject to hostile shelling than the actual line itself. Of all the hardships and vicissitudes of war, apart from the hand-to-hand fighting, from which he was officially withheld, the sapper took a full share with a pluck and tenacity second to none.

"Without you, gentlemen of the Engineers, without your co-operation, without your science, the war could not have been won. Your help will be indispensable in the future, as it has been in the past, and your country relies on your prompt response should necessity arise."

MARECHAL FOCH.

CHAPTER XIV.

THE RESERVE DEPOT IN ENGLAND.

When in April, 1916, the New Zealand Division was transferred from Egypt to France, it was decided to transfer all Base and Training personnel and equipment to England.

Sling Camp, near Bulford on Salisbury Plain, where the British Section of the New Zealand Expeditionary Force had been camped in 1914, was selected as the site of the main New Zealand depot. Unlike the procedure in Egypt, where all branches of the Service were gathered together in one large camp, each Unit in England was allotted a certain area wherein to establish its own Training and Reserve Depot. The New Zealand Engineers were located at Christchurch, the Royal Engineer Training Centre for the Southern Command, where great opportunities for improvement were afforded by the extensive stores and equipment available for training purposes and by the number of highly qualified officers and N.C.Os. on the instructional staff.

In June some 150 Engineers, Signallers and Tunnellers arrived in Sling from Egypt, and were immediately posted on to Christchurch, where they shared Jumper's Camp with the Australian Engineer Depot. After the vicissitudes of their long journey, coming straight on top of the upheaval caused by the Divisional transfer to France, they were a very ragged band on disembarking—few had even a complete uniform. They arrived at their Depot, then a few tents in a bare paddock, in no better case. However, few difficulties could long withstand the genial influence of summer in Christchurch, combined with the kindly assistance of Lieutenant-Colonel Keen, Commandant of the R.E. Station, and within a few weeks the Depot was firmly established. In addition to reinforcements constantly arriving from New Zealand, all men discharged from military hospitals rejoined the Depot before returning to France. In July the 12th and 13th Reinforcements arrived, the one from Egypt, the other from New Zealand direct, but the ensuing slight congestion of the Depot was relieved by the end of August, when the Signallers were despatched to Hitchin, to a new depot of their own.

Training commenced at once under instruction provided by the R.E. Station. Trench works and mining were carried out on St. Catherine's Hill, a large shingly knoll on the out-

Field Companies and Field Troop.

skirts of Christchurch, and a very pleasant spot for the purpose, though entirely unlike anything ever seen later in France or Flanders. The river Stour, flowing past the foot of the Hill, gave unlimited opportunities for bridging experience, and the daily presence of large bodies of interested fair spectators is reputed to have had a stimulating effect on the work of the susceptible sappers.

The Hill was crowned by the remains of an old Roman fort, whence a glorious view of the surrounding country was obtainable. On one hand the dark green mass of the New Forest stretched away for miles; below, the courses of the rivers Avon and Stour could be traced winding like silver threads across the rich countryside; and away to seaward the white cliffs of the Isle of Wight seemed strangely close, while the immediate foreground was seldom without the interest of a gipsy encampment.

The system of training carried out was both comprehensive and thorough. All reinforcements on arrival from New Zealand were required to go through a nine weeks' course at the R.E. Training Centre, which commenced with a "refresher" in infantry training, and included instruction in trench and similar field works, wiring, demolitions, construction of hutments, tramways, light railways and deep dugouts, tunnelling and bridging of all types. The appliances available for bridging instruction were on a particularly liberal scale, including pontoons, spars of practically all dimensions generally used, casks, decking, and great quantities of general material.

Many of the N.C.Os. on the instructional staff of the R.E. Centre were old regular soldiers, long since finished with parades and uniforms, but glad to come back to the square in the hour of need to do their share in training younger men for the front. Most of them still retained a fair "punch." One in particular will be well remembered. His chief delight was to secure a squad just arrived from New Zealand. To them, after a good round turn on the parade ground, he would give the command "Stand Easy," and proceed to relate a little story. In his extreme youth, it would appear, he had once been presented with a box of leaden soldiers, which forthwith became the pride of his life, prized beyond all other possessions. During one of the periodic migrations of his family, these soldiers were unfortunately lost, but his mother, in her efforts to assuage his grief, had assured him that he would find them again some day. "Yes, and by God"

The Reserve Depot in England.

he would growl in conclusion, "I've found them again to-day!" Another, amid frenzied exhortations to his squad to turn on their toes, could be heard roaring "Toes! I said, Toes! T-o-e-s don't spell 'eels." Not that these little peculiarities were entirely confined to the veterans. A corporal recently arrived from New Zealand, lecturing his command on the value and importance of the N.C.O., wound up an impressive speech with the assertion that the "Non-Com. was the mouthorgan of the Commanding Officer."

Later on, in addition to the experience of Engineering works gained on St. Catherine's Hill, the New Zealand Engineers had the advantage of a training ground of their own at King's Park, Boscombe. Here their own instructors brushed up men returning from hospital, or on tour of duty in England, and here also men who had passed through the R.E. course on the Hill were kept up to the mark until required for service in France.

Early in October, in breaking weather, the Christchurch Camp was abandoned in favour of billets in Boscombe, a near suburb of Bournemouth. A billet in England meant lodging in a private house, with, in the earlier days, board also provided by the householder. This was unsatisfactory. Some parsimonious billet owners would accommodate nine or ten men and feed them scantily; others, more generous, found the military appetite a tax on their resources. The householders of Boscombe were by no means unanimous in welcoming the attentions now thrust upon them, but a few weeks experience of the simple and docile New Zealanders soon altered all that, and in future years accommodation was always offering in excess of requirements.

However, on 26th October, while the sappers were still in the first flush of enthusiasm over their new homes, an unexpected calamity fell upon them. The Depot was ordered to Brightlingsea. Leaving the Drivers in Christchurch, all other ranks departed for their new station. The rigours of the journey were somewhat alleviated by kindly old gentlemen in London who waved their hats to the brave lads as they marched by. A Coldstream Guardsman, not to be outdone in courtesy to the strangers, volunteered to act as guide, and eventually steered the party safely to the wrong railway station.

Brightlingsea, in Essex, is described in the guide books as one of the most popular East Coast watering places, the first yachting centre in England, and the home of the "Shamrock" crews. The skippers of these craft were reverently pointed

Field Companies and Field Troop.

out on the street, while civic pride also centred about the town's position as a daughter of one of the famous Cinque ports, whose customs and privileges it still shares. The town enjoys the further reputation of being the original of Sunwich Port, made famous by W. W. Jacobs in "Many Cargoes." All of this and more may be true. To the New Zealanders it appeared but a cold, wind-swept, unattractive little town, albeit inhabited by wonderfully kind and good-natured people, who did all in their power to entertain their visitors.

Training at Brightlingsea was similar to that at Christchurch, save that the pontooning was carried out over an arm of the sea, with a tidal rise and fall. Small permanent bridges in the vicinity were also constructed at intervals. During one of these bridging experiences, some weary sappers, with the laudable intention of introducing a little Oriental colour into their drab existence, hauled on the ropes with weird imitations of an Egyptian labour gang. The R.E. Major in charge stopped the practice, comparing them unkindly with "blacks" he had known in the East, much to the secret delight of the Gyppo impersonators. Despite such small diversions, the work commenced to pall on the old hands, who became apt to prefer the storeroom fire to handling frosty cables on a grey December day. That the kindly old Major was not entirely ignorant of their wiles was evidenced by his frequent command—"Sergeant, call the Roll!" The Brightlingsea Depot was in the special defensive area of England and formed part of the East Coast garrison. Complete instructions were issued to the Engineers for the manning of their trenches in the event of invasion though, in the complete absence of rifles or other offensive weapons, their ultimate role was not so clearly defined.

Dancers were well looked after in Brightlingsea, others less advanced in social graces had to content themselves with a picture show. The New Zealand Engineers' Orchestra came into great prominence, and was soon brought up to full strength. Football, both Rugby and Soccer, flourished as ever where New Zealand troops foregathered. Devotees of the former had trouble in finding expert opponents; two of the best games were against the officers of the 66th Division, and the A.S.C., both at Colchester. Soccer players found a wealth of eager antagonists among the naval men stationed at Brightlingsea.

The arrival of reinforcements soon increased the Depot strength above the reserve required, and on 20th November 50 men were reluctantly transferred to the Machine Gunners.

The Reserve Depot in England.

Early in the New Year, 1917, to the delight of all ranks, the Depot was ordered back to Christchurch. Winter conditions being still in evidence, the billet system was taken up again in Boscombe. In place of previous arrangements for board, all rations were now cooked at a central Depot mess. This system gave more satisfaction to all concerned and remained in existence till the close of the Depot.

With the return of spring, the sappers went under canvas once more at Christchurch on the pleasant banks of the River Stour adjacent to the old R.E. Barracks of the town. These barracks had an extensive history and had often seen British soldiers depart for French battlefields in days gone by, notably in the time of Napoleon, when Christchurch was a great artillery centre. The Stour, in addition to its usefulness in connection with training purposes, provided boating and bathing facilities, which were a constant source of pleasure to the sappers all through the summer months.

Early in 1918 the Christchurch Depot was extended to include the former New Zealand (Maori) Pioneer Battalion Depot, which had been on Salisbury Plain, where the winter climate was thought to be somewhat rigorous for Maoris just arriving from the north of New Zealand. At the same time it was arranged that the New Zealand Tunnelling Company and the New Zealand Light Railway Operating Company should also make Christchurch their base. These changes considerably raised the strength of the Depot and necessitated an increase of staff, while the increased importance of the command was met by the appointment of Major G. V. Barclay of the 2nd Field Company as Officer Commanding with the rank of Lieutenant-Colonel.

For a time the good folk of Christchurch and Bournemouth were inclined to be suspicious of our Maori soldiers, but it only required closer acquaintance with their invariable good behaviour and cheerful disposition to change all that, and ere long they were general favourites with the community. As an athlete the Maori soon gained a reputation, winning practically everything at the Aquatic Carnivals promoted by the R.E. authorities.

On the return of the Depot to Christchurch a Regimental Band had been organised, and had been successful, despite great difficulty in maintaining its strength owing to the constant departure of men for the Front. With the increased status of the Depot, permission was given to draw permanent bandsmen from hospitals and other Depots and from men with long service overseas, and with the appointment of a Bandmaster, the Regimental Band then became a recognised

Field Companies and Field Troop.

institution, and quite a feature of the town and district. In addition to service on route marches and parades, with a weekly visit to the New Zealand Hospital at Brockenhurst, the Band made frequent visits to numerous other Hospitals and Convalescent Camps about Bournemouth, where its attentions were much appreciated.

Within easy reach of the Christchurch camp were many places of historic or scenic interest, such as the Old Priory Church, dating back to 1036, or the Rufus stone in the New Forest marking the spot, near Lyndhurst, where William Rufus was slain, while many of the little villages of the district were well worth a visit to anyone moved by rustic beauty. Not that it was necessary for the sappers to go far afield to find distractions for their leisure moments. All municipal resources in the way of sports grounds, baths and parks, existing in Christchurch, Bournemouth, or Boscombe, were thrown open to them unreservedly, while the extreme kindness of the private citizens to the New Zealand boys could not possibly have been surpassed. Football of course flourished mightily, and the fame of the Depot was carried far and wide by victorious teams.

The Committee of the New Zealand War Contingent Association in London early established a Soldiers' Club in connection with the Depot, and this proved a great source of pleasure and comfort to the men. Refreshments were always available, while concerts and cinema entertainments took place several times weekly. The care of the Club was undertaken by a Committee of local ladies, who gave unceasing service throughout the existence of the Depot, and will always be gratefully remembered by all New Zealanders who experienced their many kindnesses.

Another Club greatly appreciated by the boys was the Hostel of the New Zealand Y.M.C.A. in Boscombe. Originally established on a small scale, this Hostel ultimately became a large institution, where not only local but any visiting Colonial soldiers were ever welcome, and were always treated with the greatest kindness and consideration.

Towards the end of the war, the Engineers' Depot was called upon by New Zealander Headquarters to undertake constructional and repair works in connection with the hospitals and various other buildings occupied by New Zealand troops, and on occasion a considerable number of men were employed on this kind of work. The construction and erection of crosses on New Zealand graves in the United Kingdom was also undertaken by the Depot. Another extension of programme was marked by the introduction of agricultural instruction into the daily activities of the Depot. This mainly

The Reserve Depot in England.

took the practical form of growing potatoes and other vegetables for immediate consumption, and served a useful purpose without starting many men on an agricultural career.

The charms of life in the Depot, losing nothing by report, occasionally appeared unduly attractive to men in the Flanders trenches, weary of war with its dull monotony of mud and shells. There seems no reason why troops in training should not have enjoyed as much fun as possible in their leisure moments. But the cold fact sticks in the minds of many well qualified to judge that, in general, whatever the reason, reserves coming to the Companies in the field after a long spell in the Depot never showed the same grit and spirit as earlier reinforcements trained in a harder school.

From the time the Depot returned from Brightlingsea until the final demobilisation of the troops, it remained in the Bournemouth district, at Christchurch in summer, and at Boscombe in winter, growing in size until at times it held 500 to 600 men. In March, 1917, a system of exchange had been arranged by which officers and non-commissioned officers with long service in the field were given a turn of duty in the Depot, and were replaced in France by similar ranks from the Depot, to the mutual advantage of all participating. In June, 1918, the same arrangement was extended to the sappers, but by the time two drafts of 60 men each had arrived from France hostilities had ceased.

When the trend of events pointed clearly to the early closing of the Depot and to the departure of the New Zealanders, many kind sentiments of regret were expressed by local residents. The Civic Council of Bournemouth even passed an official resolution extolling the virtues of the colonial soldiers, which was duly conveyed to those modest gentlemen; while the Mayor entertained the officers of the Depot at a farewell dinner, where further occasion was taken to express the admiration of the hospitable townsmen for the good behaviour of the New Zealand soldiers.

The last public appearance of the New Zealand Engineers in Bournemouth was at the opening of the new Art Gallery, when they furnished a Guard of Honour for Her Royal Highness, Princess Beatrice. In the nature of the case, no adequate return for all the kindness heaped upon them could possibly be made by the New Zealanders, but the presentation of a New Zealand flag to the Mayor of Bournemouth, as representative of the Borough, was a slight act of courtesy much appreciated by the citizens, and one which will happily associate all memories of the overseas soldiers with some recognition of their errand and of the imperishable bond which drew them Home.

Signal Troop.

CHAPTER XV.

SIGNAL TROOP, N.Z.E.
Served with N.Z. Mounted Rifle Brigade, 1914-19

This Troop, although a member of the New Zealand Engineers Signal Service, was a complete unit, and worked independently of its sister unit, the Divisional Signal Company. Formed at the outbreak of war for service with the Mounted Brigade, it remained with that force throughout. It came into being imbued with the ideals and traditions of the Engineer Service and, being so closely allied with our magnificent Mounted Rifle regiments, assimilated their ideals and traditions as well. With these as a foundation, we find the Signal Troop throughout the war to have been an enthusiastic, hard-working and persevering body of men, who never ceased in their efforts to render the Brigade efficient communication, and who at times performed many meritorious feats of endurance and gallantry in the course of their duties.

The territorial Signal Troops all had their headquarters in country districts, and on account of the infrequency of their parades had little opportunity of receiving regular elementary instruction. During the annual camps, the various troops carried out only troop training, and were never exercised in their proper function as a Brigade signal unit. Brigade commanders therefore had no rapid means of keeping in touch with the various regiments, and the signal service was not so well prepared to take the field as some of the other arms.

The Signal Troop, being a specialist unit, was not enrolled in any particular district, its members being drawn mainly from the Signal Units of the four Territorial Mounted Brigades, the balance being motor cyclist despatch riders, tradesmen, and telegraphists from the Post and Telegraph Department. The strength was one officer, one staff sergeant-major, and thirty-six N.C.O.'s and men main body and first line reinforcements. Each district's quota first assembled in the district mobilisation camp, and after receiving an issue of uniform and other necessaries proceeded to Awapuni training camp. The whole troop was assembled by 18th August, when final equipment was issued and intensive training commenced. The troop's first O.C., Lieut. (now Lieut.-Colonel) E. J. Hulbert, lost no time in impressing on all ranks the

Signal Troop, 1914-19.

necessity for hard work and study, his efforts being ably assisted by Staff Sergeant-Major A. G. Baker, R.E. and the N.C.O.'s, with the result that in a very short time all ranks improved wonderfully in efficiency. There were constant rumours about embarkation, etc., which kept everyone on tenterhooks, and on several occasions the Troop was standing by ready to move. The daily exercises and horse-training were varied by the working out of tactical schemes including treks and night work. A section was also sent to Wellington to a warship in port for instruction in naval signalling and the international code, and this also added to the interest of the work.

On 24th September a move was made, the Troop proceeding to Wellington and embarking on H.M. N.Z.T. No. 10 (s.s. "Arawa"). Six men were detailed to the flagship (s.s. "Maunganui") for communication during the voyage. At last everyone thought the great adventure had really begun. But next day the whole force disembarked without any reason being vouchsafed to the rank and file. Half the troop remained in Wellington for further training in naval signalling, the remainder with the horses going to Hutt Park, Petone, for training. Almost three weeks were spent in this way with everyone's hope of an early departure gradually waning. However, on 15th October all ranks again embarked, and this time it looked like business. Last farewells were again said, and early next morning New Zealand's army set off into the unknown.

The men were soon aware that all was not as it should be, for in Cook Strait a nasty swell with a fair amount of wind was met, and for the next two and a half days the landlubbers were very busy finding their sea-legs. Right from the commencement of the voyage the Troop was kept hard at work—there were ten men on the "Maunganui" and twelve on the "Arawa" continuously engaged in intercommunication among the ships of the convoy, and the remainder had to look after the horses. Any spare moments were spent in flag-wagging or buzzer reading. Thanks to the efforts of the O.C. the Troop's quarters were more comfortable than those of the infantry soldiers, due to the necessity for watch-keeping on the bridge and poop, and the need for sleep during the day for the men on night watches. It was a source of much gratification to be able to put up a notice on one's cabin door "Signal Troop—not to be disturbed," and to hear the irate remarks of the ship's adjutant regarding the Gentlemen of the Signal Troop.

The voyage need not be described in detail. The outstanding event was the capture by H.M.A.S. "Sydney" of

The Emden.

the German raider "Emden" on 9th November. This was of special interest to the Troop for the reason that Private Falconer, who first picked up the S.O.S. call from Cocos Island, was at the time attached to the unit, whereby it happened that the troop signallers were the first to give warning to the flagship of the presence of the enemy cruiser. The following report of the day's happenings issued by the O.C. Troops "Arawa" has an unusually historic value:—

Exit "Emden."

9th November, 1914—

6.31 a.m.—10/777 Private W. P. Falconer on duty H.M.T. "Arawa" picked up from Cocos Island "S.O.S." and "strange warship at entrance" sent repeatedly. He woke Wireless Operator Raw. In a few minutes Emden tried to block out message by continuous interruption. Raw tuned his receiver differently and managed to keep reading Cocos message through "Emden's" block. Immediately reported to the Naval Transport Officer and tried to get the "Melbourne" also the "Maunganui," but other stations working blocked the message.

6.45 a.m.—"Waimana" said "signals quite good" but could not get the "Maunganui."

6.50 a.m.—Signalled successfully to the "Maunganui" by semaphore.

7.4 a.m.—"Maunganui" got message through to the "Melbourne."

7.10 a.m.—H.M.S. "Sydney" left for Cocos Island.

9.32 a.m.—"Sydney" sending code messages, "Emden" trying to block by working at the same time.

9.47 a.m.—Everybody ordered to stop signalling.

11.7 a.m.—H.M.S. "Sydney" to H.M.S. "Melbourne": "Enemy beached herself to save from sinking."

11.27 a.m.—"Pursuing merchant collier."

11.28 a.m.—H.M.S. "Minotaur" first spoke asking for movements of enemy.

11.41 a.m.—H.M.S. "Sydney" to all stations: "Enemy beached and done for."

Noon— "Casualties: Two killed and 13 wounded."

November 10th, 1914—

6.15 a.m.—H.M.S. "Sydney" reported:—
No further apprehension re "Emden," ashore on

Signal Troop, 1914-19.

North Cocos Island; foremast and three funnels down and she has surrendered, while "Sydney" is intact and proceeding to Direction Island. Do not know when she will rejoin convoy. She is remaining to take off all guns and will probably land wounded prisoners on Direction Island. She is also to report on condition of cable.

(Signed) G. N. Johnston,
Lieut.-Colonel,
Officer Commanding Transport "Arawa."

The day's work consisted of care of the horses, signalling training, and a little musketry. All ranks worked with a will, and thanks to their care landed all the mounts at Alexandria in good order. Although the loss of horses throughout the New Zealand force was small, it can safely be said that the Signal Troop record in this respect was an enviable one. The eight weeks' voyage was of immense value from a training point of view, and by the end of the voyage all ranks, especially those employed on the ship's bridge, were fast and accurate both at despatching and receiving messages. Alexandria was reached on 3rd December, and the Troop arrived at Zeitoun the following night. All preconceived notions concerning the heat of Egypt were shattered on this night—owing to a slight misunderstanding the guide lost himself, and the Troop was stranded all night, everybody becoming firmly convinced that the place was some degrees colder than the Southern Alps.

From then on till the end of March, 1915, was a period of solid training, first unit, then brigade and divisional operations. Everyone soon had a very intimate knowledge of the country for miles around (not forgetting Cairo). Visibility was not so good as the text-books would have it, a low-lying haze over the desert being a great hindrance to helio work. During February the Brigade made a trek of four days to Bilbeis, a native village some forty miles east of Cairo. On the fourth day an attack was made on the rest of the N.Z. and A. Division, who had taken up a defensive line about five miles from camp. In the early morning a Troop motor-cyclist succeeded by bluff and strategy in getting through the enemy lines and secured information regarding the location of their main force. He immediately returned to the Brigade, and his information enabled the Brigadier to so make his dispositions as to avoid the main force and break through at a thinly held part of the line.

Towards the end of March the Troop marched to the Nile barrage, and spent two days there receiving training

Lieut. Col. E. J. Hulbert, D.S.O.
First Commanding Officer of Signal Troop.

In Egypt.

in crossing streams by swimming the horses and rafting the stores. Throughout this period of training particular attention was paid to co-operation between the Regimental signal sections and the Brigade Troop, and the beneficial effect of their early understanding was of inestimable benefit throughout the war, and especially during the Palestine campaign.

The Troop's equipment was attended to on arrival in Zeitoun. Some signalling and telegraph gear was not available in New Zealand and had to be obtained in Cairo. There were many demands on the Ordnance store from all units, but the O.C. by great persistence and a little flattery managed to secure everything needed. The riding saddles supplied in New Zealand were quite useless, being merely light stock saddles of poor quality—the D's pulled out the first time they were used. Universal pattern military saddles were secured for all the horses. The Troop's quartermaster did valiant work in securing clothing for the men, although he was a good deal imposed upon by them. Should he ever secure a supply of breeches or boots and leave it in his store a few minutes, the whole lot would mysteriously vanish and be replaced by old clothing. He was in continual trouble on account of not being able to balance his stock books. Nor were these his only troubles. One Saturday night two sappers who had over-stayed their Cairo leave were arrested by the Military Police and locked up in Bab el Hadib barracks. The next day the Quartermaster was despatched to take the delinquents over and escort them to camp for punishment. With his usual good nature he allowed them to adjourn to a nearby restaurant for refreshment, and immediately lost them. After searching for some time he had to return to camp and report his dereliction of duty to the O.C., only to find that his prisoners had arrived home long before him and been already sentenced.

There were many regrets and downcast faces when the infantry moved off to their first great undertaking, leaving the Mounteds behind to swelter among the sand and flies. Then came news of the great landing and of many casualties. Everyone was very impatient to get away to help, and great was the joy when moving orders were received. Of course regret was expressed at leaving the horses, to which the men had become greatly attached, but the knowledge that at last the Brigade was to have its chance compensated for the parting.

The Brigade embarked at Alexandria on 6th May, and five days later landed on Anzac Beach. Difficulties were immediately encountered—all the technical equipment had been put on another transport and had to be hunted for there

Signal Troop, 1914-19.

among a thousand and one other items of cargo. However, it was all discovered and landed safely.

Immediately on landing the Brigade was rushed into the line on Walker's Ridge, then the left flank of the Anzac position. The N.Z. Infantry were at the time at Helles and did not return for some days. Owing to the almost continuous fighting which had been going on since the landing, there was indescribable confusion among the various telephone lines on the Ridge. Artillery and area lines were inextricably mixed up, and there were numerous dead lines. A serious effort was immediately made to establish an organised telephone system—the only way to discover working lines was to cut the whole bunch and relay. The artillery lines in use were soon discovered on the arrival of sundry irate Artillery linesmen, with whom peace had to be made. The trenches at the time were narrow and were constantly being enlarged and altered, so that the lines had to be continually shifted to suit the defensive scheme. The Signal office was at first merely a 6 x 3 hole cut into the side of the hill, with a canvas roof, and during a bombardment was not exactly a health resort.

On the night of 15th May the left flank was extended to No. 2 post, and the next morning the position was connected by telephone. This being the first dangerous job the Troop had to do the O.C. decided to take an active part in it himself, and with the assistance of a small party the line was laid along the beach in view of the enemy. The squad received a lot of attention, fortunately suffering no casualties.

The Turkish attack on 18th May gave the Troop a good baptism, and the men upheld the name of New Zealand with credit. The heavy shelling cut the lines in all directions, and all hands were at work throughout the action, with the result that the Brigade had perfect communication at an anxious time when constant touch with all parts of the line was more than necessary. As soon as the attack was over, the lessons learned during the action were applied, and all lines were laid in grooves cut in the sides of the trenches, being secured by pegs and other devices. The system of duplicating lines was extended, and alternative signal posts were established to be used if the station in use became untenable.

On 29th May the Brigade sent a squadron to take and occupy a post in advance of No. 2 outpost, the squadron being accompanied by a telephone section under Corporal Waymouth, and communication established. The post was heavily attacked and surrounded, and the telephone line cut. During the next thirty hours during which the post was defended, communication was maintained with Brigade Head-

Gallipoli.

quarters by visual—both stations were under continual fire and a number of casualties were sustained. The post was relieved by a Canterbury squadron on the morning of 31st May.

The next few weeks were uninteresting although there was always plenty of hard work. All lines had to be examined daily, any bare wire repaired and loose lines refastened. The continual traffic of ration parties, casualties, working parties and reliefs disturbed the lines considerably, and only constant attention ensured any chance of successful communication. Sickness levied its toll on the personnel, and this meant additional work for those remaining on duty. All the men were keen and stuck to their duties till forced away by the Medical Officers.

The high standard of efficiency of the Troop was demonstrated in a marked manner early in this campaign. Very strict instructions had been issued that all messages containing orders and reports must be sent by morse telegraph and not telephoned. Some of the Brigades, however, had not sufficient men with a knowledge of "buzzer" reading to staff their offices. All ranks of the New Zealand Troop had received thorough training in this work, and the Troop was requested at various times to lend sappers to other less efficient units.

Towards the end of July, reinforcements began to arrive and there was indubitable evidence of "something doing." The man in the line was left very much in the dark as to the nature of the operations intended, although the signallers heard a little on account of the nature of their duties. All instruments and other equipment were thoroughly overhauled and preparations made for something big. The very nature of the Brigade's part in the great operations which commenced on 6th August, and took such a terrible toll of our manhood, depended in a measure for their success on the perfection of the communication arrangements. The Signal Troop men had a full realisation of their responsibility, and the manner in which they carried out their tasks earned the hearty commendation of the Brigadier and Staff.

A telephone section moved with the Headquarters of each regiment laying the line as they went—Wellington to Table Top, Auckland to No. 3 post (the scene of the action in May), Canterbury and Otago to Bauchops Hill. The arrangements were carried out perfectly and without a hitch—in fact a party under Corporal Hinton, by taking a short cut, reached their objective before some of the storming troops, rushed and cleared an enemy trench, and were able to report to Brigade Headquarters that "the Signal Troop had occupied ———

position." This party rendered a further valuable service. Just near where they reached the enemy trench an exploder was connected up to an elaborate system of land mines. The Turks on account of the sudden onslaught of our men could not fire the mines, and thus in all probability many lives were saved.

It would be difficult to name any individuals of outstanding merit during this night, but the sections under Corpl. T. G. Hinton and Second-Corporal W. Findlay were both responsible for particularly fine efforts. These N.C.O.'s showed initiative and courage of a high order, and the tasks could not have been otherwise than successfully accomplished under such leaders. The Troop Sergeant also rendered valuable service by establishing communication with two regiments whose telephone sections had become separated in the dark and the general confusion of the attack. Not having received any progress reports from the regiments or any signals from the linesmen for some time, he organised a scratch telephone section and set off straight across the country in the direction of the attack. A few minutes after leaving Brigade Headquarters a wounded squadron commander was met, the telephone was connected up, and the officer made a personal report to the Brigadier regarding the position.

The next morning two linesmen, whilst employed in relaying the lines by more direct routes, captured a small party of Turks at the point of a pair of pliers, their only available weapon. This incident drew attention to the disabilities under which the signallers laboured in regard to self-defence, and the Troop shortly afterwards was armed with revolvers.

The following days during the terrific fighting on Chunuk Bair were anxious ones, and many valuable lives were lost. The lines were continually shelled and needed unceasing attention. On 8th August Sapper P. W. Bramwell was killed whilst patrolling the lines on Bauchop's Hill, and Sapper H. Wells whilst on duty at No. 3 Post. Sapper H. E. Voyce, a Main Body member of the Troop, who had been awarded a commission in the Imperial Army shortly before the April landing, was also killed at the Suvla Bay landing on the 7th.

On 21st August the Brigade, much depleted in numbers, moved further to the left flank to take part with the 4th Australian Brigade in an attack on Hill 60. This action, although not a complete success, was a brilliant effort, and the signallers again did their part creditably. The linesmen, on account of their continual patrolling of the lines, gained a valuable knowledge of the positions of the various troops, and the condition of things in front. They rendered good

Fighting at Hill 60.

service in directing reinforcements, ammunition parties, etc. Sapper A. L. Caselberg never ceased all night in this useful work, and in addition brought back several wounded when not otherwise employed. He was subsequently awarded the Distinguished Conduct Medal for his efforts.

On the 28th August what was left of the Brigade was thrown in to complete the capture of Hill 60, and after a desperate hand-to-hand encounter lasting all night accomplished the task. The Signal Troop again carried out its duties in a creditable manner, but not without loss—two of the best and most popular of the troop being among the fallen. Time and again the telephone parties went across the open amidst a hail of bullets in their endeavour to establish communication. Sapper A. G. Wainscott discovered Turks advancing along an unguarded sap and threatening our rear. Realising that the rifle and bayonet at the moment were of more immediate necessity than his telephone, he held up this advance alone till assistance came. His gallant action would have doubtless been rewarded by high honour had it been seen. Another sapper who had managed to establish his telephone post in the front line had himself and instrument thrown some yards along the trench by a shell which burst in the ground beside him, but nothing daunted he continued sending the message on hand. Sappers Caselberg, Marsh, Bourke, and Ranstead also performed great deeds during this nerve-wracking night.

Second-Corporal W. Findlay and Sapper W. Gibb both gave their lives in their efforts to serve the Brigade. The communication trenches were terribly congested, so in order to save time the sappers made a dash across the open with the telephone. Both men possessed all the qualities necessary in the making of good soldiers, and their deaths were mourned by comrades of all ranks.

A round-up of signallers available on the morning of the 29th revealed that the total strength (Signal Troop and four regiments) was twelve men, the normal strength being one hundred. The remnants of the Brigade were relieved on the 31st by an Imperial Infantry Brigade. The New Zealand Brigadier, however, had to remain for a few days till the relieving Brigade Commander and his staff were thoroughly conversant with the situation. The Brigadier, however, insisted that his Signal Troop should remain with him and supervise the communication till he was finally relieved. The work was particularly strenuous at this period, for with a personnel of twelve as just mentioned six telephone posts had to be maintained, in addition to the patrolling of lines and other duties. All ranks were on duty sixteen hours or more per

Signal Troop, 1914-19.

day and, although everyone was more or less sick and worn out after the strenuous actions of the month previous, all struggled on gamely, having a full realisation of the need of the service.

The Brigade was finally relieved and went to Lemnos early in September for a rest and reinforcements. There was, however, very little rest for the members of the Troop—large numbers of reinforcements arrived and the new signallers, Troop and Regimental, were given a course of training averaging eight to ten hours per day. However, special rations were the order of the day for the veterans. A daily issue of eggs and stout was made, and grapes could also be obtained at (for a time) a very reasonable price. The hot mineral springs at Thermos were within easy walking distance, and these were specially welcome. After existing for about five months on a cup of water per day which had to serve all ablutionary requirements, the luxury of being able to indulge in hot baths with an unlimited water supply can readily be imagined.

A sapper who had established a reputation at Anzac for his coolness under fire was one of the pioneers in the establishment of the numerous crown and anchor schools which abounded in the vicinity of the camp, and is reputed to have laid the foundation of a fortune by the profits derived from his enterprise.

At the beginning of November the Brigade, much refreshed, and once more effective, returned to Anzac. The climate which, on departure, was still of a summer heat, had during the stay at Lemnos grown cold and was now very wintry. After a few days in Taylor's Hollow, the Brigade was ordered to take over the line extending from Hill 60 to the foot of Chunuk Bair, held by an English Territorial Division. Just as the move was being carried out a fearful blizzard commenced and raged for some days. The outgoing Division stayed in its bivouacks till the storm ceased, and the New Zealanders, although holding the line, had to make the best of things in the open.

The work in this sector as far as communications were concerned was very heavy. The line being thinly held, the demand for numerous telephone posts was ever pressing. Although only a Brigade was holding the area, communications had to be maintained on a Divisional basis. The normal equipment of the Troop (six telephones) was naturally of little use, and after some negotiations arrangements were made to take over the whole of the equipment of the outgoing Division. This relieved the situation, and the Troop was able to take over the signal office all standing. Next day

The Evacuation.

Brigade Headquarters decided to move. Right through the campaign this was a great habit with Brigade Headquarters: they would decide on their position, the signallers would lay lines everywhere required, and as soon as the office was fairly established someone in authority would order a move. It seemed to be their standing joke on signallers. On this occasion, however, Headquarters were much blessed, for not half an hour after the N.Z. office had shifted, a heavy shell exploded right on top of the vacated office, killing or wounding the whole of the signallers of the ingoing Brigade on duty, and completely demolishing the office and equipment.

Things were fairly quiet on the Brigade front, but the lines of communication were long and entailed continual attention. The linesmen were on duty day and night repairing breaks and overhauling damaged lines. The weather was bitterly cold and wet, and working conditions were most unpleasant. One great cause for annoyance was the habit of men in the trenches of cutting a piece out of the telephone line when they wanted a pair of boot laces. The wire, being unusually strong and flexible, was also in great demand for tying up bivvies. The feelings of an overworked linesman who, after struggling for perhaps an hour or more searching for a break, found a gap in the line which suggested the use of the missing piece for either of the above-mentioned purposes, can better be imagined than described.

On 1st December rumours of evacuation began to be noised about and were received with feelings of dismay. It was realised that the position, on account of the wintry conditions and shortage of troops, had developed into a stalemate, but retirement had never been thought of by anyone in the ranks. However, orders in great detail came along, and it began to be realised that remarkable organisation was going on to effect the evacuation with as little loss as possible. The most optimistic person could not see the movement being completed without great loss of life, and the pessimists predicted a terrible disaster. All sorts of schemes were adopted to deceive the enemy—the linesmen became more active, laying new lines daily and reeling them up at night. The daily percentage of departures reduced the Troop on the last day to the O.C. and three men, Sergeant A. G. Wainscott, Sappers H. V. Fairlie and J. Bourke. All but necessary gear was discarded in preparation for a quick getaway. Earlier parties took with them as much technical equipment as could be carried, the O.C. with his usual foresight considering that instruments would be more difficult to replace than blankets and clothing, and acting accordingly. The wisdom of this

Signal Troop, 1914-19.

was demonstrated later. The last day, as it wore slowly on, seemed a lifetime, and as the zero hour drew near everyone was keyed up to a pitch of nervous excitement. Gradually as the time for evacuation approached the last reports began to come in over the wires: "Hammond's Hope post withdrawn," "C.M.R. now withdrawing," "Bluff post evacuated," "W.M.R. retiring." It was noticeable that each office as it closed exchanged the signallers good-bye call (GB). As soon as the last regiment passed Brigade Headquarters the Brigadier sent off his last Gallipoli message, "All regiments withdrawn N.Z.M.R., Brigade Headquarters now moving." The Signal Office was then closed, wires cut in every direction, and the last of the Troop, and incidentally the last of the Brigade, set out for the beach and safety at the regulation pace. To this day these men still wonder at the success of the evacuation and bless the good angel that must have been hovering over them.

On arrival at Lemnos next morning the party was entertained by the Navy on board the vessels in port. They were given hot baths and a substantial breakfast, which were much appreciated. The lads in blue could not do enough for our boys, and were keenly interested to know all the news.

The Brigade embarked for Egypt on 23rd December, the troop being among those on the "Hororata." Christmas Day was spent on board, and Alexandria was reached on the 27th. The Brigade returned to Zeitoun camp, arriving on the 28th. All hands were overjoyed to see their horses once more, and the faithful animals were the first beings with which everyone renewed acquaintance. The next few days were spent in re-equipment both of personal kit and signalling equipment. It was in this that the wisdom of the O.C. in salving telephones was made manifest. The Ordnance stores were very short stocked, but in spite of this in three days the O.C. was able to report to the Brigade Commander that the Signal Troop was fully equipped and ready for further action.

As the next operations were to be on the Suez Canal zone it was realised that the Troop's ten motor cycle despatch riders would be of little service. All except three motor cycles and all the bicycles were exchanged for horses. The next few weeks were spent in troop drill and training in packing gear on the saddles in such a way as to minimise the risk of sore backs. Some of the reinforcements possessed only a meagre knowledge of horsemanship, and had to be licked into shape for mounted work. One very keen soldier much over military age had long experience of riding the ocean waves, but was somewhat "at sea" on horseback. The

DESPATCH RIDERS OF A.N.Z.A.C. MOUNTED DIVISION.

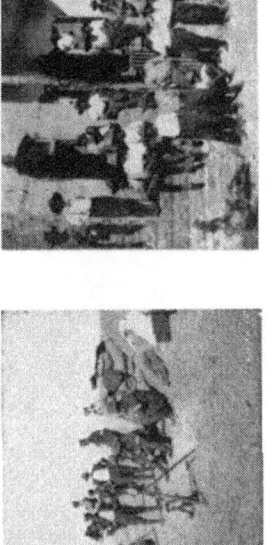

A SIGNAL STATION.

THE SIGNAL TROOP AT JAFFA.

SIGNAL OFFICERS AND N.C.O's AT SERAPEUM.

No. I. Well-clearing Party, Khalassa.

No. II. Well-clearing Party, Khalassa.

Canvas Reservoirs and Horse Trough at Khalassa.

Work near the Suez Canal.

O.C. when ordering the Troop to change direction on the march found it necessary to couch his order in the following terms: "Troop—right wheel—Sapper ———— port your helm."

On 23rd January the whole Brigade set out by route march for the Canal, and on the 29th arrived at Serapeum on the west bank of the canal some eight miles south of Ismailia. The journey was interesting but the weather atrocious, heavy rain falling nightly. There were no shelters of any kind, and the men had to make the best of things by lighting large fires and sitting round them. The firewood consisted of railway sleepers of which there was an abundance; the owners were not present at the time, but it is believed that the N.Z.E.F. subsequently had to foot the bill for the "firewood."

The Serapeum camp was about a mile from the Suez Canal, alongside the irrigation canal. Training operations were immediately commenced and particular attention was paid to instruction in laying telephone cable rapidly. One of the N.C.O.'s had designed a spindle with winding gear and the sappers soon were able to lay the cable from horseback at full gallop. The O.C. Divisional Signals could not believe that cable could be laid at the rate of half a mile a minute, and had to see the operation before he was convinced. The sand in the vicinity had a hard crust, and the despatch riders were able to take part in the operations. Various Brigade operations were carried out, and an attack on troops of the New Zealand Division was also made.

There were numerous gazelle in the desert in the vicinity of the camp, and these graceful animals were much sought after on account of their beautiful heads, which made handsome ornaments when mounted. The motor cyclists were able to secure a number, the chase being quite exciting. For ten to fifteen miles the animals could extend the machines, and it was not until the gazelle had tired that the despatch riders could get near them.

On 6th March the Brigade took over a section of the Canal Defences east of Ferry Post from the New Zealand Division, which was withdrawn preparatory to its departure for the Western front. The Brigade Headquarters were established at Railhead, Ferry Post. The A.M.R. and C.M.R. held the line on a front of about six miles. The majority of the telephone lines had already been laid and consisted of air line to Regimental Headquarters and buried ground line from Regimental Headquarters to squadron posts. These posts were also connected laterally along the whole front, and regiments were connected direct to the regiments on their immediate

Signal Troop, 1914-19.

flanks. A line was laid from Headquarters A.M.R. to an advanced night post some six miles out. The desert here was all soft sand and conditions under which patrolling and maintenance work was carried out were the reverse of pleasant. The troop had been supplied with six fast camels for despatch riding. These unlovely animals were not much appreciated, and an early opportunity was taken to give them away. The N.C.O. who had charge of them simply took the beasts to G.H.Q. and left them in front of the Signal office, getting well away before any questions could be asked. The motor-cycles sent with the troop from New Zealand had always given trouble, and the opportunity was seized of securing a complete issue of new "Triumphs" which had just arrived from England. The machines sent from New Zealand were gifts to the Expeditionary Force, and all second-hand. Of the ten machines no two were the same model, and the old adage about "never looking a gift horse in the mouth" could very well be applied to these. But for the fact that the riders were all expert mechanics, the despatch work would have been in an unfortunate position.

During this period Captain Hulbert's sterling qualities were accorded recognition by his appointment as Staff Captain of the Brigade. This position was usually held by an officer of the Staff Corps with special training, but Captain Hulbert had given indubitable proof of his capabilities by successfully performing the onerous duties of Brigade Major during the evacuation of Gallipoli. Sergeant-Major R. T. Patrick, who had been in temporary command during the last two months on Gallipoli, was granted a commission and became C.O. of the Troop in succession to Captain Hulbert.

After about three weeks at Ferry Post the Brigade returned to Serapeum Camp, where the newly formed Anzac Mounted Division was being concentrated. The Signal Troops of the Australian Light Horse Brigades were old friends of Gallipoli days and needed no introduction. The same good feeling which had grown up between the Australian and New Zealand infantry also existed among the Signal Sappers, who had made many friendships over the 'phone on the long night watches.

On 6th April the Brigade marched out en route to Salhieh, an Egyptian village on the western edge of the Nile delta. These continual moves were of value to all in learning to pack camels, and the men soon became expert in their endeavours to get all their equipment and personal gear aboard without having to abandon anything. This practice proved a great help when on 23rd April orders were received to move at short

In the Desert.

notice to Kantara. At dawn on the 24th the Canal was crossed and the Brigade commenced the great campaign which ended in the final rout of the Turks across the Jordan in the plains of Moab.

The threatened attacking forces, however, had withdrawn, and the Brigade bivouacked at Hill 70, about seven miles east of Kantara, remaining till 12th May. Various patrols were carried out daily and communication was maintained by heliograph. On the 12th the Brigade moved to Bir Et Maler and from then on till July carried out reconnaissances of varying proportions. Here hard work for all ranks engaged in communication work began in earnest. All regiments were connected by telephone to Brigade Headquarters, the offices being open day and night. The permanent defence posts occupied at night were also connected. From daylight till dark a visual signal station was maintained on Katib Gannit, a prominent sand hill some three miles from camp. This station kept in touch with whatever parties were out on reconnaissance, and transmitted reports to N.Z.P. by telephone. This work was trying in the extreme—it was summer and there was no protection for the signallers from the burning heat of the sun. The constantly shifting sand and the glare of the sun upon it were detrimental to the eyes. Very often, on account of the demand for signallers, the men after a long day had to do a watch at night and then go out on another patrol next morning.

Although there was no shortage of sunlight, heliograph signalling presented considerable difficulties. A low lying haze made the locating of patrols uncertain, and very often they could be found only by working out their position on the map and aligning the helio on the bearing ascertained. As they moved frequently the signallers had often very little time to pick up the various stations with which they were expected to keep in touch. The old telegraph line from Kantara to El Arish was still standing although in bad order. This line was overhauled as far as Bir el Abd and proved of great value during reconnaissance for keeping touch with Brigade and Divisional Headquarters. A section of the troop had an unenviable experience whilst engaged on overhauling this line during a reconnaissance by one of the regiments. Through some misunderstanding the regiment withdrew without warning the party. An enemy patrol, which had followed the regiment in, came on the party with one man up a pole and the other two busily engaged with the intricacies of the cable-laying apparatus. The men's rifles were of necessity on their saddles—it is said that the evacua-

Signal Troop, 1914-19.

tion of the position, if not orderly, was quite smartly carried out.

The camel transport, which was universally employed at this time, caused a lot of extra labour in maintenance duties. The camels had an uncanny faculty of becoming tangled up in the telephone lines and frequently caused havoc among the wires, and often the telephonist, who had the receiver strapped to his head, found himself being dragged out of his office. Even if the wire did not break, the insulation was invariably stripped for a distance necessitating either the replacement of the piece, or much work reinsulating the damaged cable.

D.III. cable, a much stouter cable than the D.I. and D.II. previously issued, was here made available, and the slight extra weight and labour in handling were amply compensated for by the better signals and greater immunity from damage. D. mark III. telephones had also entirely superseded the old D.II. and were much appreciated by all who had to use them. The staff and regimental officers especially cursed the older instruments, which prevented the person using them from taking notes, as they required the use of both hands whilst speaking.

On 24th June the Brigade was relieved by the Second Australian Light Horse Brigade, and returned to Hill 70 for a rest. Telephones and all equipment were overhauled and faulty ones replaced.

On 19th July the first information was received of the Turkish advance on the Canal. The Brigade was strengthened by a regiment of Yeomanry and the 5th A.L.H. Regiment, and maintained patrols along and to the south of the old El Arish road between Dueidar and Quatia. These patrols were equipped with telephones, and reported to Headquarters by tapping the old telegraph line.

On the morning of 4th August the attack on the Romani position was made, and the Brigade immediately moved out to operate on the enemy left flank. From this date to the Bir el Abd battle on 9th August all hands were at work continuously, and acquitted themselves with distinction. Visual communication was maintained with the Brigades on the flanks and visual and telephone within the Brigade and with Anzac Headquarters. The work throughout was excellent both as regards speed and accuracy, and on three days in particular was carried out under heavy shell fire. The Brigade, being in the centre of the line of advance, received a good number of reports from the flank Brigades intended for Anzac Headquarters, and the Divisional Commander frequently

A Quiet Christmas

made N.Z. Headquarters an advanced Divisional Headquarters. The Troop therefore had a good deal of extra work in handling Divisional messages.

On one occasion good information was obtained by teeing in to the old telegraph line, which was found to be in use by enemy headquarters. The Brigade interpreter used the 'phone and took notes of various conversations and messages, thus giving our troops an indication of the Turkish intentions. On 6th August whilst the Brigade was in action against the enemy at Ogratina, some cool work by Sapper J. E. Hollywood in repairing the telegraph line was noticed by the Divisional Commander, Major-General Sir H. G. Chauvel. The General immediately inquired the man's name and personally recommended him for the Military Medal.

The Brigade remained as an advanced guard to railway survey and construction till December, moving forward ahead of the work. A wide front and long flanks were maintained and much cable was in use. Visual stations were always maintained by night as well as by day in case of breaking of the lines. This often happened as ration convoys and troops, placing great faith in the telegraph system, always used the wire as a guide to the various outposts. Pigeons were often taken on long distance reconnaissances and proved very reliable.

On 10th November telephone equipment, continuous appeals for which had been made since the outbreak of war, was issued to the Regiments. Hitherto all cable laying and establishment of telephone posts had been done by the Brigade Signal Troop, but the small allowance of cable and instruments made it impossible to satisfy all demands for communication, and at times outposts had to send reports by mounted trooper. This entailed waste of horse flesh, reduction of men in the firing line, and also great loss of time when earlier information would have been valuable.

The year ended with the capture of El Arish and Magdhaba. The latter action was especially trying to the men. In addition to the ordinary difficulties encountered in maintaining communication in action, the men were dead tired. They, in common with the rest of the Brigade, had had no sleep for three nights, and the strain was severely felt in a job where clear eyesight was essential. The Brigade bivouac was reached on Christmas Eve, but everyone was too exhausted to take part in any celebration. In addition the force was far in advance of any canteens or supply depots, and all ranks had to make their Christmas dinner off bully and dry rations.

Signal Troop, 1914-19.

The next operation was the attack and capture of the Rafa position on 8th and 9th January. This was a great success, the honours being with the New Zealand Brigade. The Brigade operated for the first time on turf, and it was a magnificent spectacle to see the whole Brigade, in artillery formation with Headquarters in the lead, moving across a level grass plain at the gallop to take up its first position. The Turkish State telegraph line was immediately cut by the Troop linesmen. Brigade Headquarters were practically in the firing line throughout the day and received quite a lot of attention, the signal stations having to be frequently moved on account of their drawing fire. Visual signalling and runners were employed, all telephone equipment having, under general orders, been left behind. Regiments could only be communicated with by runners as there was no cover for flag or helio. However, as Brigade Headquarters were not more than four hundred yards from the regiments, not much time was lost. At 4.35 p.m., when the final assault was made, the whole of Brigade Headquarters joined in mounted, the amusing spectacle being noticed of a sapper endeavouring to impale a Turk on a flagpole.

The Troop's work during the action was of a high order, and so impressed the Brigade Commander that he congratulated the O.C. and one of the section leaders during the day on the particularly smart despatching of an important situation report. On the Brigade's return to El Arish he made special reference on a Brigade parade to the good service rendered by the Signal Troop in the Rafa battle.

As the Brigade was now out of the desert, the motorcycles were brought into requisition and rendered useful service. The despatch riders were all experienced men, and the rapidity with which they could deliver messages reduced the visual work considerably, and also saved a great deal of horseflesh.

On 26th March the first battle of Gaza took place. It was a trying day for the troop, chiefly on account of the difficulty of keeping in touch with Divisional Headquarters. The weather was dull and helio working intermittent, and A.V.A. was almost out of flag signalling range. At dusk lamp signalling was attempted, but the Divisional lamp was a poor one and could not be read even with a telescope. Resource was then had to the wireless, only to find that the Divisional station had been dismantled. A special word of praise must be given to the motor-cyclists, who found their way in the dark in rough country to and from Divisional Headquarters. The communication forward to the regiments

Gallant Actions.

was good, a party moving with each regiment and laying the line as the advance was made.

The next three weeks were spent in outpost work. On 17th April the Brigade crossed the Wadi Ghuzzeh at Shellal to carry out a reconnaissance preparatory to the second battle of Gaza, which took place on the 19th. This was another anxious day for the Signals. No one seemed to know where Divisional Headquarters were, and all reports had to be sent through Desert Column Headquarters. Communication within the Brigade was excellent, and the sappers carried out their duties in a gallant manner. The battlefield was practically flat, without a vestige of cover. A section under Corporal Wilson laid a line to the C.M.R., galloping right up to the firing line. A visual station under Corporal Anderson was maintained under heavy shell and rifle fire on a small knoll in advance of Brigade Headquarters, which was itself continuously shelled and bombed. One shell scored a direct hit, smashing the instruments and severely wounding a member of the section.

The telephone lines were frequently broken and the linesmen were continually under shell fire whilst repairing them. Sapper Giffney was awarded a well-earned decoration for his gallantry. Although wounded he gamely continued repairing the line and only collapsed on his return to Brigade Headquarters after completing his task. The despatch riders also had an exciting day, having to encounter a barrage on their way to and from the various units.

From this date right up to 24th October the time was spent in holding an outpost on the Wadi Ghuzzeh from Shellal to Fara and patrolling in the direction of Beersheba. The whole Brigade bivouacked in the vicinity of Tel el Fara, the regiments doing the daily patrols alternately. Besides the usual telephone arrangements a permanent signal station was maintained on the Tel, keeping in touch with the various troops out on reconnaissance. Each night a line of listening posts was established some two to three miles in advance of the trench system. These posts were each connected by telephone to Brigade Headquarters, so that early information of any enemy movement might be given. Between these tours of duty (lasting three weeks) the Brigade rested on the beach at Marakeb.

The arrangements for training reinforcements for the Troop and Regimental Signal sections had hitherto been somewhat haphazard. A permanent training cadre of three N.C.O.'s from the Troop was now established at the New Zealand Depot. These instructors were relieved every six months

Signal Troop, 1914-19.

by others from the front, so that the training was carried out according to the requirements of existing conditions. Selected men attended the various courses at the Imperial School of Instructions, Zeitoun, and the majority of the men also had a few weeks at the Army Telegraph School, Alexandria. Two men were also sent to the last mentioned school to undergo a course of training as telegraph mechanicians. These mechanics were of great service during operations extending over lengthy periods, as they were able to keep the Troop and regimental instruments in repair and so prevent any shortage of 'phones.

Means of communicating with aeroplanes were at this time being devised, and practices in signalling with klaxon horn, lamps and ground strips were carried out on several occasions. Each unit of the Brigade was supplied with a distinctive ground signal in order that it might be identified by our 'planes on reconnaissance.

During a period of continuous patrolling and reconnoitring such as this the demand for signallers was enormous. Every patrol both day and night was ordered to take out signallers, with the result that the few trained men on the establishment of units were much overworked. A system of borrowing signallers from other units was adopted, but was most unsatisfactory to all concerned.

On 19th July whilst on reconnaissance the Troop was heavily bombed, Sapper H. M. Wiles being killed and Sapper D. Olver so severely wounded that he died a few days later. Five of the Troop's horses were killed and five wounded during the bombing.

On 24th October the Brigade commenced its long march to get into position for the big push, which commenced with the capture of Beersheba on 31st October and ended with the surrender of Jerusalem on 9th December. At 9.10 a.m. on the 31st the Brigade commenced its attack on Tel el Saba. The attack went well and the fort fell into our hands at 3.30 p.m. The communications were by helio and flag except with A.M.R. who were connected by telephone on account of the heavy fire preventing visual signalling. The conditions were good for signalling and everything went off without a hitch throughout the day.

On 4th November the Brigade went into the line Ras el Nagb—Tel Khuweilfeh. Whilst going into action the Troop was bombed and Sapper T. McMahon, a skilled telegraphist and fine soldier, was killed outright. The next three days were arduous and anxious. The telephone lines were taken over from the outgoing Brigade, but were so bad that they

BRIDGES ERECTED OVER THE RIVER RUBIN.

Capture of Jaffa.

had to be relaid at once. This was done at night under great difficulty in bad country. The line to Divisional Headquarters was found to run forward for a distance into enemy territory and then back through an exposed valley under continual fire. A telephone party which was laying a line to a post on the right found on arrival that the position was still in the hands of the enemy, the patrol having taken up its position on the wrong hill.

During this period the horses were without water for a period of seventy-two hours, and even then had to travel some sixteen miles to get a drink. Although the men themselves were suffering from thirst, they walked the whole distance and led their mounts in order to save them all possible suffering. Such, however, was the care and attention lavished on the steeds that four days later they were able to make a continuous march of over fifty miles.

On the 11th the Brigade set out to rejoin the Division at Hamemeh, some fifty-two miles north.

On the 14th the battle of Ayun Kara took place. This action will ever be remembered by all who took part. The gallant advance of the Auckland and Wellington men, and the great defence by the Auckland regiment against the Turkish counter-attack in the afternoon were an inspiration to all. The Signallers at Brigade Headquarters did everything possible to give all the assistance they could to the much tried regiments. Visual signalling was utilised until the counter-attack came, when a telephone line was run to the A.M.R. This line was connected to the battery R.H.A. so that the Auckland C.O. could indicate where he wanted artillery support. The line was often severed by the enemy shells, but the sappers, realising its value, strove hard to maintain the connection, although they were working in a shell and bullet swept area.

On 16th November W.M.R. entered the town of Jaffa and two days later the whole Brigade moved there. The regiments bivouacked in and around the German village of Sarona and Brigade Headquarters were established in the abandoned German Consulate. The Jaffa post-office had been completely denuded of all telegraph and telephone instruments, but the various lines were in good order, and were used for connecting up the Brigade units. The troop was billeted in a large empty house, some of the men even enjoying the luxury of beds. They were able to make various additions to the army rations and, the famous Jaffa oranges being also available in unlimited quantities, all ranks soon recovered from the strain of the three weeks' fighting and marching.

Signal Troop, 1914-19.

On the 24th the Brigade made a demonstration across the river Auja, capturing enemy posts at Sheikh Muannis and Khurbet Hadrah. These posts were held that night by the Brigade in conjunction with the 161st Brigade (54th Division). The posts were all connected up by 'phone to outpost and Brigade Headquarters, and signal lamps were also aligned in case of attack. A heavy enemy attack developed at 3 a.m. on the 25th and most of our lines were soon destroyed. The whole action was in plain view from advanced headquarters just south of the Auja, so it was considered unnecessary to repair the lines.

An outpost line was then established along the south bank of the Auja and held till 4th December, when the Brigade took over the line Yehudiyeh to a point some three miles north of Ludd. The next six days constituted a period of misery, discomfort and unceasing hard work under the worst possible conditions. The rain was incessant, and the whole area from front line posts to the horse lines near the Jaffa-Ramleh road was a veritable quagmire. All the lines were in an indescribable tangle. There had been frequent changes of units and readjustments of the defence area, and each succeeding command had made alterations to the communication system. The lines were bared in many places and the insulation was perished; it was impossible to read signals from Divisional Headquarters. The regimental posts were at once attended to, communication being established from front to rear and from flank to flank. The Brigades in the adjacent sectors were then connected to our Brigade Headquarters, and flank posts connected to the nearest posts in the next sector. For the first two days Anzac Headquarters could only be communicated with through the neighbouring Brigades. There was a shortage of regimental signallers and the Troop had to assist in maintaining the signal stations at some of the forward posts. The shelling was heavy during the whole period and the lines suffered considerably. All ranks were thankful when relief came and the Brigade was able to go back to Richon Le Zion.

This ended the Brigade's share of the fighting in this sector. Although Lieut. Patrick, who was awarded the Military Cross, was the only recipient of any decoration for gallantry, there were other members of the Troop who would certainly have received recognition for their deeds, had it been possible to award decorations for consistent gallantry throughout a campaign, as well as for isolated acts often no more gallant but more theatrical. Names readily called to

Christmas Gifts Arrive from N.Z.

mind in this connection are those of Sergeant H. V. Farlie, Corporals S. O. Dillon and H. H. Wilson. Sergeant Fairlie was conspicuous throughout the campaign for fine work of a high standard. His efforts were especially gallant at Khuweilfeh, when he went out and repaired an important line, a job which the linesmen of another Brigade had jibbed at as being too dangerous. Corporal Dillon and his section were responsible during the attack on Beersheba for a smart piece of work which had important results. At one stage of the advance on Tel el Saba visual communication with the Auckland regiment became impossible owing to the flat nature of the ground and the proximity of Regimental and Brigade Headquarters to the enemy. There were two alternative routes for a telephone line, along a dry watercourse or across the absolutely flat intervening ground, a distance of some four to five hundred yards. The watercourse was crowded with led horses and a line through it would have been at once destroyed, so "over the top" was the order. Corporal Dillon and a comrade set off at a gallop, and laid the line by the method practised at Serapeum, incidentally drawing a heavy burst of enemy fire, but escaping without casualties.

Christmas, 1917, was spent at Esdud, at that time the railhead of the military railway. The weather was atrocious, but, as the bivouac of the Troop was in the sandhills, the disagreeable mud was avoided. The men fared well for Christmas luxuries. A New Zealand parcel mail had arrived with numerous seasonable gifts; a representative was sent down the line to purchase a few extras not included in the rations, and the Brigade canteen also distributed largesse to all hands. The troop cook must also be complimented on his efforts to put on a spread worthy of the occasion.

On 12th January, 1918, the Brigade returned to Richon, the next three weeks being spent in general training, with inspections by the Desert Corps and Divisional Commanders.

On 9th February Brigade Headquarters, Signal Troop and W.M.R. left for Jerusalem, arriving there the following morning. The Troop was billeted in a monastery in Bethlehem. W.M.R. arrived on the 11th and bivouacked at Mar Elias. The next week was spent in visiting the Holy City and its many historic spots. Everyone took a keen interest in the Holy places, which were pointed out by the guide.

The Division commenced its advance on Jericho through the hills east of Bethlehem on the 19th. The road soon deteriorated into nothing but a goat-track. Enemy posts

Signal Troop, 1914-19.

were located in strength east of El Muntar, and at 3 a.m. the following morning they were attacked by all regiments. Communication with the regiments was established by visual and telephone, the lines being extended as the advance continued. Visual communication was also maintained with Anzac Headquarters on El Muntar and the 60th Division at the Greek hostel on the Mount of Olives. The position was captured just after midday and the Brigade moved on to come into contact with further enemy posts at Neby Nusa. These posts were rushed at dawn and the Brigade then reached the Jericho plain without further opposition. There was a thick mist, with rain falling, and, as Divisional Headquarters had detained the Brigade wireless set at El Muntar, the report of the capture of Jericho had to be sent back by a Troop despatch rider.

The Troop despatch riders had followed the Brigade over hills almost too steep for goats. At times the whole party would have to carry the machines one at a time over places where it was impossible to even wheel them. The handling severely damaged the machines, none of which had a footrest or silencer intact at the end of the journey. Corporal Hornig arrived on the plain just in time to be sent back with the news that Jericho had fallen. His route back was by the main road, which had not yet been traversed by our men, and he had to take the chance of striking mines or enemy troops. He had to carry his machine over some large blow-outs, and round some spots which appeared to be mined. His machine collapsed near Talaat el Dumm, but the advancing infantry being met shortly afterwards, the message was despatched by telephone. The N.C.O. reported the suspicious places in the road to an Engineer officer, and a number of mines were subsequently discovered.

The Brigade immediately sent patrols to the Dead Sea and the banks of the Jordan. On account of the mist and rain communication was maintained by Lucas lamps, which had just been issued, and proved their value at once.

On the 22nd the Brigade, less A.M.R., which was left to patrol the Jordan Valley, departed from Jericho and marched back by easy stages to Richon le Zion. During the next few weeks the Brigade and Regimental signallers received further instruction in communication with aircraft. The officers and N.C.O.'s were attached for a week to the 14th Squadron Royal Air Force stationed at Junction Station. They received instruction both on the ground and in the air, experiencing the joys of flying for the first time. R.A.F. officers also

Attack on Hill 3039

visited the Brigade and addressed the officers on points of interest to both services.

On 13th March the Brigade again left Richon for the Jordan Valley, and on the 23rd crossed the river for the first time. After combining with the 60th Division attacking the enemy posts in the foothills, the Brigade set off up a mountain track to carry out a raid on the Hedjaz railway at Amman. The weather was bad, and the only communication available was the Australian wireless station on loan to the Troop. At 12.50 p.m. on the 25th the Moab plateau was reached, but owing to the bad weather and difficult roads Divisional Headquarters and the Light Horse Brigades did not arrive until the following day.

On 27th the attack on the town of Amman, which was strongly held, commenced. The Brigade soon struck trouble and was held up for some hours. The ground was so soft that it was impossible to move except on the formed tracks. After crossing the railway line at Kissir Station the Brigade took up a position for the night. During the day communication was maintained by visual with all units and Anzac Headquarters. As soon as the position was fixed lines were laid to all posts and Regimental Headquarters.

The next day A.M.R. made an advance in the direction of Hill 3039, but could not get far. Good observation posts were found, however, and the telephone line was extended from A.M.R. Headquarters to direct the artillery fire.

On the 29th a general advance was ordered, but the enemy force had been strengthened and held commanding positions. The Brigade advanced to the foot of 3039, suffering considerable loss. Telephone parties moved with the regiments and kept in constant touch with Brigade Headquarters. The enemy shells searching the hollows in rear of the advance for led horses damaged the lines frequently, and visual had occasionally to be resorted to. The enemy observation, however, was good, and fire was immediately opened on any signal station seen. Telephonic communication was established with Anzac Headquarters at 12.45 p.m. During the two previous days all messages had been sent and received by flag or lamp—a slow method during an action such as this. The wireless station made many efforts to assist but its signals were drowned by the big German station at Amman.

At one-thirty the following morning the Brigade, with the Fourth Battalion Camel Corps attached, began a further advance on Hill 3039, and gained their objective after a brisk

Signal Troop, 1914-19.

fight. The telephone lines were carried forward with the attack, and rendered valuable service both by forwarding progress reports and enabling the respective commanders to co-operate with each other in the advance. The various machine gun sections were also connected with each other and with the squadron commander, and were of great assistance in securing effective co-operation throughout the squadron. Two lines had been run from Brigade Headquarters, one to A.M.R. and one to C.M.R., and a line to the Camel Battalion branched off at the jumping off spot of the attack. The three units were then further connected by a cable running across the front close up to the front line.

At daybreak the enemy commenced a series of counter-attacks, and from then on till after dark, when orders to withdraw were received, our men had a terrible time. Attack after attack was launched on the thin line, and gallantly repulsed. The Troop had a big day's work and carried it through with distinction to all concerned. The shelling and rifle fire chewed up the lines time and again, and every available man was engaged patrolling the wires all day. The main lines were bridged in several places to assist continuous touch, and even then all lines were discontinued at times. It was difficult to single out any individual sapper for his work during the day, but Sappers J. R. Robertson and W. Lockie were responsible for a fine effort during a particularly heavy attack in the afternoon, for which the former was later awarded the Military Medal.

It should be remembered that during the whole of the stunt the men were working and fighting under indescribably bad conditions. An arctic blizzard raged, the cold if anything being more severe than the great blizzard at Anzac in November, 1915; the ground everywhere was a quagmire, and the men, having just come from the heat of the Jordan Valley, were but lightly clothed.

The telephone played a useful part in the withdrawal, the C.O.'s of the various units working back along their cable and covering each other's withdrawal alternately. The numerous casualties were evacuated with difficulty, and it was not till four o'clock next morning that the Brigade reached the Divisional concentration area. During the next twenty-four hours the Brigade acted as a rearguard to cover the withdrawal of the troops.

It is worth mention that during these operations $26\frac{1}{2}$ miles of cable were used, all of it being abandoned owing to it being required till the last moment to assist in the withdrawal.

Summer in the Jordan Valley.

During the action the Brigade lost Lieuts. H. Benson and A. Hall, signalling officer of the C.M.R. and W.M.R. respectively. They were both gallant and efficient officers whose places it was more than difficult to fill. Captain Hinson, C.M.R., who was also killed, was the regimental signalling officer previous to Lieut. Benson, but had been appointed adjutant shortly before these operations.

The Brigade now commenced its summer stay in the scorching and dusty Jordan Valley. On the 18th April it co-operated with the 60th Division in a demonstration against Shunet Nimrin, and on the 30th took a minor part in an attack on Es Salt and the enemy position at Shunet Nimrin. The plain between the east bank of the Jordan and the Moab foot-hills was very flat and there was some difficulty in employing visual successfully. A telephone line was run to the advanced regiment, and the motor-cyclists kept touch with the other units and also between the regiments and their forward patrols.

On 10th May the Brigade went into Desert Corps reserve, being bivouacked at Talaat ed Dumm in the vicinity of the Inn of the Good Samaritan. Although there was little in the way of work the conditions were unpleasant owing to the dust, heat and insanitary nature of the area. Great relief was felt when on the night of the 29th the Brigade was sent to Bethlehem for a fortnight's rest. Brigade Headquarters was established in a hostel some few miles north of Hebron and the Troop had a most picturesque camp in the garden attached. Everyone had a good rest and spent the time in visits to Jerusalem, and in various sports.

The Brigade left for the valley again on 13th June, and on the 16th took over the No. 4 section of the Jordan defences from the Third Light Horse Brigade. All lines were taken over from the outgoing Brigade, so the relief was quickly effected. The defences consisted of a series of redoubts along the front with advanced observation posts, both redoubts and posts being manned day and night. The whole area was connected up to Brigade and Garrison Regiment Headquarters by metallic circuit. All lines were duplicated by an earth circuit. Fullerphones were used to avoid any induction. Alterations in the system were soon found necessary. The metallic circuit was found to have been laid in advance of the redoubts in several places, so the lines had to be taken up and relaid on a safer route. Then the Garrison Regiment decided to move its headquarters, and of course

Signal Troop, 1914-19.

all the wiring had to be adjusted to fit in with its new position. Some objection was next made to the unsuitable position of Brigade Headquarters in case of attack, so a battle headquarters was established and a full-dress rehearsal took place. The idea of a battle headquarters immediately appealed to the Garrison Regiment, so a further alternative system of communication had to be installed. On the 27th the bivouacks of the Troop and support regiments were shelled heavily by a big gun nick-named by the men "Jericho Jane."

The men felt the strain of the continual work in the hot weather severely, and there was a number of evacuations to hospital on account of malaria. Owing to the nature of the work it was impossible to take advantage of the cool nights for labour, and therefore the sappers toiled daily under a scorching sun. The temperature averaged 115 in the shade, so the heat in the sun can be better left to the imagination. Fortunately there was plenty of cold fresh water handy to the bivouac, and any spare moments were usually spent under an improvised shower bath.

The Brigade was relieved on 19th June by the 5th Mounted Brigade (Yeomanry) and proceeded to Talaat et Dumm as Corps reserve. From there a move was made to Bethlehem on the 27th. The 19th August found the Troop again in the Jordan Valley, the Brigade taking over its old line and that of the adjacent Brigade. The Brigade front extended from the hills on the west of the valley to the junction of the rivers Auja and Jordan. The Brigadier had under his command in addition to the N.Z. regiments two battalions of the British West Indies regiment, two battalions of Jewish Fusiliers, one heavy battery, one field artillery and an Indian mountain battery. The Troop had a really busy time satisfying the demands of this cosmopolitan force, and some of the conversations over the wires, heard in the signal office, were amusing. The two systems of communication previously existing had to be adapted to fit in with the new arrangements of the defence sectors, and the Troop had a strenuous time. As a big operation was in view there was an enormous increase in the traffic over the wires.

Whilst in this position the Troop was using and maintaining 110 miles of cable—a big job for 32 men, as a number of these were employed as telegraphists, despatch riders, drivers, etc. Practically every means of army communication was in use. The Brigade office consisted of a sounder, vibrator, three D3 and two ringing telephones, and a 30 line exchange. A visual station kept touch with patrols, and the wireless station was also working. Aeroplane pilots, old

Approaching Amman.

friends of the 14th squadron, often dropped reports or sent a few words on the klaxon horn. Carrier pigeons were kept in two advanced posts.

On 21st September the Brigade initiated its part in the great operations which were destined to terminate in the complete overthrow of the Turkish armies in Palestine, Syria and Arabia. By a rapid night march the Brigade enveloped the Turkish force at Damieh bridge. The Troop laid a ground line from its old headquarters to Khurbet Fuseil, and there joined on to the Turkish air line, and was in touch with Anzac Headquarters almost immediately on arrival at Damieh. The W.M.R. captured a Divisional Headquarters with all its equipment intact and placed us in possession of some useful telegraph equipment. Touch was maintained with AVA by telegraph, wireless and visual.

On the 23rd the Brigade made a rapid march up the hills and occupied Es Salt, communication being maintained en route by helio, and on arrival by helio and wireless. An enemy air line was also repaired and put through to Anzac Headquarters.

The following morning Anzac Headquarters arrived at Es Salt and the Brigade moved on to Suweileh, preparatory to an attack on Amman of unhappy memory. The attack commenced the following morning and was brilliantly successful. Communication during the action was by visual forward and to the flanks, and by visual and cable to Divisional Headquarters. The despatch riders were hampered by shortage of petrol, but did some smart work in rough country.

C.M.R., by the rapidity of their advance, captured the big German wireless station in perfect condition, and it was in use by the wireless operators attached to the Brigade shortly after its capture. Slabs of guncotton had been fastened to the engine and instruments, but the enemy had not had time to fire the charges. This station proved of great value to G.H.Q. and Desert Corps. These two stations were too far apart to communicate direct, and the Amman station was brought into use as a transmitting plant. Some amusement was caused when our men sent out their first signal on the enemy plant. G.H.Q. were astonished to hear its code call from an unmistakably Telefunken instrument, and could not be persuaded to acknowledge the signal until it was advised by telegraph of the situation.

On the 30th the Brigade moved to Kastal, some fifteen miles south of Amman, and took over as prisoners the remnants of the Turkish army in the Hedjaz. The task was a most unpleasant one, as dead and sick Turks were lying

Signal Troop, 1914-19.

about in all directions. The air line was intact, and there was no hitch regarding communications till during the night some hostile Bedouins cut the line in several places. A pack wireless set was secured at Kastal and found to be in good order.

This was the end of operations so far as the Brigade was concerned, and on the 3rd the long ride back to the coastal plain commenced. The deadly malaria now made its presence felt, and over half the Troop was sent to hospital. Those remaining had a busy time, each man having to look after three or four horses in addition to carrying out his ordinary duties as telegraphist, linesman, etc.

On 14th October Richon le Zion was reached and a great welcome was given our men by the colonists. They had always looked upon the New Zealand Brigade as their deliverers from the thraldom of the Turk.

The Troop was fortunate throughout these final operations in having such fine senior N.C.O.'s as Sergeants C. T. (Yank) Marsh and J. G. Russell. Yank left New Zealand with the second reinforcements, and had been in every action and stunt both on Gallipoli and in Palestine. He was a glutton for work and everything he undertook was faithfully done. Russell was an experienced telegraphist and rendered valuable service in the organisation of the signal office during the extremely busy period preceding the operations.

The next weeks were spent in fitting out all ranks with winter clothing and new equipment. A Brigade rifle match was held at which the Troop arranged telephone communication at the butts and firing points in the usual style, and also succeeded in coming second in the teams event. This was a remarkably good effort, as the Troop had only thirty-two men to select from compared with a regiment's five hundred odd, and in addition the sappers had very little opportunity of enjoying any rifle shooting.

From November till May, 1919, there is little of interest to record. Pending demobilisation, lectures under the N.Z.E.F. Educational scheme were given daily. The Troop took part with the Brigade in quelling the Egyptian riots in March and April, 1919. Brigade Headquarters were at Tanta and communication was maintained through the State Telegraphs and by the Troop despatch riders.

The Troop returned to New Zealand by the "Ulimaroa" and "Ellenga" leaving Suez on 30th June and 23rd July respectively.

Return to N.Z.

It would not be fair to close this history without reference to the great service rendered the Troop and Brigade by the W4 Australian wireless section, which was attached to the Troop right through the Sinai and Palestine campaign. When the New Zealand Signal Troop was mobilised in 1914 no wireless equipment was available, and instead of a wireless section some motor-cycles additional to establishment were sent. The deficiency was never made up by the New Zealand Government, although it was many times stressed that the New Zealanders were not doing their share of the technical work of the Anzac Mounted Division. The O.C., Anzac Signal Squadron, however, had a soft spot in his heart for the New Zealand Troop, and kept it supplied with a wireless section, often suffering inconvenience himself in order that the New Zealand Brigade might not be without its services. In several big stunts the wireless was at times the only means of communication with Headquarters. Among others may be mentioned the advances in August and December, 1916, the Beersheba attack on 31st October, 1917, and the Amman operations in March, 1918. The staff always had an objection to using the wireless on account of the necessity for cyphering and decyphering messages, and the Signalling Officer usually had this job thrust upon him.

The quality of the communications of the New Zealand Brigade was a constant cause of envy among the other Mounted Brigades, both Australian and Imperial, and not infrequently did the Divisional Staff find N.Z. Headquarters a useful report centre. Commanding and Staff Officers who, at the beginning of the war, were disposed to regard any man not using a rifle as an encumbrance, gradually came to realise the immense value of their signallers, and towards the finish of the campaign took a great interest in them and were continually clamouring for a larger establishment in their signalling sections. Of course the tremendous development of the campaign, never comprehended in pre-war establishments and text books, was partly responsible for the demand, but the saving in man power and horseflesh effected by the use of efficient communications was finally realised and taken advantage of to the full. Unfortunately efficient means of communication and expert signallers could not be produced in a day, and for a time the demand was present but not the signallers. This meant much extra work for the trained men available, but such was their enthusiasm that they worked almost continuously for long periods at times, and gave efficient service in addition to doing the ordinary every-day jobs of a camp, and

Signal Troop, 1914-19.

caring for their horses. These horses needed more than ordinary care too. Talk about an infantryman being something to hang things on—a signaller and his horse in full marching order resembled a whole ordnance store.

At the beginning of the war the means of communication and the allowance of equipment were both much below requirements. The Signal Troop commenced operations with a number of flags, six telephones of an unreliable and antiquated type, four Begbie signalling lamps, cumbersome, noisy, and with a range of only six miles, and four heliographs. The telephone wire allowed was 6 1-3 miles supplied on small reels of about 300 yards, but without any practicable method of laying or picking up. In the Brigade's last position before the big push in September 1918 there were in use over one hundred miles of wire—the telephones (50 odd) were up-to-date and efficient models, and the signalling lamps had a range of 15 to 18 miles. Telephones especially were in great demand, and C.O.'s and Staff were very keen to have a 'phone in every imaginable place, sometimes overlooking the difficulty and impracticability of establishing and maintaining this means of communication on some posts. The telephone being a somewhat delicate instrument, the rough handling it often received entailed constant labour for the Troop mechanics, who were continually employed in maintaining the various instruments in a serviceable condition.

The Signal Troop, being composed of men from all districts and not having any association with a particular province, was for a time left in the cold when gifts from Patriotic Associations in New Zealand were being distributed. For instance the ──────── Patriotic Association, when forwarding a consignment to the soldiers of their district, would address the parcels "to the men of the ──────── regiment." Although it was doubtless intended that all soldiers belonging to the province should share in the distribution, the method of addressing the parcels prevented men of such units as the Signal and Field Troops, Field Ambulance and A.S.C. from receiving gifts. It is only fair to state that, as soon as the position was explained to the Regimental commanders, they asked for the numbers of men from their districts serving with the technical units, and saw that they were included in the distribution.

The history of the Signal Troop cannot be considered complete without some reference to the work of the Regimental signallers. Successful communication could never be maintained without the closest co-operation between the Troop and regimental sections, and this co-operation was developed

Return to N.Z.

and continued right from the time when the Brigade was first camped together at Zeitoun till the last shot was fired in 1918.

In conclusion the writer wishes to make his apologies to any old members of the Troop who may feel aggrieved at not being mentioned in this history. There were so many gallant incidents worthy of record that it is impossible, after the expiry of from four to eight years, to recollect more than a small percentage of them. It is also impossible to remember the names of all sappers in sections of which only the N.C.O.'s have been mentioned, although it is realised that every member nobly performed his share in the action described. This history has been written with the object of placing on record the part played in the Great War by the smallest unit of the New Zealand Expeditionary Force. No apologies are offered for what might appear to be undue flattery of the Troop's doings. The respect in which the New Zealand Troop was held in the field can best be ascertained by inquiring from an Australian Light Horse sapper or an English Yeomanry signaller, who were most closely in touch with the Troop and are best able to judge.

Field Troop.

The Party which Demolished the Asluj Bridge.

Demolishing the Railway South East of Beersheba

Asluj Railway Station, South East of Beersheba.

CHAPTER XVI.

N.Z. FIELD TROOP ENGINEERS IN PALESTINE.

The complete defeat of Jemel Pasha's Force of 15,000 Turks, Germans, Austrians and Bedouins by the British, Australian, New Zealand and Indian Force on the 2nd February, 1915, was followed by eighteen months of scouting and minor raids in the desert.

In March, 1916, when the New Zealand Division left Egypt for France, the original Field Troop, which had done most valuable work on Gallipoli, left Egypt also, as it had been absorbed into the newly formed 3rd Field Company New Zealand Engineers. The Troop had been disbanded because at that time it was considered of greater importance to complete the establishment of the Divisional Engineers than to keep these well trained specialists in Egypt, where there were no immediate prospects of making full use of their services. So the members of that experienced Troop became the nucleus of the 3rd Field Coy., the remaining vacancies being filled with men from the disbanded Otago Mounted Rifles and reinforcements which had arrived from New Zealand since the evacuation of Gallipoli. With the exception of Signallers, no Engineers therefore accompanied the New Zealand Mounted Brigade, which, under Brig.-Gen. E. W. C. Chaytor, C.B., proceeded West of the Suez Canal on the 24th April, 1916, as part of the newly formed Australian and New Zealand Mounted Division (or called shortly "Anzac Mounted Division").

The absence of the Engineers was soon felt though, for a few hours after crossing the Canal, the Brigade had penetrated about twenty miles into the waterless desert, and the troops and horses became dependent upon the Camel Transport Company for their water supplies. One camel carried 28 gallons of water and, as there were about 105 officers, 2264 other ranks and 2817 horses to keep supplied, it is easily understood that at times, on account of shortage, men and horses learned what real thirst was.

The Turkish troops, which the Anzac Mounted Division had crossed the Canal to repel, were driven off and our men took up temporary positions at Hill 70 and nearby defences

Field Troop Engineers.

which had been constructed under the supervision of two N.Z. Field Coy. officers before their departure to France. From these position many patrols set out to explore the country in front, but only a waterless area was found.

It was soon realised, that if the water difficulty was to be solved the Engineers' assistance would be necessary, so it was decided to form a "Pioneer Troop." Its chief duty was to divine, locate and develop as great a supply of water as possible, and the Troop soon discovered that hard work and the digging of many wells at selected positions in the desert were rewarded with success, and before long it had the Brigade supplied with a number of watering places.

There was no official establishment for the Troop and accordingly no special tools or equipment were available for its use, but sufficient shovels, axes and sandbags were obtained, and these enabled the men to do most useful work, although elaborate arrangements for watering points could not be made with such scanty tools. The Brigade had one or two canvas water troughs, each to hold 600 gallons, but these could not be taken from Brigade Headquarters because they were needed for storing the daily water supply brought by the Camel Train.

Pumps were not available, but each Mounted man possessed a canvas bucket and tether rope and with these he was left to devise his own means of getting the water out of the wells. Often the supply was small and the men would then have to get into the well and bail out the water with a tin.

On 3rd August a force of 18,000 of Turkey's best troops, accompanied by many Germans and commanded by General Von Kressenstein, attacked the Anzac Mounted Division and some English troops at Romani, about 30 miles South East of Port Said on a front of seven or eight miles. The enemy suffered a heavy defeat on 4th and 5th August, and our forces pursued them for about twenty miles into the desert. Again the need of more Engineers was felt, for the water was scarce and mostly had to be carried over the desert, the Troops otherwise being unable to remain away from the established water points for long.

About this time it was decided to supply the urgent needs of food by rail, and water was pumped through pipes laid across the desert. These, being supplemented with camel transport, relieved matters considerably, but later on the troops travelled faster than the railway constructing gangs, and the everlasting shortage of water was felt once more.

Spear Point Wells

The Australian Light Horse Brigades formed and trained the 1st Field Squadron of Engineers at Kantara on the Suez Canal. It was officered by a Major of the Royal Engineers as officer commanding, and five Australians. The Mounted Division at that time was composed of the New Zealand Mounted Rifles, and the 1st, 2nd and 3rd Australian Light Horse Brigades. Each Engineer Troop was therefore to be attached to one Mounted Brigade to attend to its requirements from an engineering point of view. Just prior to their departure from the training area the G.O.C. of the New Zealand Expeditionary Force in Egypt ordered that Trooper H. G. Alexander of the C.M.R. and Sergeant S. G. Brown of the A.M.R. be commissioned and attached to the 1st Australian Field Squadron for instruction. These appointments were most beneficial in many ways. For a whole the senior acted as assistant to the O.C. Field Troop attached to the New Zealand Mounted Brigade, the junior being retained at Squadron Headquarters as Adjutant and spare officer in case of casualties in the Field Troops.

Almost the whole of the Field Troops' work during the early part of the campaign consisted of water supply, so each was supplied with the full complement of pumps, troughs, four feet square well-frames in timber and iron, all loaded on to wagons. These wagons did not travel well in the sand and shortly afterwards the horses were used for packing the lighter gear, the heavier articles, such as well linings, forge, anvil, Abyssinian well, etc., being loaded on camels. The camels, however, were too slow for the well linings, which were usually required shortly after halts. No faster transport was to be obtained, so some means of overcoming the drawback had to be devised. Spear Point wells of $2\frac{1}{2}$-inch diameter piping were made. These were somewhat similar to the Abyssinian and Norton Tube. Their length was 3 feet 6 inches, with extensions each 3 feet 6 inches. In order to enable the hosing of the service pumps to be attached to the well, special brass unions had to be made with female gas thread for screwing into it or extension and male L.C.C. thread for screwing to suction hose. Patent strap carriers were also made so that the Spear Points and extensions could be quickly strapped on to a pack horse to ride firmly and safely, provision being made to protect the threaded ends. Wire netting baskets were also made to ride on top of the pack saddle and carry the brass union, couplings and other smaller accessories such as driving clamp, etc. With these Spear Points water could be found at most places on the route from the Suez

Field Troop Engineers

Canal to El Arish, a distance of 100 odd miles, at a depth of from 8 to 25 feet below the surface. The water was always brackish, in some places more so than others.

In December, 1916, Sergt. H. A. Lockington of C.M.R. was granted a commission and attached as 2nd officer to the 3rd A.L.H. Brigade Field Troop.

Until 19th December, the enemy's headquarters had been located at the coastal town of El Arish, but afterwards he retreated to Magdhaba in the vicinity of the wells.

The Anzac Troops had followed fast and, overtaking the enemy at Magdhaba on 23rd December, commenced a battle immediately in spite of having travelled a distance of fifty miles within the previous three days. After half a day's fighting Magdhaba was captured. This proved an important gain, for it enabled supplies to be forwarded by sea from Egypt.

Magruntein, another formidable position at Rafa on the borders of Palestine, was captured on 9th January, 1917. This practically cleared the Turks from Sinai and preparations were made for the attack upon Palestine.

In March the Army was greatly increased, the mounted troops being more than doubled, so a second Field Squadron was formed. A New Zealand Field Troop was once more organised and became a part of the 1st Australian Field Squadron. The senior New Zealand subaltern received authority to obtain the required personnel from the various regiments. As previous experience had proved that the establishment was too small, an increase was made from one officer and thirty other ranks to two officers and fifty other ranks. The officers were 2nd Lieuts. S. G. Brown and H. G. Alexander. 2nd Lieut. Alexander was under orders to train a Troop of men, picked from the 1st Field Squadron, for special railway demolition work, which needed great care and quiet working both day and night.

A railway running from Ramleh to Beersheba and thence to the Wadi el Arish presented possible dangers to our troops, because when the intended attack on Gaza commenced it would have been possible for the enemy to use this railway for transporting troops to attack our flank and rear.

Eventually, at dusk one evening during May, in conjunction with the Field Troops of the other brigades, the New Zealand Field Troop, heavily laden with gun cotton, primers, detonators, fuse and other necessaries, set out from camp. The railway line was reached at 7 a.m. after an all-night march.

Railway Demoliton at Asluj

Orders had been received to push ahead with the destruction but to cease at 10 a.m. An advance screen of our troops, after having a brush with the enemy outpost, protected the working party, and by the appointed time for cessation every rail for fifteen miles had been cut. A fifteen arch masonry bridge at Asluj was also destroyed.

As the Division was resting at this time the Troop, with assistance from the Regimental working parties, made roads in and out of river beds and other difficult places to allow guns and horsemen to pass through quickly.

This being a malaria area much antimalaria work was done, chiefly by draining off all stagnant pools which were the breeding places for mosquitoes in the Wadi Ghuzze.

At this stage our Army was entering on the limestone country, the water being chiefly obtained from deep wells of native construction; the wells varying in depth from fifty to two hundred feet deep.

The pump equipment issued to Field Troops in the first place was a general service suction and force pump, capable of lifting from a depth of 26 feet, the capacity of each pump being 600 gallons per hour, operated by two or more men on the handles. At this stage each Field Troop was issued with what was called a "deep well pump." It was a plunger type operated with a rocking shaft from the top of the well, coupled to the bottom rocker by cables. The pump, whith the necessary piping and equipment, weighed 30cwt. and required a G.S. waggon with six horses to transport it. The necessary transport was added to the complement of each Troop. Upon receipt of these deep well pumps the Troops were ordered to train their men in rapidly installing them, and the best time accomplished for rigging them on a 200ft. well was $3\frac{1}{2}$ hours. The water had to be pumped by hand to the surface manually.

The capacity of the pump was only 600 gallons per hour, which meant, with only one well available for a Brigade watering, that over 50 hours' pumping would be entailed to place 30,000 gallons of water on the surface. This amount was consumed daily by a Brigade, if fully supplied. Frequently a Field Troop was called on to water two or more Brigades as they might be occupying the only available water in the locality, which was being operated by the Division's forces. When one considers that in action a Brigade strength has to be watered inside of two hours it will readily be understood how inadequate the deep well pump was for the purpose. The worst

Field Troop Engineers

factor was that it could only be transported by waggon and the country into which our forces were about to advance was impassable in most places for wheeled transport to reach the wells.

After the trials of installing the deep well pump and realising its inadequacy, the O.C. Anzac Field Squadron, Major Alexander, called a conference of all Field Troop officers, who were instructed to make experiments and improvise a more efficient means of raising water from the deep wells.

All realised the plight the Division would be placed in for water unless some more efficient method than the deep well pump could be provided. There were quite a number of ingenious lifts introduced by the respective Field Troops, all of them being an improvement on the pump, and all could be transported by pack horse.

The N.Z. Troop, along with the others, was busy experimenting and several lifts were evolved—one, a conical leather tube with a holding capacity of 30 gallons and operated by cords attached to each end of the tube, introduced by 2nd Lieut. H. A. Lockington, was considered the best of all improvised lifts. A demonstration was given before the G.O.C. 2nd Mounted Division, the Engineer in Chief and the C.R.E., who decided to supply each Troop with one of these conical leather tubes or buckets, made from good serviceable leather.

To operate the bucket light sheer legs, made telescopic for packing on horse, were erected over the well top with a block at the top for one draught rope and a roller for the second draught rope, on ground level. The bucket had an iron ring and handle at the large diameter end, to which the rope leading through the block on sheer legs was attached; the smaller end just had the second rope attached thereto. The cordage was always kept lighter than the weight of bucket so that, when ropes were detached from the horse drawing it, it would drop of its own weight to the bottom of the well. The large end of the bucket being weighted with the iron handle and ring always proceeded down first and thus ensured a fill each time, for when the horse was attached to lift it, the two ropes being so wet that they lifted it up in the form of a U, the big end received the water first and the bucket filled. One diameter being so much larger than the other prevented the water spilling out of either end, for the smaller end did not have sufficient weight to effect the larger diameter end, and the weight of water in the large end was restricted

The Horn Bucket.

from spilling out through the smaller orifice by the reduction in size from 18in. diameter large end to 8in. diameter small end.

To control the ropes when tripped to allow the bucket to drop, a couple of posts were set apart equal to the depth of well, these posts supporting a guide wire to which the draught ropes were attached by a ring This allowed a second horse to be standing in position to hook on immediately when the bucket reached the bottom, and the relieving horse returned, taking up its position whilst the other horse was in draught. The block carrying the rope attached to the large end of the tube was set seven feet higher than the roller over which the second rope, attached to the small end, passed. Consequently when the bucket reached the top of the well the large end was raised higher than the small end, when the water emptied from the smaller end into a receptacle, and by the time the bucket had taken a position of 45 per cent. it was emptied.

The total weight of bucket and equipment for a 200 feet well was 250lbs. which could be comfortably packed on two horses. After practice it was found that it could be assembled on a well in 20 minutes and, with relays of horses working for short intervals, as much as 4500 gallons per hour have been raised with this type of bucket, from a depth of 50 feet.

When wells of very large diameter were found, two of these buckets would be put into commission, one travelling down whilst the other was being raised. In this case the ropes from the two buckets were attached together at the required length and passed through a block set the necessary distance from the well on the ground level. The horse, being attached to these ropes, travelled backwards and forwards, being turned at the ends without unhitching.

At El Arish the British Forces had converged with the sea and from here onwards, during a period of many months, the work of developing water was greatly minimised. Along the sandy beach within about 12 feet of high water mark fresh water could always be obtained in abundance at a depth of from 12 to 20 inches. A similar backing up of the fresh water by the sea was found on the beaches at Gallipoli during previous operations.

There was a conglomerate stratum here which had been pushed up like the edge of a saucer by the action of the sea waves, and the fresh water from inland was finding its outlet over this lip; if this subterranean stratum were driven through, the salt water was reached. During stormy weather the waves

Field Troop Engineers.

went over this saucer lip and contaminated the fresh water, when a move further inland had to be made for good water.

On the Palestine shore, although there was an ample supply of water, any attempts to dig deeper only let the water away. So long, shallow, open trenches were dug in the sand.

While preparations for a further offensive were being carried out by our forces, the Turkish forces had been busy building a strong line of defence from the Mediterranean through Gaza, Hariera and Sheria to Beersheba. South of these positions was the steep-banked Wadi el Ghuzze. At times the bed of the river would be quite dry, whilst at others it was often flooded. This area was the scene of many old past battles and still another fight was shortly to be added to the list.

On 26th March occurred the first battle of Gaza, during which the N.Z.M.R. Brigade entered Gaza and captured two enemy guns, and on April 17th, 18th and 19th, was fought the second Battle of Gaza. Before, during and after both of these battles the chief concern of the Field Troop was the provision of water.

Until October, very little fighting was done, and the period was chiefly taken up by training, preparing water points, rifle ranges, re-equipping, etc.

In the past the Field Troop had been known as "D" Troop, commanded by Lieut. Alexander (vice Lt. S. G. Brown invalided to New Zealand); Lieut. H. A. Lockington was second officer. In future it was to be known as the New Zealand Field Troop. An amusing episode occurred about this time. The Troop requisitioned for five horses as replacements or remounts. Imagine the pleasure of the Officer Commanding when five donkeys arrived on the scene!

For over six months the Turks had been strengthening their positions and considered them impregnable. These defences extended from Gaza south-east for a distance of 20 miles. In the centre was Hariera-Sheria, which protected the railway running from Beersheba to Lydda. Further east were defence works protecting Beersheba, but the area between here and the Dead Sea was a desert waste which the enemy considered impossible ground for troops to traverse. But this was not sufficient to hold up our forces. Assisted by the warships near the coast, they bombarded the strongly entrenched enemy forces at Gaza, attacking the South West of Beersheba with Infantry. The mounteds in the meantime had traversed the unguarded desert and, working to the East, attacked the Beersheba garrison. This advance necessitated a 35 miles

The Khalasa Wells.

journey by night, but the men were keen, and after a day's battle and heavy fighting Beersheba was captured.

Before these operations the Field Troop was kept very busy. It had moved with the Field Squadron and concentrated its energies chiefly on developing water supplies preparatory to the main attack. In this it was fairly successful, having found several useful wells. Two wells at Khalasa were allotted to the N.Z. Field Troop. A reconnaissance had been previously made and the Troop's officers had been informed of the surface condition of these two demolished wells. Instructions had been received to make the necessary preparations for material required, etc., and to furnish an estimate of time required for the work of clearing the wells. This was done and the estimate of time given was 72 hours.

Upon arrival at Khalasa these two wells were a sorry spectacle for the Engineers. Above No. 1 well there had been a masonry building with two large iron tanks set on the top. The building had been demolished along with the top portion of the masonry lining of the well to a depth of about 15 feet. No. 2 well was not so badly damaged, but the lining was blown out for about the same depth as No. 1.

The O.C. Field Troop, Lieut. Alexander, took charge of No. 2 well and 2nd Lieut. Lockington was in charge of No. 1 well. A strong boom with swinging arm and wooden buckets, capacity of half a ton each, and tackle had been provided for raising the spoil. These were soon erected on both wells and the surface spoil rapidly removed from the top; the surrounding ground, being a loose gravel and free running, had to be retained in place by a false lining of corrugated iron brought for the purpose, held in place by inside frames of timber, and the damaged masonry lining of the wells caught in the same manner.

All went well on both wells until No. 1 was cleaned down for 20 feet when a tangled mass of railway rails was encountered, these having been bent and thrown down the well by the Turks before demolishing it, and it was such a locked mass of metal that it took the most strenuous efforts of the Engineers and working party four hours before they could get any of the rails free, that being accomplished with a quadruple watch tackle with 60 men pulling on it.

The diameter of No. 1 well was 7 feet, and it allowed of only four men working there at a time, but despite this the men handled as high as 15 tons per hour of spoil from the well. No. 1 well entailed 600 tons of spoil being removed

Field Troop Engineers

and No. 2, 400 tons. The two wells were completed in 50 hours' time, 22 hours under the estimate. This could never have been accomplished if it had not been for the hearty co-operation of the working parties, whose work could not be too highly praised; realising the importance of the water for the Army following they all worked like trojans.

General Allenby visited the wells just when completed and he congratulated all for the splendid work done in the short time. The Engineers were working practically the whole 50 hours, with the exception of an odd half hour's sleep snatched when opportunity offered, and they all worked so well and efficiently that it would be unfair to mention one without naming the others.

As showing the unorthodox methods of the colonials the following incident was one of many that occurred. The 2nd officer of the N.Z. Field Troop was sent to Cairo just previous to the Beersheba push to order the patent buckets for the water hoist. While there he secured from a Cairo foundry the necessary ironwork mountings for the equipping of the two booms for the Khalasa wells, as shown in photo. Of course not having an official requisition, he had to pay cash. The trouble was then to get them transported from Cairo to the front. They travelled as officer's luggage as far as Kantara and then when they were being put on the Desert Express the R.T. officer interfered and refused to let the mounting go forward as it was solely a passenger train. Several attempts were made to slip on unobserved with the mountings but each time unsuccessfully, as a close watch was being kept. Just before the train was due to leave a General came along. It turned out afterwards to be General Wright, C.R.E., and he suggested concealing them in his sleeping compartment. This was accomplished after some manoeuvring and the mountings reached their destination.

When the O.C. Field Squadron was informed he nearly took a fit, and when gently pressed for a refund of the amount paid he did not know what to do. Eventually he arranged for the mounting to be assembled and a demonstration given before the R.E. General Commanding Desert Corps Engineers. This was done and, after a very successful demonstration of lifting sand, Major Alexander broke the question of payment to the General and the officer received his refund.

The N.Z. Troop, having finished ahead of timetable on the Khalasa wells, immediately pushed on towards Asluj, for the Forces were now arriving and the wells at Asluj were not

Booby Traps

giving the quantities of water which had been reported as their yield.

A well 20 feet in diameter was found at Museisri. It was unlined and had been blown in by the Turks. Work was at once commenced by the Troop upon this well and, after over 100 tons of spoil had been removed in six hours, a splendid flow of water was encountered, yielding 5000 to 6000 gallons per hour, this assisting the watering of the Force quartered at Asluj.

One at Khalasa had only a few feet of the top masonry blown in by the enemy, but the ground around was shattered. This required considerable excavation to enable the workers to reach a solid bottom, but before the day was over a supply was obtained. Another at Khalasa had been badly shattered by the enemy, and considerable work was necessary in clearing the debris and timbering the walls. Water was soon reached, but the accumulation of the ages in tons of broken pots, silt, etc., hindered the use of the well. A centrifugal pump and engine were installed at each of these wells and the watering arrangements were simplified. Up till now, our troops had only sand on which to erect their reservoirs, but here there was hard ground. Excavations 30 feet square were made and the canvas container was placed in the hole.

Another well found was hewn out of solid rock, bowl shape, and several underground streams fed it at the rate of thousands of gallons per hour. One mounted division watered each day at Khalasa and one at Asluj.

At Asluj the Turks had blown in the wells and the clearing had to be carried down to a depth of 100 feet. A well, with a flow of one thousand gallons per hour, situated at Museisri near Asluj was developed on 30th October.

During the same evening a move was made towards Beersheba. After marching all night, the troops deployed and a reconnaisance was made for water. One well was found at Selim Irgeig with 60 feet of water. A tackle and horn bucket were put in use and all troops and horses were supplied.

For a while after the capture of Beersheba the Field Troop was kept busy detaching and removing Turkish mines and booby-traps. One captured pumping plant was well charged with explosive. From the magneto a wire was connected to a case of gelignite placed under the engine, and a portion of the deep-well pump was cunningly attached to another charge of gelignite. These and many other traps were removed without casualty.

Field Troop Engineers.

For a couple of days the Field Troop remained with the New Zealand Mounted Brigade at El Halak. The district here was dry, and water was scarce. The exceptionally long, dry summer preceding had made matters as bad as possible.

On 4th November a move was made with the N.Z. Mounted Brigade to Kuweilfeh, where it relieved an Infantry Division in the firing line. Rough and rocky country surrounded this part, and little water could be found.

Wells were found at Kolek and unsuccessful attempts were made to develop them. During work here an enemy airman paid a visit and, flying low, fired upon the working parties and wounded several men. Shortly after midnight the Troop proceeded to Sheria.

The next move by our fighting troops was to attack the enemy's line on its left flank at Hareira-Sheria. This was successfully carried out on 6th November, 1917. It left the enemy's force at Gaza open to frontal and flank attack and its position was hopeless. Realising this, he evacuated the town and had retired several miles northwards when our troops entered the city the next morning.

The next day saw our force occupying a line along the Wadi Hesi, having captured all the intervening ground after some gallant efforts. They also seized the branch railway from Lydda to Gaza. The capture of Joppa, Ramleh and Lydda soon followed and the enemy's only communication and line of retreat was by the road running northwards to Shechem. A move was made on 4th December to cut off this communication and two weeks of heavy fighting followed. During this fighting the Engineers had a busy time repairing roads and maintaining the water supply.

When Jaffa was captured by our forces the N.Z. Engineers took possession of an up-to-date foundry there, owned and operated by a German. Many of our vehicles had got into a precarious state after our long forced march to Jaffa, so the Engineers at once got busy at the foundry and put all the Brigade gear in order. The German's foundry staff were ordered to return to work, and in the course of two days about 50 per cent. of the staff were engaged on work for our Division, and, supplemented by the N.Z. Engineers, a large amount of work was put through the foundry. Before the Division moved out of this area all necessary repairs had been completed to vehicles and gear.

As some time was spent in this area, the A.D.M.S. Major Hercus requested to have a delousing plant installed if possible. Our Engineers constructed a steam chamber for this

Dirty Engines

purpose and linked it up with a steam plant in a brewery at Sarona, a village in the vicinity of Jaffa; and after our Division had made full use of this plant for the period of their stay, it was handed over to the following units, who readily availed themselves of this chance to separate themselves from the very attentive live stock most were carrying on their persons. The process consisted of placing the clothes in the steam chamber and subjecting them to moist steam for twenty minutes, when the steam was turned off from the boiler and the chamber was then heated by underfiring and the clothes dried in the chamber before being removed.

Along the beach north of Hamame a plentiful supply of water was found at a depth of two to three feet in the sand. Good water in abundance was obtained from large pools in the Wadi Thahharat and troughs were erected nearby. At Richon four troughs and a 30,000 gallon reservoir were installed. Later a 12 h.p. Hornsby gas engine with Tangye suction gas plant was found. The pump was a triple plunger of 4000 gallons per hour capacity.

Hebron was occupied on the 6th December and Bethlehem and Jerusalem were ours shortly afterwards. The official entry into Jerusalem took place on the 11th.

The Field Troop moved to Wadi Hanein on 12th January, 1918, to prepare the water supply for the incoming Brigade. Wadi Hanein was one of the best villages the Troop had been near. The population, mostly Jews, was chiefly engaged in orange growing. Rothschild had been very kind to these people by providing engines, mostly Deutz, and deep-well pumps for their groves. Many years had passed since the engines and pumps were first installed and it is doubtful if a proper mechanic had attended them during that period. All machinery was in a shocking state, being tied up with bootlaces, string and wire. Grease, oil and dirt were thick, but, in spite of all, the machinery was started fairly easily and ample water was procured. A few days later the troubles began, and not until bootlaces, strings and wires were properly replaced and the machinery thoroughly cleaned, were satisfactory results obtained.

Owing to very heavy rains and excessive traffic the roads in this country broke up, and endless work on repairs kept our men busy. The rains had also caused a sudden flood in the Wadi Sultan where a trestle bridge which our men had erected on the 4th January, and over which 3000 camels had passed,

Field Troop Engineers.

was washed away. This was replaced with a barrel-pier bridge and an improvised pontoon bridge.

From 20th January to 4th February a detachment of the Field Troop served with the Canterbury Mounted Rifles Regiment in the front line area at Nalin. Here it spent most of the time forming a very difficult roadway over the rocky hills, practically every yard having to be blasted out of solid rock. An obelisk, with the names of all the members of the C.M.R. Regiment who fell during the recent heavy fighting carved upon it, was erected in this area by our men .

A trek was made to Junction Station on 15th February. On arrival here cisterns were found containing respectively 30,000, 20,000 and 15,000 gallons of water. Twelve were also found in the Monastry at Mar Saba containing 120,540 gallons. In the vicinity of Hill 932, cisterns with 18,750, 12,000 and 13,800 gallons were discovered.

Many raids were made into the enemy's country, but it was not until March 21st that the Jordan was crossed in force. The object of this raid was to cut the Hedjaz railway at the ancient town of Amman so as to prevent supplies reaching the Turkish Armies in Arabia. Amman lies on the plateau to the East of the Jordan, about 30 miles North East of Jericho, and about four thousand feet above it. The river was in flood, so the Engineers built bridges to enable the troops to cross. The N.Z. Engineers, who took part in the raid, comprised a half troop under Lieutenant H. A. Lockington, strengthened by a troop from the Canterbury Regiment and one from the Auckland Regiment. The party proceeded practically due north for about five miles, parallel with the railway, and then turned east to reach the railway line.

Great difficulty was encountered with the camels. They were laden with explosives and were continually slipping on the roads, which were wet and greasy from the heavy rain; one section of sloping rock track had become so greasy that eight camels in succession did the splits and had to be destroyed. It was found necessary then to get a man supporting each of the camels' legs to prevent them from slipping before this place could be negotiated. The explosives from the eight camels, which were out of action, were divided up amongst the horsemen and carried on their mounts.

During the trek our allies, the Arabs, proved a great source of annoyance, for on nearly every hill-top they were found grouped, watching proceedings, and the advance guard had to investigate each time to ascertain whether it was a

Demolition of Amman Bridge.

Turkish outpost or not. After each of these Arab groups had been passed they collected in our rear and accompanied us on the journey, and by the time we had nearly reached the railway they had a much greater strength than our raiding party.

A hasty consultation was held by the officers of our force to consider what had better be done under the circumstances, for if the Arabs proved hostile the party would be caught between two forces. The decision was to push on and take the risk, as our force was too weak to place a guard over and hold them.

Without further incident the railway was reached and a two-arch masonry bridge located. The Engineers, with the Auckland and Canterbury men assisting, quickly had charges of guncotton placed and ready for firing. These were successfully fired electrically and the bridge completely demolished —not one stone being left in place. The time occupied on this piece of work was twenty-eight minutes, from the time the force dismounted, 200 yards from the bridge, until they returned and were marching away on the return journey to Ain es Sir. To demolish this bridge 20 cases of guncotton were employed, each case holding 20 slabs or pounds of guncotton, the guncotton being placed in four loose heaps over the haunches of the arches.

To ensure all the guncotton being fired and not blown piece of work was twenty-eight minutes from the time the the slabs of guncotton in each heap. Guncotton is made so that it will stand a considerable force or blow before exploding, to ensure safety in transport. To assist the detonator to fire the guncotton a hole $1\frac{1}{2}$ inches in diameter is left in the centre of each slab to receive what is called a primer, the detonator fitting into a hole in the primer. In addition to the electric exploder for firing the charges, four fuses were also used in case the exploder failed to operate. In connection with the fuses an incident happened which would have ended the career of all the firing party but for the presence of mind and quickness of action by a Sergeant of the Engineers. At the time it seemed very strange that no guard was found on the railway, and that the work was accomplished without any molestation from the Turks.

After the campaign had finished at Amman, when the Armistice was signed, inquiries were made regarding the guarding of the railway line, and it was found that the Turks had a strong guard on two bridges, one on each side of the

Field Troop Engineers.

one demolished, one being only 10 chains distant and the second a quarter of a mile distant, and patrols from these two guards visited the intervening railway at frequent intervals. So our party had the good fortune to slip in and do their work between the visits of the Turks' patrols.

On 30th May, the Troop returned to Solomons Pools, near Jerusalem. Here it located cisterns containing 200,000 gallons of water in addition to other supplies previously obtained. A few days later it was busy installing a three-inch water pipe from a spring to a site for troughs some 400 feet away. Near Fort Roman an old four-inch pipe supply to Jerusalem was discovered. This was improved and 6000 gallons per day were obtained. Pools containing 1,000,000 gallons of water each were also found.

During the twelve months spent in holding the Jordan line, dummy bridges were constructed across the Jordan River to lead the Turks to believe that another attack was to take place against Amman. These dummies were made of hessian, supported by three lengths of cordage, and the thick undergrowth was cut down giving an approach to each side. Aeroplane photos of these dummy bridges were most unique, for in comparing them with the bridge proper one could hardly tell which was the dummy.

While holding the Jordan line all our force, except one brigade, were on the western side of the river, the 1st Brigade A.L.H. being across on the eastern bank, and two bridges—one pontoon and one a barrel bridge—across the Jordan linked them with the Western side. The Turk was continually shelling these two bridges, and there was always the risk of his putting them out of action, when this brigade would have been isolated. It was decided to have emergency arrangements made for crossing the Jordan to allow of the force on the Eastern side swimming the horses across the river in the event of the bridges being destroyed.

Approaches were cut down to the river at both sides and an endless rope erected across the river. The horses were attached to this rope at intervals of 10 to 20 feet apart and a party of men pulling the rope guided or dragged the horses across, the horsemen holding on alongside his horse or by the tail.

Being warm weather at the time of the erection of these swimming ropes, much fun was caused when the Regiments came down to practice their horses in swimming the river; the horses relishing it as much as the men.

THE BRIDGE AS FOUND.

PLACING THE CHARGES.

AN EXPLOSION.

THE WORK FINISHED.

DEMOLITION OF THE ASLUJ BRIDGE.

Crossing the Jordan.

The length of draught rope across the river extended back about 20 yards on each bank, which allowed the horses to be led alongside the moving rope and attached without checking the movement of the draught rope; it also enabled the horses to be detached.

At 4.30 a.m. on 18th September, the British made a fresh attack on the enemy along the front from the coast to a point ten miles inland, and by 11 a.m. had gained their objectives. Further attacks were made by the Infantry on the hill positions, while the Mounted Division, having previously broken through the gap in the Turkish lines, attacked the enemy in the rear. By the evening of the 20th the Cavalry had overrun the whole country as far north as Nazareth. Those of the defeated armies who were not captured retired in great confusion across the Jordan, but here they suffered heavy casualties through the energy of our airmen.

During this last big push when the General Advance was ordered, Chaytor's force in the Jordan Valley moved north, breaking the Nazareth line held by the Turks and capturing many prisoners, the main portion of the demoralised Turks escaping over a pontoon bridge at Damieh. After crossing, the Turks chopped the bottoms out of two of the six boats carrying the bridge. The N.Z. Engineers were instructed to immediately repair this bridge, to allow our forces to follow up the demoralised Turks. Upon arrival it was seen that the boats had been too completely destroyed to allow of repair, so parties were sent up and down the river in search of timber or poles. A landing wharf was located a short distance up the river and the heavy baulks of timber were quickly dismantled and floated down to the bridge where they were manner by and floated down to the bridge where they were manned by very willing helpers—B.W.I. Troops—who climbed on to each baulk as it came along and sank it beneath the two badly damaged boats until sufficient buoyancy was given by the sunken timber to allow the force to cross over the bridge. The first of our main force crossed in less than an hour after the arrival of the Engineers at the bridge.

When Amman was reached, five locomotives were found in the Amman Railway Station yard. The Turks, before leaving, had blown the cylinders off four of the engines, and the fifth, a large pusher-engine (the duty of which had been to fall in behind the ordinary trains and assist the train up the steep incline from Amman to the main plateau above) had been seriously damaged, but the enemy failed to blow the cylinders off it as they had with all the other engines.

Field Troop Engineers.

The 2nd Brigade A.L.H., under General Riley of our forces, was hard pressed for water at Ziza, which had been surrendered to them by the Turks, chiefly owing to the shortage of water, for lack of which men were dying. The G.O.C., General Chaytor, ordered the Engineers to endeavour to place an engine in commission to convey water on the railway to Ziza, 25 miles distant, to the forces there. This was done in spite of the very inadequate equipment available.

The Turks, being short of coal, used wood for fuel on the locomotives, so all the heating of the plates had to be done with firewood.

Asbestos pulp was found on the premises. The vital parts of the engine were covered with this to protect them from the heat and the wood fire applied to heat the plates before straightening them.

After four hours furiously firing with wood it was found that our extreme heat was a very dull red and not sufficient to allow the locomotive jacks, which were applied to the extreme end for leverage, to force the plates back into position. A trip-block, or tumbler, was then arranged by taking an 8in x 8in baulk of timber (out of the station building) with a button attached at the bottom or lower slope to retain until required to trip.

The engine, 75 tons in weight, was blocked up solid at the back and held securely at sideways and then raised at the damaged front end and made to sit on this tumbler. On the jacks being removed the tumbler was tripped, when the engine suddenly dropped upon the ends of the plates, upon a setting prepared for it. The dead weight of the engine was thus brought to bear upon the bent plates. On account of its great weight the engine could not be dropped very much for fear of breaking the cast portions. By raising the engine, removing the jacks, and giving the engine four inch clear drop, the plates were forced back into position with half a dozen trippings of the tumbler. A few bolts were then fitted to replace the sheared rivets.

Whilst this work had been going on, minor repairs had been completed. The boiler was then filled with water and an attempt made to raise steam. The water leaked badly from nearly all the fire-box crown bolts—evidently the Turks had let the water out of the boiler and fired the boiler with no water in it. To prevent the fire being put out by the leakage, axle grease, of which there were several barrels, was freely used in the fire, and after adding about one cwt. of horse

Puffing Billy.

manure to the water in the boiler the leakage was sealed and steam successfully raised.

The train of loaded water was then made up. The engine crew consisted of Lieut. Lockington, the O.C., N.Z. Field Troop, as driver, an Australian Ambulance man as fireman, and Corporal Williams of Field Troop as brakesman.

After proceeding half way up the Amman incline, the engine suddenly halted just after rounding a sharp curve and the train commenced to run back down the step incline. The automatic brake was too badly damaged to be repaired and the braking system of this train was two hand-brakes, one on the engine and one on the tender, the driver purposing using the engine power for braking by reversing when required. The two hand brakes could not arrest the train from going back down the hill, but luckily the engineers travelling on it realised the danger and at great risk, just as the train was gathering speed, they sprang off and spragged the wheels of all the trucks with pieces of firewood, thus succeeding in bringing it to a halt.

Upon examining the engine, it was found that the two high pressure steam pipes leading from the boiler to the cylinders were fractured right through and the steam was escaping. The broken pipes were cast-iron, 5in. diameter, and had evidently been fractured in the collision, but had held in place until subjected to heavy vibration through taking the sharp curves, when they opened out at the fracture. It was decided to slide back the three miles downhill to Amman, leaving all the other wheels spragged. At Amman further repairs were effected.

The journey was again attempted after four hours had been spent on the above repairs and all went well until the main plateau was nearly reached, when the bolts in the crown of the fire-box commenced leaking badly—evidently our horse manure had become displaced or blown out under the vibration—and the fire was fast being extinguished. To overcome this difficulty, limestone from the side of the railway cutting was rapidly crushed to powder with hand hammers and the powder fed to the boiler with the water through the injector; after about 20lbs. of limestone had been thus put into the boiler, the leakage completely stopped and the journey was resumed.

After negotiating the big hill and running serenely along on the level plateau, the fusible plug in the crown of the fire-box blew out and the fire was soon extinguished. Immediately the steam had been exhausted from the boiler, cold water—

Field Troop Engineers.

despite the risk of breaking—was thrown on the fire bars to cool them and the driver screwed a solid bolt into the fusible plug to replace the fusible metal portion displaced. To accomplish this the driver had to make frequent visits into the fire-box, and owing to the extreme heat, it being impossible to stay in the heated fire-box more than a couple of minutes at a time, his clothes were saturated with cold water each time. After the fusible plug had been attended to, the boiler was refilled with water and steam again raised.

Some days previously our Engineers had demolished portions of the line, with a view to isolating the enemy's force at Ziza from that at Amman. Our train crew therefore needed to negotiate the line carefully and, after a little difficulty, reached Ziza, the destination, without further mishap. Needless to say everybody there was pleased to see the train as the water supply was practically exhausted when the train load of water arrived.

The 2nd Australian Brigade, together with 6000 Turkish prisoners, were at Ziza. The prisoners were so famished for water that, when they saw the overflow running away from the injector on the locomotive, they rushed over and cupped their hands and conveyed this practically boiling water in their mouths.

The engineers enjoyed a much needed sleep and rest that night as they had been engaged practically fifty hours without sleep or rest from the time they commenced upon the locomotive until reaching Ziza. They returned to Amman the next day with a valuable train load of Army stores, etc., including a large quantity of quinine which was most opportune for our malaria infected army, our supplies of quinine having run short.

For three weeks this engine was kept busily engaged transporting to Amman the valuable stores, munitions, etc., which had been captured both north and south of Amman. The repair work done on the engine proved quite a good job and remained intact despite the severe tests it was subjected to.

An armoured railway car, beautifully upholstered and driven by an oil engine, was also found at Amman. This had been used by the G.O.C. Turkish force. A feeble attempt had been made to put this car out of action but no very serious damage had been done to it. The N.Z. Engineers soon had it in commission and General Chaytor had the pleasure of utilising it on the railway for some of his journeys round his command.

Armistice.

Our forces pursued the enemy to Gilead and Deraa, where junction was made with our allied Arab forces, and thence they rode northwards along Pilgrims' Road to Galilee, Damascus and Aleppo. Troops had also advanced along the coast, and by the 25th, Tyre, Sidon, Beyrout, Baalbek, Homs, Hama, and intervening towns had been captured. This completed the victory and the Turks capitulated before any further efforts were made.

On 11th November, Armistice was signed and shortly afterwards the disbanding of the Colonial forces commenced.

CHAPTER XVII.

PERSONNEL OF FIELD TROOP ENGINEERS.

The personnel of our engineers were picked men, practically all being artisans. They were chiefly 30 to 45 years of age and many of them in private life had been occupied in business of their own. Being most versatile, it would be hard to find a finer body of men anywhere for the class of work they were called upon to do on active service. With their adaptability and ingenuity, nothing came amiss to them and, if anything from which an improvised bridge or structure could be built, lay in the vicinity, our engineers could be relied on to rise to the occasion and provide some improvised structure to answer the purpose required.

Realising the importance of their work, such as bridging, barb-wire entanglements, redoubts, water supply, etc., etc., they were always ready and willing to work at high pressure. All took a pride in their unit and always strived never to let their brigade down.

As with all units, many funny incidents occurred among the personnel and it is a great pity a diary had not been kept of such incidents with all units, for they would have well merited being collected and published. But unfortunately most of them have been forgotten.

One story relates to a trooper who had been transferred from a regiment to the troop. In leaving the regiment he had to part with his horse and take on a new mount from the new unit. Having been very attached to the horse he could hardly reconcile himself to the loss. He approached the O.C. Field Troop to try to secure the transfer of his horse to the Troop. This the officer endeavoured to do, but it being against regulations he was unsuccessful. The trooper persisted in his efforts for some three months and every time his old regiment was in his vicinity he would visit it and ask the Major for his horse. One day the Major informed him that, although it was against orders, if he got a mate for "Toby," the fancy mule of the regiment, who had lost his mate in action a few days previously, he would allow the trooper to take his horse. Thanking the Major, the Trooper undertook to supply a mule to pair with Toby. After six weeks had passed and this trooper had

Personnel of Engineers.

spent all his spare time, with leave and without, scouring the lines of all the units he came near, with the purpose of pinching the required mate to pair with "Toby," he was unsuccessful.

One morning as the O.C. Field Troop was inspecting the horse lines, a strange horse was observed there. Upon making inquiries it was learned that it belonged to this trooper, who assured the officer all was in order and that the Major of his late Regiment had given it to him the night before. Thinking there must be a tale to unfold behind this, the O.C. quietly made inquiries some time later and the facts were as follows: This man, accompanied by a companion, proceeded to his old regiment's quarters at night and arranged with his companion to hold the horse-picket in conversation whilst he himself proceeded, when unobserved, to remove from their horse-lines "Toby" himself.

Scouting clear round the camp he came in from the other end near the officers' quarters and asked for the Major. The Major came out to view the mule, and examining it closely he remarked that it was a splendid mate for "Toby" and told the trooper to hand it over to the horse-picket and tell the sergeant in charge that he was to allow him to remove his own horse.

Highly delighted, the trooper, unobserved, got Toby back to the horse-lines and fastened him in his quarters again, then boldly approached the sergeant of the horse-picket and informed him that he had the Major's permission to remove his horse from the lines. The sergeant, being in doubt, sent a messenger to the officer to inquire. Back came the messenger informing the sergeant it was correct and the trooper was to remove his horse, which was done.

Next morning, when the Major came down the horse lines to compare the new mule with Toby, much to his surprise there was only Toby to view. Being a humorist, and a horse lover, he appreciated the joke that had been put over him as much as anybody, and he took no action to have the trooper's horse returned.

One other incident was in connection with a bombing raid by Turkish aeroplanes in Palestine. The groom of the Field Troop officer always made himself a safe dug-out where possible when a new camp was set up, but the batman usually occupied it first when the area was bombed.

Upon this particular occasion, when the taubes came over and bombed the camp, the batman, as usual, rushed the

Personnel of Engineers.

groom's dug-out first. Plunging head first into the dug-out he found himself confronted by a large snake which was sitting up making ready to bite him. He scrambled out more quickly than he had entered and remarked to the groom that he could have his dug-out to himself.

One of the men entered the dug-out with a rake and killed the snake, which measured six feet six inches long.

Wireless Troop.

CHAPTER XVIII.

N.Z. WIRELESS TROOP IN MESOPOTAMIA AND PERSIA.

The Wireless Troop, although only a small unit of which very little was heard during the War, carried out some valuable work.

After being formed in New Zealand, it left on the transport "Willochra" on the 4th March, 1916, and proceeded to Colombo, disembarking there on the 26th. At this port the European population and the garrison treated our men so well, showing them the chief places of interest on the beautiful island, that they were loath to leave.

Colombo was soon left behind and the tracks of some of the 5th Reinforcement Engineers were followed to Madras. Here the heat was terrific in comparison with our own home climate, and the men, being dressed in heavy khaki uniforms, felt it severely and were pleased when evening approached with a few hours' coolness. The white population of Madras repeated the hospitality shown by those at Colombo and the men of the Troop enjoyed a few more days of sight-seeing.

Then followed a miserable train journey, in third-class carriages, usually used by the natives, to Bombay. Only two meals per day were supplied and the efforts of the men to purchase extra food at the various stations en route were unsuccessful.

Bombay was reached on the 2nd April and, when new equipment was obtained, several days of sight-seeing were once more indulged in and customs and life in the East were studied. Then a move was made by boat to Basra, which was reached on the 16th, and the Troop camped at Makina Masus where, with only one wireless set available, a certain amount of instruction was given.

On the 9th May one section left for Mudelil and nineteen days later another proceeded to Ali Gharbi. The remaining sections were incomplete through illness, which incapacitated several men.

The Australian Squadron arrived at Magil on the 4th July and the New Zealand Wireless sections amalgamated with it, thus forming what was known as "C" Wireless Troop of the

Wireless Troop.

Anzac Squadron, under the command of **Major Sutherland**, who shortly afterwards died. Lieut. W. R. H. Clarke, who had commanded the Troop since leaving New Zealand, also died at Magil Basra in July. This left the New Zealand Troop without an officer and several promotions took place "In the Field" in consequence. The ranks were also rapidly decreasing in numbers through fever and dysentery and in October only 20 men remained. It was therefore a great relief when 24 men arrived as reinforcements at the end of the month.

The Wireless sections were immediately reorganised, but within one month half the new men became ill and were sent to hospital. Matters were somewhat improved when the next reinforcements arrived on 16th December, and the Troop ranks were filled.

Just before this a British concentration had taken place up the Tigris River about twelve miles from Kut. The policy was to attack the Turks on a big scale and force their retreat to Baghdad. The assault took place on the 13th December and under General Maude's command, our troops won a victory. One force, under General Marshall, secured the waterway by advancing to Hai, and cut the enemy's communications in other directions.

General Cobbe's force was not so fortunate, for it was stubbornly resisted by the Turks who fought desperately for two months, after which all the ground between Kut and Baghdad was won and the key positions for the future offensive were secured.

Through a series of feint attacks by our troops the enemy's defence was kept centred near the Kut peninsula. Troops then quietly moved into position during the night of 22nd-23rd February, 1917, and the main attack was launched at daylight. Infantry crossed the river in pontoons and completely surprised the enemy, of whom 300 were captured. Severe fighting followed, but the Turks were too hard pressed, and Kut was once more captured by the British. Eleven months had passed since General Townshend's gallant force was compelled, through starvation, to capitulate. The re-capture of the town was a serious blow to the enemy and in addition many prisoners were taken by our troops. The Turks had been caught in a well-set trap and they lost 2000 men in extricating their main force.

Baghdad was reached on the 10th March and captured on the following day. The Wireless Troop, which had been attached to the Cavalry Division, was amongst the first batch

Mesopotamia to Persia.

of troops to enter the city. By the 24th, the whole railway from Baghdad northwards was secured after some brisk fighting.

In July, a section of the Wireless Troop accompanied a force to Hindia on the Euphrates River. Another proceeded to Belid Ruz on the mountain side of Baghdad, where it took part in the fight for the Jebel Hamrin mountains. It then moved to Bakubah on the Diala River, remaining there until November, but joined in the battles afterwards at Kizil Robat Kifri and Jebel Hamrin. Later another return was made to Bakubah.

During September the British decided to improve their positions in the vicinity of the Euphrates. The first aim was Ramadie, which was captured at the second attempt on the 29th. Over 3000 prisoners and the Turkish Army Commander were captured during this battle. Fighting then continued north-east of Baghdad, where the enemy was driven across the Diala River towards Kifri, also along the Tigris River from Tekrit, where the enemy was decisively beaten on the 5th November, 1917.

The most important operations in Mesopotamia being finished, the Wireless Troop moved to Persia where a decided change awaited it. In the former country, the heat had been as much as 126 degrees in the shade, but during the first night out from Baghdad a storm was encountered, and at midnight four feet of water was in the camp.

After three days' trek, a portion of the Troop reached Kasr-i-Shrin, an old Persian town with interesting historical buildings. Then moves took place to Surkhadiza, Khanakin, Kerind, Hamadin and Kermanshah. Kermanshah is a fairly large town with beautiful trees and gardens. Its situation is at the head of a very fertile valley and the surrounding country is rich and excellent for wheat crops, etc. On account of the Russians and Turks stealing everything of use or value, the populace was suffering through starvation. Filth abounded also, and the sights were both pitiful and hideous. It was a common occurrence to see people dying in the streets and others eating raw donkey meat or anything they could secure.

Another section of the Troop had served with the Cavalry Brigade during the severe but successful fighting at Hit and Arsa.

In June, orders were received for the Wireless Troop to proceed to France, so the scattered sections immediately concentrated at Baghdad, where the men were equipped ready to

Wireless Troop.

leave the country. It was struck off the strength of the Anzac Squadron on the 25th June and departed for Basra on the 4th July.

After about ten days it embarked for Bombay, where it awaited the arrival of the New Zealand Transport "Royal George" which carried it to Suez. By rail it proceeded to Alexandria and by H.M. Transport Indarra to Taranto in Italy. Nine days and nights of a train journey, via Ancona, Genoa, the Riviera, Marseilles, Lyons and Paris to Rouen followed, and thence by road it reached Abbeville. Leave to England was granted and on return to France all the members were taken on the strength of the New Zealand Divisional Signal Company, and the Wireless Troop ceased to exist.

Appendixes.

APPENDIX A.

Roll of Honour.

DIVISIONAL ENGINEERS AND FIELD TROOP.

No.	Rank.	Name.	Date of Death.
4/672	Sapper	Allen, J. M.	7/6/17
4/1139a	,,	Allen, L.	9/5/15
4/4a	,,	Astley, E. H.	26/6/15
4/1028	,,	Aston, F. C.	11/11/15
4/373	,,	Bateman, C. P.	30/7/15
4/2254	,,	Beaumont, W. B.	22/9/16
4/1146a	,,	Bedlington, R. P.	30/11/15
9/1777	,,	Birkett, H. L.	11/5/17
12/3560	,,	Bray, H. R.	9/4/17
4/455	,,	Bramwell, P. W.	16/8/15
26360	Lieut.	Broadgate, F. K.	30/9/18
37609	Sapper	Buckingham	30/9/18
4/692	,,	Burke, J.	22/9/16
4/94	,,	Burnett, A.	21/2/17
4/43	Sergt.	Burt, H. C.	13/10/17
4/49a	Sapper	Burton, F.	9/5/15
4/168a	,,	Bushbridge, W. J.	23/6/15
10/3210	L.-Cpl.	Byrne, J. F.	18/6/17
4/662	,,	Cameron, A.	9/8/15
4/1166a	2nd Cpl.	Cameron, F. T.	5/10/16
4/382	Sapper	Cameron, P.	17/8/15
4/697	,,	Campbell, D.	4/6/16
4/2060	,,	Campbell, E. D.	2/10/18
4/911a	,,	Carlyon, S.	1/6/15
4/701	,,	Carr, G. J.	2/9/15
4/939	2nd Cpl.	Chadwick, E. T.	29/8/18
4/700	L.-Cpl.	Charles, M. T.	1/10/15
4/660	W.O. 1	Choate, S. S.	26/5/19
6/1267	Sapper	Collins, R. M.	28/11/15
4/1144	,,	Cook, J.	11/10/18
4/37a	,,	Cooke, T. P.	26/5/15
4/1212a	L.-Cpl.	Connery. J.	21/11/16
	(Temp. 2nd Cpl.)		
4/1769	Sapper	Dadson, J. L.	8/9/16
4/894	,,	Danby, C. E.	30/7/16
11/1682	,,	Dauphin, A. H.	16/9/16
4/1113	,,	Dawson, J. M.	3/2/17
4/895	,,	Davies, S. A.	10/7/17
56263	,,	Davies, A. R. S.	1/2/18
4/1913	,,	Davis, A. E.	29/4/18
4/7	,,	de Rose, F. J.	7/3/16
4/717	L.-Cpl	Dimble, R.	27/11/17
49355	Sapper	Dryden, T. W.	14/3/18
12018	,,	Dunn, C.	7/6/17
46702	,,	Dunipace, J.	26/10/18
4/1153	,,	Eddie, D.	23/2/17
4/392	,,	Edwards, B.	28/8/15
4/2080	,,	Ellis, H. L.	30/3/17
47130	,,	Elliott, B. F.	29/8/18
4/1919	,,	Evans, R. D. J.	10/8/17
4/947	,,	Fancourt, C. L.	8/11/15

APPENDIX A.

No.	Rank.	Name.	Date of Death
4/129a	Sapper	Farrer, C. T.	29/6/16
4/188a	Cpl.	Fear, F. J. H.	20/9/16
4/343	Sapper	Findlay, W.	27/8/15
4/2083	,,	Fleming, J.	8/10/16
4/400	Sergt.	Forsyth, S. (V.C.)	24/8/18
4/2040	Temp. Cpl.	Fotheringham, W. L.	19/9/16
4/2084	L.-Cpl.	Frandsen, C. R.	21/11/18
4/1780	Sapper	Fry, R. T.	4/11/18
12032	,,	Gibbin, E. G.	3/10/16
4/732	,,	Gale, R. J.	22/9/16
4/612	,,	Gibson, B. J.	23/7/15
4/212b	Cpl.	Gorton, E. St. G.	11/1/18
6/3028	Sapper	Gray, T.	25/3/17
11/1797	,,	Grantham, F. J.	7/9/18
4/740	Cpl.	Green, C. H. (M.M.)	26/7/17
4/1928	Sapper	Greenlees, A.	10/6/17
4/901	2nd Cpl.	Griffin, J.	7/6/17
10/225	Sapper	Gwilliam, H. B.	7/9/16
4/525	Cpl	Haig, D. K.	27/7/15
4/1247a	Sapper	Halliburton, B.	11/12/15
4/406	,,	Harrison, D.	5/8/15
10/3592	,,	Haxton, G. W.	14/11/18
4/408	,,	Haynes, J. F.	6/5/17
10/2434	,,	Henderson, L. A.	21/2/17
12083	,,	Henniker, A. B.	26/8/18
4/1793	,,	Hickey, P.	23/11/16
4/1128	Sergt.	Hickson, A. G.	7/6/17
7/2268	Sapper	Hide, F. G.	14/10/11
6/3044	,,	Hollyman, H. L.	31/7/16
9/1866	,,	Hook, C. P.	3/8/16
4/411	,,	Horne, J. B.	19/7/15
4/750	,,	Howell, H. N.	19/6/15
26413	,,	Howland, L. G.	20/5/18
4/1439a	,,	Hunt, B.	24/6/15
4/1796	L.-Cpl.	Hunter, A. J.	7/6/17
4/1170	Sapper	Husband, P. J.	30/9/17
23703	Cpl.	Hutton, B.	29/9/18
4/1322a	Sapper	Inglis, A.	24/6/16
4/1940	,,	Irving, R.	30/3/17
21933	,,	Jardine, P. F.	26/11/18
4/1944	,,	Jarrett, H.	1/3/19
12047	,,	Jellyman, H. B.	16/2/17
4/762	,,	Jones, L. S.	11/8/15
4/415	2nd Cpl.	Johannessen, C. R.	12/9/16
4/1172	Sapper	Johnston, J.	1/5/17
26416	,,	Johnstone, R.	10/7/17
4/767	,,	Kay, G. M.	20/9/16
4/58a	,,	Keating, J. D.	9/5/15
4/993	,,	Kennedy, S. C.	20/9/16
4/770	,,	Kennedy, W.	10/8/15
4/1806	,,	Kenyon, B. D.	17/10/16
4/2097	,,	Lewis, C. L.	10/6/17
8/3675	L.-Cpl.	Lintott, K.	23/9/16
33175	Sapper	Logie, H. McC.	26/8/16
26640	,,	Loftus, W. J.	29/3/18
4/2016	,,	McCathie, J.	20/6/17
4/1297a	Driver	McColl, D. A.	27/10/15
4/427	Sapper	McGimpsey, R.	20/9/16

[306]

APPENDIX A.

No.	Rank.	Name.	Date of Death.
4/1001	L.-Cpl.	McGee, F. N.	5/2/18
8/3690	Sapper	McHugh, E.	13/3/17
4/1300a	,,	McKenzie, M.	19/5/15
4/626	,,	McKenzie, J.	10/8/15
4/1978	Cpl.	Mc. Kinley, W. D.	12/4/18
4/917	Sapper	McNamara, D. P.	9/9/15
	Bvt. Major	McNeill, A. G.	
7/1641	L.-Cpl.	McPherson, A.	20/10/18
4/658	Sapper	McWhirter, A.	23/9/16
12061	L.-Cpl.	MacNeill, M.	29/8/18
4/424	Cpl.	Manson, D.	31/8/15
26425	Sapper	Maisey, L.	31/8/18
35977	,,	Marsden, W.	22/10/18
4/786	L.-Cpl.	Mathias, L.	21/7/15
4/192a	2nd Cpl.	Matthews, W. J.	25/7/15
4/792	L.-Cpl.	Minton, F. J.	2/5/18
4/956	Sapper	Mitchell, W. R.	18/8/15
6/1344	,,	Morgan, W. S.	4/9/18
4/1000	,,	Muirhead, J. W.	
24717	,,	Murray, K. R.	26/11/17
4/654	Sergt.	Nairn, R. R.	2/8/15
4/233a	Sapper	Naylor, W.	10/5/15
4/1830	,,	Neason, H. W.	25/11/17
4/807	,,	Neville, J. A.	10/7/15
4/1364a	Cpl.	Nobbs, J.	21/6/17
55114	Sapper	O'Brien, L. J.	4/11/18
4/2118	,,	Paget, A. W.	14/6/17
4/819	2nd Cpl.	Parsons, H.	8/2/17
4/429	2nd Lieut.	Paine, S. W.	9/5/15
23724	Sapper	Payne, C. W.	30/7/17
4/1309a	,,	Pearson, F. G.	28/4/15
4/1314a	,,	Peddie, I.	26/7/17
26449	,,	Peters, T. E.	21/2/19
4/962	,,	Pheeley, R.	10/4/17
23725	,,	Pilkington, J.	27/6/17
4/825	,,	Porter, F.	24/8/15
4/3446	,,	Potts, C. W.	7/9/16
4/432	L.-Cpl.	Preston, F. J.	7/6/17
9/1950	Sapper	Proctor, G.	1/10/17
8/271	,,	Quayle, D.	3/8/15
4/125a	,,	Ramsey, J. K.	11/1/18
9/1634	,,	Ralph, F. H.	19/1/17
4/1392a	,,	Reid, E. H.	2/5/15
4/830	,,	Reid, J. A.	2/12/17
23726	,,	Reid, I. M.	24/3/17
12076	,,	Robertson, A. E.	31/8/18
9/2125	,,	Riddell, J. G.	2/7/18
4/232a	,,	Ridgley, T. A.	26/5/17
12074	,,	Robinson, B. C.	15/11/16
28573	,,	Rollings, E. A.	2/9/18
8/3054	,,	Rooney, J. W.	29/7/15
8/3390	,,	Ross, C.	20/9/16
4/29a	,,	Ross, H. M.	10/7/15
8/3745	,,	Rhoades, H.	24/6/18
4/124a	,,	Ruddock, E. O.	7/5/17
26459	,,	Sampson, G.	16/6/17
4/838	,,	Scahill, P.	24/6/16
10/1330	,,	Scales, G. A. M.	18/12/15

APPENDIX A.

No.	Rank.	Name.	Date of Death.
4/1195	Sapper	Schaw, A. H.	21/2/17
4/344	,,	Scrivener, C. A.	12/6/15
4/1894	,,	Shaw, W. G.	31/7/16
4/839	,,	Shore, J.	8/8/15
11999	,,	Silvester, C. G.	2/7/15
4/2136	,,	Smallholme, G. H.	2/10/19
4/1196	,,	Smith, A.	18/6/17
23735	,,	Smith, L. G.	11/7/17
53563	,,	Smith, R. C.	19/10/18
4/847	,,	Snell, J. H.	3/1/18
26471	,,	Spencer, J. A.	15/10/17
4/1849	,,	Stratford, F. G.	7/9/18
12080	,,	Stevenson, A.	30/11/17
4/1847	,,	Springall, A.	26/8/18
4/444	,,	Storer, C. B.	4/8/15
4/849	,,	Strong, M. A.	28/8/15
4/853	2nd Cpl.	Sullivan, F. J.	26/11/17
4/1851	Sapper	Sullivan, T. P. T.	31/7/16
4/2146	,,	Syme, R. M.	25/10/18
4/1616a	,,	Tester, T. L.	18/6/17
4/446	,,	Tonkin, J. R.	28/8/15
4/1355a	2nd Cpl.	Tuck, H. J.	21/8/18
28603	Sapper	Tyerman, F. E.	
4/22b	,,	Vickers, F. H.	31/5/15
4/72a	Sergt.	Wallace, A.	10/5/15
4/63a	Sapper	Warburton, P. A. E.	30/4/15
32928	,,	Walton, G.	18/8/17
4/859	,,	Welsh, F. S.	4/10/15
4/463	,,	Whitaker, C. G.	11/8/15
4/463	,,	Whitaker, J. V.	29/10/18
4/453	L.-Cpl.	Windle, H. E.	13/9/16
4/2161	L.-Cpl.	Winston, M.	28/3/17
46423	Sapper	Young, F. G. R.	8/2/17

WIRELESS TROOP.

Lieut. W. R. H. Clarke.

SIGNAL TROOP.

DIED IN EGYPT, 1915.

Sapper G. Rosevear   Sapper G. T. Scrivener

KILLED ON GALLIPOLI.

L.-Corpl. W. Findlay   Sapper H. G. Wells
Sapper P. W. Bramwell   Sapper (Lieut.) H. E. Voyce
Sapper W. Gibb

KILLED IN PALESTINE.

Sapper (Lieut.) A. Hall, M.C.   Sapper T. McMahon
Sapper Hartman   Sapper D. Olver
Sapper Lowe   Sapper H. Wiles

DIED IN PALESTINE.

Sapper G. Lynskey   Sapper J. E. Deehan

DIED IN NEW ZEALAND.

Sapper L. Hanlon

APPENDIX B.

Honours and Rewards.

DIVISIONAL ENGINEERS FIELD COMPANIES AND FIELD TROOP

THE VICTORIA CROSS (V.C.)

Sergt. S. Forsyth, 3rd Field Coy.

BREVET HONOURS.

Major G. R. Pridham, R.E., C.R.E., Brevet Lt.-Colonel
Capt. F. A. Ferguson, R.E., 1st Field Coy., Brevet Major
Capt. A. G. McNeill, M.C., R.E., 1st Field Coy., Brevet Major

DISTINGUISHED SERVICE ORDER (D.S.O.)

Major D. J. Gibbs, 3rd Fld. Coy.
Capt. F. Waite, H.Q., N.Z.E.
Lt.-Col. G. R. Pridham, R.E., C.R.E.
Lt.-Col. H. L. Bingay, R.E., C.R.E.

ORDER OF THE BRITISH EMPIRE (O.B.E.)

Lt.-Col. G. Barclay, N.Z.E. Reserve Depot
Lt.-Col. L. M. Shera, M.C., C.R.E.

MILITARY CROSS (M.C.)

Major N. Annabell, H.Q., N.Z.E.
Capt. R. J. Black, 3rd Fld. Coy.
2/Lieut. Hon. R. T. P. Butler, R.E., H.Q., N.Z.E.
Lieut. C. W. Chilcott, 2nd Fld. Coy.
Lieut. D. Doake, 3rd Fld. Coy.
Lieut. M. K. Draffin, 3rd Fld. Coy.
Lieut. E. W. George, 3rd Fld. Coy.
Lieut. A. O. Glasse, 3rd Fld. Coy.
Major A. G. McNeill, R.E., 1st Fld. Coy.
Capt. M. G. R. Newbould, 1st Fld. Coy.
Capt. H. W. Newman, 1st Fld. Coy.
Lieut. A. N. Oakey, Fld. Troop
Lieut. W. S. Rae, 2nd Fld. Coy.
Capt. G. V. Russell, 1st Fld. Coy.
Lt.-Col. L. M. Shera, O.B.E., C.R.E.
Lieut. A. W. Thomas, 1st Fld. Coy.
Capt. S. Cory Wright, 3rd Fld. Coy., attached D.H.Q.

DISTINGUISHED CONDUCT MEDAL (D.C.M.)

Sergt. A. W. Abbey, 1st Fld. Coy.
Sergt. A. T. Brokenshire, M.M., 1st Fld. Coy.
Cpl. F. J. H. Fear, 1st Fld. Coy.
Spr. E. A. Hodges, 1st Fld. Coy.
L.-Cpl. A. J. Randall, 3rd Fld. Coy.
Capt. C. W. Salmon, 1st Fld.Coy.
Lieut. C. W. Saunders, 1st Fld. Coy.
Sgt. E. G. Scrimshaw, 1st Fld.Coy.
Sgt. A. Ward, 2nd Fld. Coy.
Cpl. K. W. Watson, Fld. Trp. transf. 3rd Fld. Coy.

MILITARY MEDAL (M.M.)

Spr. R. W. Adams, 1st Fld. Coy.
Cpl. J. R. Adams, 2nd Fld. Coy.
Sergt. A. T. Brokenshire, D.C.M., 1st Fld. Coy.
Sgt. W. J. Brown, 3rd Fld. Coy.
Cpl. G. Campbell, 3rd Fld. Coy.
Cpl. J. H. Anderson, 2nd Fld. Coy.
Sgt. T. Atkinson, 1st Fld. Coy.
Spr. J. W. McKay, 3rd Fld. Coy.
Cpl. W. J. McKinley, 1st Fld.Coy.
Sgt. A. A. McMaster, 1st Fld.Coy.
Spr. H. McMillan, 3rd Fld. Coy.

APPENDIX B.

MILITARY MEDAL (M.M.)—Continued.

Sgt. B. V. Cooksley, 1st Fld. Coy.
Cpl. A. W. Danby, 1st Fld. Coy.
Cpl. J. W. Duggan, 1st Fld. Coy.
Cpl. W. G. Easton, 2nd Fld. Coy.
Sgt. C. H. Elsom, 1st Fld. Coy.
Cpl. H. Fake, 2nd Fld. Coy.
Sgt. W. J. Fix, 3rd Fld. Coy.
Lieut. H. A. Foote, 2nd Fld. Coy.
Sgt. H. E. Fricker, 3rd Fld. Coy.
Sgt. D. N. Fullarton, 1st Fld.Coy.
Cpl. J. W. Garnett, 1st Fld. Coy.
Sgt. A. E. Gibb, 2nd Fld. Coy.
L.-Cpl. J. R. Gilbert, 1st Fld.Coy.
Cpl. C. H. Green, 2nd Fld. Coy.
Cpl. F. Gleeson, 2nd Fld. Coy.
Sgt. D. Gunn, 3rd Fld. Coy.
Sgt. T. Hatfull, 3rd Fld. Coy.
Sgt. N. L. Higginson, 2nd Fld.Coy.
Lieut. F. J. Hodson, 4th Fld. Coy.
Spr. J. H. Hodgson, 3rd Fld. Coy.
Spr. J. Houston, 3rd Fld. Coy.
Sgt. A. A. Howard, 3rd Fld. Coy.
Dvr. R. Johnstone, 1st Fld. Coy.
Sgt. D. A. Kennedy, 3rd Fld. Coy.
Sgt. R. S. Knight, 3rd Fld. Coy.
Lieut. H. Linklater, 1st Fld. Coy.
L/Cpl. H. K. Mackie, 3rd Fld. Coy.
Lieut. J. J. Moore, 1st Fld. Coy.

Sgt. D. McLaren, 1st Fld. Coy.
Dvr. A. J. McLean, 1st Fld. Coy.
Cpl. T. McLennan, 3rd Fld. Coy.
2nd Cpl. L. J. Palmer, 1st Fld.Coy.
Sgt. R. G. Pearce, Fld. Troop
C.S.M. A. R. Penman, 3rd Fld.Coy.
Cpl. E. R. W. Pledger, 1st Fld. Coy.
Spr. J. K. Ramsay, 1st Fld. Coy.
Cpl. D. D. Rennie, 1st Fld. Coy.
Cpl. W. J. Riddell, 2nd Fld. Coy.
Lieut. D. Ross, 1st Fld. Coy.
C.S.M. G. C. Rusden, 3rd Fld.Coy.
Cpl. G. H. Shelly, 2nd Fld. Coy.
C.S.M. E. Smith, 2nd Fld. Coy.
Spr. A. Springall, 3rd Fld. Coy.
Cpl. D. W. Stronach, 3rd Fld.Coy.
Cpl. F. G. Taylor, 3rd Fld. Coy.
Sgt. G. H. Thorpe, 3rd Fld. Coy.
Spr. J. Tindall, 3rd Fld. Coy.
Cpl. D. N. Treleavan, 1st Fld.Coy.
Spr. J. Walker, 1st Fld. Coy.
Sgt. F. S. Wilkinson, 2nd Fld.Coy.
C.S.M. G. Williamson, Fld. Trp.
Spr. C. G. Wilson, 1st Fld. Coy.
Sgt. W. K. Wilton, 2nd Fld. Coy.
R.S.M. J. Woodhall, 1st Fld. Coy.

MERITORIOUS SERVICE MEDAL (M.S.M.)

Far.-Sgt. W. R. Blackall, 2nd Fld. Coy.
C.Q.M.S. C. Brunsden, 3rd Fld. Coy.
Sgt. S. S. Choate, N.Z.E., attached D.H.Q.
Cpl. W. A. Comrie, 1st Fld. Coy.
R.S.M. G. R. Evans, H.Q., N.Z.E.
C.S.M. P. J. Graham, 1st Fld.Coy.
Sgt. M. H. Grigg, 1st Fld. Coy.
Cpl. A. M. Heath, 2nd Fld. Coy.

Cpl. R. E. Hooker, 2nd Fld. Coy.
Sgt. C. L. Horne, 3rd Fld. Coy.
C.Q.M.S. H. S. H. Iles, 2nd Fld. Coy.
S/Q.M.S. H. J. Manning, 1st Fld. Coy., attached H.Q. London
Sgt. A. M. Oliver, 1st Fld. Coy.
C.Q.M.S. W. F. Taylor, 1st Fld. Coy.
Cpl. L. G. Waygood, 3rd Fld.Coy.

MENTIONED IN DESPATCHES.

Sgt. A. W. Abbey, D.C.M., 1st Fld. Coy.
Major N. Annabell, M.C., H.Q., N.Z.E.
Lt.-Col. G. Barclay, N.Z.E. Res. Depot (2)
Lt.-Col. H. L. Bingay, D.S.O., R.E., C.R.E. (2)
S/Sgt. R. Boswell, H.Q., N.Z.E.
Temp. Capt. J. W. Dow, 1st Fld. Coy.
Lieut. M. K. Draffin, 3rd Fld.Coy.

Cpl. S. W. Bridge, 1st Fld. Coy.
2/Lieut. Hon. R. T. P. Butler, M.C., R.E., H.Q., N.Z.E.
Spr. D. R. Campbell, 2nd Fld.Coy.
Spr. S. Carlyon, 1st Fld. Coy.
Cpl. C. R. Carr, 2nd Fld. Coy.
S/Sgt. J. S. Criffs, H.Q., N.Z.E.
Capt. T. W. Dollimore, 2nd Fld. Coy.
Lt.-Col. G. R. Pridham, D.S.O., R.E., C.R.E. (3)
Lieut. W. S. Rae, 2nd Fld. Coy.

APPENDIX B.
MENTIONED IN DESPATCHES—Continued.

Cpl. T. Drummond, 2nd Fld. Coy.
Capt. F. A. Ferguson, R.E., 1st Fld. Coy.
Capt. H. H. Fisher, 2nd Fld. Coy.
Sgt. S. Forsyth, V.C., 3rd Fld.Coy.
Major D. J. Gibbs, D.S.O., 3rd Fld. Coy. (2)
Lieut. A. O. Glasse, M.C., 3rd Fld. Coy.
Cpl. A. H. Loke, 3rd Fld. Coy.
Lieut. A. Lush, 1st Fld. Coy.
Cpl. A. W. Minchin, 3rd Fld. Coy.
Sgt. J. McKay, 1st Fld. Coy.
Major A. G. McNeill, M.C., R.E., 1st Fld. Coy. (2)
Capt. M. G. R. Newbould, M.C., 1st Fld. Coy.
Capt. H. W. Newman, M.C. 1st Fld. Coy.
Lieut. A. N. Oakey, M.C., Fld. Troop
Cpl. B. O'Connor, 2nd Fld. Coy.
Spr. H. A. O'Neill, 2nd Fld. Coy.
R.S.M. A. G. Picken, H.Q. N.Z.E.

Major B. L. R. Reeve, 2nd Fld. Coy.
Capt. G. V. Russell, M.C., 1st Fld. Coy.
Dvr. J. Ryan, 1st Fld. Coy.
Capt. C. W. Salmon, D.C.M., 1st Fld. Coy.
Lieut. C. W. Saunders, 1st Fld.Coy.
Sgt. E. G. Scrimshaw, D.C.M., 1st Fld. Coy.
Major F. W. Skelsey, 2nd Fld. (Coy. (2)
Lt.-Col. L. M. Shera, O.B.E., M.C. C.R.E.
L.-Cpl. F. Smyth, 3rd Fld. Coy.
C.S.M. J. W. C. Steele, 3rd Fld. Coy.
R.S.M. J. N. Thompson, H.Q., N.Z.E.
Capt. F. Waite, D.S.O., H.Q., N.Z.E.
Sgt. A. Wallace, 1st Fld. Coy.
Lieut. B. West, 2nd Fld. Coy.
Capt. F. C. Wilson, H.Q., N.Z.E.
Cpl. D. Wight, 3rd Fld. Coy.

II. A.N.Z.A.C. MERITORIOUS SERVICE TESTIMONIAL.

S/Sgt. R. Boswell, H.Q., N.Z.E.
Far. Sgt. H. Burford, 1st Fld. Coy.
Spr. C. H. Duff, 3rd Fld. Coy.
R.S.M. G. R. Evans, H.Q., N.Z.E.

Spr. S. F. Lane, 3rd Fld. Coy.
Sgt. J. A. Leary, 2nd Fld. Coy.
L/Cpl. A. Nuttall, 1st Fld. Coy.
C.Q.M.S. E. R. Wheeler, 2nd Fld. Coy.

MENTIONED IN ARMY ORDERS.

Sgt. J. S. L. Deem, 1st Fld. Coy.
Sgt. M. H. Grigg, 1st Fld. Coy.

Sgt. P. G. Pearce, Fld. Troop
R.S.M. J. Woodhall, 1st Fld. Coy.

Brought to the notice of the Secretary of State for War for valuable services at home towards the successful conduct of the War.

R.Q.M.S. H. Dyson, 3rd Fld. Coy.
Lieut. H. S. King, 2nd Fld. Coy.

S/Q.M.S. H. J. Manning, 1st Fld. Coy.
Lt. H. G. Alexander, Fld. Troop

FOREIGN DECORATIONS.

FRENCH CROIX DE GUERRE.
Capt. H. W. Newman, M.C., 1st Field Coy.

FRENCH MEDAILLE MILITAIRE.
L.-Cpl. H. J. Mascall, 2nd Field Coy.

BELGIUM CROIX DE GUERRE.

Cpl. J. J. Dooley, 3rd Fld. Coy.
Spr. P. M. Rooks, 1st Fld. Coy.

Sgt. A. Ward, D.C.M., 2nd Fld. Coy.

APPENDIX B.

SERBIA ORDER OF THE WHITE EAGLE, 4th Class (with swords).
Lt.-Col. G. R. Pridham, (D.S.O.), C.R.E.

SERBIA CROSS OF KARAGEORGE, 2nd Class (with swords).
Lieut. J. J. Moore, M.M., 1st Field Coy.

SERBIA GOLD MEDAL.
Sapper C. Lovell-Smith, 1st Field Coy.

MONTENEGRIN ORDER OF DANILO, 4th Class.
Lt.-Col. G. Barclay, N.Z.E. Res. Depot.

ROUMANIAN MEDAL.
Sapper G. M. Bennett, 1st Field Coy.

SIGNAL TROOP.

Major	E. J. Hulbert	D.S.O.
Lieut.	J. L. Brathwaite	M.C.
Lieut.	R. T. G. Patrick	M.C.
Lieut.	A. G. Wainscott	M.C.
Sapper	A. L. Caselberg	D.C.M.
Corpl.	L. Noble	M.M. and Bar
Sapper	J. G. Giffney	M.M.
Sapper	J. E. Hollywood	M.M.
Sapper	O. Oxley	M.M.
Sapper	J.R. Robertson	M.M.
Major	E. J. Hulbert	Ment'd in Despatches
Lieut.	R. T. G. Patrick	Ment'd in Despatches
Sergt.	H. V. Fairlie	Ment'd in Despatches
Sergt.	G. M. Ranstead	Ment'd in Despatches

APPENDIX C.

OFFICERS WHO SERVED WITH THE N.Z. ENGINEERS.

Divisional Engineers and Field Troop.

Name and Rank last held, N.Z.E.F.	Date and Rank First Appointment N.Z.E.F.	
Major D. J. Gibbs, D.S.O.	5/8/14	Captain
Major P. St. J. Keenan	5/8/14	Captain
Major A. A. McNab	5/8/14	Captain
Lieut.-Colonel L. M. Shera, O.B.E., M.C.	5/8/14	Captain
Lieut. A. N. Oakey, M.C.	5/8/14	Lieutenant
Capt. F. Waite, D.S.O.	5/8/14	Lieutenant
Capt. D. P. Simson	28/9/14	Captain
Major F. W. Skelsey	28/9/14	Lieutenant
Brevet Major F. A. Ferguson, R.E.	15/1/15	Captain
Brevet Major A. G. McNeill, R.E., M.C., (Killed in Action)	16/1/15	Captain
*Capt. M. G. R. Newbold, M.C.	2/2/15	2nd Lieut.
*2nd Lieut. S. W. Paine (Killed in Action)	2/2/15	2nd Lieut.
*Capt. R. J. Black, M.C.	10/2/15	2nd Lieut.
Brevet Lt.-Col. G. R. Pridham, R.E., D.S.O.	26/2/15	Major
Lieut.-Colonel G. Barclay, O.B.E.		
Capt. A. Beekman (Accidentally Killed)	16/1/15	Major
	16/1/15	Captain
Major B. L. R. Reeve	16/1/15	Lieutenant
Capt. F. C. Wilson	16/1/15	2nd Lieut.
Capt. H. H. Fisher	16/1/15	2nd Lieut.
Lieut. W. S. McCrorie	16/1/15	2nd Lieut.
Major N. Annabell, M.C.	15/3/15	Lieutenant
2nd Lieut. Hon. R. T. R. P. Butler, R.E., M.C.	31/5/15	2nd Lieut.
2nd Lieut. Holbrook, R.E.		2nd Lieut.
2nd Lieut. Douse, R.E.		2nd Lieut.
*Lieut. D. W. Saunders, D.C.M.	17/6/15	2nd Lieut.
*Lieut. H. M. Clark	23/6/15	2nd Lieut.
*Capt. C. W. Salmon, D.C.M.	26/6/15	2nd Lieut.
*Capt. H. W. Newman, M.C.	21/10/15	2nd Lieut.
*Capt. T. W. Dollimore	21/10/15	2nd Lieut.
Capt. G. V. Russell, M.C.	1/1/16	2nd Lieut.
Lieut. G. Simpson	1/1/16	Lieutenant
*Lieut. H. S. King	19/1/16	2nd Lieut.
*Capt. W. S. Rae, M.C.	15/2/16	2nd Lieut.
*Capt. C. W. Chilcott, M.C.	15/2/16	2nd Lieut.
*Lieut. A. O. Glasse, M.C.	1/3/16	2nd Lieut.
Lieut. P. H. Morey	1/3/16	2nd Lieut.
Lieut. F. M. Corkill	1/3/16	2nd Lieut.
*Lieut. A. W. Thomas, M.C.	15/3/16	2nd Lieut.
*Lieut. E. D. Clough	18/4/16	2nd Lieut.
Capt. S. Cory-Wright, M.C.	29/4/16	Lieutenant

APPENDIX C.

Name and Rank last held, N.Z.E.F.	Appointment N.Z.E.F. Date and Rank First	
Lieut. E. Morton	29/4/16	2nd Lieut.
Lieut. J. A. Smith	27/5/16	2nd Lieut.
Lieut. J. Keilar	27/5/16	2nd Lieut.
Lieut. P. R. Angus	24/6/16	2nd Lieut.
Lieut. H. G. Lockington	7/1/18	2nd Lieut.
Lieut. F. K. Broadgate (Killed in Action)	24/6/16	2nd Lieut.
*Lieut. J. J. Moore, M.M.	17/7/16	2nd Lieut.
Lieut. K. T. Jenssen	22/7/16	2nd Lieut.
Lieut. H. A. Lockington	1/2/18	2nd Lieut.
Lieut. A. H. Bogle	10/8/16	2nd Lieut.
Lieut. T. D. Barker	23/9/16	2nd Lieut.
Lieut. E. A. Marchant	14/10/16	2nd Lieut.
*Lieut. A. Lush	23/12/16	2nd Lieut.
*Lieut. M. K. Draffin, M.C.	23/12/16	2nd Lieut.
*Lieut. H. A. Foote, M.M.	27/1/17	2nd Lieut.
Lieut. G. W. Eaton-Turner	5/4/17	2nd Lieut.
*Lieut. D. Doake, M.C.	21/4/17	2nd Lieut.
*Lieut. B. West	21/4/17	2nd Lieut.
*Lieut. T. F. Rowe	18/5/17	2nd Lieut.
Lieut. J. W. Dow	28/5/17	2nd Lieut.
*Lieut. D. Ross, M.M.	28/5/17	2nd Lieut.
*Lieut. O. Y. Davies	29/5/17	2nd Lieut.
*Lieut. W. Hulbert	29/5/17	2nd Lieut.
*Lieut. B. L. Joll	21/6/17	2nd Lieut.
Lieut. N. L. Vickerman	14/7/17	2nd Lieut.
Lieut. C. N. Boult	14/7/17	2nd Lieut.
Lieut.-Colonel H. L. Bingay, R.E., D.S.O.	27/7/17	Lieut.-Col.
*Lieut. D. R. Mansfield	28/7/17	2nd Lieut.
*Lieut. H. H. Pavitt	8/9/17	2nd Lieut.
*Lieut. E. W. George, M.C.	21/9/17	2nd Lieut.
*2nd Lieut. C. A. Perkins	26/10/17	2nd Lieut.
*2nd Lieut. C. S. Beilby	14/12/17	2nd Lieut.
*2nd Lieut. R. G. Slyfield	2/2/18	2nd Lieut.
*2nd Lieut. H. Linklater, M.M.	24/2/18	2nd Lieut.
*2nd Lieut. O. G. Thornton	27/4/18	2nd Lieut.
*2nd Lieut. W. R. H. Duke	31/5/18	2nd Lieut.
*2nd Lieut. H. J. Reid	31/5/18	2nd Lieut.
*2nd Lieut. F. J. Hodgson, M.M.	27/1/19	2nd Lieut.

* Denotes Officers who have gained Commissions in the Field.

Field Troop in Palestine.

Lt. H. G. Alexander
Lt. H. A. Lockington
Lt. S. G. Browne
2nd Lt. A. F. Lange

Signal Troop.

Lt.-Col. E. J. Hulbert, D.S.O.
Lt. R. T. G. Patrick, M.C.
Lt. J. L. Braithwaite, M.C.
Lt. T. G. Hinton
Lt. A. G. Wainscott, M.C.

Wireless Troop.

Capt. J. W. Melville
Lieut. W. R. H. Clarke

New Zealand.

EVANS, COBB AND SHARPE, LTD.,
Printers, Bookbinders and Publishers,
Wanganui.

1927.

www.ingramcontent.com/pod-product-compliance
Lightning Source LLC
Chambersburg PA
CBHW021830220426
43663CB00005B/188